Blacks in Colonial America

BLACKS
— IN —
COLONIAL
AMERICA

by OSCAR REISS

McFarland & Company, Inc., Publishers
Jefferson, North Carolina, and London

LIBRARY OF CONGRESS CATALOGUING-IN-PUBLICATION DATA

Reiss, Oscar, 1925–
    Blacks in colonial America / by Oscar Reiss.
        p.   cm.
    Includes bibliographical references and index.

    ISBN-13: 978-0-7864-2957-8
    ISBN-10: 0-7864-2957-7
    (softcover : 50# alkaline paper) ∞

    1. Afro-Americans—History—To 1863.   2. United States—
History—Colonial period, ca. 1600–1775.   3. Slavery—United
States—History—18th century.   4. Slavery—United States—
History—17th century.   I. Title.
E185.18.R45   2006
973'.0496073—dc21   97-10009

British Library cataloguing data are available

Cover art ©2006 Pictures Now

Manufactured in the United States of America

McFarland & Company, Inc., Publishers
    Box 611, Jefferson, North Carolina 28640
    www.mcfarlandpub.com

To Elinor,
my wife of many years,
who supported my endeavors
as well as my physical being
during the research and
writing of this book

CONTENTS

PREFACE

About 50 years ago, I took a course in colonial history in college. We had no textbook, but the professor·suggested we read one book on the subject each week. This led to a lifelong interest in that period of American history. Through the years I read many scholarly manuscripts which covered various aspects of that era, but to the best of my knowledge no book solely addressed the subject of persons of African descent in the colonies, even though blacks and those people classified as blacks made up 20 percent of the population at the outbreak of the American Revolution. Many volumes on black history devote one or two chapters to this period. Most of them describe the political and social problems of slavery in the nineteenth century and the fight for equal treatment in the twentieth. I hope the present book will fill many of the informational gaps left by other works.

I am not African American. In researching this book I strove for objectivity, but as my store of knowledge increased, it became more difficult to suppress feelings of anger over the treatment to which black people have been subjected. Early in their history in America, blacks were reasonably accepted by society. Like many whites, they served out indenture contracts and went on to become landowners and merchants. With the passage of time, however, English attitudes toward this group in their midst shifted toward a more pronounced racism. This change in racial attitude, added to the financial need to get unpaid workers on a permanent basis, led to slavery, first de facto, then de jure. A major subject of the present book is how this group, who in many cases were treated as if they were a separate subspecies of man, tried to make a life for themselves in a white society.

A necessary starting point for the reader is to consider the concepts of slavery historically held by various civilizations and the eventual evolution of the concept to black slavery only. The milder form of slavery practiced in Africa, the transport of slaves to this country and their life in various parts of the colonies are presented. There were free blacks on the Eastern Seaboard almost from the start of white habitation. How they became free and lived among their neighbors is described.

This text tries to cover opposition to slavery by both blacks and whites—

1

the blacks by law and rebellion, the whites by law. There were no John Browns in the colonies. Just as the French and English tried to bring Christianity to the Native Americans (and get their furs), so the English explained the need for slavery to save black souls. Among the blacks they were more successful. White Americans, who had a mildly positive attitude toward blacks, nevertheless abhorred miscegenation, and to avoid its consequences they tried to remove the blacks from their new country. Finally, black participation in the many imperialistic wars on the North American continent is covered. Blacks fought under duress or the promise of freedom, but they rarely benefited from their participation.

The foundation of research on this manuscript is a close scrutiny of 75 years of *The Journal of Negro History*. In addition, I combed the archives of the several colonies, later states. The archives provided materials on legislation relating to black codes, duties on incoming merchandise including humans, last wills and testaments concerning property both inanimate and two-footed, and letters between citizens relating to the problem of slavery. I also combed journals of history of the 13 original states to get a feeling for the way other authors have approached this uniquely painful subject.

I did not intend for this work to be a reference book on the period it covers. I view it as an attempt to increase the store of knowledge of that early period of our history. The project was exciting to me, and I hope others will respond to it with equal interest.

I wish to express special appreciation to the staff of the University of California San Diego's library whose sixth floor was a refuge and a font of information during the long research phase. Books, archives, and state historical journals on its shelves were important sources consulted for this manuscript. The atmosphere was conducive to research and study, and I spent many happy hours among the stacks.

—O.R., *February 1997*

Chapter 1

THE CONCEPT OF
SLAVERY

In the history of mankind, most civilizations except the Essenes (of the Dead Sea Scrolls) accepted slavery.[1] The Hebrews of the Bible took slaves from among the vanquished tribes of the Middle East: "Both thy bondmen and thy bondmaids, which thou shalt have, shall be of the heathen that are around about you: of them shall ye buy bondmen and bondmaids. And ye shall take them as an inheritance for your children after you, to inherit them for a possession; they shall be your bondmen forever" (Lev. 25:44, 46). Joshua mandated that the Gibeonites become "bearers of wood and drawers of water for the congregation" of Israel (Joshua 9:21). To support their argument in favor of the concept of slavery, apologists pointed to other portions of the Hebrew Bible. An angel of God commanded Hagar, "Return to thy mistress and submit thyself under her hands" (Gen. 16:9). Noah, who enjoyed the fermented grape to excess, became uncovered while in his cups; Ham, his dark-complexioned son, observed his father in this state, and he (or, according to the literal text, his son, Canaan) was cursed to be a "servant of servants ... unto his brethren" (Gen. 9:25).

The slavery of the Hebrew Bible was mild and patriarchal in nature. The slave was part of the household, and he worked alongside his master. The status of the slave was not always permanent, despite the previous reference in Leviticus. The interpretation of the passage in Leviticus depends upon how one defines the Hebrew word *olam*. Apologists for slavery limited its meaning to the literal "forever"; opponents of slavery believed that *olam* actually meant various durations of time, depending on the subject under discussion.[2] In Leviticus, it probably represented at most 49 or 50 years. According to Jewish law, all Hebrew slaves were to be set free at the beginning of every seventh (sabbatical) year, and even those who elected to continue their condition of servitude were to be freed when the shofar (ram's horn) was sounded on the Day of Atonement every fiftieth (Jubilee) year. Furthermore, the Mosaic code protected slaves against violence; if it occurred, freedom was granted as reparation. "Slave catching" was an abomination: "Thou shalt not

3

deliver unto his master a servant which escaped from his master unto thee" (Deut. 23:16). Finally, the abolitionists interpreted the eighth commandment as a total prohibition against slavery. To take from a man his earnings was theft, but to take the earner was a compounded, lifelong theft.

The New Testament did not prohibit slavery as such, so, many portions could be interpreted to shore up one's argument for or against the practice. Thus, Saint Paul wrote to the Ephesians (6:5): "Servants be obedient unto them that be your human masters, with fear and trembling, in singleness of your heart, as unto Christ." In I Corinthians 7:20–24 Paul wrote: "Let every man abide in the same calling wherein he was called. But were thou called being a servant? Care not for it, but if thou mayest be free choose it rather. For he that is called in the Lord being a servant, is the Lord's freeman; likewise also, he that is called being free is Christ's servant. Ye are bought with a price, but be not ye servants of man. Brethren, let every man in the state wherein he is called, therein abide with God." Paul's Epistle to Titus (2:9–10) exhorts "servants to be obedient to their masters and to please them well in all things…, showing complete good fidelity." Paul's First Epistle to Timothy (6:1) advises, "Let as many servants as are under the yoke, count their own masters worthy of all honor." These statements were interpreted to favor slavery; but Paul also said, "There is neither Jew nor Greek; there is neither bond nor free, there is neither male nor female: for ye are all one in Christ Jesus" (Gal. 3:28).

The early church fathers seemed to condone slavery.[3] Saint Augustine advised slaves not to demand liberation every seventh year as per the Hebrew model, for the Apostles had clearly repudiated this un–Christian act; yet he also said, "Man who was made in the image of God and endowed with reason, was made to be lord of all heavenly creatures, but not of his fellowman." Saint Isidore was explicit: "In consequence of the sin of the first man, the penalty of slavery was brought by God on the human race, so that they whom he saw less fit for liberty, might more mercifully be punished by slavery." Saint Thomas Aquinas concurred: "Slavery rests upon the ground that there are men for whom it is better to be slaves than to be free, and that slavery is therefore an institution of human reason." Martin Luther believed in racial superiority, and he felt slavery was a necessary social institution.[4]

The Koran accepted slavery with certain qualifications.[5] A true believer could not hold a member of the faith in slavery. He was to be merciful to his slave, and he would be blessed if he liberated his slave. He could buy and sell Jews, Christians, and heathens, but not Muslims.

The ancient Greeks accepted slavery.[6] Plato justified slavery because of the natural inferiority of most men. He described a caste system wherein those who worked with their hands were not citizens; this group was not able to govern itself or to grasp the truth. Plato did not look with favor upon Greeks having Greek slaves who were captured in war; he preferred barbarians as slaves. Aristotle believed that there were two classes of slaves: a man might be a slave by nature in that he was created inferior to other men, or a man might be a slave by right of conquest. "Bodily services for the necessities of life are forthcoming from both, from slaves and from domestic animals alike. The intention of nature, therefore, is to make the bodies of freemen and slaves different.... It is manifest, therefore, that there are cases of people of whom some are freemen and the others are slaves by nature, and for those slavery is an institution both expedient and wise." The individual who was a slave by nature was of a form between man and animal. He was a man because he could understand orders; he was an "animal" because he could not formulate orders. Proper supervision of slaves required work—and the use of food as reward and punishment for wrongdoing.

The Romans were judged by history to be a pragmatic people. Slaves were the spoils of war; as such, enslavement was an act of largesse. Bondage was an alternative to killing prisoners of war. Those taken in war became agricultural workers, artisans, and gladiators. Greek slaves brought culture to Rome and dominated the professions. Many slaves were liberated and became the bureaucratic controllers of the empire. Slaves could purchase their own freedom. Those who became sick or old in service were "allowed to die of hunger and exposure." Over the course of years, slaves could obtain and keep private property. They could not be killed at the whim of their master; they could not be sent off as gladiators or treated with brutality. There were Roman officers to hear and adjudicate slaves' complaints. With the ascent of the first Christian emperors, their lot improved. The rule that forbade the willful killing of slaves was enforced. The intent to kill was deemed present if certain specified atrocious tortures were inflicted; if a slave died during ordinary torture, death was considered accidental. Crucifixion was outlawed. But, sexual union between a free woman and a slave resulted in death to both, his by burning—and a slave's testimony against his master, except in cases of high treason, resulted in execution of the slave at the stake, notwithstanding the truth of his testimony.

The early Church in the Roman Empire amassed property, part of which was in the form of slaves—and this was accepted by the early Fathers. However, manumission was made easier and was considered a Christian virtue. Spiritually, the Church placed the master and slave on an equal footing before God. They worshipped together, took Communion together, and suffered the same penalties for breaking canon law. A person born a slave could aspire to the priesthood.

Part of Justinian's code covered the slave and his status. Many restrictions on manumission were abolished. All disabilities and burdens on the freed man were removed, so that he was the equal of a free-born Roman. A free woman could marry a slave, if his owner consented. Men could marry their women slaves after they were freed; children of such a union were heirs of their free-born fathers.

During the Middle Ages, a period of almost complete Church control over all aspects of society, slavery was accepted.[7] Christians could not make slaves of other Christians, but enslavement of heathens was permitted. Christians and Jews could sell Moslems, but neither could deal in Christian slaves. So Christians could not sell Christians to Moslems; but unhappily, laws were made to be flouted, and Frankish monks purchased the children of the poor, castrated them, and sold them to the rich Moors in Spain. Popes Gregory X, Boniface VIII, Urban V, and Gregory XI threatened excommunication of traders who dealt in Christians, but this threat did not prevent Christian traders in Marseilles from selling "soldiers" of the Children's Crusade to Moslems. Christians could be sold into slavery for unlawful offenses. Under Charlemagne, a fortune-teller was given to the priests as a slave of the Church; incest too was punished by slavery.[8] In Danish and Anglo-Saxon law, those guilty of theft could be sold into perpetual bondage. If a wrongdoer was punished with a fine that he could not pay, he was given as a slave to his victim. Rapists became slaves of the women they raped. The slave in the Middle Ages was chattel and had no rights. For crimes, he could be hanged, broken on the wheel, emasculated, burned at the stake, immersed in boiling water or oil, buried alive, or drowned. Slavery gradually died out in Europe and was replaced by serfdom or villenage.

Slaves and Servants

The serf or villein was not chattel. Rather, he was bound to the land. He could not be sold off the land, but he could be sold with the land. He owed the lord his labor, and he performed any task his lord demanded. He in turn received protection. A villein fell into this state by poverty, mischance, crime, debt, vagrancy, or vagabondage. Orphans, bastards, and children of servants could be sold into villenage. Like slavery before it, this condition gradually died out in England by the fourteenth century. It persisted in parts of Scotland until the eighteenth century.

It was commonly believed that there were no slaves in England by the sixteenth century. Any slave setting foot in England became a free man, because English air was "too pure for slaves to breathe." (A slave purchased in Russia and brought to England was freed.) Yet slavery had not been entirely destroyed. In 1547, a vagabond could be put into slavery for two years.[9] He could be branded with a V, chained, and forced to work. If he ran away, he became a slave for life if caught. Fortunately, this law was repealed in 1550.

Perhaps the air of England was too pure for slavery, but the country supported permanent bondage and other forms of involuntary servitude in the British West Indies and in the North American coastal colonies. The owners of sugar, rice, indigo, and tobacco plantations needed cheap help to maintain the profitability of their estates. This could be supplied by slaves, indentured servants, paid servants, and redemptioners. The terms *servant* and *slave* were used interchangeably in the seventeenth century. In England, *slave* was a term of derision for peasants. Servants were called slaves, as were criminals in jail and children working to pay off the debts of their deceased parents. In Colonial America, *servants* referred to domestic servants, laborers, mechanics, apprentices, schoolmasters, secretaries, clerks, students in lawyers' or physicians' offices, Indians, Negroes, and "other slaves." Basically, there were two types of servants: those who served for a period of time and those who served for life. To avoid ambiguity in enumerating servants for taxation or a census, masters would add the terms *white*, *English*, or *Christian* to the list of "short-term" servants. To complicate matters, indentured servants were called slaves when punished.[10] If a servant missed church in Puritan New England, he was "to lye neek and heels that night," and he became a "slave for a week." For serious criminal offenses, servants could be sentenced to servitude for life. Political prisoners, priests, Quakers, and soldiers taken in rebellion were sent to the colonies to "serve the term of their natural lives."

Paid servants were largely a phenomenon of urban life and represented a minority of this servant group; the greater number were indentured servants. An indenture was a written contract stating the obligations of each of the two individuals involved; each retained a copy of the agreement, which was "indented" at the top so they could be matched at any time. A common indenture was a contract to learn a trade. Here is an example:

> This indenture made ye 23rd day of July ... 1696, between Bastian Congo, a Free Negro man, aged 27 years or thereabouts of the one parte and Abraham Kep [Kip] ... of the City of New Yorke Merchants ... that the said Bastian Congo for the consideration of the sum of £17 15S ... hathe put himself Apprentice unto Abraham Kip ... to dwell and serve ... until June 18 next ... Bastian Congo to provide and furnish himself with clothes and wearing apparel during the saide time ... after the expiration of the terme aforesaid ... Bastian Congo after the manner of an apprentice will serve Abraham Kip ... at the rate of 30S[hillings] per month until ... he shall fully satisfie ... the ... saide servitude and apprenticeship ... Bastian Congo well and truly shall serve the commandments of his said Masters ... he shall not doe or suffer to be done hurt [to his Masters], neither shall he purloyn waste or destroy their goods ... nor absent himself from their paid service ... [he shall] be a good and faithful apprentice and servant ... during the terme ... Abraham Kip ... [will supply] ... meate, drinke, and lodging.
>
> Bastian X [his mark] Congo[11]

To obtain passage to the New World, another form of indenture was signed.

> This Indenture made the 21st February 1682/3 [January and February of each year were written this way until the Gregorian Calendar was accepted] between Richard Browne aged 33 years of the one parte and Francis Richard-

son of the other party, witnesseth, that the said Richard Browne doth thereby covenant, promise and grant to one with the said Francis Richardson his executor and assigns, from the date of the date hereof, until his first and next arrival at New York or New Jersey and after, for and during the term of four years, to serve in such service and employment as he the said Francis Richardson, his assigns shall there employ him according to the custom of the country in the like kind. In consideration thereof the said Francis Richardson doth hereby covenant and grant to and with the said Richard Browne to pay for his passing, and to find and allow him meal, drink, apparel and lodging, with other necessaries, during the said term, and at the end of the said term to pay unto him according to the Custom of the Country.

In witness thereof the parties above mentioned to this Indenture have set their hands and seals the day and year above written.[12]

This form of indenture helped populate the English colonies. During the colonial period, probably 250,000 indentured servants reached America.[13] At least 80,000 went to Virginia. Whites in Europe were cajoled, propagandized and kidnapped by agents called "spirits," who were paid for each person placed on board a ship. Jails were emptied with the connivance of wardens. Once in America, the indentured servant was completely under the control of his master. Without his master's consent, he could not marry, engage in a trade, buy whiskey, or leave the plantation; he could not raise his hand against his master, vote, or hold office. A servant had more in common with a black slave than with his white master. White servants ran away frequently as they could blend in with white society, an option not available to black slaves. Flight from plantations became so common in Maryland that a law of 1639 called for the death penalty for those who fled. In Virginia in 1643 a second offender could be branded with an *R* on his cheek or shoulder.

The redemptioner was an individual without money for the passage to America. He promised to pay his fare upon arrival in America. He could borrow money from friends, or he could sell himself to someone on shore. If he was unable to get a master, the captain could sell him to pay his fare.

Occupying the lowest rung of the servant class were slaves. The concept of slavery was not unknown to the English planters. The Spaniards and Portuguese had used slaves before the founding of any English colony. In the British West Indies, Bermuda was the first island to use slaves.[14] The first black arrived in 1616. Governor Tucky was instructed to send Mr. Willmott to the "Savage Islands" for cattle, casaba, sugar, and "negroes to dive for pearles." The *Edwin* returned with plantains, sugar cane, figs, pineapples, "one Indian and a negroe." The black slave population grew rapidly in Bermuda; they were seized from other West Indian islands as well as from Spanish and Portuguese ships. These were "seasoned" slaves, and they brought skills learned from previous masters. They were pearl divers and agricultural workers (sugar cane, tobacco, tropical and semitropical plants). The term *slave* was first used in Bermuda in 1617. (There were probably free blacks on the island as well.)

In 1617 "Symon the Negro" was condemned to become a slave to the colony because he assaulted a child. In 1623 Bermuda had its first slave code, "An Act to Restrain the Insolences of the Negroes." It forbade trade with Negroes, restricted their movement, and prohibited their carrying weapons. From Bermuda, slavery spread to the other West Indian islands that England stole from the Spanish.

There has been much dispute as to the time of formal introduction of slavery on the American mainland. In Virginia, slavery at first was a de facto condition that gradually became de jure. The first blacks in Virginia arrived at Jamestown in 1619. A Dutch man-of-war took 20 blacks (including three women) off a Spanish frigate and brought them to the port. According to John Rolfe, "they sold us 20 Neggers" in return for food and water.[15] They were items of merchandise, but so were white indentured servants. White servants had contracts, however, and usually came voluntarily. Blacks had no contracts, and they were kept for as long as possible. There were no relevant laws in Virginia, and English laws were vague. The black servants were kept longer than the whites, sometimes for life.

Very early, the law treated blacks differently. In a census in 1624, whites were listed with at least two names, blacks with one name, or designated only as "negroes." White women were listed as married to a particular man; Negro women were not listed as married. In the census of 1625, only one Negro was identified: "John Pedro, a Negar, age 30, transported in *The Swan* in 1623." In his last will, Governor George Yardley listed his debts, chattels, servants (whites), "negers," and cattle.

Most blacks who arrived in the early days of the Jamestown settlement worked as indentured servants and became free.[16] They became property owners, and some later owned black slaves. (Anthony Johnson, a free black, owned both land and slaves. His heirs spread thoughout Virginia and Maryland and all were free.) In fact, the first runaway slave in Virginia was owned by another black.[17]

The concept of lifetime service for blacks was first seen in the ruling of a Virginia court on July 9, 1640.[18] Hugh Gwyn brought back three servants who had escaped to Maryland. The court ordered that they were to receive 30 lashes. Victor, a Dutchman, and James Gregory, a Scotsman, were to serve out their terms of indenture as well as an extra year of service to Mr. Gwyn, plus three years of service to the colony. John Punch, a Negro, was to serve his master for the rest of his natural life. The court was not always consistent, however, about such discrimination. On July 22, 1640, six servants belonging to Captain William Pierce and a Negro servant of Mr. Reginald ran away. When apprehended, Andrew Nope received 30 stripes; Richard Hill was placed on probation; Richard Cookeson had to serve the colony for two and one half years after his indenture and John Williams (a Dutchman) for seven; Christopher Miller (the leader) received 30 stripes, was branded on his chest with an *R*, worked one year with a shackle on his leg, and had to serve seven years beyond his contract; Peter Melcock received 30 stripes, was branded on his cheek, and worked three years for the colony—and Emanuel (the Negro) received 30 stripes, an *R* on his cheek, and shackles for one year. There was no mention of his service for life.[19]

During this period of flux, some blacks sued for freedom in the courts, and the judges ruled in their favor. Andrew Moore, "a servant negro of Mr. George Light, claims he came to this country only for five years" (this contention was supported by other witnesses). The court required Moore to be freed from his master, and the master paid him corn and clothes, "according to the custom of the county," plus 400 pounds of tobacco with a cask, for services performed since he should have been free. Mr. Light also paid court costs.[20] In another case, "Edward Mezingo, a negro man, has been and was an apprentice by Indenture to Col. Jns. Walker and his term of 28 years is now expired. He was judged free by the General Court in 1672."[21]

There was also some question about slavery being a state exclusively for blacks. In October 1663, the General Assembly of Maryland heard the case of a white father who was about to become an apprentice to another family. He feared that the apprenticeship would turn into slavery, and he was also concerned that his slave status would pass on to his daughter. The General Assembly of Maryland calmed his anxiety, fearing that this belief might hurt the good name of apprentices and prevent free Christians from coming to the colony as servants. (Proceedings and Acts of the General Assembly of Maryland.)

Law followed custom, and standards of usage were codified into law. Laws in Maryland in 1639 and in Virginia in 1642 set specific terms of servitude for white laborers to encourage white immigration. Blacks, who came involuntarily, could not be encouraged to come by decreasing their term of service; therefore, they were condemned to lifetime service. In 1661 a law in Virginia stated that a white indentured servant who ran away with a Negro served out his time of indenture, plus a time penalty, as well as a time penalty for the Negro. The "negro is incapable of making satisfaction by addition of time," so he served *durante vita*.[22] On December 14, 1662, Virginia proclaimed that the child followed the status of his mother; this meant that the offspring of a slave mother were slaves for life (*partus sequitor ventrum*).[23] This concept was contrary to common usage in England, where the child followed the father's status. Maryland followed Virginia in 1663. On October 3, 1670, Virginia ruled that servants imported into the colony by ship who were not Christians were slaves for life.

In Massachusetts, the niceties of custom ending in the firmness of law did not exist. The early English settlers, during wars with the Indians, made slaves of prisoners of war. In 1638 the ship *Desire* out of Salem took Indian slaves to the Puritan Colony of Providence Island[24] off Central America and returned with Negro slaves, cotton, and tobacco. Slaves were also carried to Boston from the Caribbean Islands. In 1641 Massachusetts passed the "Body of Liberties," which "outlawed bond slavery except when taken in just wars, when strangers sold themselves to us, or when sold to us."[25] This was the height of hypocrisy, however, because these exceptions were precisely the means whereby slaves were obtained.

New Netherlands accepted outright slavery early in its history. In 1626 the Dutch West India Company brought 11 male Negroes to New Amsterdam.[26] The slave population grew, because the company had difficulty enticing Dutch citizens to emigrate as servants. When England took New Netherlands in 1661, there were several hundred blacks. The form of slavery practiced there was more benign than that practiced by the English. Dutch slavery resembled that of the Hebrew Bible, as well as Spanish and Portuguese concepts.

Why Black Slaves?

Following Columbus's encounter with America, Spain set out to gather the riches of the New World. With their superiority in firepower and the wild bravery of the Conquistadors, the Spanish were able to enslave the indigenous population. The native Americans were not equipped to serve their Spanish masters, however, and death due to disease, starvation, and overwork decimated the "Sugar Islands" and Mexico. In 1495 Columbus, with 400 armored infantry, 20 horsemen, and bloodhounds, killed thousands on Hispaniola (Haiti). Those who survived died in the mines, digging for gold and silver. The population of Haiti in 1492 was believed to be 1 million; in 15 years, it dropped to 60,000. Forty thousand natives from the Bahamas were transported to Haiti to replace the dead; by 1517, 14,000 remained alive. What was seen in Hispaniola was played out throughout the Caribbean. News of the destruction reached the ears of Queen Isabella,[27] and in 1504 she issued orders that the Indians should be free from servitude and molestation. Decrees, unhappily, became diluted in the passage over 3,000 miles of salt water. In 1511 King Ferdinand decreed that the service of Indians was warranted by the laws of God and man. Bartolomeo de las Casas, "Protector of the Indians," a Dominican monk and later bishop, tried to relieve the conditions of the indigenous peoples. He turned to Cardinal Ximenes, minister to the king, and recommended that the Indians be replaced by Africans from the Portuguese ports in Africa.[27] Some black slaves had been imported to the Americas before his request: Ovando, the Spanish governor who replaced Columbus in Hispaniola, as well as the Portuguese, landed slaves in Hispaniola in 1502.[28] This first group was "Christianized" as a result of being "born in the power of Christians." Bartolomeo probably observed that blacks were able to work in the tropical climate of America. The officers of the "India House of Seville" recommended that 4,000 Africans be sent to the New World. La Bresa, a Flemish favorite of Charles V, successor to Ferdinand and

Isabella, received the exclusive patent to deliver the new slaves to their Spanish masters. (By decree, each Spaniard could take 12 slaves.) He, in turn, sold the patent to Genoese merchants, who started the commerce. By 1540, 10,000 Africans had been transported to the West Indies.

Perhaps because of their separation from the rest of Europe by the Pyrenees, the Iberians treated their black slaves differently from the way northern Europeans did; they followed Roman concepts developed centuries earlier.[29] According to Roman law, slavery was an accident, and anyone could become a slave. Therefore, blackness and slavery were not identical. Slavery was not necessarily a permanent state, and if the slave gained his freedom, he was not relegated to a lower social position. Furthermore, the Iberians had a longer period of exposure to Africans; and, particularly in southern Portugal, intermarriage was common. Hence, in Latin America, slaves could legally marry, own property, and have courts set a price on their freedom, so that they could buy their way out of slavery.[30] Very few Iberian women migrated to the New World; the men were forced to take Indian or black wives and concubines. Their offspring could join the militia, join slave patrols, and compete with whites in commerce. The more benign attitude on the part of Iberians toward their black slaves, however, did not mean that the slaves accepted their condition willingly. Like their brothers in the north, they fled, they rebelled, and they killed their owners. Slave insurrections were more successful in Latin America than in English America.

The English, and other northern Europeans, had a different perspective about blacks. Probably "racism" best described their attitude. The first real exposure to blacks for the English was in 1554, when five West Africans were taken to London to learn the language. They could then return to Africa and help the English trade with the "Dark Continent." (The original English trade was in gold, not humans.) The English were introduced to anthropoid apes and blacks at about the same period in their history. The apes were different from baboons or monkeys: they had no tails and walked like men. The English perceived a similarity between manlike beasts and the "beastlike" men of Africa. Some believed that the blacks were derived from the apes, or that apes were the offspring of blacks and some African beast. A strong notion existed that sometimes apes and blacks copulated and that apes sexually preferred and attacked black women. This attitude toward blacks was almost uniformly accepted.[31]

Thomas Jefferson, one of the greatest minds America has produced, voiced this opinion in his "Notes on the State of Virginia" (1787).[32] Jefferson noted the physical differences between blacks and whites: there were great differences in color, figure, and hair. Blacks had less hair on their bodies and faces. They secreted less from their kidneys and more from their skin; this caused a strong, disagreeable odor from their skin. They were more tolerant of heat and less of cold because of these skin secretions. Black lungs were different, and they did not extract heat from air. (This probably referred to the concept of "Phlogiston.") Blacks required less sleep; after hard labor, they could stay up until midnight for amusement despite the need to get up for more labor at dawn. They were as brave as whites, but more "adventuresome," perhaps owing to a lack of the foresight needed to recognize danger.

Blacks preferred white women sexually, as the "oranootan" (synonymous here with ape) preferred the black woman over his own species. They were more ardent in their pursuit of the female, and their love was "eager desire, not a delicate merging of sentiment and sensation." Grief was short-lived. They were not reflective, so when not laboring or involved in discussions, they slept. Their memory was equal to that of whites, but their reasoning and their minds were inferior and their thought processes limited: they could never understand Euclidean geometry. They were tasteless and dull in imagination, and they had no skill in painting or sculpture; they were more gifted in music, but they could not produce poetry. Blacks were thus inferior to whites in body and mind; and this difference, thought Jefferson, was an obstacle to emancipation. If freed, the slave had to be "removed beyond the reach of mixture [with whites]."

Physicians supported the notion of the inferiority of blacks. John H. Van Eurie, a physician, claimed that Negroes were an inferior species of man and did not originate from the same source as whites, so they could not be forced to perform the activities that God assigned to whites.[33] The Caucasian brain was 92 cubic inches, with a cerebrum, the center of intellectual function, predominant over the cerebellum, the center of animal instincts. It was therefore capable of the progress and transmission of acquired knowledge to succeeding generations. The Negro brain was 65–70 cubic inches with the cerebellum predominant over the cerebrum; it was thus unable to transmit knowledge to succeeding generations. Could those who wished to elevate the Negro improve on God and add 25–30 percent to the Negro brain and supply more to the anterior portion? A Negress could not give birth to this being. The Caucasian race has progressed; the Negro today is where the white race was 4,000 years ago. Negroes never advanced beyond the hunter; they could temporarily advance when in contact with whites, but, this disappeared if the contact was broken. God permitted some amalgamation between races, but the mulatto or hybrid to the fourth generation was as sterile as the mule or most animal hybrids are in the first generation. (The concept of the mulatto's sterility was advanced to show that whites and blacks were similar but not identical. Most people discarded the sterility concept when they observed the mulatto's ability to procreate. They solved the dilemma by showing that a dog and a wolf, similar but not identical, could produce fertile offspring— like the mulatto.)

Another physician, Samuel M. Cartwright, described two illnesses common to blacks.[34] It is difficult to know whether this was written tongue in cheek to make light of a difficult problem, or whether the physician was serious and a product of his upbringing in Louisiana. According to the doctor, "poor slave working habits were due to a disease called 'dysesthesia aethiopica.' (The overseer called it rascality.) The sufferer was apt to do much mischief which appeared intentional. He destroyed or wasted everything he touched, abused livestock, and injured crops. He did his tasks in a headlong, careless manner, treading down with his feet or cutting with his hoe the plants he was supposed to cultivate, break up his tools, and spoiling everything. These accidents were due to the stupidity of mind and insensibility of the nerves induced by the disease."

The second disease was "drapetomania." This was a disease of the mind that caused Negroes to run away, but with proper medical advice it could be cured. The first symptom was a surly and dissatisfied attitude. To prevent progression, the cause of the discomfort had to be removed. If no cause was discerned, then "whipping the devil out of them" was the "best preventive measure against [their] absconding."

Not only were blacks inferior by nature, but the color black had a negative connotation.[35] In early England, white was on top of the scale, superior; black was on the bottom, inferior. Black meant dark, deadly, malignant, pertaining to death, baneful, sinister, foul, atrocious, wicked. White was pure, stainless, spotless, innocent, free of evil intent, and innocent. The English felt that the degree of inferiority was proportionate to the degree of pigmentation.

The eighteenth century could be described as the period of classification. Following the work of Linnaeus, everything had to be compartmentalized. The theory of the "Great Chain of Being" was developed. At the top of the scale was God, then the archangels, the angels and the Europeans (white). Farther down were American Indians, Laplanders and Malaysians, among others. At the bottom were blacks, who were inferior to whites. They were probably of the same genus but of a different species. Edward Long, in his book, *The History of Jamaica* (1774), described the Negro in animal terms. He claimed that the ape had almost the same mental power as the Negro. They acted similarly and engaged in sexual intercourse together. He believed an ape would be a suitable husband for a Hottentot female. Furthermore, apes resembled blacks more than blacks resembled whites. Long concluded with the belief that slavery was a structure of divinely ordained nature. The ape had dominion over his slaves, the lower animals; the white had dominion over his slaves, the Negroes.[36]

English anatomists described differences between blacks and whites. John Hunter, the famous English surgeon, graded animals according to their "facial angle." He believed that he could examine a skull and decide whether the individual was white, Asiatic, American Indian, black, "oranoutang," or monkey. Dr. Charles White claimed that the Negro more closely resembled the ape. His skull size showed lesser capacity. Dr. White believed that mankind was divided into several species, and they did not all derive from Adam and Eve.

In 1787, Samuel Stanhope Smith, president of Princeton and a Presbyterian minister, published an essay, "The Causes of the Variety of Complexion and Figure in the Human Species." He believed that the human species, did not come from several stocks but from one; the differences in men's appearance were due to natural causes, like climate and living habits. He was a dim light, however, in a sea of darkness. Others felt that heat caused blackness. The skin thickened in heat and bile became more active, coloring the middle layer of skin. Charles Jones believed that all people were white before the Tower of Babel. After Babel and the confusion of tongues, God changed manners, customs, habits and colors, so humankind would have no recollection of its former, united state. Hugh Williamson believed that climate, food, education, and habits determined color. He believed in the inheritance of acquired characteristics: America was a white country, and Negroes living here would gradually become white.[37] Dr. Benjamin Rush, the most prominent physician in colonial and federal America, believed that the color and facial characteristics of the black were a result of leprosy; the darkening of the skin and thickening of the nose and lips were observed in lepers. He believed that, in time, that blacks could become indistinguishable from whites. (It should be understood that Benjamin Rush was a vociferous opponent of slavery.)

Once society accepted the inferiority of the black, on the ground that he was of a lesser species, the next step was to keep him separate, and finally to demonstrate the benevolence of the slave system. Black indentured servants and slaves had more in common with white servants than either class had with their masters. They did much the same work side by side. This affinity between black and white servants was amply demonstrated by Bacon's Rebellion in 1676 in Virginia.[38] Free men and indentured servants—both black and white slaves looking for freedom—joined Bacon because they had no hope for free land or a future in a province controlled by a handful of white men.

The authorities recognized the need to separate future potential revolutionaries, and this was most easily accomplished along racial lines. The law identified slavery with blackness, and the slave codes restricted Negroes more tightly than white servants. The idea of the inferiority of blacks was pounded into white consciousness from the legislature, the courts, newspapers, and the pulpit. By the start of the Civil War, 3,000 major slaveholders controlled 8 million poor whites and 4 million blacks. That they were not completely successful in separating the races was seen in the presence of many children of mixed parentage. Society considered the "mulatto an abomination and a troublesome element in society."[39] Virginia in 1662, Maryland in 1663, Massachusetts in 1688, Connecticut and New Jersey in 1704, Pennsylvania and New York in 1706, South Carolina in 1712, Rhode Island in 1728, and North Carolina in 1741 all passed laws against "fornicating with negro women." Men were whipped in public for this transgression, and the rule of *partus sequitor ventrum* made the offspring slaves. Far more serious to the authorities was the union of white women with black men. In Virginia in 1691, a law fined the woman or sold her into service for five years, and the offspring was bound out for 30 years. Similar laws were passed in Maryland, Pennsylvania, and North Carolina.

The benevolence of slavery with respect to its victim was repeatedly expressed by slaveholders and their sympathizers. George Fitzhugh, a lawyer in Virginia, believed that the Negro was a grown-up child and had to be governed like a child; the master was his parent or guardian.[40] The black was improvident and he did not plan for the future; he wouldn't save money for his old age, and he would become a burden on society. The Negro was inferior to the white, and he would be outwitted in free competition, which would lead to his extermination; he could not earn as much money as whites. If left to his own devices, he would become idolatrous and a cannibal or be devoured by others. His slavery would be worse in Africa, and he would be heir to all vices and crimes. Slavery Christianized, protected, supported and civilized slaves, who were governed better than the free laborers in the North. Northern laborers beat their wives while slaves did not. Slaves were the happiest and freest people on earth. Children, the aged, and the infirm did not work but received the necessities of life; they were not oppressed by cares or labor. The work of the woman slave was not hard, and she was protected by her master from her husband. Men worked no more than nine hours per day in good weather, and they rested on the Sabbath and holidays. Negroes luxuriated in ease and could sleep anytime. The master cared for his slaves, and his wife was their housekeeper, nurse, and mother.

Others claimed that "equality" among the races was fundamentally wrong. "The great truth is that the negro is not equal to the white man; that slavery—subordination to the superior race—is his natural and normal condition" (Alexander Stephens).[41] Slaveholders took "low, degraded, savage Africans and civilized and improved them" (John C. Calhoun, whom we will meet later as a leader in the "colonization movement," accepted the benefits of slavery). Slavery was the natural and beneficent state of an innately savage people. "It has elevated him from the depths of barbarism and brutalism to a degree of civilization and usefulness, and happiness which he never would have reached through any other instrumentality"[42] (J.H. Van Eurie).

Chapter 2

AFRICAN ROOTS

Blacks, who composed one-sixth of the population of the new United States, were, with their progeny, the survivors of the trip across the Atlantic Ocean, with an occasional detour to the West Indies. The minute details of their life and society in Africa are beyond the scope of this chapter, but a general outline follows. Slaves were taken from the Senegal River area in the bulge of West Africa south for 3,000 miles to the southern tip of present-day Angola.[1] In addition, some came from East Africa in what is now Mozambique. Early Yankee slavers, to break the English monopoly on the slave trade, sailed around the southern tip of Africa to the east coast to pick up their share of "black gold." The holds of the sailing ships could be filled with dark black people from Central Africa, dark brown individuals from tribes of the Bantu group in East Africa (whose ancestors had thousands of years of contact with Indians, Arabs, and Malaysians), and, rarely, light-skinned natives from Ethiopia, Somalia, and the Sudan.[2]

Africans had no written history, but oral tradition described a unified West African state founded before the birth of Christ. Ghana (also called Kumbi or Walata) could boast 744 kings by A.D. 300.[3] This was a confederacy of settlements from Senegal to the upper Niger River. It was divided into provinces and smaller units governed by a hereditary ruling class. The inhabitants were predominantly farmers and herdsmen. By the tenth century, Muslim incursions brought changes to this agrarian society, which resulted in increased prosperity, power, and growth. At the acme of its power, Ghana could field an army of 200,000 warriors. Traders from Ghana crossed the Sahara desert carrying ivory, slaves, and gold. They returned from Muslim countries with wheat, fruit, sugar, textiles, brass, pearls, and salt. In 1076 the Almoravides brought their Muslim religion to Ghana. Unhappily, this incursion was followed by a waste of resources in religious wars, compounded by an extensive and persistent drought. The end result was a decline in Ghana's power by the end of the eleventh century. Accompanying this decline was the growth of Melle (Mali) to the west, which grew in influence from a small enclave in the seventh century to a powerful kingdom in 1235. Under the native Muslim Kecla dynasty, it reached from the Atlantic Ocean to Lake

Chad. Storytellers described the required pilgrimage of one of its emperors to Mecca in 1324, whose camel train spread to the horizon. Melle declined and was replaced by Songhay. Under the Sonni dynasty, Songhay defeated Melle, to become the greatest power in West Africa, but the Sonni family was overthrown in 1493 by Askia Mohammed. The limits of this kingdom extended from the Berber country in the north to the Mossi and Benin states in the south. Askia made the required pilgrimage to Mecca, where he learned administrative skills. He appointed chiefs (*noi*) over provinces and cities, and governors (*fari*) over subdivisions of his empire. Cities in the empire, like Gao, Walata, Timbuktu and Jenne, grew in wealth, and schools of law, surgery, and geography were founded. Timbuktu may have had a population of 100,000 and could boast of the University of Sankore, where scholars converged. Askia was eventually overthrown, however, by invading Moors.

West Africa saw the rise and fall of smaller kingdoms as well.[4] The Mossi states, the kingdom of Kanena-Bornu, Hausa city-states, Benin, Dahomey, and Ashanti each had their periods in the sun.

William Bosman, a slave trader under the Dutch flag, described the classes of society to which he was exposed.[5] The king was the apex of the pyramid and was often considered sacred. When he died, his successor was usually chosen from his family by an "electing family." The "enthroning family" invested the new king with the powers of office. The matrilineal line more commonly produced his heir, but in some kingdoms the patrilineal line was used. Occasionally the new king could be chosen from outside the former king's family: a member of the third level of society. The king had a court composed largely of trusted family members. There were also greater and lesser dignitaries, eunuchs, pages, bodyguards, artisans, doctors, historians, genealogists, astrologers, and slaves. Money to support the court came from royal lands, export and import duties, property taxes, and special levies. Conquered people, controlled by the military, sent tribute. The second level below the king consisted of the *caboceros*, or civil fathers, who supervised cities and villages. There was a set number of *caboceros*, and new members were taken from families of an inner circle. Occasionally a member of the general public could advance to this select group. These were usually older men, and this was a lifetime appointment. Below the civil fathers were the rich, who were thought to be special because they had become wealthy. They had to show proof of their great wealth with big, expensive parties and gifts, practices similar to those of Native Americans of the northwestern United States. The fourth group was that of the "common people," who tilled the soil and otherwise produced the wealth of society. Below them were the slaves.

Slaves were criminals, debtors, prisoners of war, and family members sold into slavery. The practice of Slavery had existed in Africa for centuries. Slaves were largely of the household variety, and they were counted as part of the family. They could be punished like children or other relatives by the head of the house. The slave could own property and other slaves, and could purchase his own freedom. Slave women who married free men became free. The slave could testify as a witness and inherit his master's property. The bondsmen worked in the house but rarely in the field. Therefore, slaves were a sign of wealth rather than producers of wealth. Unhappily, they could be sold away to the Middle East or, later, to European traders. They could also be used for religious rituals and were occasionally sacrificed in the worship of their master's ancestors. The nature of African slavery was modified by Muslim incursions. Women were taken for harems, for example, and men for military duty or menial tasks. They were obtained by purchase or conquest. Black kings, connected to Islam, remove and cooperated with the newcomers in establishing the slave trade to which Europe was heir.[6]

Politically, the basic social unit in West Africa was the family, composed of the progeny of a single ancestor, usually on the maternal side. The oldest male of the family was its leader. The family frequently occupied a village. Several families sharing a more remote common ancestor formed a clan, and several clans could come together to form a village state or tribal seat. These could merge to produce a small kingdom, and several kingdoms could join to form a federation or "empire."[7]

The houses in the villages were built of red clay or earth covered with woven rushes or palm leaves. Both men and women wore a vestlike garment reaching to the knees, with long, wide sleeves. Men wore drawers beneath the shirt. Their diet was composed of millet, fish, milk, rice, poultry and fruit. The people understood fermentation and drank palm wine. Early movies in the United States showed "Africans" cooking missionaries in a large pot. Cannibalism, however, probably did not exist to any extent, though it was sometimes imputed to other tribes. This concept then spread to white slavers. Many slaves feared they were being taken on board ships to be eaten, and this was one reason for their high suicide rate (to be discussed in Chapter 12).[8]

Monogamy was the usual practice, but polygamy was accepted if the husband could afford it. The suitor paid his future wife's family because he was taking her away from them (although she remained a part of her birth family after marriage). The cost of this first wife was paid by the head of the man's family. To obtain future wives, the male had to amass the required wealth himself. This kept polygamy to a minimum.[9]

Among the fourth class (the "common people"), social stratification was based upon the kind of work performed. Farmers were the highest category, but they did not own their own land, which belonged to the community and was distributed by "the master of the ground." Below the farmer was the herdsman, then hunters and fishermen, then those involved in construction, navigation, commerce, and gold mining, and finally those involved in the processing of commodities like soap, oil, and beer. These were not hard and fast demarcations. A miner going into agriculture could elevate his status in the community.

Iron smelting was a very old technique in Africa, and evidence of iron-work has been found in many parts of the continent. Artisans could also work with gold, silver, bronze, and copper. The blacksmith was an important member of the community. He made tools, agricultural equipment, weapons, and armor. His most common product was probably a tool resembling a hand axe used by farmers to till the soil. He recognized the need of intense heat for metal-working and devised a bellows made of reeds.[10]

A village could excel in the production of one or several items, and trade among villages was important. Trading goods were carried along rivers and the coast. Large fairs were held twice a year for trade, and these also worked to disseminate skills throughout the area. The medium of exchange was the cowrie shell and occasionally bars of iron or brass. However, barter was probably more common.

Religious beliefs varied, but generally monotheism existed, in the belief in a High God who had created the world and all its creatures.[11] However, each tribe had its own tribal deities. There were no categorical distinctions between life and death. Temporal and spiritual relationships were fluid. The oldest members of society were closest to their ancestors; therefore, they had a favorable position with the gods. They became the respected story-tellers, advisers, and historians. They accumulated wisdom over the years and had an assured place in the social structure of the community. Africans carried this concept with them when transported to America to a life of bondage.[12] Animism, the belief that spirits were present in every object, animate or inanimate, was a fairly general concept of religion throughout sub–Saharan Africa. Spirits had power over one's daily life. The spirit of a dead relative was worshipped, although spirits of long–dead ancestors had greater power than those of the recently deceased. These spirits "lived" near the living members of their family and watched over them; they were intimately involved in family affairs. Spirits were believed to occupy rocks, trees, earth, and sky. The village had a priestly class who were the patriarchs of the family. The priests could commune with spirits and conducted worship services. Human sacrifice was rare, but the blood of chickens, goats, and sheep was regularly sacrificed to a god. Other offerings included songs, prayers, and fermented drinks. There was a strong belief in magic, and its practice was widespread. An individual could carry around magic in an amulet. Sorcerers could divine the future.[13]

Proper burial of the dead was a sacred obligation of the family. Relatives were buried days to weeks after their demise. They were placed in cemeteries or under the floor of the hut they had inhabited during life. The burial chamber was not closed until all members of the family had presented offerings and were involved in the rite. Following the intrusion of the Arabs, many accepted Islam, and they were accepted as equals. Christianity did not take hold early in African exposure to this "white" religion.

Art was functional and related to daily activities. Artists produced masks and statues to be used in religious practices. Artisans worked with wood, glass, gold, ivory, terra-cotta, and clay. Craftsmen produced tapestry, pottery, and filigree.[14] Music was predominantly percussive with the use of tom-toms. Flutes, violins, harps, zithers, xylophones, and trumpets, however, were also used. Musicians composed lullabies, and songs for dancing, working, and religious ritual. The common form of song was a "call and response": a solo voice would sing the call, and the chorus would sing the response.[15]

African medicine was based on fetishism. Diseases were caused by an evil spirit, and the efficacy of therapy depended on the benevolent spirits that were infused into the patient: the "good spirit" chased the "evil spirit" out of the patient's body. The *abeabok* was the apothecary/village doctor. These "magicians" traveled from village to village treating the ill. They were knowledgeable in herb therapy and surgery. The herbs used to treat a disease were trade secrets, and the native doctor went through a long apprenticeship to learn his trade. The native doctor was not the witch doctor, however. The witch doctor in Africa most closely resembled a Christian Scientist or a psychiatrist in the West. He worked directly on the soul, and he drove out the disease by driving the "idea of the disease" out of the patient's mind. The witch doctor dealt with malevolent invisible spirits; some of these spirits, however, were human. Therefore, his methods often took the form of a criminal investigation. He was called in to assist in the discovery and connection of people responsible for disease (damage to another person). He probably acted something like a polygraph and could watch the accused's responses to his incantations.

For society to function, there had to be laws governing the activities of the individuals of that community. The Africans had laws relating to property, morality, and protection of life. The form of the law in some ways resembled that of medieval Europe. Occasionally ordeal by combat was used to decide disputed cases. There were no written laws, but narrators could describe ancient customs and usages, which were then employed as precedents to adjudicate a case before law. Witnesses testifying in "court" took an oath to tell the truth. New laws were formulated at a popular assembly (town meeting), and the town crier would proclaim the new decree at dusk, when everyone was at home. In this way, no one could claim ignorance of the law.[16]

Chapter 3

THE SLAVE TRADE

According to Booker T. Washington, the Europeans started to steal black Africans for service in Europe as early as A.D. 990.[1] The Moors "without curly hair" also had an active trade in slaves with the countries of southern Europe and the Middle East. The Arabs brought their "black ivory" to Cyprus for further European distribution; these blacks were trained to be house servants, because there were plenty of white serfs to work the land. The Spanish merchants of Seville imported yellow and "black gold" from West Africa early in the fifteenth century, because Juan de Valladod (a black) was made judge and mayor of all Negroes and mulattoes, both free and slave, in Seville and the archbishopric surrounding it in 1474.

The Portuguese were the originators of the slave trade in Christian Europe. Prince Henry the Navigator (1394–1460), third son of King John I of Portugal, founded a navigation college at Sagres on Cape Saint Vincent in 1419. His purpose was to discover new lands (where he could turn a profit) and to bring Catholicism to the heathen. He assembled geographers, cartographers, and naval architects to build fleets and send them to Africa. During his campaigns against the Moors in 1415 and 1418, Moorish prisoners of war related stories of gold and slaves beyond the Sahara Desert. Henry preferred the sea route to these riches rather than crossing the desert. By the time of his death, Portugal had explored 2,000 miles of the West African coast. In 1486 Bartholomeu Dias reached the Cape of Good Hope, a way to the riches of the Indies without traversing Moorish lands.[2]

One of Henry's captains, Antem Gonsalvez, captured three Moors. To obtain their freedom they gave the captain ten Negroes. He brought those unfortunates to Henry in 1442, who in turn presented them to the pope.[3]

Under King John II in 1482, the fort at El Mine on the African Gold Coast was built. Other forts at Cape Verde and on the Niger River followed, and the African slave trade had its beginning.[4] (The Catholic Church under popes Eugenius IV and Nicholas V sanctified the project as a means of rescuing the souls of the benighted blacks.) Unlike the rest of Europe, southern Portugal needed blacks for work, because the area was underpopulated due to war, epidemics, and emigration. By 1550 Lisbon was said to have more people with black ancestors than those with white ancestors only. The Portuguese did not share the English attitude toward blacks, and intermarriage was common.

Following the European "discovery" of America, the world was divided between Spain and Portugal, the two Catholic naval powers. In 1493 Pope Alexander VI (who was of Spanish birth) drew a "demarcation line": a line 370 leagues (1,500 miles) west of the Cape Verde Islands was drawn from north to south. Everything west of the line belonged to Spain, everything east of it to Portugal. This effectively locked Spain out of securing and transporting Africans. The Spaniards initially used the indigenous population of the New World as slaves, but these people were not able to perform the duties required of them. Spain then turned to Africa, a Portuguese monopoly. The tide of African slave importation into the New World started in 1501, with slaves carried in Portuguese ships.

For about 100 years, Portugal was the major, though not the only, player in the trade. The Spanish monarchy tried to control the extent of the trade with duties and licenses, but the plantation owners needed healthy black bodies. They encouraged foreign interlopers to bring in help beyond Spanish official control. In 1562 John Hawkins, with three ships and 100 men, financed by English merchants, left Plymouth for Sierra Leone. He took 300 blacks and carried them to Hispaniola without opposition and with great profit. The Spanish monarchy learned of this invasion when Hawkins sent two ships loaded with hides and other commodities, picked up in Hispaniola, to the Spanish mainland. His second trip in 1564 had four ships, including the *Jesus*, Queen Elizabeth's ship. He picked up 400 slaves at Sierra Leone and carried them to the northern coast of South America, west of the Orinoco River. Hawkins returned to England with gold, silver, pearls, and other jewels, clearing 60 percent on the investment. Queen Elizabeth, delighted with her share of the booty, knighted Hawkins. His crest was a black African bound and captive. His third trip in 1567 carried 450 slaves in six ships. However, Hawkins did not follow the procedures of the trade. Rather than dealing with African chiefs for human bodies, he raided villages and captured his own. The Africans fought back, and many of his crew died of lockjaw from wounds received in battle. He was able to gather 150 people. Hawkins then allied himself with one "king" fighting another and was able to fill his complement. He landed his cargo at Rio de la Hacha on the northern coast of South America. This time, the planters refused to do business, so he attacked the town and destroyed its defenses. The planters then bought 200. Hawkins in turn was assaulted off Vera Cruz with the loss of four ships, his bullion, and most of his men. The captain landed in Cornwall in 1589 with little to show for his effort.

John Hawkins was not the only intruder, only the most famous. Many adventurers, before and after him, traded with Africa for gold, ivory, pepper, and pearls. John Hawkins's father, William, was active in the trade, as were other English, French, Danish, and German captains. Formally, their monarchs might have looked askance at this illegal trade, but informally many were partners in these ventures. In an attempt to control the competition of an unregulated slave trade, Elizabeth I of England in 1588 granted a monopoly to merchants of Exeter and London to carry commerce to the area between Senegal and the Gambia River for ten years. Other patents were given, including one to William St. John in 1618 by King James I covering the entire coast of West Africa. It was administered by the newly formed Company of Adventurers of London, but it failed. In 1631 Nicholas Crispe received a monopoly from Charles I for 31 years. In 1660 Charles II granted a charter to the Company of Royal Adventurers into Africa. This was to be primarily a gold-mining venture, but it too failed. (Interestingly, Charles II ordered all gold taken from Africa engraved with an elephant to distinguish it from other English coins. These were called guineas to commemorate their site of origin.) In 1663 the company received a second charter and a new name, "The Company of Royal Adventurers of England Trading into Africa." They received a monopoly for commerce in slaves, the true gold of West Africa. It must be remembered that the patent was only a piece of paper, and its owners had to fight for the area given to them and then defend it against other interlopers. The company built forts to protect the property seized from Portugal, the "rightful" owners of West Africa according to the Papal Declaration of 1493.[5]

In the seventeenth century, the Dutch were more active than the English in attacking Portuguese control of the African trade. The Dutch West India Company, chartered in 1621, had among its privileges the monopoly to bring slaves to the Dutch colonies in the New World. The Dutch, in their long war for independence from Spain, did much of their fighting at sea and against the colonies of their oppressors as well as the Portuguese. In 1637 they seized Saint George of El Mine, the oldest and strongest Portuguese fort on the Gold Coast. The Dutch continued to chip away at Portuguese possessions until 1660, when they signed a peace treaty with Spain and Portugal. They returned control of Brazil to the Portuguese and received control of the Guinea coast in return, gaining legal possession of what they had captured in the previous 40 years. The new owners now had to fight off the other intruders. The English, with some help from the French, actively attacked the Guinea coast. These activities led to a naval war in 1665. In the Treaty of Breda, on July 21, 1667, each country kept what it had seized. (England was now in possession of New Netherlands.) The Dutch were still the leaders of the slave trade until the end of the century, when they were supplanted by the English.[6]

The Spaniards, like their neighbors on the Iberian Peninsula, were not permitted to keep their possessions in the New World. The Dutch seized Curaçao, Saint Eustatius, and Tobago by 1640.[7] The French Company of the Islands of America took Guadaloupe, Martinique, Marie-Galante, Saint Lucia, and Grenada. The Danes grabbed Saint Thomas (Virgin Islands). The voracious English occupied Saint Christopher, Barbados, Nevis, Antigua, Montserrat, and Jamaica, as well as the coast of North America. These islands, with several growing seasons each year, could supply the demands of Europe for tobacco and sugar, and the mother countries encouraged their merchants actively to participate in the slave trade in order to work the land. What had been a "trickle" in the sixteenth century (900,000 slaves) became a torrent in the seventeenth (2,750,000), and a deluge in the eighteenth (7,000,000).

In the seventeenth century, the French monarchy granted patents to its merchants (French Company of the West Indies, Company of Senegal, Second Company of Senegal, Company of Guinea, the Royal Company of Senegal). These were for the most part unsuccessful, probably due to the enormous appetite of the English. The French companies carried approximately 3,000 slaves per year to their colonies. But after their defeat in the War of the Spanish Succession, the French left England in control of the slave trade until its termination in the nineteenth century.

Throughout this period, Spain, despite the loss of many areas to the European naval powers, still controlled large regions of the New World. Spain did not cross the "Demarcation Line" and never carried African slaves to America. Spain depended on the *asiento* (contract) with a foreign power or company to supply the necessary labor. In 1517 Charles V, heir to Ferdinand and Isabella, granted the first patent to a Flemish favorite (La Bresa) to carry 4,000 slaves to Cuba, Hispaniola, Jamaica, and Puerto Rico. He in turn sold the monopoly for 25,000 ducats to Genoese merchants.[8] Throughout much of the sixteenth and seventeenth centuries, Portugal held the *asiento*. This did not interfere, however, with the illegal slave trade by other European powers to Spain's American colonies, with the collusion of Spanish planters. In 1696 the Portuguese Guinea Company was given the *asiento* to deliver 10,000 tons of Negroes to Spain's New World territory.[9] In 1702 the French Guinea Company received the *asiento*; it was to deliver 38,000 slaves to the Spanish West Indies during a period of ten to twelve years.[10] In 1713, after Queen Anne's War ended with the Treaty of Utrecht, England received the contract. England had to deliver 114,000 pieces of "India" of both sexes and all ages during a 30-year period. England kept the *asiento* for the remainder of the century, and during this period Spain signed ten such treaties for a total of 500,000 Africans. In none of the treaties were there any specifics regarding the humane treatment of the cargo.

The British Slave Trade

Every European nation with possessions in America gave a monopoly to a company of its merchants to deliver slaves to its possessions. The dawn of the eighteenth century showed the British to be in control of much of the territory that required slaves in agriculture. Add to this the *asiento* legally to supply the Spanish colonies with black laborers and one can appreciate the statement of Malachy Postlethwayt: he claimed that the money from the slave trade probably fueled the English Industrial Revolution.[11] The monopolies granted by British monarchies to groups of merchants were unsuccessful for the most part. Capital had to be raised to buy ships and trading commodities. "Factories" (forts) had to be built on the African coast to hold and train new slaves as well as to fight off trespassers. Monopolies tended to get administratively top-heavy. The recipients of the slaves rightly complained that the prices demanded for the "merchandise" were too high. Finally, the "in group" could not supply all of the merchandise demanded by the American planters.

The Cabo Corso Castle, owned by the Royal African Company, provides an example of the expense incurred by a private company to remain in the trade. The castle was a fort constructed in seven years, with outerworks, platforms, and bastions built of brick, lime, and tarras (plaster). Inside were apartments for the director general, factors (traders), writers (clerks), mechanics, and soldiers (mercenaries). Other parts were given over to arms magazines. There were warehouses, storehouses, granaries, and guard rooms. They had repositories (pens) for slaves, as well as vaults to store rum (an important trade commodity). The fort was defended by 74 great guns, as well as small arms, blunderbusses, buccaneer guns, pistols, swords, and cutlasses. The fort had storage space for tools required by brickmakers, bricklayers, armorers, gunners, and gardeners, as well as a chapel for prayer. Many small boats were needed to carry slaves from the fort to ocean-going vessels. Seamen, stevedores, messengers, and workmen passed between the fort and these vessels. While waiting to be transferred for the trip abroad, the slave started his "education" in the fort. Some were trained as smiths, carpenters, armorers, masons, stonecutters, sawyers, and brickmakers. A semiskilled black brought a higher price on the market.[12]

The "Glorious Revolution" in 1688 resulted in the banishment of the Stuarts and the crowning of William and Mary. With the new regime, the concept of free and open trade (only to British subjects, that is) developed. In 1688 the Royal Africa Company lost its monopoly and later declared bankruptcy. In 1750 King George II opened the slave trade to all of his subjects, from the Port of Saller in South Barbary to the Cape of Good Hope. What British merchants had been doing illegally during the monopoly now became legal. By an act of parliament, any merchant could participate in the trade if he paid the British government 10 percent of the value of the commodities shipped out of Africa. This money was then paid to the Royal Africa Company to pay for the upkeep of its forts in Africa.[13] The merchants complained about the cost, however, because the company did not maintain the forts properly, and all the forts were above the Volbe River. They argued that no duty should be paid for trading below the Volbe. Also, the traders wanted to be able to purchase barter goods for the African trade outside the British Empire; this concept contravened the basic tenets of mercantilism, and it was disallowed.

In a very short time, the individual merchants were supplying more slaves than the Royal Africa Company. They did it more cheaply, and they paid the government more money in taxes. The government used the money to subsidize the company, and this assistance sustained it for several years. Initially, the parliamentary annuity was £10,000, but that sum increased yearly. Finally, it was discovered that the company was padding its costs, and the monopoly was formally revoked. However, market forces accomplished sooner what the government did later. The company ended its participation in the slave trade in 1731 and declared bankruptcy. The independent slavers formed the Company of Merchants Trading in Africa in 1750, and any slaver could join for a 40-shilling initiation fee. It was controlled by nine directors, three each from London, Liverpool, and Bristol. The trade in humans increased geometrically. In the 100 years ending in 1786, more than 2 million blacks were carried to the British colonies. The Company of Merchants functioned until 1821, when the trade was suppressed.

Early in British involvement in the slave trade, the centers of activity were London and Bristol. During the eighteenth century, Liverpool supplanted all competitors. Between 1751 and 1787, one-tenth of all ships leaving Liverpool were slavers. By 1788, 90 slavers left that city each year. They carried 2,700, sailors as well as manufactured goods for trading worth between £80,000 and £90,000. In 1795 Liverpool controlled five-eighths of the British trade and three-sevenths of the entire European slave trade. The net profit from carrying slaves and other merchandise reached £250,000 per year. The ripple effects from the trade provided work for joiners, shipwrights, ropemakers, gunmakers, coopers, blockmakers, bankers, lawyers, merchants and investors. Factories to supply the goods were opened for the production of iron, copper, brass, beads, lead, and sails. Between 1783 and 1793, 878 ships from Liverpool were slavers; they carried 303,737 blacks worth £15,186,850. Merchants' profits reached £1,700,000.[14]

American Involvement in the Trade

The beginning of New England's involvement in the slave trade is subject to debate. A ship out of Salem, Massachusetts, brought slaves to Boston in 1638.[15] In 1639 Hartford had black slaves. The other contender for the dubious honor of bringing the first slaves was the Rainbow, in 1645.[16] The ship reached Africa only to find a line of English ships waiting to pick up a cargo. Captain Smith suggested that the waiting captains arm their sailors and raid a town. For his part in the action, Smith received two slaves. When he returned to Boston, he was arrested and convicted of murder, man-steal-ing, and sabbath-breaking (the raid was carried out on a Sunday). However, Smith was eventually freed because the crime was committed outside of Mas-sachusetts' jurisdiction. The colony paid to return the slaves to Africa.

Americans, as British subjects, were licensed to join the slave trade pro-vided they paid 10 percent of their profits to the Royal African Company. Boston was the main port of departure for the ships, but gradually, Rhode Island replaced Massachusetts as the center of the trade. By 1750 Newport had 100 ships in the slave trade. Early slavers brought their cargo to the West Indies for "seasoning," because slaveholders feared those fresh from Africa. They could handle "home-grown" servile slaves, but Africans were rebellious. Toward the end of the slave-trading period, Africans were brought directly to the colonies. Newport, Rhode Island, became the major port for incoming slaves.[17] From there, they were shipped throughout the colonies. Connecti-cut, involved to a lesser degree, sent manufactured goods to the West Indies and brought in seasoned slaves.

Just as the slave trade was important to the industrial growth of England, so it represented a tremendous boost for New England. The New England-ers recognized early that the rocky, infertile soil could not support a grow-ing population. They turned to fishing, shipbuilding, and sailing to supple-ment their wealth. In addition to the gold brought in from the sale of slaves, capital was generated by shipbuilding for the trade, as well as through the employment of seamen. Massachusetts and Rhode Island had a major indus-try in rum production. This commodity, preferred by African "kings," was used to barter for bodies. It also paid for sugar and molasses from the West Indies used in its production. New England factories also turned out woolens and cotton goods, copper and brass vessels, firearms, handcuffs, chains and instruments of torture, spermacetti candles, and gunpowder used in the trade.[18]

British merchants owned 86 percent of the ships used in the colonial slave trade, and these brought in 89 percent of the slaves. However, most British ships in the eighteenth-century slave trade were built in the Ameri-can colonies. New England produced the greatest number, but Bermuda, Virginia, and South Carolina had productive shipyards for the trade. Two types of ships were produced. The larger ones, carrying about 72 slaves per ship, were built for the direct Africa-to-eastern-seaboard trade (mostly Vir-ginia, Maryland, and South Carolina). Smaller ships, which carried about 14 slaves per vessel, were traveled between the West Indies and East Coast ports. These ships carried other commodities as well. The larger, more costly ships were primarily owned by English merchants, because capital could be raised more easily in London and Liverpool. The smaller ships were frequently owned by colonials. The American ships, plying the West Indian trade, car-ried manufactured goods and food. They picked up "seasoned" slaves and raw materials for the distilleries. Land in the West Indies was too valuable to grow foodstuffs, so these and clothing for slaves were imported in colonial ships. The English large ships left England with manufactured goods, which were traded for slaves in Africa. The slaves were carried to the West Indies or to a mainland southern port where they were traded for raw materials. Sugar, tobacco, rice, indigo, turpentine, and masts were carried to the home islands, the "triangular trade."[19]

The slave trade from New York began with the Dutch. The Dutch West India Company had the monopoly for the Dutch colonies. Ships for the triangular trade run were outfitted in New Amsterdam. They traveled to Africa, then to Curacao, and back to New Amsterdam. After New Netherlands was ceded to the British, the Royal Africa Company took over the monopoly. In the last decades of the seventeenth century, New York traders sailed around the Cape of Good Hope to Madagascar for their cargo. They then traveled to southern ports as well as to New York City. Early in its involvement in the trade, New York took a back seat to Boston and Newport. However, a series of events in the middle of the eighteenth century resulted in a rapid growth of New York's share in the transport of human cargo. Jamaica's sugar production grew to supply the increased European demand, and more black hands were needed. South Carolina and Georgia needed bodies to produce rice and indigo. (It was at this time that Great Britain opened Europe to American rice, which resulted in a doubling of acreage to raise the grain.) Furthermore, the Royal Africa Company went bankrupt, and the *asiento* became a dead issue. During the French and Indian War, trade decreased because of French seizure of ships and increased insurance rates. The victorious conclusion of the war ended the French threat and trade rebounded. Between 1715 and 1769, 4,398 slaves were brought to New York. Most came directly from Africa, while some came from the West Indies and a few from South Carolina. Smaller ships were used in the New York trade, because a large cargo of slaves would glut the market. The demands in the North were minimal compared with those in the West Indies and the Deep South. Slaves for the New York market were frequently landed in New Jersey, because that colony had no duty on slaves. Overall, New York traders delivered few Africans to the West Indies and the plantation South. Most slaves imported into New York were used to work the large estates along the Hudson River. A few went singly and doubly to smaller successful farmers who could afford to buy them.[20]

Most ships from New York were 40 tonners, with a crew of seven or eight. Most were built for the West Indian trade, but some went to Africa. They could carry only a small cargo, but they were fast, capable of making a one-way trip in 40 days. On average, they spent about 16 weeks trading on the African coast. Although they carried fewer slaves, they were able to make the round-trip more rapidly. A shorter time spent on the ship meant a healthier cargo on arrival in New York; there were also fewer deaths and less disease among the crew. The slaves were kept on board until they were sold. This might require two or three weeks, because the demand was light. The traders tried to reach New York in the late spring or summer; since the need for slaves dropped in the cold months, and the buyer had the added expense of purchasing warm clothes. Most successful traders realized a profit of 50 percent on their investment.

The American Revolution stopped the slave trade temporarily. It restarted, however, after the hostilities ended, and it was needed to restore fortunes destroyed in the war. Liberty took a back seat to economics. Prior to the war, many colonies had posted large import duties on slaves to curb their import and to encourage white immigration. These duties were uniformly vetoed by the royal governors under orders from the Privy Council and the Council on Foreign Plantations in London: the slave trade was too important to the mother country's finances to allow any tampering by the colonials. After the war, Rhode Island permitted traders to bring their cargo to Newport if they could not sell it elsewhere; however, they had to re-export that cargo within one year. Those trying to flaunt the law were fined £1,000 per ship and £100 per slave. (It should be remembered that British forces occupied Newport for much of the war and destroyed its prosperity; so perhaps this law was an attempt to restore the city to its previous position.) Connecticut and Massachusetts passed similar laws in 1788. Virginia closed its ports to slavers in 1778, as did Maryland in 1783. North Carolina placed a prohibitive duty on imported slaves in 1786, but it was repealed in 1790. In 1791 North Carolina forbade importation of African slaves. South Carolina closed its port to slaves until 1803; it was reopened until 1808, when external slave trade became illegal. Georgia excluded foreign slaves in 1798.[21]

The new United States suffered severe trading problems as a result of its newfound independence. The nation was now outside the favored trading status accorded all members of the British Empire. However, Americans still needed English manufactured goods, which led to a negative balance of trade. To recoup their losses of gold, the merchants turned to the West Indies. The plantation owners of the islands needed American foodstuffs and ships to carry their produce, but all European nations had "navigation acts" similar to Great Britain's, which excluded American ships. So, Yankee captains depended on smuggling and other evasions to keep their merchant marine afloat; many carried foreign registry forms. The Americans' difficulty was solved by two incidents outside their control. First, in the 1780s, Spain opened the slave trade to all ships. Second, the Napoleonic wars led to a greater portion of trade carried in neutral (American) ships. By 1793 the United States and Great Britain controlled two-thirds of the slave trade. In 1794 the United States alone controlled more than 50 percent of the market. Although

American ships carried fewer slaves per ship from Africa (approximately 44, compared with 68 for Great Britain and 155 for France), they controlled the intra–Caribbean trade.[22]

The Trip

Slavery existed in Africa long before European penetration, and so the structure for gathering and moving slaves was already present. Individuals were sentenced to slavery for adultery, thievery, destruction of fetishes, and debt. During periods of famine, individuals could sell themselves, as well as part or all of their families into slavery. Gambling sometimes led to slavery, and a person could gamble himself into bondage. Some were kidnapped and sold (called *sanyared*). A significant source of slaves was prisoners of war. Following European intervention, "wars" represented the major source of bondsmen.[23] According to Booker T. Washington, 3.2 million individuals were transported to the New World from the Niger Delta in 200 years. Total numbers removed from all of Africa reached 18 million. White traders carried French brandy, rum, iron bars, linen, brass kettles, glass buttons, beads, brass rings, bracelets, medals, bangles, gunpowder, musket balls, muskets, clothing, knives, red calico, and silk. The arms were the most important items because they could be used in "war" to procure slaves from tribes not yet introduced to gunpowder.[24] The trader approached an African chief with gifts, in return for which he would give the European permission to trade in his domain. The chief appointed men of his entourage to assist the trader. These were the *cabocers*, who gathered the victims for sale. Prices were agreed upon in advance with the chief. The price varied with age, sex, location of the trading post, and the time at which the trade occurred. In the mid–eighteenth century, a healthy male might cost £20 or 110 gallons of rum or one-half hogshead of brandy or 12–14 iron bars.[25]

Slaves were taken in raids on unsuspecting villages, which were surrounded while the inhabitants slept. Huts were set afire, and the survivors were rounded up and marched away. Venture Smith was a victim of such a raid. He lived on the Guinea coast until he was seized by members of another tribe who had guns. His father was tortured and killed to force him to divulge the site of his buried wealth. The child believed that there were 6,000 warriors in the party. The raiders moved the coffle (a slave caravan of chained blacks) in a westerly direction. They laid waste to villages as they passed, enslaving the inhabitants and carrying off their livestock for food. The train eventually reached a "castle," where the slaves were kept for market. A slaver from Rhode Island was the buyer: Venture Smith was sold to Robertson Mumford for a few gallons of rum and a piece of calico. He was named Venture, because he was purchased as Mumford's own venture. That day 260 slaves were sold to fill up the ship's cargo space.[26]

William Bosman, a Dutch slave trader, described the trade at the port of Whydah in West Africa. The white trader paid £100 to "Customs of the King and the Great Men." For this, he received free license to trade. Before dealing with others, the trader had to purchase all of the king's slaves at a set price, which was usually one-quarter to one-third above the going market price. The regular slaves were taken out of their prison and assembled on a large plain. Surgeons from the ships examined them. The "commodities" were stripped naked: the sick were set aside. These were the *invalids*, or *machions*. Included among the sick were people thought to be more than 35 years old, those with maimed extremities, absence of teeth, gray-headed, eyes covered with a film, and venereal disease and other diseases. The well were separated, numbered, and listed according to purchaser. They were branded on the chest with the name of the company to separate them from British or French purchases, as well as to prevent the black seller (*slaffee*) from switching them for a poorer grade. Prices were set. A woman was valued at 75–80 percent of a male. The slaves were paid for in bartered goods or in the currency of the trader's country of origin. The slaves were then returned to prison until they were sent out to the ship. The "goods" not accepted for purchase were killed because of the expense of keeping them or sending them back home. After the sale, the cost of upkeep fell on the new owners—this was about two pence per day per slave. To save money, the slaves were transferred to the ship as soon as possible. They were moved in long canoes paddled by free blacks called *krumen*. The slaves were kept naked unless the captain ordered them covered. The "cargo" was fed three times a day, and the food was "better than they received in their own country." The men were kept on one side, women on the other. The slaves' better rations suggested to them that they were being fattened for their captors' future meals. To prevent this, many rebelled and tried to kill the Europeans. Often the rumor of cannibalism was started by one slave. If discovered, he was shot in the head, and the rumor then subsided.[27]

The slavers were not above "picking up a bonus." One tribal chief brought a coffle of slaves taken in war. After concluding his business, he was invited on board ship for dinner. He was drugged and awakened at sea—now a member of the coffle.[28] The captain of the ship received a monthly salary plus other "perks of the trade." Of every 104 slaves taken on board, for example, he received four of these slaves for making the purchase; the cost of carrying his slaves was paid by the ship owners. If he delivered his cargo to the West Indies and picked up another coffle for sale on the mainland, he received 2.5–5 percent of the value of the new "cargo." The captain could also use his personal slaves as crewmen, and he pocketed their salaries.[29] The captain's bonus was not shared by the crew, who put their lives on the line in any voyage to Africa: a Guinea-bound ship rarely returned with more than one-half of its original crew.[30] Thomas Clarkson examined the rosters of ships leaving Liverpool from 1786 to 1787. Of 3,170 sailors who shipped out, 1,428 returned; 642 died (20 percent); and the rest deserted or were left behind due to illness. Of those who returned, many went from the ship to a naval hospital and never recovered. Sailors not aboard slavers had a lower mortality rate. Twenty-four West Indians sailed out and lost only six crew members; on 24 slavers, the death rate was 216. The loss of seamen on slavers was greater than on all other English trading vessels combined. Death was caused by the usual hazards at sea, as well as tropical diseases and insurrection by the "cargo."

The literature is replete with mortality statistics on the six-week trip from Africa to the West Indies or mainland ports. Some believe that one of three slaves died on the "middle passage." If 18 million left Africa during the "trading period," then perhaps 6 million died. Lord Palmerston, who opposed the slave trade, believed that of every three blacks taken from the interior, one reached America. According to the tables kept by the Board of Trade between 1680 and 1688, the Africa Company shipped out 60,783 "pieces of merchandise" and delivered 46,394—a loss of 23 percent. In business terms, this was a loss of principal. These slaves were paid for in Africa, and failure to deliver them for sale at their destination was a serious loss.

The slaves were brought on board the ship in chains. For the first few days, they were kept packed in the hold of the ship. They were forced to lie "spoon fashion" on their sides to conserve space. A fully grown male received eighteen inches' width by six feet of length; women received five feet ten inches of length by sixteen inches; boys five feet by fourteen inches; and girls four feet, six inches by twelve inches. Lord Palmerston commented that they had less room than a corpse in a coffin. Crowding was so intense that the British Parliament passed a law restricting the numbers of slaves to no more than five slaves per three-ton capacity in a ship of 200 tons.[31] Like so much unpopular legislation, this was not obeyed by the ships' captains.

An English ship's surgeon left a description of conditions on board a slaver. Men slaves, upon boarding the ship, were fastened two by two with handcuffs on their wrists and cuffs riveted on their legs. They were sent to a compartment, separate from the women, who were not cuffed. Boys were kept in a third compartment. They were all below deck. The slaves were placed on their sides. The height between layers prevented an upright posture except when under the grating. Platforms were built between decks to stow more slaves. In each compartment were three or four conical buckets for the "cargo" to relieve itself. Some were unable to reach the bucket and relieved themselves where they lay. The buckets were too small for the purpose they served and overflowed before they could be emptied daily. At eight in the morning, the slaves were brought up on deck. A chain passed through rings on their shackles was attached to two ring-bolts on the deck. Fifty to 60 were chained this way. If the weather was good, they remained on deck until four or five in the afternoon. Their diet consisted of horsebeans (horse-eye beans, a West

Indian leguminous plant) boiled to a pulpy consistency, as well as boiled yams and rice. Occasionally they received a small feeding of beef or pork. They also received "slabber sauce" made of palm oil, flour, water, and pepper. Slaves were fed at eight in the morning and at four in the afternoon, and were served in a bucket. Ten blacks sat around the bucket and fed themselves with a wooden spoon, which was frequently lost and not replaced, and the individual was forced to feed himself by hand. The ration of water was one half-pint per meal, presented in a bucket with a pannekin (a utensil with a straight handle, like a sauceboat). Food was eaten on deck in good weather and below deck in bad. If the voyage was long, rations were cut in half. If the slaves refused to eat in an attempt to commit suicide, shovels with hot coals were placed near their lips with the threat of forcing them to swallow the coals. One captain poured melted lead on the heads of those who refused to eat. Other captains used a *speculum oris* to force open the victim's mouth. The "cargo" was forced to dance for exercise and to "dispel melancholia." Refusal resulted in a whipping with a cat-o'-nine-tails. Music was provided by a drum or tub. The slaves were forced to accompany the dance with song. Women received beads as a diversion. Another diversion was sex. The ordinary seaman could have sex with the female slave if she consented, while officers could take their pleasure without consent. The blacks suffered from seasickness, and many died, particularly the women. Between decks the ships had five or six air-ports on each side which were four by six inches. About 1 in 20 ships had wind-sails. (These were ducts made of sails with an opening to the wind. The forward movement of the ship forced air down to the farthest reaches of the hold.) In bad weather, these were closed, and the holds became hot and toxic, leading to fevers and fluxes (dysentery), with many deaths. The floor would be covered with blood and mucus from the flux. Those who fainted were brought on deck where some died. Slaves who sickened were taken to the under half deck and laid on bare planks. The rocking of the ship caused the skin to be rubbed away over the bony prominences. Some lay in mucus and blood, and the flesh was more easily rubbed away, causing severe pain. The surgeon applied plasters, which were of no help. Bandages were removed by the patients. Every morning, the surgeon went below to make rounds. Several would have died during the night and were still cuffed to their mates. Both were taken on deck, and the dead were thrown overboard. Insurrection was common and was suppressed with bloodshed, though some were successful. Some slaves were able to jump overboard, but were eaten by sharks, which always followed a slaver.[32]

A similar story was told by the African Gustavus Vassa to show the English the horrors of the slave trade (1789). According to the writer, most slaves were captured in military expeditions by African chiefs. The narrator, Vassa, was kidnapped. When he was brought on board the ship, he saw a large copper pot with boiling water next to a group of chained blacks, and so he believed he was going to be eaten. The captive was placed under the deck where there was a great stench. He could not eat and was flogged to stimulate his appetite. Some were whipped to death. The slaves were chained and kept below, so they could not learn how the handle the ship. They were packed together and sweated, producing an overwhelming stench that was responsible for many deaths. (Ships miles to the leeward side of a slaver could pick up the stench.) Tubs were placed around for toilet use. Children fell in and were almost suffocated. Many did suffocate from lack of air in the far reaches of the hold. Vassa weakened, and he was brought on deck without chains in an attempt to revive him. The crewmen caught and ate fish. They threw the uneaten part back overboard despite the cries of hunger from the blacks, who were flogged if they attempted to steal some of the fish. Finally the ship reached Barbados. Merchants and planters were welcomed on board. The whites examined the "merchandise," who cringed because of the fear of being eaten. Old slaves from the island were brought on board to quiet them and reassure them that the whites were not cannibals. The slaves were taken on shore and placed in parcels. At a signal, the buyers rushed in and chose those they preferred without any interest in family groups.[33]

The practice of cannibalism was attributed to one tribe by another, perhaps like frightening misbehaving children with the bogeyman. The blacks believed whites were human flesh-eaters, and those marched west from the interior believed they were heading for the pot. The white slavers encouraged this belief, but they attributed the horror of cannibalism to slavers of other nations. This fear was supposed to prevent slaves from running away (they might be caught by the others). The captain of the ship tried to dispel this fear to prevent insurrection or suicide. When slaves were taken on board, some sadistic crew members rekindled this anxiety. They drank red wine, which the slaves assumed was blood. Many rebelled, hoping they would be killed immediately.[34]

Suicide was attempted frequently. In some tribes, it was a form of religious martyrdom. The suicide believed that it would end his suffering and that he would return home. When the other slaves saw the body, they put their head bandannas on the suicide, because they believed the clothing would accompany the individual home and greet friends and family. The danger of suicide was highest when the slaves arrived in the new land, particularly among the Africans of high station at home. It was not uncommon for groups to do it together. Certain groups, like the Ibos, were more prone to do away with themselves. Some groups committed the act in a specific way—by hanging or cutting their throats. Others drowned themselves, relating this act to the trip over the water. Still others believed that they would fly back home, carried by the "magic chains" they tied to their bodies before jumping. They carried food and water to accompany them on the flight. In an attempt to discourage suicide, the master might cut off the suicide's head and place it on a pole. Other slaves were paraded around the pole and asked how the suicide could fly home without his head. Some mutilated the body, while others resorted to burning it and spreading the ashes. Still others threatened to kill themselves and follow the slaves back home to beat them endlessly. Finally, others resorted to dismembering the corpse, because such a corpse could not return to Africa. Gradually, with time in America, the suicide rate dropped. Over the centuries of slavery, however, the number of successful suicides reached the hundreds of thousands.[35]

The Triangular and Straight Trade

Much attention has been paid to the triangular trade, from England to Africa to the West Indies and back to England, and from New England to Africa to the West Indies and back to Boston or Newport. This was typical until 1740; after that, most trips from New England went to Africa and returned to their original port. The purpose of the original trip was to drop slaves off for "seasoning." During this period of two to three years, the black was introduced to clothing, the requirements of plantation agriculture, and fear and respect for the white man. The mortality rate during seasoning might approach 30 percent.[36] The early site for seasoning was usually Barbados, though later, other British colonies received their share of new slaves. In the British West Indies, it was felt that it was cheaper to work the slave to death and buy a replacement than to give him proper care. Barbados in 1764 had 70,708 slaves. Over 17 years, 38,843 were imported, while none were exported.[37] This would mean 109,551 living slaves in 1780. In fact, there were only 68,270 alive in 1780. The slave population would decrease by 50 percent in 23 years.

Continental slaveholders did not trust imports from the West Indies, who they believed, were undesirable laborers, belligerent, old, or infirm. The colonial legislatures frequently shared this concern and placed a higher duty on West Indian blacks than on Africans. (Rhode Island excluded Africans from duty; New York's duty in 1702 was 15 shillings on Africans, 30 shillings from elsewhere; and Virginia leveled a 10 percent tax on these from Africa, 20 percent on those from the West Indies.) It was believed that the best slaves came directly from the Gold Coast (Coromantees). They were "hardy, serviceable, docile and sensible." The Mandingoes from the Gambia River region were "strong, agreeable and capable of great labor." Individuals from Calabar, the Bight of Biafra, and Angola were undesirable, but they would be taken if nothing better was available.[38]

Generally, the profit on a voyage was great. Fortunes were amassed by New England merchants who later left the trade to become leaders of society and politicians. This was not unlike the situation of the English absentee plantation owners who became enormously wealthy on the sugar plantations of the West Indies. Their money was passed down through generations and allowed their progeny the leisure to become leaders in England. Individuals of less wealth could "purchase shares" in a single trip with an excellent return on the investment. A slaving round-trip usually lasted one year, and the investor could realize up to a 50 percent return on his principal. However, not every trip produced a profit. Excessive time at sea, excessive time hunting for cargo along the African coast, epidemics of smallpox, dysentery, yellow fever, and malaria on board ship, suicide, and insurrection on board, with the necessary fatal punishment of the leaders, destroyed much of the profit. The merchant and captain faced other business problems. A glut of trade products (particularly rum) on the African coast, for instance, would raise the cost of the "merchandise." There was often a need to sell the "cargo" immediately on arrival, because the slaves were debilitated from the long voyage. The slave merchants on shore might fail to pay promptly, and the interest on the capital would eat into the profits. Finally, the slaves could become sick after docking, frightening away potential buyers.[39] This last problem was described in a letter in Massachusetts (1718): "Several were struck down with smallpox and flux" even after they landed. Those who were sick were returned on board the sloop to prevent the illnesses' spreading to the rest and becoming known, "whereby ye sale would have been greatly Prejudiced. One of the articles in this consignment turned out to be blind, and some suffered from a strange distemper of sore eyes which was owing to their 'Feeding on Rice only.'"[40]

The mortality rate of the slaves in the West Indies was great, and there was a constant demand for replacements. The arable land was divided among a few plantations, with white overseers and a contingent of soldiers to prevent insurrection. The idea of settling small independent white farmers on their own land did not fit in with the grand economic design of the owners and government officials. This was not the situation on the mainland, however, where colonial governments (including those in the Southern states) were more interested in attracting white servants who would become independent farmers. They could be counted upon to take up arms against the encroaching French and Spaniards just over the border, but white farmers could not compete against slaves, particularly in the plantations of the South. Therefore, duties were placed on imported slaves to prevent them from becoming an overwhelming majority and a potential danger to the whites. The colonial governor, appointed by the Crown, usually vetoed these laws if he discerned their true purpose to be an attempt at the restraint of imported blacks. If the duty passed his surveillance, the Council on Foreign Plantations struck it down, for the slave trade represented too great a part of Britain's wealth to be interfered with by the colonials. Duties, however, were passed if the law was worded properly by the colonial legislature. Thus, Maryland raised £40,000 on duties to help support the war against France (the French and

Indian War).[41] Twenty shillings were added to the basic 20 shillings on imports. In 1704 Maryland passed a duty of 3 pence per gallon on rum and other spirits, 20 shillings per Negro for government expense, and 20 shillings per Irish servant to prevent the importation of too many Irish Papists.[42] (It should be remembered that Maryland was founded as a haven for Catholics.) Virginia was able to pass import duties to help build its capital; to pay debts from the French and Indian War; and to pay for "public needs." The real purpose of the duty was against "a trade of great inhumanity" and to prevent "retarding the settlement of the colonies with more useful inhabitants."[43] In 1771 Maryland placed a duty of £5 per head to build and maintain county schools; failure to pay the duty resulted in a fine of £20 per head plus court costs.[44] In New Jersey, "the Act Laying a Duty on Slaves is Calculated to Encourage the Importation of white Servants for better Peopling that county, a law something like that in Pennsylvania having evidently had that effect."[45] In 1773, Pennsylvania placed a duty of £20 per slave. Virginia and North Carolina followed in 1774, as did Georgia in 1775.[46] After the French and Indian War removed the French danger from their borders, the wealthy merchants and landowners (who controlled the colonial legislatures) could more openly express their fears and demands. Part of this was seen in ever larger duties on slaves, which threatened the merchants of Liverpool, London, Bristol, and Lancaster. In 1769 Virginia placed a 15 percent duty on imported slaves on top of an already existing tax of 10 percent. Pennsylvania in 1772 added a £10 duty in addition to its pre-existent duty.[47]

Prohibition of the Slave Trade by Government

The duty placed on imported slaves by colonial legislatures was a covert attempt to suppress the introduction of more slaves in favor of white servants. Laws overtly prohibiting the trade were attempted throughout the eighteenth century. Quaker Pennsylvania led the other colonies in this endeavor: laws of 1712, 1714, and 1717 were passed but vetoed by the governor. The Massachusetts General Court (legislature) passed similar laws in March and June 1774, but these too met the same fate. Rhode Island and Connecticut followed Massachusetts's lead the same year. In 1787 the Rhode Island legislature decreed that no resident was to be involved in the trade to Africa, and that the fine would be £100 per slave and £1,000 for the vessel. In 1791 the Providence Society for Abolishing the Slave Trade could bring suit in any court in the state in any case related to the abolition of slavery. The Continental Congress, on October 24, 1774, in the Non-Importation Covenant, stated, "We will neither import nor purchase any slave imported after the first of December next; after which time we will wholly discontinue the slave trade, and we will neither be concerned in it ourselves; nor will we hire our vessels; nor sell our commodities or manufactures to those who are concerned in it." This was ratified by representatives from the Northern and Southern colonies. However, nothing came of it.[48]

In the original draft of the Declaration of Independence (June 28, 1776), Thomas Jefferson wrote,

> He [King George III] has prostituted his negative for Suppressing every legislative attempt to prohibit or to restrain an execrable Commerce, determined to keep open a Market where men should be bought and sold and that this assemblage of Horrors might want no fact of distinguished die. He is now exciting those very People to rise in Arms among us, and purchase their Liberty of which he has deprived them, by murdering the people upon whom he also obtruded them. He has waged cruel war against human nature itself, violating its most sacred rights of life and liberty in the persons of a distant people, who never offended him, captivating and carrying them into slavery in another hemisphere, or to incur death on their transportation to the other. This warfare is the warfare of the Christian king of Great Britain determined to keep open a market where Men should be bought and sold ... he is now exciting those very people to rise up in arms against us.

When the Declaration was ratified, this paragraph was removed, and this statement was inserted in its place: "He has excited domestic insurrection among us and has endeavored to bring on the inhabitants of our frontiers the merciless Indian Savages...." Jefferson's private notes explained that the removal of the paragraph in question was an attempt to placate South Carolina and Georgia, "who had never attempted to restrain the importation of slaves; and who on the contrary still wished to continue it...." Northerners were castigated as well. Although they had few slaves themselves, "yet they had been pretty considerable carriers of them to others."

In 1781 the Articles of Confederation gave the individual states power to regulate the slave trade along with all other forms of commerce. Fortunately, the Articles of Confederation were replaced by the Constitution in 1787. This document protected the foreign slave trade for 20 years. Article II, Section 9, stated: "The Migration or Importation of such Persons as any of the States now-existing shall think proper to admit, shall not be prohibited by congress prior to the year 1808, but a tax or duty may be imposed on such Importation, not exceeding $10 for each Person." In an attempt to obtain Southern acceptance of this clause, Article IV, Section 2, was added: "No person held to Service or Labor in one State, under the laws thereof, escaping to another, shall, in consequence of any law or Regulation therein, be discharged from such Service or Labor, but shall be delivered on claim of the Party to whom such Service or Labor may be due."[49]

In March 1794 the new Federal government passed "An Act to Prohibit Carrying the Slave-Trade from the United States to any Foreign Place or Country."

No citizen or resident of the United States shall build or prepare a ship to go to any port to carry on the slave trade to a foreign country or to pick up slaves in a foreign country and transport them and sell as slaves. Every such ship is forfeited to the United States. It can be seized and prosecuted in any circuit or district court where it is found and seized. Anyone involved in building, loading, equipping the ship knowing the purpose of its use is fined $2,000, one-half to the United States, one-half to the one who prosecutes [informer]. Any foreign ship leaving for the coast of Africa, suspected of being involved in the Slave Trade.... any citizen may declare his suspicion to a customs officer.... The ship's officer must leave a bond to the Treasurer of the United States that no slaves will be taken on in Africa. Any citizen of the United States involved in the Slave Trade will be fined $200 per negro, one-half to the United States, one-half to the informer.

The law was approved on March 22, 1794, by "G. Washington, Pres." The law was strengthened in 1800: it was "unlawful for any resident of the United States to own a ship in the slave trade," and the ship would be forfeited for the use of the informer. Anyone transgressing the prohibition paid a sum equal to double the value of the property in the ship, and double the value of the interest he had in the slaves carried in the ship after passage of the law. It was unlawful for a resident of the United States to serve on board such a vessel: a fine of up to $2,000 and jail for up to two years was the penalty. The same sentence was given for service on a foreign ship in the slave trade. Any commissioned ship could capture a slave ship: its value, except for the slaves, would be shared by the crew of the capturing ship. The crew of the captured ship would be brought to a civil authority of the United States. District and circuit courts had adjudication in these cases. Any further forfeitures under this act which had not been disposed of went equally to the informer and to the United States. If prosecution was first instituted on behalf of the United States, the United States received all of the money. This law was signed on May 10, 1800, by John Adams, President. In February 1803 Congress prohibited the introduction of slaves into any state that had forbidden the slave trade by law. (Virginia had passed such laws in 1778 and 1785, as did Georgia in 1793, South Carolina in 1792, 1796, 1800, and 1801, North Carolina in 1791, and Maryland in 1796.)[50]

As the 20-year protection of the slave trade in the Constitution reached its last days, President Jefferson on December 2, 1806, reminded Congress that the date approached when it could prohibit the slave trade. He further urged that no ship be sent to Africa to pick up humans if it could not return before January 1, 1808. The law of March 2, 1807, stated that "no importer will hold right or title to any person of color, nor to his service, who is brought into the United States or territories in violation of this law." For equipping a slaver, the fine was $20,000 and forfeiture of the ship. For transporting Negroes, the fine was $5,000 and forfeiture of the ship and cargo (blacks). For transporting and selling slaves, the fine was $1,000–$10,000, plus five to ten years in prison and forfeiture of the ship and Negroes. For knowingly purchasing imported Negroes, the buyer was fined $800 per Negro plus forfeiture.[51]

Section 8 of the law attempted to prevent interstate commerce by water. It stated that no ship of less than 40 tons was permitted to transfer any person of color to any port for the purpose of selling him as a slave; the fine was $800 per person taken on board.[52] In Section 9, the captain of a ship of greater than 40 tons, sailing coastwise within United States' jurisdiction, who transported a person of color for service or labor, had to make out duplicate manifests on each Negro (with his complete description). One such manifest was delivered to the collector at the port of embarkation and debarkation, and the captain took an oath that the Negro had not been brought into the country after January 1, 1808. Any ship not observing these regulations was forfeited to the government, and the master was fined $1,000 per slave. If a captain landed slaves and failed to deliver the manifest, he was fined $10,000. The law went into effect on January 1, 1808. The responsibility of enforcing of the law was divided among the secretary of the Treasury, secretary of the Navy, and the State Department.[53] Slaves removed from ships involved in trade were sold; the money was divided between the government and the informant.

The Slave Trade Act of 1819 called for the resettling in Africa of liberated victims of the slave trade.[54] President James Monroe, in cooperation with the American Colonial Society, used the colony of Liberia as the site of the federal government's African Agency. Congress voted $100,000 to suppress the trade, but the amount voted each year decreased due to Southern influence. At this time too the president could dispatch cruisers to the coast of Africa to interdict the trade. In 1820, as part of the Missouri Compromise, Congress defined slave trading as piracy, punishable by death.[55]

All of the laws described here were on the books, but they could not be enforced. The navy was small, and the coastline was large. Navy officers, frequently Southerners, were not anxious to chase the slavers, and courts did not enforce the laws too vigorously when criminals were apprehended. Between the time the Missouri Compromise bill was passed and the end of the Civil War, only one captain was hanged (Nathaniel Gordon in 1862).[56] Furthermore, the money was too tempting for the amoral merchants and their captains. For example, Captain James Smith was captured and sentenced to two years in prison and a $1,000 fine. He claimed the trade was carried on openly after being outlawed by the nations of Europe and America. According to Smith, New York was the chief port in the world for the trade. Most ships were fitted out there, with an occasional ship from Boston or Philadelphia. About 25 slavers left New York the year he was apprehended. Large shipping houses were involved, and many merchants owned shares in the vessels. British men-of-war on the African coast were no problem to the captains. When hailed, they ran American flags up the masts. When boarded, they showed American papers, which precluded a search. Smith claimed he could pack in 664 slaves. If he took his cargo to Brazil, a much shorter trip, he could carry 800. Boys and women were kept on the upper deck, while the stronger men were placed on the "slave deck." They were not chained below, because "they would die." The crew had orders to be strict with the "merchandise" for the first week to show them who were the masters; they eased up by the second week. At night, the slaves were packed in so tightly that they could not sleep on their backs. Many died during the trip and were thrown overboard. The captain said that he could fit out his brig for $13,000, and he sold his cargo in Cuba for $220,000. Smith declared that slaver captains belonged to no country and did not obey any country's laws. They defended themselves when in harm's way against any aggressor.[57]

The early years of the nineteenth century saw most of the slave trade banned by the major nations of Europe. Great Britain outlawed it in 1807, the Netherlands in 1814, France in 1818, Spain in 1820, and Portugal in 1830. In 1830 Britain abolished all slavery in its West Indian colonies and compensated the owners for their loss of property ($100 million). And Britain went one step further: it signed individual treaties with the various nations which permitted warships to stop and board each other's merchantmen to search for slaves.[58]

The External and Internal Slave Trade

In the seventeenth century, trade on the North American continent was haphazard. Four years after the first settlers arrived in Maryland, Lord Baltimore asked his agent to acquire ten Negroes to work his land. His younger brother, Leonard Calvert, first governor of Maryland, asked for 14 Negro men and 3 Negro women between 16 and 26 years of age. Small ships plying the West Indies might pick up a few "incidental" slaves to fill the cargo space containing sugar, tobacco, molasses, and salted beef. These were "peddled" by the captains in port. This was particularly the case in the North, where the demand for black laborers was minimal. The large slavers carrying several hundred humans, sponsored by merchants of Liverpool and London, learned early to bypass the northern ports of Boston, New York, and Philadelphia. The merchants in these Northern cities owned the smaller craft in the West Indian trade. Some of the smaller ships made the trip directly to Africa when potential buyers showed a preference for blacks directly from Africa rather than the "seasoned" slaves of the West Indies. Gradually, a definite pattern developed in the Southern ports. In the Chesapeake Bay area, Liverpool-based ships dealt with factors or agents. The agents received and sold the slaves. They also stored tobacco and other products used by the planters to pay for their purchases, which eventually found its way to England. The agent earned a commission for his work. He frequently acted as a banker as well: planters, often without cash, paid with bills of exchange, and these were converted to credit in London. The agent also took paper money and tobacco, which he discounted. If necessary, the factor extended credit to his customers at very high interest rates. A dealer also worked on consignment. When he received notice of an incoming cargo, he advertised in newspapers and through handbills. In times of glut, when several large ships were due in port at the same time, prices and interest rates dropped.[59]

Charleston, South Carolina, became a major port of call later than the Chesapeake Bay area. It eventually became the center between Maryland and Saint Augustine, Florida. Slave ships docked at Sullivan's Island, where they remained in quarantine for ten days, or longer if disease was obvious on board. After this period, planters came to pick and choose. New lands south and west of Charleston had opened for rice and indigo production and planters came from as far as 150 miles away. Their demand for black hands was great, and they drove up the prices. The price paid for a slave was determined by many factors: the preceding harvest; the cost of freight to and from the west; insurance costs; war (locally on the border, or formally by the mother country); and weather (in unusually rainy periods, more slaves died of pneumonia).[60] The slaves' home area was an important consideration: Senegambia was preferred over the Guinea coast, Sierra Leone, and Angola. Cash or credit in the purchase was factored in as well. A slave bought on credit cost more, and the planter might be charged as much as 25 percent per year in interest. For his work, the agent received 8–10 percent of the sales. During the latter part of the eighteenth century, Sullivan's Island became the largest slave port in America. In 1787 the port was closed to the trade, perhaps as a result of the post–Revolutionary ardor for freedom and liberty. However, with the approach of the deadline ending the external trade in 1808, the port was thrown open in 1803. The demand for slaves in the South and West grew to a point where more than 39,000 slaves, carried in 202 voyages, were brought into Charleston in five years.[61]

On the North American continent, 90 percent of the external trade was carried on between April and October. Work decreased on plantations as winter approached, and the planter had to feed and clothe his relatively nonproductive laborers during this period. The farther north, the more the planter had to spend on warm clothing. In addition, cold American winters killed off many new slaves before they became acclimated. None of these considerations existed in the West Indies, however, where perpetual summer reigned, and slavers docked at any time of the year.

The internal slave trade was more a phenomenon of the nineteenth century, but it had its beginnings at the end of the eighteenth. In Virginia and Maryland, the oldest states with a plantation economy, tobacco cultivation eventually sapped the fertility of the land. After the invention of the cotton gin, cotton production became a major plantation product. This, too, was destructive of the land; and so farmers diversified, and fewer slaves were needed. In addition, the legal cessation of the external slave trade in 1808 caused Virginia and Maryland, and later Kentucky, to become slave breeding and exporting states.[62] Internal slave-trading firms like Woolfolk, Saunders and Overly of Maryland and Franklin & Armfield of Virginia purchased and sold slaves to the Deep South and West. Baltimore, Washington, Richmond, and Norfolk were active exporting centers, while Montgomery, Memphis, and New Orleans were the importing centers. Franklin & Armfield picked up slaves and stored them in a stockade in Alexandria, Virginia. The firm had agents scouring the countryside to fill out the shipments. The stock came from individual plantation owners who could not afford to keep all their slaves; slaves sold to settle the debts of an estate; slaves who had committed serious crimes and were sent out of the state to avoid executing them, and free Negroes and slaves who had been kidnapped. When an adequate supply was amassed, it was sent by ship or overland to Natchez or New Orleans. As described earlier, the African Slave Trade Act of 1807 stated that only ships over 40 tons could be used to transport slaves between American ports. The owners of these ships were permitted to pack in as many humans as possible. At the port of destination, usually New Orleans, the slaves were checked for illness before they were permitted to enter the city. The merchant could insure his cargo for 1.25 percent of its value. Those slaves shipped overland walked to the Ohio River, where they were placed on boats to carry them to Natchez or New Orleans. Women were tied together with a rope around their necks. Men wore an iron collar, which was padlocked, and these were chained together. A slave coffle traveled 20–25 miles per day. Occasionally, the boats would stop on the banks of the Mississippi River, and planters would gather for first pick. Before they were presented at their ultimate destination, the slaves were washed and shaved, then gray hairs were plucked out or their hair was dyed. They were stored in a "flogging room" equipped with a flogging paddle (so as not to leave marks), then dressed and brought to the auction block. They often received liquor or a little money "to brighten them up." The merchandise was examined by the buyers to check their health, as well as to check for old scars of flogging—too many scars suggested an unruly slave. If a slave described by the seller as healthy died prematurely, the buyer had recourse to the court.[63] Those among the slaves with skills brought more. Lighter-skinned blacks brought less, because they could escape and blend in more easily with the free population.

Chapter 4

THE SLAVE'S LIFE IN COLONIAL AMERICA

It is impossible to make general statements about the life of the slave in continental North America. Many variables determined how he lived out his time: Did he live in the North or the South? Was he on a small farm or a large plantation? Was his owner a Puritan or an Anglican? Was he an urban or a rural dweller? Was he a house servant or field hand? Was he an artisan or an agricultural worker? And was he dark or light? In this chapter, many of these variables will be covered.

Housing

Like everything else in the slave's life, his living quarters were often described with a subjective rather than an objective view. One archaeological study provided a straightforward description of his "home." It was a one-room frame dwelling with a dirt floor which measured 17 by 20 feet. The cabin had at least one glazed and shuttered window. There was one door with a plate stock lock and a brick chimney with a dirt-floored brick hearth. This provided accommodations for seven or eight adults, with perhaps a sleeping loft for children. Digging in the earth floor brought up lead shot, gun flints, and percussion caps, which suggested that these inhabitants had access to firearms, legally or illegally.[1] The cabin was built of logs without windows or floors. Crevices between the logs allowed in light, cold, and rain. There was a door on wooden hinges. The cabin also had a fireplace for cooking and heating.[2] According to Philip Foner, crevices between the logs were daubed with mud, and light and ventilation were provided by holes in the walls covered by wooden shutters. The chimney was built of mud and sticks, and caught fire frequently. Furniture was built or found by the cabin's inhabitants. Boxes were used for sitting or storage. Gourds, wooden buckets, and a wash barrel contained the water needed for cooking and washing. The occupants slept on planks with wooden pillows or on mattresses stuffed with corn husks.[2]

Schoolcraft saw slavery as a benefit granted to the blacks by their white owners. She described the plantation of the offspring of one of the original proprietors of South Carolina (Wyndham). There were 60 or 70 field Negro
houses; every black family was allowed a house to itself unless they "chose to
invite others to live with them." The houses were whitewashed twice a year
to promote health and to keep the boards from rotting. The windows were
painted green.

> No poor on the face of God's earth are so comfortably housed, fed and clad,
> as the Southern plantation negroes. They certainly have everything necessary
> to life and godliness.... Only compare their thoroughly ventilated, healthy
> houses, and their families around them with the dens, and holes, and cellars,
> and tenements of the white poor of New York, and other great cities. Negro
> houses on the coast plantations are built on pillars, and made of oak founda-
> tions, boarded up with pine boards. They are usually 15 feet square, have four
> windows, and have a partition between sitting and sleeping room. They are
> one story with a loft for storing provisions. In back of every house is a spot
> for a garden, poultry coop, and pig pen. The brick chimneys are immense, six
> to eight feet wide. They can burn as much wood as they can take from the
> forests.

On a very large plantation with many slaves, the slave quarters formed almost
a small village. There were household cabins, workhouses, a children's house
(nursery), a sick house and bachelor's quarters. The living accommodations
of the "house slaves" were of better quality and close to the main house, so
they could be available on short notice.[3]

In the middle states and New England, where the farmer or wealthy
urban dweller owned one or two humans, the slaves slept in the master's
house, often in the loft with the master's children.

Clothing

Wearing apparel had to fit weather conditions. Johann Martin Bolzius,
clergyman of the Salzburgers in Carolina and Georgia, described the slaves'
clothing in a questionnaire sent to him from Germany. He claimed that blacks
went naked in the summer, except that the men wore a cloth rag that hung
down from a strap around the waist. Women had petticoats, but their upper
bodies were bare. Children were totally naked. In the winter, they had shoes,
and they wore a woolen blue or white camisole, cloth pants that reached to
their shoes, a wool cap, but no shirt. Negroes who accompanied their master
to town were dressed better, and skilled Negroes who lived in Charleston were
well dressed. He believed it cost about 4 shillings to clothe a Negro each year.
(The questionnaire was dated 1767.)[4] In eighteenth-century South Carolina,
slave clothing was stipulated by law, but this was not enforced. Fabric suitable for negro clothing included Negro cloth duffels, osnaburgs (coarse linen

of flax and tow), blue linen, check linen, coarse "garlix" [*sic*], coarse calicos, check cottons, and Scotish plaids. Favored male slaves were dressed in full livery and rode as attendants on painted coaches.[5] (The specific types of cloth described in the law may have been a means of identifying runaway slaves.) As seen through the rose-colored glasses of Schoolcraft, the clothing of children and older Negroes was made by trained black seamstresses under the supervision of the mistress of the plantation. The master bought planes, an all-wool cloth used by all the inhabitants of the plantation; this cost one dollar per yard. Slave women wore a white shirt with a blue bodice; men wore white pants and a blue coat. Women covered their heads with a red kerchief or turban, while the men had red wool caps.[6] According to Otto and Burns, summer wear was coarse cotton, "jeans," and flannel. Slaves were given thread, needles, buttons, scissors, and brass thimbles. Generally, clothing for men and boys was the same as was the clothing for women and girls. They wore coarse woolens in the winter and cotton in the summer. They wore no underwear, and the men were not given shirts. Strong shoes were supplied for winter wear.[7]

In one case, the administrative council of a small community, probably in Virginia, took up the problem of clothing a Negro woman on October 19, 1692: "Whereas Mr. Ebenezer Taylor, late schoolmaster.... It is thought reasonable that a negro woman belonging to the sd. schoole should be clothed at the charges of the Schoole master she being almost naked. It is therefore ordered that the sd Taylor provide ... one new cotton waistcoat and pettycoat, three yards of good new canvis for a shift, one pare new shoon and stockins."[8]

Food

The Puritan slaveholder in New England treated his Indian and black bondsmen in the patriarchal manner described among the Hebrews of the Old Testament. They were almost family members and ate at the common table. Similarly, the small farmer of the middle colonies usually worked side by side with his slaves, and their food intake was equal. The urban black was adequately fed. He also had money that he earned and could buy any additional food and drink that he felt he needed. The plantation economy of the South was different. Often, as in the West Indies, land was too valuable to grow foodstuffs, which had to be purchased. If the slave depended on the master's largesse, he would develop caloric and protein deficiencies. The basic food supplied to the slave was Indian corn or yams. A working man or woman received a peck or two gallons of corn per week, distributed on Sunday. Working children received half this amount, and little children received about one quarter. In the Deep South, two pecks of unhusked rice was substituted for corn. Protein was supplied in the form of salt fish, salt beef, or salt bacon, approximately three and a half pounds per week. Each worker received a quart of salt each month. Occasionally, molasses was used to cut down the meat ration. According to the Reverend Bolzius, slaves were fed potatoes, unsold rice, Indian corn, and beans. Women and children received the same food in lesser amounts. An adult received 20 bushels of grain per year. Bolzius believed food cost per slave per year was 20 shillings.[9] Schoolcraft, who saw the slave as a pet of his owner, said that every plantation had a butcher to kill animals: "When a great bullock is killed for negroes, they make 20 gallons of soup ... and divide it." They received a food allowance weekly as "determined by law or experience." This included corn, rice, peas, sweet potatoes, molasses, fish, beef or bacon. All writers agreed that the slave had to return to his cabin after work, start a fire, grind his grain, and prepare his nightly meal. In addition, he prepared the food for two meals to be eaten the following day during 15-minute breaks from work. The cabin usually contained one cooking kettle, so everything was thrown in to create a stew; this was dished out into individual bowls. Occasionally, the master supplied his workers with ceramic dishes for their food. Grain was an important part of their diet. This was ground to produce a meal to which enough water was added to create a consistency that would support an upright spoon. A pat of this was positioned between oak leaves and placed in the ashes to produce "ash cake." When dropped on a hoe and baked, it was called "hoe-cake." Fortunately, the slave had the use of a piece of land to grow food to supplement his family's rations. He worked his land on Sundays and on holidays and after he had completed his assigned tasks for the plantation. On his plot, the bondsman grew cabbage, cauliflower, cowpeas (black-eyed peas), corn, turnip, and rutabagas. He also had chicken coops, rabbit hutches, and pigpens. The animals were fed from the slave's rations, and they were butchered for the slave's use, or they could be sold to merchants or to the slave's owner. According to Mrs. Schoolcraft, a plantation slave near the coast had a "canoe" made by hollowing out a log; at night, he could fish for prawn, crabs, clams, turtles, and fish.[10] (That a plantation owner would allow a slave to have a boat is unlikely, particularly if the slaves knew about Spanish Florida to the south with its offer of liberty to escaped slaves.)

Illness and Health Care

The slave, like his white master, suffered the usual ills of a society ignorant of the basic concepts of the pathophysiology of disease. In addition, he developed illnesses related to his work, food preparation, and genetic makeup. Yaws, the "country distemper," was predominantly a disease of blacks. It was seen most commonly in the first generation of slaves from Africa, but others, particularly children, could become infected. The illness was caused by an organism resembling that which caused syphilis, and the patient developed skin, nose, mouth, and bone lesions. White physicians treated it like syphilis with mercurial unguents. A black "herb doctor," James Papaw, was given his freedom in 1729 by Governor William Gooch of Virginia for his treatment of this disease. Papaw used four ounces of the bark of a Spanish oak tree plus two ounces each of the middle bark of a pine tree and "the root of sumack that bears the berries." These were boiled together to create a strong decoction. The patient drank one pint "milk warm" and one-half pint cold; this caused a "strong vomit." For six weeks after this initial treatment, the patient drank one-half pint in the morning, at one in the afternoon, and at night. The skin sores were washed with the same decoction five or six times a day until they healed. During the treatment period, the patient's diet consisted of broth, gruel, and panada (bread boiled to a pulp and flavored with sugar or nutmeg) four times a day. No meat or alcohol was consumed.[11]

Malaria was a serious problem as far north as New York City, but it was devastating in the South. In South Carolina and Georgia, where heat and standing water were required for rice cultivation, it decimated the white population. The disease favored the importation of blacks and discouraged the immigration of white servants, resulting in a markedly skewed ratio of blacks to whites in the Deep South. Vivax, a mild form of malaria, was probably brought from England; Falciparum, a malignant form, was carried by the Africans to the Western Hemisphere. The slaves were said to be resistant to malaria, and to a degree this was true. The red cells of many blacks lacked the Duffy antigen, which was needed by the malarial organism to gain a foothold in the host's red cell. Approximately 30–40 percent of the slaves from West Africa carried the sickle cell trait, which protected them from Falciparum malaria. Unfortunately, this condition was a two-way street: the sickle trait also predisposed the individual to pneumonia, which worked like a scythe on the black population.[12]

Intestinal problems, from dysentery and food spoilage, were common. Lack of refrigeration, preparation of food after a long day in the field, and the ingestion of the midday meal, prepared the night before and carried through the heat of the day, easily explained these problems. Worms were a universal problem among children, but slaves, young and old, were affected. In a description of rattlesnake root, a panacea against most diseases, discovered by Dr. John Tennent, the writer claimed, "He has found it almost a specific in Pleurisy [pneumonia] which are the most fatal of all Diseases in this Clymate amongst the Negros and Poor Peoples…. It is a specific against worms … where most of the children that dye, and most of the Negros, dye of worms."[13]

Fever, considered as an illness rather than as a symptom of many illnesses, was treated with tartar emetic. Ten grains were added to water, and the patient took a tablespoon every 15 minutes until vomiting occurred, accompanied by a sweat that broke the fever, at least temporarily. For "feverish indispositions" and sore throats, the patient received Glauber's salt, a laxative; a teaspoon every six hours for four doses was advised. If the patient had pleurisy or a continued fever, he received a mixture of 40 grains of nitre, 20 grains of camphor, and 2 grains of tartar emetic divided into four doses; a tablespoon in thick, cold gruel was prescribed every six hours. Rheumatism was treated with a rub of spirits of wine and gum camphor. If a patient showed evidence of venereal disease, he received Chubbs pills or corrosive sublimate in Northern rum; a spoonful was consumed each morning. Mercury cured syphilis if it didn't destroy the kidneys first. For bile or "jaundas" (probably yellow fever), calomel was used. (This too was a form of mercury.) Sores on the limbs were very common due to working conditions. Hog's lard and beeswax, melted together and applied on lint or linen, covered the lesion. Overseers believed that most slave problems were due to malingering, and they frequently started therapy with red pepper tea, which worked "like a dose of salts." (In his diaries, George Washington wrote that he did not believe slaves were sick unless they had a fever. This was treated by bleeding.)[14]

Ninety percent of slave births were attended by black midwives, as were 50 percent of white births. If a baby could not be delivered normally, a white doctor was called, who frequently destroyed the baby in the uterus and delivered it in pieces. Miscarriage, due to hard work and falls, was common. Infant mortality was high from infantile diarrhea, but the mother would become pregnant again very soon. A "good breeder" might have 15–20 pregnancies during her fertile years, and she brought 25 percent more on the auction block. During pregnancy, her work load was decreased, and after she gave birth, her family received more food and clothing. She was allowed to nurse her child for only three months, and her duties were limited for three weeks until she got her strength back. Newborns were cared for by their older sisters. If the plantation had many slaves, a house was set aside as a nursery under the supervision of an old slave woman.[15]

No plantation had a physician in residence. Some planters, like George Washington, kept a physician on retainer. For the most part, the owner or his overseer acted as the physician to the plantation's inhabitants. Generally, he purchased a book that described symptoms and prescribed the "cure." A cabinet, containing the most commonly used medications could be purchased from England or in the large urban centers of America. An old slave woman and occasionally the mistress of the plantation were the nurses. If the patient failed to thrive under the overseer's care, the slave might find a black "herb doctor" to try for a cure. The slave was an expensive commodity, and his owner would then turn to a doctor to "protect his investment."[16]

It is difficult to determine the life expectancy of the slave in eighteenth century America. Among the white people, if infant mortality and children's death below five years are factored in, the average white male at birth could expect to reach 30 years. The female's life was shorter due to childbirth, consumption, and pneumonia. It was believed that a field hand lived about 15 years after he started adult work at age 12–14. Surprisingly, Virginia mortality statistics showed that more blacks died of "old age" than did whites.[17] The definition of "old age," however, was not mentioned.

Marriage and Family

Slave marriages tended to be unstable and frequently were of short duration. As a group, the only slaveholders who took slaves' marriages seriously were the Puritans.[18] Adultery was a serious sin and marriage a sanctified institution, even among bondsmen. A marriage ceremony was performed, and the participants were expected to stay together for life. If slaves were sold, the owner tried to sell them as a family unit. Among other groups, only a deeply religious master tried to promote morality and avoid licentiousness among his possessions. Under these conditions, slave unions could last a lifetime. The father then became an important part of the family, and he frequently worked nights and Sundays to provide his family with small "luxuries" like extra food and clothing. The children benefited by having a strong father figure in the cabin; however, this was an unusual situation. Statistically, 32.4 percent of 2,888 slave unions were dissolved by the master; the average marriage lasted about six years.[19]

The typical slave marriage was not sanctified by a clergyman. In some cases, perhaps with a devoted house slave, a minister might be present, but he rarely performed the ceremony. The closest formality to marriage was "jumping the broom," with the promise that "you will cleave to him only, so long as God, in his Providence, shall continue his and your abode in such place (or places) as that you can come together." They were "married" until the master sold one partner away. In many states, the slave code prevented real marriage. A slave could not enter into a contract and marriage was a binding contract, so their marriage was called a contubernium, literally a sharing of the tent.[20] The closest institution in society today would be that of the "significant other."

On large holdings, the master preferred that his slaves marry within the plantation. Marrying someone from another plantation meant that the "husband" would have to take time to walk over to see his wife. Also, the offspring of the union would belong to the wife's owner. Occasionally, to avoid lost time and progeny, a master would purchase his male's consort. The "husband" who visited his wife, usually for sexual gratification, was not considered a father figure by the offspring. The mother became the dominant figure in the slave family, and she provided for the children's needs. Very early in its life, the baby was turned over to its older siblings or to an "old woman" for care. The care of children by older siblings created an important bond—if the parents were sold away, the children could maintain a semblance of family. The damage produced by separating children from their mothers was recognized by state authorities. The Louisiana legislature, for example, prohibited separation of a mother from her child who was less than ten years.[21] Like most humane legislation regarding slaves, unfortunately, this was not enforced.

Sexual promiscuity was encouraged by the owner. If a couple was not fertile, he separated them and gave each a new mate, because the purpose of "marriage" was the production of more slaves. A good "breeder" was a prized possession. If a slave union was broken by the sale of one spouse, the remaining individual was forced to take another sexual partner. Breeding was so important to the owner that he would push young girls of 13 into a relationship. In some areas, a woman with ten live children could receive her freedom; the children, however, would remain with her ex-master. The males' input into the breeding process was not overlooked. Strong, potent men were hired out as studs to other planters to produce a strong breed of children.[22] In addition, the owner could take a comely slave at will, and the offspring of this "union" was added to his working population. In some situations, the white father accepted parental responsibility, and he educated and freed his child.

In the larger communities of the North, as well as on small farms, breeders were not prized. The problem was lack of space in the homes and inability to find a use for the children. Two classified advertisements in the *New York Mercury* bear this out: "June 3, 1765. To be sold a likely Negro wench, about 30 years old, with her two children, the elder a Girl between 3 and 4 years; the other a Boy about one year. She is a very good Conditioned Wench and can do all Manner of House Work: The only reason for selling her, is because she breeds; which her present Master and Mistress are adverse to; they being advanced in years." On December 12, 1765, this appeared: "A very likely Negro Wench, about 27 years old, with a Male child 5 months old: She is very handy, faithful and honest: sold for no fault but getting children."[23]

The end product of the breeding process was the child, who belonged to the master. Generally, nursing was permitted for about three months. It was believed, as it is still in many quarters today, that nursing prevented pregnancy, and the master wanted his "machine" to reproduce as frequently as possible. However, removal of the child from his mother's breast exposed him to infantile diarrhea with its attendant mortality. If children survived the childhood illnesses and the diseases of poor nutrition and poorer hygiene, work was soon found for them. At five or six, they became messengers. They fanned the white family when they ate and acted as pages when the white family went out for a drive or visit. As the children aged, they were introduced to field work. They might start as water carriers to the adults working in the fields. They also attended the livestock, drove the wagons filled with produce out of the field, and kept crows out of the field by running, jumping, and screaming.[24] According to Schoolcraft, boys and girls were not sent out to the fields until they were 14–16. They were expected to do one-third the work of an adult, a workload that was increased as they became stronger. They were supervised at all times, because otherwise they would not work. She felt it did not pay to whip them, because of their devil-may-care attitude and because "their nerves [were] too obtuse" for them to remember that they had been punished an hour earlier.[25]

Holidays and Celebrations

On Sunday the slave was relieved of his duty to his master. He could relax, go to church, or work on his own plot to earn extra money. In addition, there were two main periods of relaxation—summer lay-by and Christmas. The lay-by was at the end of the cultivation period when the bondsman's duties were decreased and he could work for himself.[26] Christmas was a special holiday when the slave was free of all duty from three to six days. This period acted as a steam valve or cathartic to ease the tensions built up in a year of servitude. The owner encouraged license and unruliness with the hope that the slave population would then be more docile during the rest of the year. During the Christmas break, the slaves were occupied with the John Canoe (Jonkonnu) festivities. First recorded in America in 1774, this holiday came to the southern mainland from the Caribbean, and probably originally from the Guinea coast. The strongest male on the plantation dressed in bizarre clothes, wore ox horns on his head; covered his face with a mask; and placed boar tusks in his mouth. He danced around the festive site, followed by his retinue of "drunken women." The slaves frequently used the celebration for more serious activities. Under the cover of the festivities they stole to supplement their needs, made plans to run away and executed them, and prepared for insurrection. They also showed resentment of their servile state under the cover of comedy. The slave might use his "fancy" costume to mock the poor whites in the area. The activities were carried out by the field hands, because the house slaves abstained from the excitement—they saw themselves as a "higher class." The master seemed to enjoy the festivities, but he was fully aware of the undercurrents and tightened security on the plantation to avoid trouble.[27]

During this period, individual planters provided feasts for their own slaves and those of neighboring plantations. The participants put on their best clothes and ate meats, vegetables, and other delicacies denied them during the rest of the year. Long tables were set in front of the main house; men sat on one side, women on the other. The meal was followed by dancing. Then the slaves visited the main house, where they received presents from the master.[28] Mrs. Schoolcraft described the festivities: "The Negroes in the south are allowed three or four days every Christmas for a jubilee, and I so vividly remember the patriarchal benevolence, my father's countenance exhibited, when out of his abundant larder he contributed everything necessary to these jovial feastings among his slaves. Some of them spent the holy days in playing on the violins and other instruments, for their young friends to dance by; others went from place to place, to visit their neighbors, and others held prayer-meetings, where most of the night was spent in singing psalms in religious exhortations, and in prayer."[29] In addition to Christmas, the slaves might be invited to partake in significant celebrations of the white family, such as birthdays or anniversaries.

Work

The bottom line of the entire institution of slavery was profit derived from keeping humans at a subsistence level. In the eighteenth century, for the small farmer who could double his output with an additional pair of hands, or the small factory owner who owned or hired slaves at lower rates than white workers, a return on the investment was possible. In the cities, where slaves were used as cooks, butlers, and coachmen, the return was prestige rather than dollars. Slaveholding was important to the economic and social status of whites in the colonial period and remained a uniform measure of wealth during the Revolution because of the distortions produced by inflation.[30] Wealth was measured in numbers of slaves rather than in money. For example the possession of 20 slaves in the pre–Revolutionary South made one a "man of means," a good-sized plantation had at least 70 slaves.[31]

The plantation slave system gave the white owner freedom to gain additional schooling, to obtain military training, and to go into politics. This small elite group provided the leaders of the government in Southern states. As Mrs. Schoolcraft explained, "The exemption from manual labor supplied by slaves of South Carolina to the sons and daughters of Carolina forms one of the chief characteristics of southern life. It produces a class of elevation and refinement not achieved under any other system. This caused the filling of this colony with gentlemen of aristocratic taste and refinement."[32] Their lifestyle resembled that of the nobility of Europe, and, like their European counterparts, they were in debt to the lower class merchants and traders.

The foundation of the plantation system was the work produced by the owner's chattel. There were two classes of workers: the house slave and the field slave. The house slave was the "aristocrat."[33] This distinction was set up by the blacks and accepted by the whites. The domestic servant was more "sprightly, better clad, more intelligent and animated, apes polite manners, and imitates the polished airs of the well-bred white folk." The field hands constituted the lowest order of slaves, "the last and lowest link in the class of the human species." Field hands were "coarse, filthy, brutal and licentious, liars, parasites, hypocrites and thieves." The house servants were usually chosen from among the more intelligent slaves, particularly the mulattoes. It was believed by both whites and blacks that mulattoes were more intelligent because of the presence of white blood. The mulattoes considered themselves superior, but this sense of "superiority" fragmented slave society because they felt closer to their white masters than to their "brothers."

House slaves brought their children into this work; they married within this group; and they stayed with the white family for generations while the field hands were bought and sold. The domestic ate and dressed better, often from the table and closet of his master. Occasionally a house slave was married by a white minister. Their children were raised with the white children, and not permitted to associate with the children of the field hands for "fear of picking up their ways." Some were taught to read and write despite laws prohibiting slave education. The house servant was in constant attendance on his master, and he had to wear a "mask of servility all day." The field slave had his nights free from white observation, when he could be himself. Few house slaves ran away; those who did disgraced the "class."[34] The field hand did not trust the house servants with plans of flight or insurrection, because their allegiance was to the master. They were known to leak insurrection plans to secure their position with the whites.

Among these "aristocrats" the highest individuals were the body servants. At the top of the pyramid was the "black mammy."[35] She cared for the young white children, and was second in command to the mistress. A child raised by a mammy had the cachet of aristocracy. She was practically a part of the family, and her ideals were those of the whites. Unlike other slave women, she was considered self-respecting, independent, loyal, forward, gentle, "captious," affectionate, true, strong, just, warm-hearted, compassionate, and fearless. She was clothed in silks and velvet, though secondhand of course. Her white charges frequently taught her to read and write. If she did not sleep in the room with the white children, she lived with her husband and family in a cabin, finer than that of the other slaves and close to the "big house." She had no real home life of her own, however, until she became too old to care for her master's children. She and her children were usually safe from sale and corporal punishment. In a large house, she might have younger assistants or "nurses" to care for the children. The mammy was usually the daughter of a previous mammy and grew up as a playmate of the whites. As she grew older, she took on maid's duties and gradually moved into the highest position among the servants. The mammy was wet nurse for the mistress's children, so that the mistress could "get back into shape" as soon as possible; though this duty deprived her own offspring of necessary subsistence. As substitute mother, she bathed, dressed, fed, put to bed, and trained the master's children. Many of her charges cared more for her than for their natural mother. She taught them etiquette, position in the plantation hierarchy, and proper respect for different individuals they might encounter. She was permitted to discipline the young white children for transgressions. As the children grew older, she was their confidant in love affairs and was often consulted in their choice of a mate. Mammy was present at her "children's" weddings. To her mistress, she was the oldest, dearest, closest friend. When she passed on to her final reward, she was buried in a proper coffin in the white family's plot with a marker, and the master conducted the burial service. Her husband was usually the butler, driver, gardener, mechanic, or foreman. He might belong to another master, but his conjugal visits came more easily. Overall, the house slaves did not produce wealth. Instead, they represented a draw on the family's finances in the name of prestige and social position.

The field hand produced the wealth that supported the system. The small planter with five or six slaves worked in the field with them as their overseer, while the large planter hired a white overseer to assume responsibility for production. In addition, many colonies had laws requiring a specific proportion of whites to blacks, in order to suppress the constant danger of slave insurrection. A small Southern farmer could not compete with slave labor and frequently lost his farm. All of his instincts should have made him an opponent of slavery. However, he was bombarded by propaganda from the church, newspapers, and political leaders about the benefits of slavery. Negroes were his biological inferiors and could go on a murderous rampage if they were set free. Because the poor white was superior to the slave, he could always aspire to own one or several slaves and join the upper class. It was this landless group that produced the overseer.[36] According to Patrick Henry, he was the most "abject, degraded, unprincipalled [sic] man."[37] The cruelty of the overseer was indirectly caused by his employer, because the hired man had to bring in an adequate crop to keep his job. He signed a contract each year that listed his salary and supplied a house, an allowance of food, and a slave servant.[38] His duties were listed in the contract and included the care and control of the slaves; the amount and kind of labor performed; care of tools and livestock; and his social behavior. He kept daily records of all plantation activities and reported to the owner at specific periods. He assigned the work to the slaves; policed and inspected their quarters to search for weapons; treated sick slaves; punished malingerers and rebellious blacks; and prevented sabotage and stealing. Most overseers remained on a plantation for just two or three years because they rarely met the production demands of the owner. The overseer's life was little better than that of the slaves he controlled. He could not fraternize with the slaves, and his employer's family considered him socially inferior. He could not entertain guests or leave the plantation without permission. Like the slave, he had to hunt, fish, and grow crops to supplement his food ration. His food was similar to that of the slaves in kind and preparation. His "genetic superiority" sustained him through a very unhappy life.[39]

Below the overseer was the driver or foreman. He was a slave hated by the other field hands. The driver supervised his charges minutely. He was usually the strongest slave on the plantation, with a presumed judgment capacity above that of the ordinary slave. His job was a lifetime occupation. In addition to supervising the work of the others, he watched the other slaves' deportment in and out of the fields. He reported daily to the overseer and received his tasks for the following day. In return for his work, he received more food and better clothes. The driver had little free time after work, so the owner compensated him by having other slaves work his plot of land.[40]

The workday could last from dawn to dusk, with two short periods free for food and rest. During the harvest, the work day could last 14–18 hours. To prevent the overseer from pushing his charges beyond human endurance, several colonial legislatures passed laws regulating their work. A law in South Carolina of 1740 stated, "Whereas many owners of slaves, and others who have the care, management, and overseeing of slaves, do confine them so closely to hard labor that they have not sufficient time for natural rest, Be it therefore enacted, that if any owner of slaves, or other persons, who shall have the care, management or overseeing of slaves, shall work or put such slave or slaves to labor more than 15 hours in 24 hours ... every such person shall forfeit a sum not exceeding £20 nor under £5 current money, for every time he, she, or they shall offend."[41] The law was on the books, but its enforcement was questionable.

Slave work was produced under the gang system or the task system. The former involved a group of slaves under an overseer who worked until the overseer decided when to stop. In tobacco and sugar cultivation, there were certain steps that had to be completed before the next step was started. These steps required supervisors and were best served by the gang system. The task system required the slave to do a set amount of work. When he finished, his workday was done, and he could then work his own plot. Rice and cotton production were simple and could be worked with the task system. The task system worked well in South Carolina and Georgia, where owners left the area in the summer to avoid malaria. The amount of work specified for the day's task was set by custom. If the owner tried to raise his slave's output, his neighbors reproached him, and his slaves sabotaged his livestock and tools. The task system increased the autonomy of the slave for a good worker could complete his task by midday and spend the rest of the day producing wealth for himself. Many were able to accumulate enough money to buy their freedom.[42]

The Salzburgers in Georgia were family farmers. They were morally opposed to slavery, but slaves were necessary to get communities started in the Deep South. To prevent the accumulation of large numbers of slaves, they were initially limited by their church leaders to 500 acres of land. The Reverend Johann Bolzius described a slave's output on a small farm. He believed a black could work six to ten acres of corn, beans, pumpkins, rice, and potatoes; on old land, he could work six acres. A field hand could cultivate five acres of new land in rice per year; on old grassy land, he could manage three acres of rice.[43] Men and women were expected to produce the same amount of work in planting and cultivating, but men were expected to do the heavy work required to clear the new land (chopping down trees and removing roots). Women could cut the brush and carry it away. Children were expected to hoe potatoes, feed chickens, and shoo birds from the field. New land was fenced in with split poles 12–13 feet long and four inches thick. Each slave split 100 poles from oak and fir each day. At night, slaves burned the cut brush. They planted potatoes at the end of March. After the potatoes, Indian corn was planted, about one-half acre per worker per day. Then a worker would furrow for rice, one-quarter acre per worker per day. Rice was sown and covered, one-half acre per day; After this, the slave could weed one-half acre of corn. Beans were planted between the furrows of corn. Children weeded potato patches, then they weeded one-quarter acre of rice each day. When agricultural work was at a low point, slaves worked in and around the house. Corn was cut at the end of August or September. Pumpkins, planted between corn furrows, also ripened at this time. White beets were sown in July and August. In the middle of August, all male slaves worked on the roads for four or five days. After Christmas, peas, beans, and cabbage were planted and trees were pruned. Fences were mended, and new lands were cleared for cultivation.

On a large plantation with many hands, work was divided into quarters. Young children of nine or ten were "quarter-hands." As they grew stronger, they became half-hands, then three-quarter hands, and finally full hands when they were fully grown. As they aged and became more feeble, they retrogressed in the same manner. The very old slave was finally removed from the field, and sedentary work was found for him. A full hand set to digging drains in clean meadowlands was expected to dig 1,000 cubic feet per day. He could hoe one-half to two-thirds of an acre of rice or one-half to one acre of cotton, corn, or potatoes daily. He could chop and bring in one cord of wood per day.[44]

Rice and indigo production used many slaves, who worked plantations of Georgia and South Carolina, and as far north as Cape Fear, North Carolina. A proper rice plantation required 30 slaves and one overseer. Each slave produced four to five barrels of unpolished rice, each weighing about 500 pounds. This could be produced on two acres of land. Indigo cultivation complemented the rice: rice was grown only on land that could be flooded, while indigo grew upland adjacent to the flooded areas. Indigo cultivation ended in the summer, so the slave was free to harvest the rice. During the winter, the slave threshed the rice with a hand flail, which removed the outer hull. Polished (hulled) rice was loaded into barrels that held 600 pounds. Unhusked rice brought two and a half cents per pound, while polished sold for three and a half cents. Each slave produced 2,000–2,500 pounds of polished rice, which came to $70.40–$87.50 per year. If he produced an equal value in indigo, his yearly production of wealth was $150–$175 per year. When not involved with rice cultivation, the slave cleaned out canals and ditches and repaired the dikes.[45] According to the Reverend Bolzius, to keep one slave cost 12 shillings for clothing, 2 shillings for tax, 28 shillings for food.[46] Basic upkeep came to 2 guineas, or about $10 per year. A slave cost $150–$200. If he had 15 productive years, his depreciation was $10–$15 per year. Therefore, during his productive years, he produced $125–$150 per year. From this would have to be subtracted his nonproductive or minimally productive years.

Cotton production was responsible in large measure for the politics of nineteenth-century America, but it had its origins in the eighteenth century, the beginning of the Industrial Revolution. In 1733, John Kay invented the flying shuttle, which doubled the production of a weaver. John Hargreave's "spinning jenny" in 1761 increased the production of yarn. Richard Arkwright's water frame produced strong cotton yarn, and in 1773 he produced an all-cotton calico. Samuel Compton developed the "spinning mule" in 1779, which produced high-quality thread and yarn. Edmund Cartwright in 1785 invented the power loom for weaving, and later introduced James Watts's rotary action steam engine to the production of cotton textiles.[47] In 1785 cylinder printing of cotton was introduced, and in 1786 acid bleaching produced clean white cotton fabric. The bottleneck in cotton use, however, was the separation of the seeds from the raw cotton. A slave could separate seeds from one pound of short staple cotton in one day, while long staple cotton could be separated from its seeds by passing the bolls through rollers that separated the seeds. One slave could produce ten pounds of cotton this way. However, long staple cotton could be grown only around Sea Island. In 1791 the United States produced 190,000 pounds of cotton, while England's factories imported 28 million pounds.[48] Eli Whitney's cotton gin removed the bottleneck. Whitney, a recent Yale graduate, took a position as a tutor in Savannah, Georgia. He heard about the problem of separating seeds from the bolls, and in ten days he had the solution.[49] The cotton boll was pulled through wire teeth on a revolving cylinder. The fiber passed through narrow slots in an iron breast-work too small to allow the seeds to pass. It could run on manpower, horse-power, or waterpower, and one man could clean 150 pounds of cotton daily. With steam power, one man could produce 1,000 pounds per day.[50] By 1800, 35 million pounds of cotton were produced, and almost 18 million pounds of this "white gold" went to feed England's hungry machines.

Cotton supplied work for the slave throughout the year. It was suited to the gang system, with close supervision by white overseers, and it could employ young, old, and infirm slaves in the various stages of production. Cultivation started in March and April, and picking began in August. A field was picked over three times until it was finished in December. The picker pulled a sack with a strap that went around his neck or chest; the mouth of the sack was chest high. The filled bag was emptied into a basket. A good worker picked 200 pounds of cotton daily. When filled, baskets were carried to the gin house for weighing and "sweating"; it then went to storage in the cotton house. In January and February the cotton was ginned, pressed, baled and sent to a shipping depot.[51]

In the agricultural South, tobacco was an important product. It was the main agricultural product of seventeenth-century America. It was the currency of exchange in early Maryland and Virginia. As with sugar production in the Caribbean, it was the reason for importing Africans to the mainland. However, it destroyed the land. By the mid–eighteenth century, the market in Europe was glutted, and new agricultural products took its place.

If a white inhabitant of colonial America were to be questioned about the mental capacity of the blacks in his midst, he would probably claim that the African was probably a lower species who was fit only for simple agricultural work under the control of a white overseer. There was adequate evidence to the contrary, however. The Reverend Bolzius, when questioned about the cost of slaves, said a good field hand sold for £28–£32. A sawyer was £4–£6 more, a cooper £50–£70, a carpenter £70–£107. A black female field worker cost £26–£33, but a house worker was valued at £35–£57. Bolzius pointed out that the bricks and fired stones used to build Charleston were produced by slaves.[52] Clearly, the Africans were valued for doing more than simple agricultural work.

Few plantations were large enough to keep full-time slave sawyers, coopers, or carpenters. The slaves skilled in these occupations were too valuable to keep as field hands, and they frequently were sent to neighboring urban centers. Life in the towns was better for the bondsmen than it was on the plantation: their food was better, and there was less corporal punishment. Urban slaves were able to learn to read and write despite the prohibition by law, and they learned about independent living. However, they still had restrictions on movement, were required to have passes, had to obey curfews, and they could not ride in public vehicles. There were strict laws against "loitering" (this actually meant meeting with other blacks, free and slave).[53]

Slaves were involved in all aspects of iron production in the Chesapeake Bay area. Colonel Alexander Spotswood built several furnaces using slaves as early as 1716. There were 65 iron works in this area, most run by slaves, when the American Revolution started. These foundries produced most of the iron used in the colonies. Slaves were used in unskilled duties like woodchopping and casting, some were semi-skilled and were miners and coalers, while others were trained in highly skilled jobs like foundering and blacksmithing. The skilled slave was rewarded with more food and better clothing.[54] At the Oxford Iron Works, Abram, a slave, managed a blast furnace. Four furnace keepers were slaves. Fillers, who dumped measured amounts of ore, charcoal, and limestone into furnaces, were slaves. The owner, David Ross, used slaves as blacksmiths, potters, and refinery workers; he had 220 slaves at his foundry, supervised by a white carpenter, a miller, and a manager. Many of the slaves could perform two or three tasks. Some black workers cared for the machinery, and they could rebuild it when necessary. The slaves' output was controlled through punishments and incentives. Punishment included verbal abuse, denial of new clothing, transfer to a harder job, and whipping. Incentives included more food and special clothing. One potter was permitted to have a special stamp to mark his work as a sign of distinction. If the product received outside commendations, the slaves were notified, which built their pride in the product. A very important incentive was the assurance that the slave family would stay together. Skills were passed down from father to son, and slave parents were given complete charge of raising their children. Most foundries employed an "overwork system" to reward slaves for overproduction. The excess output resulted from slaves' coming in after regular working hours. At the Elk Ridge plant, the slave received as much money for overtime as a free white worker. The money could be used to purchase food, fancy clothes for his family, or eventually his own freedom.[55]

In the South, slaves worked in the early textile mills. In 1776 Daniel Heyward had 30 slaves making cloth from cotton and wool. They were supervised by a white spinner and weaver. The first cotton mill in South Carolina to use spinning jennies was operated by slaves.[56] Finally, in the North, slaves, working alongside free blacks, were printers, rope makers, gold- and silversmiths, and cabinetmakers.

Most plantation owners were in debt because of the purchase of slaves, seeds, and the necessities of life on credit, as well as because of living above their means. (The interest on credit purchases could reach 25 percent per year.) They could not sell off their slaves too easily, because this would lower their social position and would bring moral chastisement from their neighbors for "breaking up families." A solution to this problem was to hire out their chattels. During the year, there were periods of slack time, and the owner could hire out his bondsmen's work dealing directly with an individual who needed "temporary help." The concept of hiring became important enough that some individuals could work full time as agents or middlemen. Agents used advertisements like this in local newspapers to notify owners of their function and location: "Wanted to hire, twelve or fifteen Negro girls from ten to fourteen years of age. They are wanted for the term of two or three years. E.H. & J. Fisher." Hiring might be for the day, week, month, or year. The busiest time for hiring was around January 1, and the hire usually ran for 50 weeks until just before Christmas. The individual who hired the black was responsible for feeding, clothing, housing, and payment of the yearly slave tax. As in all business dealings, problems developed, and the courts had to adjudicate. In Virginia in 1806 the court decided, "Where one hires a slave for one year, that if the slave be sick or run away, the tenant [renter] must pay the hire; but if the slave dies without any fault of the tenant, the owner and not the tenant, should lose the hire, because such death was an act of God."[57]

Slave hiring was important in the budding growth of industry in the South. Before the American Revolution, slaves working in iron foundries generally belonged to the owner of the factory. After the war, they were hired from neighboring plantations or from slave-hiring markets. Iron masters traveled to the Piedmont area of Virginia to markets in Pittsylvania, Louisa, Spotsylvania, Orange, Abermarle, Amherst, Nelson, and Fauquier Counties. By the turn of the century, nonmasters would pay $55–$67 per year for a vigorous, skilled slave. The slave owner specified the type of work his man might do to prevent injury or death to his property. The slave could work "for himself" nights (after an 11-hour day), Sundays, and during the Christmas break (if the hire was for more than one year). He received money that he could spend at the foundry store for clothing, coffee, sugar, and tobacco. At the end of the year, he received any residual money he did not spend.[58]

The slave could hire himself from his master. The slave paid his owner "freedom dues," a set amount of money for a fixed period of time. The slave could then hire his time out to others. The slave usually went to town and competed with free black and white artisans for all types of work. He was able to compete successfully, with resulting white unemployment and increased animosity directed against the slave, not the system. These town blacks were "free slaves," and many escaped to become truly free. Many remained in town as "free slaves" and opened businesses and sometimes hired other slaves. Over a period of time, the entrepreneur could save enough money to buy his freedom and then buy his family. Southern states had emancipation laws that forced the slave to leave the state within a fixed period of time after gaining his freedom (the presence of free blacks was feared as a site for stealing, fencing and promoting insurrection). To remain in an area while he worked to free his family, the individual and his previous owner set up a trust, whereby the money he earned was set aside until enough was accumulated to cover the total cost of his family. Then all were freed and could leave the state as a family.[59]

Chapter 5

AFRICANS IN NEW ENGLAND

Massachusetts

Historians have written thousands of pages about the beginning of slavery in Virginia, the oldest English continental colony. Was it gradual? Did it follow court decisions? Was it de facto, then de jure? It was Puritan Massachusetts, however, the colony that produced judges Sewall and Cushing and other advocates of emancipation, that first accepted slavery. The first mention of a black in Massachusetts was in 1633 when the Indians saw an individual darker than anyone in the tribe—they called him "Abimacho," the devil. They reported him to the English authorities, who took him to his master. (He may have been a slave or an indentured servant. Africans had lived in England for about a century before this incident, and many were baptized Christians. English common law prohibited the enslavement of a Christian.) He was listed as an "estray," a term usually reserved for cattle and other livestock that wandered away from the field.[1] The earliest mention of black slavery was in 1638 in Governor John Winthrop's diary. In 1639, a black woman mentioned her slavery. Her master tried to mate her with another black, but she kicked him out of her bed, because such behavior was "beyond her slavery."[2]

In 1637 the Puritans defeated the Indians in the Pequot War. Many captives were taken. According to Puritan concepts, all savages were the children of the devil and had to be subjugated or exterminated.[3] Indian slavery, consequently, became an accepted institution. However, like the Spaniards a century earlier, the English discovered that the Indians did not endure "the yoke." In 1638 William Pierce, captain of the *Desire* out of Salem, transported Indian slaves to the Puritan colony of Providence off the coast of Central America.[4] He returned with black slaves as well as tobacco, cotton, and salt. This first shipload was followed by others from Barbados and other islands in the West Indies.

The Puritans had to wrestle with the concept of slavery. Slavery was a sacred privilege the Almighty was pleased to grant his elect. They believed that God had given them heathen Indians and blacks as part of their inheritance. However, slavery robbed a man of the fruits of his labor and removed the primary motive for industry and frugality. It also had a bad effect on the owner, who lost the "Puritan ethic" of hard work. Perhaps it was this battle of the conscience that led to the "Body of Liberties," a meeting of men of the colony, in 1641.[5] The leaders proclaimed there was to be no bond slavery, villenage or captivity in Massachusetts except for (1) those taken in just wars, (2) those who sell themselves or are sold, and (3) those who are judged such by authority. The decree may have acted as a soothing salve to the inflamed conscience of its authors, but it was ludicrous at best. The first proviso covered the Pequot Indians conquered in a "just war." However, it could also be applied to slaves taken by one African chief against an unarmed village in a "just war" for profit. The second covered black slaves and indentured servants sold to the Puritans by a ship's captain. The third clause covered those already in slavery, as well as those condemned to a form of slavery for a period of time under this provision. In 1643, the Puritan theocracies of Connecticut and New Haven joined Massachusetts in the New England Confederation and accepted the terms of the Body of Liberties.[6]

The decree contained a clause that determined the treatment of slaves in the region for the next 40 years. The bondsmen "shall have all the liberties and Christian usages which the law of God established in Israel requires."[7] Consequently, blacks and whites received equal treatment before the law. Blacks received police protection. Black testimony against whites was accepted in court. The bondsman had access to legal counsel. Blacks and whites were punished equally for fornication (10–20 lashes or a fine of 40–50 shillings). Illicit sex between members of different races was punished the same way as it was when members of the same race were involved. Racial intermarriage was legal until 1705; if children resulted from the union, the father was responsible for the support of the offspring. The punishment for rape or manslaughter was the same for both races. A slave owner could be tried for manslaughter if he killed his slave.

Despite this more "benign" attitude toward slaves, the leaders of Massachusetts did not want blacks in their midst. Blacks had different facial characteristics and could not mix with whites. Blacks could not be good servants, because they yearned for freedom and would escape at any opportunity. White indentured servants could not compete with slaves, and they would not immigrate to the colony. Without new immigrants, the daughters of the colony would remain spinsters, and the population of the colony would not grow. Blacks were not permitted to develop military skills. White servants would join the militia for the protection of the community. The long, cold winters resulted in decreased productivity, but slaves still had to be fed and clothed properly. The poor soil did not lend itself to "group agriculture."

Toward the end of the seventeenth century, a change developed in the slave laws; which began to resemble the oppressive laws of the South. The reasons for this change are difficult to understand. Massachusetts slaveholders did not have large numbers of slaves, in relation to whites, and rebellion was not a serious consideration. (In 1715 Massachusetts had 96,000 whites and 2,000 blacks, while South Carolina had 6,250 whites and 10,500 slaves.[8]) Perhaps they feared a mixture of the races. Perhaps they worried about giving this "different group" so much freedom. Perhaps, too, Massachusetts slave traders who were discouraged from bringing their cargo to New England learned about the treatment in other colonies and brought these concepts to Massachusetts. Finally, there was an infusion of other groups into Massachusetts which diluted the Puritan theocracy. In Barbados small plantation owners were being crowded out by the large owners. Between 1643 and 1647, 1,200 whites left Barbados for New England.[9] The West Indies had the harshest slave codes in the New World, and the whites brought these concepts with them. Whatever the cause, a stricter slave code became a part of the Massachusetts body of laws. In 1670 children of slaves could be sold into bondage.[10] This was a significant change from the Body of Liberties. The original ruling did not cover children of slaves born in the colony, who, as such, could be presumed free. In 1680 blacks could not board ships without permits. In 1693 no white could trade with slaves, to prevent stealing of the master's property. A law of 1703 prohibited slaves from being on the streets after 9:00 P.M. This rule was extended to free blacks as well. Another ruling in 1703 made manumission more difficult: the owner had to deposit a £50 security bond with the government for each slave freed, which would be used if the freedman became a charge on the community. This decree may have been used to prevent a master from freeing an old or infirm slave who would require community support. A master could not prevent his slave from marriage, but intermarriage was forbidden (1705). A minister who performed the marriage ceremony between a Christian and an infidel was fined £50. The decree was passed for the "Better Preventing a Spurious Mixt Issue." Black offenders were banished, while the white consort was made responsible for the support of the child. Between 1652 and 1656, free blacks were permitted in the militia. This was rescinded in a law of 1707. They were required to perform "community service" equal to the time whites spent in military training. They had to answer all fire alarms and perform all duties required by the whites at the fire. Free blacks could not entertain slaves in their homes without the express permission of their owners; if a violation was discovered, the fine was very high and beyond the capacity of the free black to pay. He was then taken to the House of Correction, and his labors were hired out at one shilling per day. No black could defame or strike a white—the punishment was flogging. No one was permitted to sell alcohol to a slave.[11] In 1718 the legislature prepared a bill to "encourage importation of white Male Servants, and preventing the Clandestine bringing in of negroes & mulattoes."[12]

Despite the restrictions placed on slave activities, there was an active movement to train blacks and prepare them for freedom. Many Puritans believed slaves should learn to read, so they could interpret the Scriptures. To this end, Cotton Mother, the leading cleric in New England, started a school for blacks and Indians in 1717. Nathaniel Pigott tried to start a school in 1728. The Quakers, a persecuted minority in New England, urged the education and training of slaves to prepare them for their ultimate goal, universal emancipation.[13] With the passage of time, the theocracies of the Puritans in New England were invaded by other Protestant sects. The Society for the Propagation of the Gospels and Dr. Bray's Associates brought Anglicanism to New England. As a result of this exposure to the Protestant religion, some blacks became Congregationalists, Quakers, or Anglicans, although these groups were not anxious to admit blacks into their midst. By the outbreak of the Revolution, most blacks in Massachusetts were considered "infidels."

Of greater significance to the slaves than learning to read and conversion to Christianity was the movement to emancipation. The success of this movement was demonstrated in the census of 1790: no slaves existed in Massachusetts at this time. "The Selling of Joseph" (1700), by Samuel Sewall, chief justice of the Superior Court of Massachusetts, was a landmark in the fight to destroy slavery.[14] The tract was allegedly written as a result of a case tried before the judge. In this case, John Saffin leased land and livestock to Thomas Shepherd. Saffin sent his slave, Adam, to work for Shepherd, with the promise of freedom in return for seven years of faithful service. Adam proved unsatisfactory to Shepherd, but he demanded his freedom after seven years. Sewall found in Adam's favor. In his writing, Sewall equated Joseph's experience with manstealing and manstealing with slavery, proving the moral liability of slavery from the known immorality of manstealing (which was prohibited in Exodus 21:16). Manstealing was included among the capital offenses in the Massachusetts Body of Liberties (1641). Sewall then proceeded to describe how slavery weakened the colony's society. He also attacked the commonly held belief that blacks were descended from Ham, and the opinion that "evil must be done, that good may come of it" (referring to the notion that slavery was a good for blacks because they would be exposed to Christianity). The jurist destroyed the belief that blacks were "taken in just wars in Africa." He tried to raise doubts that Abraham, father of the Hebrews, had slaves. Sewall claimed there were restrictions on slavery among Jews. A Jew could not enslave another Jew. Since Jesus had said all people were one, therefore all people were Jews and consequently slavery fell under the prohibition in Leviticus (25:44–46) against Jews enslaving Jews. The judge also attacked the "Trade of fetching negroes from Guinea."[15] (Many Puritans were directly and indirectly connected with the slave trade.) "Liberty is in real value, next unto life: None ought to part with it themselves, or deprive others of it, but upon most mature Consideration.... It is most certain, that all men, as they are the Sons of Adam, are coheirs; and have equal Rights unto Liberty, and all other outward Comforts of Life.... Through the Indulgence of God to our First Parents After the Fall, the outward Estates of all and every of their children, remains the same, as to one another. So treat Originally and Naturally, there is no such thing as Slavery."

Saffin did not take his loss kindly. He attacked Sewall's arguments and used his rights as an Englishman to publish "The Negroes Character":

> Cowardly and cruel as those Blacks Innate,
> Prone to Revenge, Imp of inveterate hate.
> He that exasperates them, soon espies
> Mischief and murder in their very eyes.
> Libidinous, Deceitful, False and Rude
> The Spume Issue of Ingratitude,
> The Premises considr'd, all may tell,
> How near good Joseph they are Parallel.[16]

Others joined Sewall in print to support his attack upon the institution of slavery. In 1729 Elihu Coleman, a Quaker minister in Rhode Island, wrote "A Testimony against that anti–Christian Practice of Making Slaves of Men." He claimed that slavery was the mother of vice and against the laws of nature and God. Nathanial Appleton in 1767 published "Considerations of Slavery," followed by the Reverend Samuel Webster of Salisbury, who wrote "An Earnest Address to My Country on Slavery" in 1769.[17] The war against slavery was joined by the legislature, individual communities, the courts, and the slaves themselves. The colonial legislature had to tread very lightly, because all laws had to be approved by the governor, whose primary interest was the mother country and its finances. However, Massachusetts did pass a law in 1705 placing a duty of £5 on each slave brought into the colony.[18] This was described as a revenue act, and the governor acceded. In 1767 a law that failed to pass called for the cessation of slave importation and the abolition of slavery; it passed the legislature but was not signed by the governor (1771). A law passed in 1774 placed a fine of £50 per slave imported and a £250 fine on the purchaser. This was vetoed by the governor. In 1757 a £500 fine was levied on anyone who kidnapped a slave and sold him out of the colony. The local town meetings dealt only with collective consciences of the townspeople and were ahead of the legislature in their demands. In 1701 Boston instructed its representative to vote for the abolition of the slave trade. Salem in 1755 and Worcester in 1765 voted to oppose the slave trade. Sandwich followed in 1773 and added that slave children should be freed on their twenty-first birthday. A Boston town meeting instructed its representative to the General Court (legislature) to work for a law abolishing slavery. Ten months later, Boston voted for the emancipation of slaves within the city's limits.

Unlike the situation in Southern colonies, slaves in Massachusetts had recourse to the courts to protect their rights. They also had money to pay for legal representation. Most legal activities were on a local level and did not have colonywide effects; however, they frequently mirrored society's objections to slavery. In 1707, John Clark, Esquire, justice of the peace, convicted whites of assaulting blacks in five separate cases. He caused a Boston lawyer, John Peak, to put up a bond to appear in court for "Civil treatment toward his Negroman, Primus."[19] Jenny Slew, a slave in Ipswich, sued John Whipple for her freedom in 1766; she won and received an award of £4 for his restraint of her liberty. A slave received his freedom in a Boston court in 1770; a jury in Plymouth County gave Caesar his freedom from Richard Greenleaf because it was "his right." Cabot Dodge received his emancipation in 1774 because no law of the province existed to hold a man to serve for life."[20] Felix Cuff, a slave in Waltham who served during the Revolution, took the Massachusetts Constitution literally—it proclaimed that "all men are born free and equal." He induced a group of slaves to join him in flight and hide in "Devil's Den" in Snake Rock, but they were chased and attacked by a posse under Lieutenant Hastings. The slaves beat the posse back, went to the village, and "prosecuted Hastings for riot." The community supported Cuff, and he and his followers retained their freedom.[21]

The slaves were active in the fight for their freedom, sometimes with quiet dignity, which pricked the conscience of the whites, sometimes as "Uncle Tom," and sometimes as active participants before the courts and legislature. John Jack, a slave in Concord, left this epitaph: "God Wills us free; Man Wills us slaves, I will as God Wills, God's will be done. Here lies the body of John Jack, a native of Africa, who died March, 1773, aged about 60 years. Tho' born in a land of slavery, he was born free; Tho' he lived in a land of liberty, he lived a slave. Tho' not long before Death, the grand Tyrant gave him his final emancipation, and set him on a footing with kings."[22] Compare the elegance of John Jack with the obsequious "will" of Peter, a slave of Thomas Fleet of Boston, who left his money to his master's children and their playmates: "To Thomas Fleet Jr., 10 shillings & a pair of buckles—but not to be worn for three years. John Fleet, five shillings, Anne Fleet, five shillings, Elizabeth Fleet, five shillings, Simon, five shillings, Nathan Bowen Jr., five shillings, Thomas Oliver, five shillings." Peter then assured his master that he did not get the money by "Roguery in anything belong'd to you or any body else, I got it honestly; by being faithful to people ever since I undertook to carry ye Newspapers, christmas-days, and New-years days." He then talked of other money, "but I had so much dealing with a wench." He and his wife (Love) were not "great Drinkers not Smooker," and "I have a little more with than I use to have formerly against ye wenches."[23] This will was probably shown to his master, so he "could be patted on the head." Of greater significance, though, was the ability of both to read and write. The actions of individual slaves to seek freedom through the courts was described earlier. In addition, bondsmen joined together to petition the Massachusetts General Court (legislature) for their rights. In 1773 a group petitioned for the right to earn money to purchase their freedom.[24] Later that year, a group petitioned for their freedom and a grant of unimproved land for a settlement of their own.

The penultimate act in the march of the slaves to freedom was the Massachusetts Constitution of 1780. Article I of the Bill of Rights stated, "All men are born free & equal, & have certain natural, essential & inalienable rights. Among which may be reckoned the right of enjoying & defending their lives & liberties; stated, that of acquiring, possessing & protecting property, in fine, that of seeking & obtaining, their safety & happiness." Did this apply to black people? The same high-sounding language was present in the Declaration of Independence, but it did not apply to slaves. It took the Quok Walker case, decided by Chief Justice Cushing, to put the final nail into the coffin of slavery in the Bay State.[25]

There were at least six cases involving Quok Walker, Nathaniel Jennison, and John and Seth Caldwell between 1781 and 1783. Quok was purchased by James Caldwell in 1754 when he was nine months old.[26] According to Quok, his master promised him his freedom when he reached his twenty-fourth or twenty-fifth birthday. James Caldwell died intestate, and his wife received one-third of his estate, including Quok. According to the slave, the widow Caldwell promised him his freedom at age 21. The widow then married Nathaniel Jennison, who became Quok's owner. In 1781, when he was 28 Quok ran away and started to work for John and Seth Caldwell (they were younger brothers or sons of James, the original owner). Jennison discovered where Quok worked, and went to the farm and used force to bring his "property" home. Quok filed a civil suit for £300 against Jennison on assault and battery charges. At this trial Quok claimed he was a free man. The Inferior Court of Common Pleas on June 12, 1781, found in favor of Quok and fined Jennison £50 plus costs. Jennison's lawyer, John Sprague, appealed the decision to the Supreme Judicial Court of the County. The new trial was to take place in Worcester in September 1781. Sprague, however, did not appear. Quok's lawyer, Levi Lincoln, asked for a reaffirmation of the earlier judgment, plus increased costs. The court concurred in February 1782. Jennison then appealed to the Massachusetts House of Representatives to reverse the decision because of Sprague's neglect. At the same time, Jennison pursued the Caldwell brothers, bringing a civil action against them in June 1781 at the original Inferior Court of Common Pleas. He accused them of luring his slave away and thus depriving him of six weeks of work from Quok. The court found in favor of Jennison, and the Caldwells appealed to the Supreme Judicial Court in Worcester in 1783. Levi Lincoln represented the Caldwells. In his brief, he argued against slavery. He attacked it as being against the law of nature and God. There was a higher law, and the quality clause of the Declaration of Rights of the Massachusetts Constitution was an extension of this higher law. Judge Cushing charged the jury, "slavery is in my judgment as effectively abolished as it can be by the granting of rights & privileges wholly incompatible & repugnant to its existence. The court are therefore fully of the opinion that perpetual servitude can no longer be tolerated in our government."[27] The jury agreed with Lincoln and declared slavery contrary to the Massachusetts Constitution.

Connecticut

Connecticut was a "kid brother" of Massachusetts, and its laws and regulations followed those of the larger colony by one year or two. It was a Puritan theocracy founded by the Reverend Thomas Hooker in 1636 in Hartford.[28] New Haven, which would later become part of the colony of Connecticut, had black servants or slaves as early as 1644. Records in Hartford described an incident wherein a black slave, Louis Builuce, was killed by his master, Gysbert Opdych.[29] By 1680 slavery was an accepted institution in that colony. Connecticut's governor reported to the Board of Trade in England that "sometimes three or four blacks per year come from Barbados and they are sold for £22 a piece." These individuals may have been indentured servants, although £22 was a lot of money for an indenture that lasted a few years. As in the Northern theocracy, these slaves had their rights protected by the courts. However, Connecticut developed a slave code more stringent than that in Massachusetts. In 1660 a law prohibited blacks from acquiring military training in the militia. No black mulatto or Indian was permitted to wander outside of his community. If a ferry operator carried a slave without a pass, he was fined 20 shillings. An innkeeper could not sell alcohol to a slave (1703). A black who threatened to strike a white was whipped (1708). To prevent a slave from stealing his master's property, no white could purchase anything from a slave without an order from his master; if apprehended, the purchaser had to return the property plus double its value. If he had disposed of the property, he paid three times its value. If unable to pay, he received 20 lashes, and the slave received 30 lashes (1708). A slave was not permitted in the street after 9:00 at night without a pass. If picked up, he was brought to a justice of the peace and would receive ten lashes unless his master paid 10 shillings to release him. Anyone harboring another person's slave was fined 10 shillings, half to the government and half to the informer (1723). If a free person entertained a black in his home after 9:00 P.M. without a certificate from the slave's master, he was fined 20 shillings. If a slave slandered a white, he received 40 lashes, and his master was fined for the slave's misbehavior. If the master refused to pay, the slave was sold to cover costs

(1730). Free blacks had to carry a certificate of freedom. If they were mistaken for slaves and did not have the certificate, they were taken before a magistrate and had to pay court costs.[30]

In the years preceding the Revolution, Connecticut had 6,562 slaves. This represented a substantial portion of "private property," and to remove this property without recompense was contrary to English law. Nevertheless, like Massachusetts, Connecticut had individuals who urged emancipation by the free will of their owners or, if necessary, by law. Ezra Stiles, Jonathan Edwards, and Levi Hart were forerunners in the battle against involuntary servitude.[31] In 1774 Connecticut prohibited the importation of slaves because they were injurious to the "poor and inconvenient"; the fine was £100 per slave. In 1788 no Connecticut ship's master was permitted to engage in the slave trade: the fine was £50 per slave and £500 per ship.

New Hampshire and Vermont

In 1623, a charter was granted to Ferdinando Gorges and John Mason for territory north of the Plymouth Bay Colony.[32] It was divided, and Mason took the future New Hampshire and Gorges took Maine. There was little activity in these areas until 1679, when New Hampshire became an entity separate from Massachusetts.[33] There were very few slaves in the entire colony, and there was little legal activity related to them. In 1684 the governor freed a slave who belonged to a resident of the colony. In 1714 no servant or slave was permitted to be away from his master's property later than 9:00 P.M. unless he had permission. Some protection was afforded to the slave by an act of 1718. If a master willfully struck out the eye or tooth of his servant or maimed or disfigured him, that servant was given his freedom plus an award of money. The purposeful killing of an Indian or black servant brought the death penalty to the master. (The term *servant* was used here; *servant* and *slave* were used interchangeably. Also, Indians were "slaves" rather than "indentured servants.") The colony tried to reduce the numbers of blacks with an import duty in 1761; this was vetoed by the mother country. After the Revolution, the importation of slaves was declared contrary to the new state's constitution (1784).

Vermont in 1777 had a constitution that prohibited adult slavery.[34] However, slavery existed in Bennington until the 1780s. A will of John Armstrong, probated in 1782, listed in his estate a "negro boy—value £60."[35] The attitude toward slavery in Vermont was summarized by Royall Tyler, a justice of the Vermont Supreme Court. A Virginia planter pursuing his runaway slave came before Justice Tyler. The Virginian brought all the necessary papers proving his ownership, but the court refused to return his property. The planter's lawyer, in exasperation, asked what would be considered sufficient evidence of the planter's ownership of the slave. Tyler replied, "A quit claim deed of ownership from the Almighty."[36] Vermont was admitted to the union in 1791. In Vermont's constitution, its bill of rights stated that no person could be a servant or slave after the age of 21 unless by his own consent or in payment of debts or fines. It was the first state to outlaw slavery by law.[37]

Rhode Island

Rhode Island, founded by Roger Williams in 1643 as a haven for religious liberty, "outlawed" slavery in 1652. Its legislature proclaimed,

> Whereas there is a common course practiced among Englishmen to buy negers, to that end they may have them for service or slaves forever; for the preventing of such practices amongst us, let it be ordered, that no black mankind or white being forced by covenant, bond or otherwise, to serve any man or his assignees longer than ten years, or untill they come to bee twentie four years of age, if they be taken in under fourteen from the time of their coming within the liberties of this Collonie. And at the end or terme of ten years to sett them free, as the manner is with English servants. And that man that will not let them goe free, or shall sell them away elsewhere, to that end that they may be enslaved to others for a long time, hee or they shall forfeit to the Collonie forty pounds.[38]

The law effectively outlawed adult slavery on the books. However, while the rest of New England had a black population of about 3 percent of the total in the eighteenth century, parts of Rhode Island had a slave population that made up 16–25 percent of the total. Throughout slaveholding society, the greater the number of slaves, the stricter the slave code, and despite the law of 1652, Rhode Island had the strictest code in New England.[39] A law in 1703 stated that Negroes or Indians, free or slave, seen on the streets of any town after 9:00 at night, without a certificate from their master or a legal excuse, could be picked up by any inhabitant and delivered to the constable. The constable kept him "secure" until the next morning. The miscreant was then brought to a justice of the peace. If the justice found him guilty of breaking the law, he received up to 15 lashes in public. If the lawbreaker was "incorrigible," he could receive more than 15 stripes. Anyone who sheltered a black or an Indian after 9:00 without the permission of his master was fined 5 shillings, which was used to help the poor in the community. In 1708 the fine was raised to 10 shillings. Also, the housekeeper was forbidden from serving Indians and blacks hard liquor. If a housekeeper who was a free Indian or black was found guilty of entertaining a slave, she lost that position and had to work for a private family for one year, with the salary for her work going to the community. If the offender was unable to pay the fine, she could be subject to ten lashes. A law of 1714 declared that no boatman was to carry a slave on his ferry without a certificate from his master. If guilty, he paid the master for his loss of property plus a fine of 20 shillings. In 1728, if a master freed a slave, he had to deposit £100 security in the event that the new freedman became a charge of the community. The legislature in 1751 repeated the law prohibiting free blacks and slaves from the streets after 9:00 P.M. It also prohibited trade with a servant or slave to prevent theft of the owner's property. To prevent shipmasters from carrying runaways out of the colony, a law of 1757 fined the shipmaster £500 if a slave was found on board. The owner of the slave could sue and receive double the value of the slave. If an owner suspected that his slave was on board a ship, he could make application to the master before witnesses: "This is taken as full proof of his knowledge if his slave is on board. If the master of the ship refuses owner to search ship, this will be taken as proof he has knowledge that the slave is on board."[40]

There were also laws to control the import of blacks into the colony. A law of 1712 ordered shipmasters to report to the governor the names and number of passengers landed in the colony. Similarly, they could not carry away from Rhode Island any passenger without the governor's permission. The fine was £50.[41] Those planning to leave the colony posted a notice ten days before the date of departure. There was also an import duty of £3 per Negro and 40 shillings per Indian. An act of 1715 used some of the duty money to fix the streets and build bridges. If a shipmaster did not list all of the slaves on board, he was fined £6 per slave above the number listed. If the slave remained in Rhode Island less than six months, the duty was returned. The duty on slaves was repealed in 1732 by the English Board of Trade.

How could a colony that prohibited slavery by a law in 1652 have the highest percentage of slaves in New England? There are two reasons. First, the citizens of Rhode Island became the greatest slave traders in the colonies. At the peak, 90 percent of the slaves brought to America were carried in vessels registered in Rhode Island. Between 1709 and 1807, 939 voyages carrying 106,544 Africans went from Newport, Rhode Island, to Africa, the West Indies, and the Southern colonies. This represented jobs for seamen, investment for financiers, and markets for the products of Rhode Island's distilleries.[42] Second, an unusual plantation economy developed in the Narragansett area. The slave traders of Newport needed livestock and other produce for foreign trade, and so large livestock and dairy plantations developed in the area of South Kingston, North Kingston, Charlestown, and Exeter. The soil was fertile and produced a good quality of grass to support livestock. The area also had a milder climate with shorter winters. Furthermore, it was not controlled by a Puritan hierarchy that preferred small, single-family farms. The land was a site of dispute between Rhode Island and Connecticut, and its status and ownership were unstable, so anyone who wanted to gamble could purchase acreage cheaply from the Narragansett Indians. In 1671, 500 acres in Kingston could be purchased for £28. In the eighteenth century, some families owned thousands of acres used for livestock and the production of "Rhode Island cheese" and other dairy products. This produce was shipped to the Southern colonies and to the Caribbean. Slaves were easily purchased and transported from nearby Newport. Some planters owned 20 slaves. In 1730 South Kingston could count 498 slaves. The heyday of this plantation economy however, had passed by 1770. The available land was all taken, families grew, and plantations were divided among children and grandchildren; consequently, land could not be used for grazing. With these changes, slavery became less economical. The presence of Quakers in the area caused the manumission of Quaker-held slaves. By the dawning of the Revolution, this "Southern" economy was only a memory.[43]

The tide against involuntary servitude turned in midcentury and became a torrent after the Revolution. In 1746 a law was passed against privateers, who captured free blacks in the Massachusetts Bay Colony and sold them as slaves in Rhode Island. If caught, they repaid the purchaser the cost of the "slave."[44] In 1774 Rhode Island freed any slave brought into the colony after that date.[45] However, if a master had a slave in another colony and brought that slave into Rhode Island, he kept the slave. If he left the colony, he had to take the slave and his progeny with him. If a shipmaster could not sell his cargo of slaves in the West Indies, he could bring them to Rhode Island. He posted a £100 bond per slave, which would be recovered if he removed the slave within one year. If a slave was brought to Rhode Island to be set free and he became a charge of the community, the carrier paid a £100 fine and the receiver paid a similar fine. The slave was then sent out of the colony. A law in 1779 prohibited the sale of slaves outside the state against their will.[46] In 1783 the Quakers presented an act to the assembly to free the slaves; it was shelved until the next session.[47] In 1784 a law was passed stating, "No person born in this state on or after March 1, 1784 shall be slaves."[48] These children were to stay with the slave mothers, and the expense of their support ultimately fell on the community. The town council could bind these children out as apprentices or support them in other ways between their first and twenty-first birthdays for males and their first and eighteenth birthdays for females. These children were to be schooled and taught a code of morality, paid for by the town. All slaves freed by their owners who were unable to support themselves were supported by the community like other paupers, rather than by their former owners. However, they had to be judged sound of body and mind by the town council if they were between 21 and 40 for males and 18 and 40 for females in order to fall under this clause in the law. In 1785 this law was changed. The children were to be supported by the owner until they were 21. If the owner freed the mother, he was no longer responsible for her children. No slave freed after age 30 was to be supported as a pauper. In 1785 any slave who enlisted in the army and became sick and unable to support himself would be cared for by the overseers of the poor in his community.[49] This money came from the general treasury. Finally, in 1787 Rhode Island forbade ships of that state from engaging in the slave trade, with a fine of £1,000 per ship.[50] This law could easily be sidestepped, however, by registering the ship in another state.

Chapter 6

AFRICANS IN THE MIDDLE ATLANTIC COLONIES

New York

In 1624 the Dutch West India Company seized an area comprising what would later be Connecticut, New York, New Jersey, Pennsylvania, and Delaware, naming it New Netherlands. Slaves were introduced one year later. Eleven black men, seized by privateers from Spanish and Portuguese ships, were landed in New Amsterdam. Between 1623 and 1636, about 2,300 blacks were seized in this manner. Some were released, and others were taken to New Netherlands as slaves to fill a labor shortage. The original slaves were the property of the company rather than of individual owners. These men cut timber, burned lime, and built Fort Amsterdam at the southern tip of Manhattan, while others worked in agriculture. Some blacks may have fought alongside their white masters against the Indians, but they were probably baggage handlers and support troops rather than actual combatants. The slaves were under the supervision of an employee of the company, the "Overseer of Negroes," who received 25 florins each month and 100 florins in "board money."[1] Two years after the introduction of male slaves, three black females were introduced into the colony. They were used as household help by the executives of the company.

After four years of total control of all activities in the colony by the company, with resulting financial reverses, the policy was changed to allow individuals to develop the settlements. (This was the start of the patroonship system in the Hudson River Valley.) Company slaves were leased to the settlers as well as to the local governments. The City of New Amsterdam requested and received three blacks to work as garbage collectors and to perform other heavy work not fit for white hands. The leasing system failed to slow the red ink, however, and the company began to sell its slaves to pay its debts. The need for blacks by individual owners soon outstripped the supply, and in 1648 the company discovered that slave trading from Curaçao and Brazil was more lucrative than using the slaves themselves. In 1651 the company let out a contract for the licensee to bring slaves from Africa (largely Angola) to New Amsterdam. The traders paid a duty of 15 guilders per slave to the director and council. The following year any inhabitant of the colony who could afford to fit out a ship for the slave trade was permitted to bring slaves to the port.[2]

Slavery under the Dutch, and particularly for those slaves owned by the company, was far more "benign" during the 40 years they controlled New Netherlands than the subsequent period under the English. Bondsmen owned by the company had basic rights.[3] They were admitted to the Dutch Reformed Church and were married by its ministers. Their children were baptized. Slave families were kept together. They could testify in court, sign legal documents, and bring civil actions against whites. A slave was permitted to work after hours, and he was paid on a scale equal to that of white workers. The company built a hospital in New Amsterdam for soldiers and slaves in 1660.[4] Company slaves were promised their freedom in return for faithful service. In 1644, 11 slaves petitioned for and received their freedom; their wives were also freed, and they were given plots of land to work for their support. Each family promised to deliver to the company one hog and 23 bushels of corn, wheat, or vegetables each year. They also served the company as paid laborers when they were needed. Their children remained slaves of the company, however. In 1646 the company granted a second manumission. The freedmen in this group paid only eight bushels of wheat per year. The company discovered that rearing the children was an excessive burden, and they were returned to their parents and eventually freed. In 1665 the company freed its last nine slaves, who were given "half liberty." They worked part-time for the directors. This group was given complete freedom before the English occupation in 1664.[5]

The last years of Dutch control of the Middle Atlantic area saw the conversion of the company from a predominantly agricultural and Indian trading enterprise to a slave-trading business. In 1655 the slave ship *Witte Paest* sold its full cargo of slaves from Guinea for 1,200 florins per slave.[6] As a result of the large profit, the directors planned to make New Amsterdam a central slave market for North America. Many slaves brought to New Amsterdam were sold in Maryland and Virginia. In addition to the profits realized from the trade, the company received a 10 percent export tax on those slaves shipped south to the English. In the last five years of Dutch control, six slave ships reached New Amsterdam by way of Curaçao with about 400 slaves. Some of these were sold locally to merchants, tavern keepers, butchers, and company officials.[7] Terms of purchase were kept so easy that all economic classes, except the very poor, were able to own one or more human beings during this period. It is possible that this ease of purchase was an attempt by the company to entice Hollanders and other Europeans to migrate to the colony.

The Dutch and English were maritime rivals in the seventeenth century, and they engaged in declared and undeclared wars at sea. On August 27, 1664, during one of these wars, Colonel Richard Nicolls forced the surrender of New Netherlands to the British, and the English king gave the territory to his brother, the Duke of York. Under British rule in 1665, slavery was recognized as a legal institution, but the duke prohibited Christians from being held in bondage.[8] The Naturalization Act of 1683 fully recognized slavery, and the duke's prohibition against Christian slaves ended in 1706; baptism did not lead to emancipation after this date. English slave laws were harsher than Dutch statutes. Slaves were chattel and served for life. Their masters could inflict any punishment short of mutilation and death. Freed blacks were denied civil rights. Any crime committed by a black against a white was severely punished, while white crimes against blacks were largely ignored.[9] Governor Edmond Andros tried to prohibit cruel practices, and he urged that blacks be instructed in Christianity. Queen Anne in 1702 supported the governor, although her motives were more financial: she wanted a sufficient supply of salable Negroes at moderate prices.[10]

With the growth of the black population (in 1771 New York State had almost 20,000 blacks in a total population of 168,000) and the development of the urban centers of New York City and Albany, larger concentrations of blacks existed. It became easier for groups of slaves to come together to "plan." This led to more stringent laws being added to the slave code. The colonial assembly as well as the urban councils tried to supervise the activities of the blacks. In almost every colony and in most urban centers, there were laws against "entertaining blacks in one's home." In 1693 the grand jury in New York indicted three whites for "Entertaining of Negroes in their houses contrary to the law."[11] The intention of the ban was not explicitly stated, but presumably its purpose was to prevent too many blacks from congregating to plan insurrection; to prevent the sale of liquor to them; and to prevent fencing of stolen goods. The Common Council of Albany instructed its constables to remove blacks and Indians from taverns on Sunday. The tavern owner was fined 6 shillings per person removed (1702). An earlier law of 1680 restricted blacks from consuming alcohol, but obviously this could not be enforced. Like the laws against entertaining blacks, the tavern laws were passed to prevent blacks from congregating in secret.[12] An assembly law of 1702 prohibited trade with a slave without his master's consent; the recipient of the goods was fined £5 plus three times the value of the item. The owner could punish his slave as violently as he wished, short of a threat to life or limb. The law also stated that no more than three slaves could congregate at one time except for the master's benefit. If they were discovered, the justice of the peace could order a whipping of up to 40 lashes plus a prison sentence. A "whipper" served this function, and he could be a black. Later a "common whipper" was employed, and he received 3 shillings per whipping. The duty then went exclusively to whites.

A slave was punished for striking a white, regardless of the provocation. A free man who concealed a slave was punished. In Albany laws were passed in 1705, 1715, and 1745 punishing a slave with execution if he were found more than 40 miles north of Albany—it was presumed that he was on his way to Canada with information about Albany's defenses against the French. This law was permitted to expire in 1750. New York City prohibited slaves from its streets at night without a lantern with a burning candle (1710). No free black could own real estate in New York City (1712). Also, New York passed a law defining capital and lesser crimes and their punishment.[13] Capital crimes included murder or attempted murder of a free man or slave, rape or attempted rape of a free woman, burning or willful damage to a house, barn, stable, outhouse, or stalks of corn or hay (the firing of these lesser structures could be used as a signal to start an insurrection) and burglary. If the preliminary investigation of a capital crime suggested guilt, the slave was imprisoned. The justice of the peace called two other justices and five freeholders (property owners) to act as judge and jury. (The slave's owner could have him tried by a 12-man jury if he paid a fee.) The slave could not challenge the freeholders or jury. If convicted, he was executed. The mode of execution depended on the severity of the crime. Hanging was usual, but those convicted of unusually heinous crimes were burned at the stake. Other slaves were forced to watch the execution. In many cases the corpse was left in place for days to remind other slaves of the punishment for offenses against whites. Prior to execution, the slave's owner could call one or several people to appraise the slave's value. (In a law of 1705 a slave over 15 who appeared fit was valued at £30.) The appraisers sent their judgments to the justices. If there was a substantial variation in the several appraisals, the justices had the final word. This amount plus the cost of prosecution was divided among the slaveholders in the county. Minor crimes by slaves included selling goods to others without the permission of the master, assembly of several slaves, and bearing arms. These crimes were tried by one or several justices of the peace. Punishment was usually a whipping; the slave was rarely jailed, because this represented a loss of work time for his master. If he assaulted a white, he was whipped and imprisoned for 14 days. Petty larceny led to a fine of up to £5 and a whipping. His master could be sued to recover the value of the loss by the victim.

Colonial New York City had the largest concentration of blacks in the middle colonies.[14] Perhaps with the Negro Revolt of 1712 still in mind, the New York City Council codified its slave laws in 1731. No more than three blacks could assemble on Sunday. Blacks could not carry weapons. Slaves were not permitted on the streets after dark except with their master. They had to carry one lit lantern for every three blacks in the group. No more than 12 blacks were permitted at a funeral, aside from the carriers and gravediggers and presumably the minister. No blacks could use the streets in a disorderly fashion. Gambling was forbidden among blacks, because the white authorities believed this led to stealing. In New York City, slaves were permitted to bring their own produce to large markets for private sale. The city council disallowed this practice in 1740, however, in response to the fears of the white population, who believed that the blacks were spreading disease in their fruits and vegetables, and that they had access to the city water supply, which they could contaminate with poisons "known only to themselves." In addition, there was always the fear of allowing too many blacks to congregate in one place. Finally, black merchants represented a threat to the profits of the white merchants. Violators of this ordinance were whipped unless their owner paid a fine of 6 shillings. Neither the approaching Revolution nor the activity of the forces of emancipation stopped the passage of restrictive legislation against slaves and blacks in general. Perhaps fears engendered by the Negro Conspiracy in 1741 forced a continuation of repressive laws. In 1773 liquor sale to slaves was again outlawed. If guilty, the tavern keeper lost his license for three years. If more than three slaves were found together and they could not prove they were doing their master's work, they received up to 40 lashes. If a free person entertained a slave in his house without permission of the owner, he was fined £5 per day, which went to the owner in compensation for loss of work. If free blacks entertained slaves, their fine was doubled. After the Revolution, while corporal punishment and execution were still carried out, jailing became more common. Laws of 1790 and 1801 called for the deportation of a black after he had served time in jail for a serious crime.

Large slaveholdings in the urban centers and small farms were not economically viable. A rich urban merchant might have one or two slaves in his home, and a small farmer might have that number as well. However, by 1800 there were 20,663 slaves in New York State among 8,439 slaveholders.[15] Presumably the large landowners in the Hudson River Valley had a plantation economy similar to that in Narragansett, Rhode Island, and these patroons owned many slaves. A review of probated wills shows this to be the case. The appraised value of these humans was frequently listed, and the wills demonstrated the owners' attitude toward their slaves—they were chattel and were listed among the silverplate, cattle, horses, and wheat. Colonel Lewis Morris in 1691 left an estate including 22 Negro men valued at £440, 11 Negro women worth £165, six boys worth £90, two "garles" worth £24 and 25 children worth £125. Before the humans, Morris listed spirits, molasses, sugar, wheat, and plate. After the slaves were the oxen, cows, bulls, horses, and swine. (Colonel Morris's estate was probated in New York, though his plantation and iron foundry were actually in New Jersey.)[16] In 1791 Thomas Garton of Ulster County had a Negro man, woman, and suckling child, one old Negro man, one woman of 32 years, four males between 10 and 18, three males between 6 and 8, and three females below 5 years.[17]

These wills also give some insight into the social mores of the white owners. Ephraim Trapp in 1755 declared, "I leave to my true and faithful slave

Clarinda her freedom, together with three slaves, *viz* a negro man named
Will, the father of said Clarinda, and a man named Staford, brother of said
Clarinda, and a negro wench called Diana. I give to my natural son, Uriah,
begotten of the body of the said Clarinda, his freedom and all the remainder
of my estate."[18] Trapp left money to send Uriah to a good school in Great
Britain until he was 14. Clarinda was to stay with him. Unlike Trapp, Thomas
Hadden in 1761 had two families for whom he provided. "I give to Mary
Wems and to my wench, Rose, the use of my house and lot for six years. I
leave to my negro children their bedding and clothes and to my wench, Rose,
£25. To my negro boys Francis and Robert £20 each. My executors are to sell
10 sheep which my two oldest negro boys have, and put the money at interest for them. At my death, all my negroes are to be free, and my executors
are to bind out the children to trades, also to take care they are learnt to
read."[19] In his will, Hadden also left money to his legitimate wife and children. Benjamin Stymets in 1750 may have had pangs of conscience about his
behavior. He left to his wife and eight legitimate children his estate, while
"my negro woman 'Cate' and my two negro children are to be sold by my
executors to pay debts."[20]

Some slaves were manumitted in their masters' wills for faithful service.
In 1750 Eve Scurlock, "victular ... and tavern keeper.... In consideration of
the extraordinary fidelity, faithful service, and good behaviour of my negro
slave Caesar, and my four other slaves, I manumit them and set them free
from all manner of slavery & bondage. I leave Caesar £4 and a pair of hand
irons, and one-half the firewood, soap, candles, six slates, the English Books
& a small looking glass. To my slave Anthony I leave the tools he commonly
works with in the carpenter's trade. To my slave Ann £3 & some household
utensils, and my homespun clothes & the cupboard I put my clothes in."[21] In
1774 Kesia Dean Spinster gave "Jacob his absolute freedom ... my negro
woman Letitia her freedom and to my girl Jerusha ... all such beds and bedding they call their own & all my wearing apparel, my pots & kettles ... sell
all my estate & from proceeds to pay to my negroes £50 each."[22] Only one
master freed his chattel in the spirit of liberty espoused by the Declaration
of Independence. Thomas Townsend stated in 1777, "Whereas I am now in
possession of some Negroes, & taking the matter under solid consideration,
being our fellow creatures, do feel a freedom in my mind to set them fully at
liberty, believing it to be consistent with the will of kind Providence, who
had created all Nations with one blood. And I do set them free, being two
negroes & three children."[23] Matthew Franklin (bachelor) had no slaves in
1780, but he recognized the need to train freed slaves for a life in the community: "My executors are to put at interest £150 the interest to be applied
to use of providing poor negro children books & also towards paying their
schooling, them that their parents did belong among the People called Quakers."[24]

As in other Northern colonies, there were groups in New York that saw the evil of the white race's holding the black race in perpetual servitude. The movement for manumission was started and fueled by the Quakers. In 1767 the Society of Friends questioned the premise that slavery was consistent with Christianity. Four years later New York Quakers would not sell their slaves except to liquidate an estate. Committees were formed to visit individual Quaker homes to urge manumission. By the outbreak of the Revolution they were ostracizing members who continued to keep blacks in bondage. This activity was extremely effective—no Quaker owned slaves in New York by 1787.[25]

In 1785 the New York Manumission Society was chartered, with John Jay as its president and Alexander Hamilton as its secretary. They petitioned the New York legislature to rule against permanent black bondage. They urged the legislature to prohibit slave owners from exporting their bondsman out of the state. An important part of their activity was to teach freedmen to read and write. To this end, African Free Schools were started.[26]

The driving force for total emancipation had to be the legislature, which had to balance the shame of bondage against the rights of private property. In 1777 John Jay and Gouverneur Morris urged the insertion of a clause in the state constitution which banned slavery; this was defeated. The legislature freed any black who had served three years in the recent war. After the war (1785), the legislature authorized the manumission of all slaves under age 50 without posting a security bond if the slave had a certificate of his ability to provide for himself. Any slave brought to New York and sold after 1785 was freed, and the seller was fined £100. At this time too, blacks were given a trial by jury for capital offenses. In 1786 "all negro slaves become the property of the people of this state, by attainder or conviction of any person whomsoever, and now in possession of the Commissioners of Forfeitures, he and they are hereby manumitted." This meant that slaves who became wards of the state when the master's estate was confiscated were emancipated. If they could not care for themselves, they fell under the care of the overseers of the poor. Two years later, the purchase of a slave with intent to sell him out of state was made illegal; the individual was fined £100, and the slave was freed. To calm the anxiety of slaveholders about their property, a fine of £5 per day was imposed on anyone who harbored an escaped slave. If the slave died while hidden, the concealer paid the owner the appraised value of the slave. Finally, a law of 1799, signed by Governor Jay, freed all slaves born after 1799. However, if the slave's mother was a slave, he or she served her master, until age 25 for women and age 28 for men. The master could release the child before his first birthday to the care of the overseer of the poor if he did not wish to incur the expense of rearing the child. After 1801 it was made difficult to bring slaves in or ship them out of the state. Those New Yorkers traveling out of the state with slaves had to bring the same number in when they returned. In 1809 slave marriages were made legal, and freed slaves could acquire an estate. The following year, only travelers (those staying in the state less than nine months) could bring slaves into New York. Also, the children of slaves who were to be freed at 25 or 28 years of age were freed at age 21 if their owners did not teach them to read the Scriptures. The complete end of slavery finally came in 1827.[27]

New Jersey

The history of Africans in New Jersey can be divided into the Dutch period, the Proprietary period, the Royal Colony period, and the Post-Revolutionary period. New Jersey was a part of New Netherlands until 1664. The Duke of York, who received New Jersey as part of the "gift" of New Netherlands, divided it between two of his retainers, Lord John Berkeley and Sir George Carteret (the Quinpartite Deed of 1676).[28] New Jersey was named after the English Channel Island, whose governor was Sir George Carteret. West Jersey was sold by Berkeley to John Fenwick, a recent convert to Quakerism.[29] The Proprietary period ended in 1702 when both Jerseys were joined with New York into a royal colony. New Jersey once again became a separate colony in 1738.

The Dutch introduced slavery into New Jersey. The first black mentioned was a gift to Jacob Stoffelson of Ahimus (Jersey City). Just as it developed in New York, slavery was a relatively benign form of the "institution." Blacks held property, married legally, obtained an education, and could look forward to manumission. The term *slave* was first used in legal documents in the "Concessions of 1664."[30] The division of the colony in the Proprietary period resulted in a marked difference in attitude toward involuntary servitude. West Jersey came under the domination of Philadelphia Quakers. A Quaker law in 1676 stated, "All & every person, & persons inhabiting the said province, shall as far as in us lies, be free from oppression & slavery." East Jersey encouraged slavery. Any settler relocating in East Jersey received 60 acres of land per slave in 1665. This dropped to 45 acres in 1666 and to 30 acres in 1667. West Jersey was given over to large farms where slaves could be used, but Quaker influence prevailed and resulted in a low density of blacks in that part of the state. East Jersey had small urban centers and farms, but the desire for free laborers resulted in a larger proportion of blacks. Early in the Proprietary period, slaves were treated more like apprentices and free servants. Toward the end of the period, their rights were curtailed, and the beginning of a strict slave code was legislated.[31] In 1675 anyone "transporting" a slave was fined £5. For concealing a bondsman, the fine was 10 shillings per day. A law in 1682 prohibited the purchase of articles sold by slaves; the fine for breaking the law was £5 for the first offense and £10 for the second. If a slave offered a white an article for sale, the white could whip the slave and receive a reward of half a crown from his master. The same year, a law stated that masters had to "clothe and feed their slaves adequately." At this time, too, the sale of strong liquor to bondsmen was prohibited except for medicinal purposes. On March 2, 1682/3, a message was sent to Indian Sachems to confer with the whites about their "entertainment of Negro Servants." That same year, a treaty was signed with the Indians which prohibited their trade with slaves.[32] A statute in 1694 prohibited slaves from carrying guns, pistols, or dogs into the woods unless accompanied by their master or another white with the consent of their owner. A slave could not have hunting equipment that did not bear his master's mark. No white could give, lend, or rent guns or pistols to slaves. No one could harbor a slave for more than two hours. If a slave was found more than five miles from his home without his master's consent, he was returned home and the finder received a reward proportionate to the mileage.

The trial and punishment of slaves was spelled out in 1695. For murder or other felonies, the slave was tried by three justices of the peace and 12 men in the county where the crime was committed. (New Jersey was the only colony that had a 12-man jury for slaves. The slave could also be sworn in to give testimony.)[33] If the defendant was found guilty, they could sentence and execute him. If the slave stole, his owner reimbursed the injured party; he then hired someone to whip the slave publicly, but no more than 40 lashes were permitted.

The Royal period coincided with the accession to the throne of Queen Anne (1702). During the early period, there was some humanity shown to the slaves. Anne called for the death penalty for a white who deliberately killed a Negro or Indian and a harsh penalty for maiming him. She urged that bondsmen be taught the tenets of Christianity leading to baptism. (A law of 1704, however, denied freedom to slaves who accepted Christ.[34]) The humanity of the sovereign did not spread to this side of the ocean. A letter to the queen in the archives referred to an act of 1704 for "Regulating Negro, Indian, & Mulato Slaves within This Province of New Jersey." According to the letter writer, one portion of the law "inflicts inhumane penalties on Negroes, etc., not fit to be confirmed by Your Majesty, and therefor we humbly offer that said act be repealed."[35] Nevertheless, the code became more onerous. In 1704 earlier statutes were re-enacted. For instance, a slave could receive up to 40 lashes for stealing 6 pence or more. If the value was between 5 and 40 shillings, he received 40 lashes and a *T* was branded on his cheek. The constable received 5 shillings for whipping and 10 shillings for branding; he could be fined 40 shillings if he did not carry out his task with vigor. A black convicted of rape or attempted rape was castrated; he remained in jail until the "operation" healed, while his master paid the cost of keeping him under lock and key. In 1713 no free black could purchase, inherit, or own land or tenements. If such property fell into a black's hands, it reverted to the Crown. Without land, the freedman could not vote or hold public office. Sellers could circumvent the law by leasing it to blacks for 999 years. In that same year, slaves were permitted to be sworn in as witnesses in trials of other slaves. Jury trials for slaves were no longer mandatory. Slaves could be tried by three justices of the peace plus five freeholders, and agreement among seven could result in a judgment. However, the slave's owner could still demand a jury trial. If his slave was executed, the owner would receive £30 for a male and £20 for a female. Castration for rape was replaced by corporal punishment (too many died from the "operation"). A slave was severely punished for striking a Christian (presumably white) or attempted rape of a white woman. Two justices of the peace could pass judgment and order corporal punishment. Manumission was also made difficult. The owner posted a security bond of £200. From this, the ex-slave could be paid £20 per year if he fell on the community for support. If a slave was freed in a will, the heirs posted the £200 security unless they declared this part of the will invalid. In 1751 no liquor could be sold to slaves without the owner's permission. Five or more slaves were not permitted to congregate. Slaves could not be out after sunset except for attendance at church or a funeral. A trapping decree was approved in 1759: no one could own or use a steel trap weighing more than three and a half pounds. A black received 30 lashes for a violation, while a white paid a £5 fine.[36]

The early Revolutionary period, with its ideals of liberty, had no immediate effect on the slaves. Between 1774 and 1783, one slave was freed in New Jersey.[37] Slaves were needed to produce supplies for the army at the cheapest prices. The new state constitution in 1776 gave suffrage to anyone with an estate of £50, including blacks and women. In 1807, however, this was amended to restrict voting to free white males. In the years between the Revolution and the total emancipation of all slaves, laws passed to control slaves became less burdensome. With one major exception, most laws concerned preparation of bondsmen for eventual freedom. In 1798, the legislature codified all previous laws relating to involuntary servitude. At this time, any black or other slave who entered the state without license was subject to arrest. Freedmen had to carry with them a certificate of freedom given by their previous master.[38]

The fight for total manumission, started by the Quakers in West Jersey, was gradually taken over by the legislature. However, it was not until 1846 that slavery was totally abolished in this Northern state. (At least the term *slavery* was abolished.) As early as 1696, the Quakers of West Jersey joined the Philadelphia Quakers in urging their communicants to refrain from the import and use of slave labor.[39] The work of John Woolman of Mount Holly, New Jersey, in 1743 is cited as the start of the crusade against bondage. He was preceded, however, by John Hepburn in 1715, who preached to his neighbors that they risked damnation by holding slaves.[40] What the Quakers initially requested only of their coreligionists they later expected all New Jersey residents to accept. By 1758, they opposed the import, sale, and retention of slaves in the entire colony. They also started schools for black children to prepare them for a future as freedmen.[41] ·

The colonial, and later the state legislature, attacked slavery on two fronts: first, through the use of duties to restrict importation of blacks; and second, through laws that led to gradual abolition. In 1717 a duty of £10 was placed on any Negro, Indian, or mulatto imported into the colony.[42] The express purpose of the duty was to encourage white immigration; it expired in 1721. Attempts to pass similar duties in 1739 and 1744 were thwarted by the assembly itself and by the royal Governor. As a "duty-free port," New Jersey became a point for the import of slaves to be smuggled into Pennsylvania and New York, which still had duties on their books. The reasons given for the veto of the duty of 1744 were described in the Archives of New Jersey.[43] It was stated that the people of New Jersey, particularly the farmers, would suffer from the duties (£10 on slaves from the West Indies, £5 on those from Africa). It was claimed that many white laborers left New Jersey on expeditions to the West Indies and few returned. Many also signed up for privateering expeditions, which resulted in a decreased supply of labor and a consequent increase in wages they could demand from farmers and merchants. Furthermore, Ireland had perfected its linen manufacturing processes, so New Jersey could not expect laborers from there. Finally, Great Britain engaged in wars on the Continent, and potential workers served in the army instead. In 1762, a £2 duty was placed on slaves entering East Jersey and £6 on those entering West Jersey. An import duty act passed by the New Jersey Assembly in 1765 was repealed by the Lord's Commissioners for Trade and Plantations. In 1767 a £10 duty was passed; this was raised to £15 in 1769. Appended to this last duty law was a ruling that required a £200 bond for manumission. The owner had to maintain his ex-slave in a "proper" manner. If he could not provide for his ex-slave who could not care for himself, the freedman received support from the colony like any other pauper.[44] The duties and other restrictions on black immigration had only a moderate effect on the black population of the state. Throughout the eighteenth century, approximately 10 percent of the inhabitants were black.

Legislative activity for emancipation developed slowly after the Revolution. Initially, individual slaves who had served in the Revolutionary army were freed by legislative mandate. Prince, Cato, Cudjo, and Peter Williams were manumitted, as were slaves of Tories who had fled the states. In 1786 the legislature prohibited the importation into New Jersey of slaves who were brought into the country after 1776. This law also made manumission easier. Able-bodied slaves between 21 and 35 years of age could be freed without a financial obligation of their master to cover potential pauperism. The new freedman was supervised very closely, though. If he committed a felony or two acts of petty larceny, he was jailed, then exiled from the state. If he returned before his period of exile was over, he was sold to labor for the duration of the exile period. No freedman from another state was permitted to enter New Jersey. The ex-slave could not leave his county without a certificate signed by two justices of the peace and the county clerk. A statute in 1788 prohibited the sale of a slave from the state without his permission; this prevented the sale of slaves to the South because the owner saw abolition on the horizon. The master was forced by law to teach his slave to read and write before his twenty-first birthday in preparation for eventual freedom. In 1798 it was made illegal to bring slaves into the state for sale or servitude. Slaveholders who lived in New Jersey and had slaves elsewhere were exempt from this provision, however. The Gradual Abolition Act of 1804 protected the property rights of the owner.[45] No slave who was living before 1804 was freed, but slave children born during or after 1804 were the beneficiaries. These children had to work for the master until males were 25 and females were 21. The master could abandon these children to save the cost of raising them while they were unproductive. Then the state stepped in and assumed responsibility. The state boarded these children out, often with their ex-master, who received a monthly stipend for their support (about $3 per month). Tax money was used to compensate the owners for the loss of the child's services. In 1820 manumission was made easier, and children of slaves were freed, but they served an indenture period. Finally, in all legal material, the euphemism *apprentice for life* was substituted for *slave* in 1846. Children of these "apprentices" born after 1846 were free.[46]

Pennsylvania and Delaware

In 1681 the area west of the Delaware River was given to William Penn by Charles II in lieu of repayment of a debt of £16,000. Charles "threw in" what is now Delaware, so Penn could have a seaport.[47] This action offended Marylanders, and the boundary between Pennsylvania and Maryland remained unclear until 1767, when Charles Mason and Jeremiah Dixon "drew their line." Penn, a converted Quaker, brought 100 coreligionists with him in 1682, purchased land from the Indians, and laid the foundations of Philadelphia. Blacks preceded the proprietor by almost 50 years.

The Dutch had slaves working along the Delaware River in 1639. Penn preferred slaves to white servants, because "they worked for life." Within three years of the founding of this new colony, a shipping firm from Bristol, England, delivered 150 slaves to the "City of Brotherly Love," where they were snatched up by the Quakers.[48] By the turn of the century, 1 in 15 Pennsylvania families owned one or several slaves. But the need and desire for free black labor did not go unchallenged. As early as 1688, Francis Daniel Pastorius penned a memorial against this practice for the Germantown Quakers. This epistle was sent to the Yearly Meeting in Philadelphia (the governing body of the Quakers in the Delaware River Valley), but it was tabled, probably because the leading Quakers of Philadelphia were slaveholders. It was not until 1696 that the Yearly Meeting reacted adversely to the concept of slavery. They announced their opposition to the importation of slaves and tried to improve the spiritual condition of the heathen in their midst. This reversal probably followed the diatribe against slavery by George Keither in 1693.[49] While Quaker leaders and philosophers railed against slavery, many Friends held on to their slaves until the period of the Revolution. Craftsmen invested time and money training their slaves, and manumission meant a substantial loss of property. Quaker-owned slaves worked in the retail trades and on farms. In 1761 the Quaker population of Philadelphia was 12.8 percent, but they owned 16.9 percent of the slaves in that city.[50]

Wherever a group of "different" people were kept subjugated, laws had to be passed to keep them under control. Pennsylvania, under Quaker control, was no exception. Less than 15 years after the first boatload of blacks was brought to Philadelphia, the beginning of a slave code passed the legislature. In 1700 laws were on the books which distinguished blacks from other servants.[51] Blacks could be tried in courts presided over by two justices of the peace and six freeholders. The death sentence was meted out for murder, robbery, or rape. Attempted rape of a white woman led to castration. Stealing was punished by whipping. Blacks were not permitted to carry firearms without a license. A statute in 1721 prohibited the sale of alcohol to bondsmen without the permission of their masters. They could not fire guns without permission. In 1726 racial intermarriage was forbidden. Blacks were not permitted to go more than ten miles from their homes without a written pass from their master. Slaves had to be off the streets by 9:00 at night. No more than four blacks could congregate at one place. A decree also forbade masters from hiring out their slaves; perhaps this prevented slaves from acquiring money for illegal purposes or congregating in large groups in the city. Manumission was made more difficult. A £30 security bond had to be posted for each slave freed. Decrees against free blacks were passed by the assembly. Vagrant free persons (blacks) could be bound out as indentured servants.[52] Free blacks could not keep slaves. Freedmen could not trade with slaves without their master's permission. A black could be sold back into slavery if he married a white woman. If they believed that black children were not being raised properly, justices of the peace could bind out the children of free blacks without their parents' permission until males reached 24 and females reached 21. In 1732, 1738, and 1741, Philadelphia prohibited black "tumults" on Sundays and in the courthouse square at night. Tumults were defined as parties, funerals, and church services.

As in the other provinces, Pennsylvania placed duties on imported slaves. The reasons included distaste for the institution by Pennsylvania's ladies, the fear of insurrection by large numbers of bondsmen, the preference for white immigrants (German and Scotch-Irish), and the need for money to run the province. As early as 1700, a duty of 20 shillings was placed on each imported black; this was raised to 40 shillings in 1705. The assembly tried to prohibit all importation in 1712, but this was disallowed by the Crown, influenced by the Royal Africa Company. A £5 duty was similarly disallowed. (This followed the black insurrection in neighboring New York in 1712.) A duty was reimposed in 1722, but it was lowered to £2 in 1729. The duty was raised to £10 in 1761, and it was to remain in place until 1768.[53] According to Lieutenant Governor John Penn, the money raised was used to pay owners of slaves who were executed for capital crimes.[54] (By an earlier law, they received two-thirds the value of the slave from the state.) The rest of the money was used for "running the state." After three years, the duty raised £650 per year. In 1773 a duty of £20 was passed; this totally destroyed the slave trade to Pennsylvania. During the Revolution, all importation of slaves was prohibited.

During the eighteenth century, the importation of blacks was inversely proportional to the immigration of white servants. The number of slaves reached its peak by 1720. At that time slave prices were low and white labor was scarce. However, instability and poverty in Europe resulted in a great migration of white Europeans to the middle states, and the demand for slaves decreased temporarily. Despite Quaker opposition to war, Pennsylvania was involved in the wars with France on the North American continent. Many white servants were taken into the army, and the scarcity of white labor resulted in an increase of slave importation, which persisted until the end of the Seven Years' (French and Indian) War. Between 1759 and 1765, 1,243 slaves entered the Delaware River Valley; most came directly from Africa. Peace was followed by a massive white migration into the province, with a concomitant drop in slave importation.[55]

The decrease in slave importation after the war was one of several causes of the decrease in the slave population of Pennsylvania. Added to this was decreased family contact. (Slaves were frequently owned singly, which made cohabitation difficult.) There were more males than females. Slave women were passing their reproductive period without replacement by young women. Infant mortality among slaves remained high. Finally, manumission rates increased, as the push to free slaves by Quakers was joined by Presbyterians and then by Anglicans. In 1767 there were 1,392 slaves in Pennsylvania; this dropped to 673 in 1775.[56] The free black population varied inversely with the slave population. Many escaped slaves from the Southern colonies found freedom and protection in Pennsylvania. In 1790 there were 10,274 blacks in Pennsylvania; of these, 3,737 were slaves.[57] According to William Dunship (1806), "Philadelphia has more free people of color than any place in the union. Most of them are vicious and degraded, but many are useful and respectable. They are hired as servants by the month. Cooks and waiters for parties, mechanics (a sailmaker has many apprentices and journeymen), a clergyman."[58] The writer described a rural cemetery, beautifully situated, which was for blacks. "There are black teachers of orthography and black manufacturers of tombstones."

In the eighteenth century, the Quakers were in the forefront of the abolition movement wherever they settled. Philadelphia, as the hub of Friends activity, was one of the earliest sites of activity for emancipation. George Fox, the founder of the Quaker religion, opposed the institution. The memorial of the Germantown Quakers, previously described, was followed by that of the Chester City Friends, who urged the governing body in Philadelphia to prohibit members from purchasing imported slaves. The Yearly Meeting, controlled by merchants and slaveholders, only cautioned members against buying slaves brought into the province.[59] Despite these efforts, the manumission movement was only minimally effective before the middle of the century. In 1754 the Philadelphia Yearly Meeting issued an Epistle of Caution that slavery was wrong. The Quakers prohibited importing or buying slaves in 1758. They encouraged Friends in the Delaware River Valley to give up their slaves. At this time, they were joined by Presbyterians influenced by the Great Awakening. The Philadelphia Yearly Meeting urged their communicants to teach their slaves to read and write, to educate them in Christianity; and to train them in an occupation to prepare them for eventual freedom. Anthony Bezenet, William Sturgeon, a man named Bolton, and others were actively involved in teaching blacks. Bezenet convinced the Philadelphia Monthly Meeting to open a school for African children. The first class had 22 pupils (1770), and the curriculum was opened to adults, who came when they were able. Between 1770 and 1775, 250 blacks received instruction. Dr. Brays Associates (Anglican) opened a school for blacks in Christ Church.[60]

The Gradual Abolition Act was the capstone of the arch leading to freedom. The Pennsylvania Archives of November 8, 1778, described a letter from the council (the appointed upper house of the legislature) to the assembly (the elected lower house):

> The past assembly received a bill to free negro children born of slaves. This would be an easy and gradual abolition of slavery. Those in slavery should not be freed because they are not competent for freedom. All import of slaves to be stopped. This is the best time to start freeing of slaves. The numbers of slaves are few in Pennsylvania and have been decreasing by the plunder of our late invaders. [If slaves reached English lines, they were evacuated when English troops withdrew.] In divesting the state of slaves we will save the cause of humanity and offer God our gratitude for his deliverance of us from thraldom. We will show Europe our character for justice and benevolence. Europeans have been astonished to see "a people eager for liberty holding Negroes in bondage."[61]

The Gradual Abolition Act of 1780 decreed that no child born after passage of the statute was a slave. Black and mulatto children would be servants until the age of 21. Other regulations included the following: all slaves were registered; owners of slaves were liable for their support; blacks would be tried in courts like others; the jury would put a value on a slave in a sentence of death in order to compensate the master; the reward to slaves who captured runaways would be the same as for white servants; only those slaves registered by their owners would be considered slaves except runaways from other states; slaves taken from the state could be brought back and registered; and no black or mulatto other than infants could be bound for indenture for more than seven years. Masters could not separate husbands, wives, and children. Penalties were described for taking blacks or mulattoes out of the state. To safeguard blacks from slave catchers from other states, emancipated blacks were given "freedom papers."[62] (Indentured servants carried papers describing the duration of their indenture.) To protect blacks from having their papers stolen or destroyed, registries for these papers were set up, such as the Pennsylvania Society for Promoting the Abolition of Slavery and for the Relief of Free Negroes. The registry also kept marriage and birth certificates, certificates of freedom and identity, statements of character, certificates allowing blacks to seek employment, and papers, passports, and certificates to prevent impressment. Certificates of freedom showed how many were freed by birth, will, manumission, and purchase by themselves, by family and by benevolent groups of people, and those freed when their masters left with the British. Also registered were work agreements through indenture. The society used its records to act as counsel to blacks who were kidnapped. (Kidnapped free blacks were sold into slavery in Southern states.) The society asked the governor of Pennsylvania to intervene in flagrant cases of kidnapping and sale. A later amendment to the statute declared that any Pennsylvania ship involved in the slave trade was forfeited to the state.[63]

Masters from other areas who wished to free their slaves without legal complications in their native states took advantage of the law and brought their slaves to Pennsylvania. For example: "The bearer, Nanny, with her daughter Hagar, were brought by me to Philadelphia from Dover in June 1785, where they remained with me until this day, having by the laws of Pennsylvania become free in six months after they came to the state. When I brought them up it was my intention they should become free by their stay in Pennsylvania. Nanny received wages from me for the time she has been with me here. s/May 14, 1788—Edward Telshman."[64]

Pennsylvania preceded the federal government in outlawing the slave trade. Both the Gradual Abolition Act and a decree in 1788 prohibited Pennsylvanians from engaging in the nefarious trade. Unhappily, laws were made to be broken, particularly if they offended some of the people. In 1800 the schooner *Prudence* brought 17 Africans to Pennsylvania, while the *Phoebe* brought 100 Africans in that year.[65] It must be remembered that most Africans brought directly from Africa had ritual scars on their faces and bodies, and could not be passed off as native-born slaves. Most likely Pennsylvania acted as a way station for new slaves to be sold in the South.

The earliest European settlers of present-day Delaware were the Swedes and the Danes. These northern Europeans opposed slavery, and the institution was unable to gain a foothold until they were dispossessed by the Dutch. The latter group introduced slavery in 1636. The Dutch were barely able to settle in before they were evicted by the English. Delaware remained a part of Pennsylvania until the proprietor gave the southeastern counties the privilege of a separate administration in 1703 (Charter of Privileges).[66] A legislature was formed, but Penn was still governor. Slaves existed in Delaware, but the first legal mention of slavery was in the slave code in 1721. Slaves could be tried for heinous crimes by two justices of the peace and six freeholders. If a slave was executed, the assembly paid his master two-thirds of his value. Slaves could not congregate or bear arms. Adultery and fornication were severely punished. The child of a white mother and a slave father was bound out until it reached 31 years of age. In 1739 a law pertaining to indentured servants had an amendment to void manumission if a security bond was not posted. Children of free blacks could be bound out if they were not raised properly. In 1767 a security bond of £60 was required to emancipate a slave to ensure the county against dependency and illegal activities. (Delaware's early slave code resembled the code of Pennsylvania.)[67] Unlike the other Northern colonies, Delaware did not produce any voices against involuntary servitude, and its attitudes toward its bondsmen resembled those of its neighbors to the south. Like other states temporarily smitten by the spirit of liberty in the Declaration of Independence, Delaware wrote a constitution that prohibited the export and import of slaves, but in 1787 a state law repealed this sanction. Unhappily, the exuberance was temporary, and Delaware accepted the bondage of its blacks.

Chapter 7

AFRICANS IN
THE SOUTH

Virginia

Virginia, the first permanent English colony on the shores of continental North America (1607), was the template for the development of black-white relations in the rest of the South. Most English colonies in seventeenth-century America were founded by religious dissenters who came to practice their religion as they thought proper (although to the exclusion of all others). By contrast, Virginians were Anglicans who came to make money for themselves and their sponsors. This meant physical work, which was foreign to the leaders of the group. Later in the century, it became apparent that the best way to make money for the few was a plantation economy built on the backs of stolen Africans.

Twelve years after the colony's founding, in 1619, 20 blacks, including 3 women, disembarked in Jamestown. In 1618 Governor Samuel Argall of Virginia sent the *Treasurer* to the West Indies, supposedly to obtain and deliver a load of salt and goats. At sea, the *Treasurer* met a Dutch man-of-war, and the two attacked a Spanish frigate carrying over 100 blacks. The attackers took the "cargo" and sailed for Virginia, though they were separated by a storm. Several weeks later, the Dutch ship sailed into Hampton Roads, where the black cargo was traded for goods and supplies.[1]

These new immigrants were treated as indentured servants, not as slaves. Most of these early blacks had been baptized on the African coast or in the Spanish colonies, and in 1619 it was still illegal for an Englishman to enslave Christians. The sale of indentured servants by captains of ships was a common practice in early colonial history. The Africans were traded for public provisions, and therefore they became "servants of the state" (similar to their position in early New Netherland). They were assigned to officers of the colony and to planters associated with the administration of the colony. Also in 1619 100 young men and boys arrived from London to start their indenture contract.[2] Both groups were treated in a similar fashion, and both would become freeholders in the colony if they survived the "seasoning" period and the depredations of the Native Americans. The blacks survived this early period better than their white co-workers. In the decade of the 1620s, black arrival was slow. The *Treasurer* brought one woman; the *James* brought Antonio in 1621; the *Margaret and John* brought Mary; in 1623 the *Swan* brought John Pedro. In 1623 Anthony and Isabel married and produced William, baptized in the Church of England. A head count in 1623 showed 1,275 whites and 22 blacks. Two years later there were 23 blacks and 1,095 whites and Indians. In 1629 a cargo of blacks captured from a Portuguese ship was exchanged for 85 hogsheads (a cask, often referring to a certain amount of liquor or occasionally other stored material) plus five butts of tobacco (also a term for casks equal to two hogsheads).

The black and white indentured servants had more in common with each other than the whites had with the owners of their indenture contracts. The servants worked, lived, and ate with each other; they also socialized and bred. Their masters saw a danger in this intimate relationship and tried to drive a wedge between the two races. At first, this was done through different work assignments. African women worked with the men in the fields, while white women worked around the house. Then, whites were listed with a given and a family name, blacks with only a given name. For example: "A muster of Mr. Edward Bennett's servants included Wassell Wibling and Antonio, a negro, in the *James* 1621. ...Mary, a negro woman in the *Margaret and John* 1622."[3] A court record for Essex County: "September ye 10th, Ano Dom 1694. Certificate according to Act of Assembly is granted to Captain Richard Haile for two hundred & fifty Acres of Land for the Importation of five persons into this Colony by names Patrick Bradley, Elinor Corkeley, Andrew, Guy, Anne, Negroes."[4] In the first true Virginia census in 1629, blacks were listed separately from Englishmen.[5] In 1630 Hugh Davis was whipped in public for defiling himself (sleeping) with a black woman.[6] Laws against miscegenation were passed in 1662, 1691, 1696, 1705, 1753, and 1765. By the end of the seventeenth century, intermarriage was illegal. In 1640 all inhabitants, "negroes excepted," were expected to bear arms for the security of the colony. The Anglican church, allied to the rich planters, helped to create this schism. Anglican priests preached that the blacks were not Christian and that they were different. When blacks began to undergo baptism in the church, a new reason for separation was needed so the church preached that there was a defect in the black's character solely related to being black.[7] Eventually, the black was deprived of civil rights, his position in the community was lowered, and he fell outside the protection of the law. Finally, the site of origin of slaves had its effect. Early in the century, blacks came from the West Indies where they may have worked for two or three years. They were accustomed to the white man's ways, wore the same clothes, and had picked up enough English to communicate with whites. Later in the century, slaves were imported directly from Africa. They spoke no English and could not communicate with white workers. It should be noted that since they came from different tribes they could not communicate with each other either.[8]

These attempts at separation were not uniformly successful. In 1676 Nathaniel Bacon led an insurrection of freedmen, servants, and slaves against the authorities. White free men joined because they had no hope for a future while the authorities, supported by the wealthy planters, were in control. They felt closer to the servants and blacks than they did to the rich. After Bacon's sudden death in 1676, the authorities offered amnesty to those who would put down their arms, and the rebellion collapsed. After the insurrection, fewer indentured whites were imported. They were replaced by blacks who were severely restricted in their activities.[9]

Early in the century, blacks who completed their indenture were free to obtain land; several took advantage of the head-rights law to obtain large grants of land. Anyone who imported servants, white or black, received 50 acres of land per individual. In one case, Richard Johnson, a black, purchased an indenture contract and kept a white man in servitude.[10] However, by 1670 a black was forbidden to keep a white servant. Black landowners treated their black servants as their white neighbors did. For instance, Anthony Johnson, a Negro, was accused of holding a black as an indentured servant "longer than he should or ought." Johnson told the court that he had a claim on the servant for life, and he won his case (1640).[11] From this decision one may assume that the concept of lifetime servitude already existed before the court's decision.

The acceptance by society of service for life by society predated its acceptance by law. Most authorities cite the case of John Punch as a landmark decision by the courts. In 1640 Hugh Gwyn brought back to Virginia three servants who had escaped to Maryland. Two were white, and John Punch was black. The court ordered that all three were to receive 30 lashes. The whites were to serve out their terms of indenture plus a penalty of one year to the owner and three years to the colony. The black could not be punished by increasing his term of servitude, because it was for life.[12] The next step in the descent of the black into slavery was to make his progeny servants for life. In 1646, Francis Potts sold a Negro woman and boy to Stephen Charlton "to the use of him forever." In 1652 William Wittington sold to John Pott "a negro girl and her issue for their lifetime."[13] What was accepted practice was written into law in 1661. According to this legislation, blacks could not be punished by adding time to their period of servitude, because they served for life. The decree further stated that if an English servant ran off with a black, he would serve his penalty time plus that of the black, because time could not be added to the black's lifetime of servitude.[14] The following year a statute was added to the laws of Virginia stating that the child took the status of the mother (*partus sequitor ventrum*).[15] This decree was diametrically opposed to common law, which conferred the father's status on the child. If the usual condition applied, slavery would slowly have reached a point of extinction: while many white masters produced offspring with their slaves, many fewer white women engaged in miscegenation. The old common law against Englishmen enslaving Christians was next to be struck down. By a law in 1667, baptism did not change the status of the convert. Three years later, it was decided that all non–Christian servants who came to Virginia by ship were slaves for life. Those blacks who came by land (that is, from another colony) had to serve 12 years, and children had to serve until the age of 30. Finally, this loophole was closed in 1682 when all servants, except Turks and Moors, brought to this country whose native religion was not Christian were slaves.

Within a period of 50 years of their arrival in Virginia, the position of blacks was written in stone. They were slaves upon whose labor the plantation economy existed. The need for white indentured servants decreased while the importation of blacks increased. In urban areas, there was still a need for white artisans. Virginia offered white artisans a five-year exemption from taxes except on land. This attempt was unsuccessful, however, because the mechanics, once in Virginia, could purchase land, buy or rent a few blacks, and become "wealthy" planters.[16] Of necessity, the planters overcame their belief in black inferiority and inability to learn. They "apprenticed" their slaves to craftsmen, and the blacks were able to produce a product equal to that of their teachers. The white was usually skilled in one craft, but the black became reasonably skilled in many fields. (It is said that Monticello and Mount Vernon were built largely by slave labor.) This development further limited the immigration of white mechanics. The increase in the value of these skilled slaves was offset by an increase in rebelliousness following exposure to free men, and because of their capacity to make tools and weapons of insurrection where they worked.

By the turn of the eighteenth century, there were about 6,000 blacks in Virginia, most of them slaves.[17] With this large group held in subjugation, laws had to be passed to control them and keep them servile. The first problem was how to treat this individual, who was both a person and a nonperson. As a person, he was liable for crimes and punished accordingly. He was also titheable for revenue in the colony like the white. As a nonperson, he was dealt with in law as property. Like a horse or cow, he could be inherited, bought, sold, and taken in payment for debt. The theft of a slave was tried as a felony. Prior to 1705, he was chattel, like livestock. A law in 1705 made him real estate, and he could not be moved. However, a later court ruling made him real estate and chattel that could be used for paying a debt. In 1748 he became the personal estate of his owner and was not considered as real estate.[18]

For white people, the commission of a capital crime went to a general court or to a special court of "oyer and terminer" (a high criminal court).

County courts handled civil cases and lesser crimes. The decision of a lower court could be appealed to the general court of the general assembly. In slave cases, a county court had jurisdiction with no appeal from its decision. In a capital offense, the governor issued a commission of oyer and terminer, usually made up of judges of the county courts. There was no jury. If the defendant was proved guilty, he was executed in ten days. In cases of conspiracy or insurrection, punishment was carried out sooner. By a law of 1705, a slave could not be a witness or call other slaves as witnesses. A statute in 1732 prohibited a slave from giving testimony except in the case of another slave in a capital offense. If it was believed that he had given perjured testimony, he received 39 lashes and his ears were nailed to the pillory. Patrick Henry, who wanted liberty or death, was governor of Virginia in 1778 when he signed a law amending a previous statute in 1764. The new legislation stated that the

> governor was empowered to direct Justices of each county to be empowered to try, condemn & execute or otherwise punish or acquit all slaves committing capital crimes in their county. These men are to check into all Treasons, petit Treasons [attempt at murder of someone to whom subservience is required; that is, a wife of her husband, a servant of his master] or Mispresions [a misdemeanor resembling treason but which did not carry the death penalty] thereof, Felonies, Murders, or other Offenses, or Capital Crimes whatsoever, committed or perpetrated within the said county, by any Slave or Slaves whatsoever. The justice of or any four justices meet at the court house to try slaves brought up by the sheriff of the county. You will pass judgment & execute or acquit.[19]

On rare occasions, usually posthumously, the courts found in favor of the slave. A notice from Williamsburg, November 23, 1739, read: "This day seven of the nine malefactors who received sentences at the last General Court were carried from the public prison to the usual place of execution & were hanged, viz, Charles Quin, an overseer, & David White, an accessory, from Essex County; for the murder of a negro belonging to Col. Braxton by whipping him to death in a most cruel & barbarous manner."[20] From the *Virginia Gazette*, April 21, 1775: "William Pitman, being found guilty by the jury, received sentence of death from the General Court for beating his negro boy to death. This man has justly incurred the penalties of the law, & he will certainly suffer, which ought to be a warning to others [to] treat their slaves with moderation, etc."[21]

In addition to the laws passed to control the black's position before the courts, statutes were passed to control his daily life. As early as 1639, slaves could not bear firearms. If a slave was caught with a firearm, the constable administered 20 lashes. An exception to this law existed on the frontier; with his master's permission, a slave could bear firearms to ward off marauding Indians. No free black could hold an office of the church, military, or civil authority (1705). For raising his hand against a white Christian, he received

30 lashes.[22] A slave could not absent himself from his plantation for more than four hours. If found on another plantation, that owner was fined 200 pounds of tobacco. A slave could not leave his plantation unless he had a certificate describing the circumstances of his absence. If the slave was absent without a certificate, he was taken by force; if he resisted, he could be killed, and his killer would not be prosecuted for this offense.[23] This threat of death was posted at county courts and parish churches every six months. The minister had to read this law to his congregation every September and March; his failure to do so resulted in a fine of 600 pounds of tobacco. If the slave ran away a second time, an *R* was branded on his cheek. Whites who traded with slaves were jailed for one month, and any possessions the slave had obtained was confiscated and sold. If a slave traded with whites with his master's permission, the master was fined £10. More than five slaves meeting together "to make insurrection" were guilty of a felony and were executed without benefit of clergy. A slave who killed another slave was executed with a minister present. A conviction of burglary brought the death penalty without clergy. Manumission was made very difficult. A slave could be freed for "merit" but only if the governor and council agreed on the meritorious act. If freed by his master only, the slave could be seized by the church warden and resold. The money was used for the needs of the parish. If a slave was freed by the civil authorities, the colony paid his master his assessed value. A freed slave had to leave the colony within six months; if discovered after this period, he was fined £10, which was used to transport him out of the colony. This was an improvement, however, over a law of 1705 that re-enslaved the freedman if he failed to leave.[24] No free blacks were permitted to immigrate into Virginia (1793).[25]

Underlying most slave laws was the fear of insurrection. In areas with small numbers of blacks well dispersed throughout the white population, individual killings of white masters through frustration and rage were occasionally reported. However, with increasing numbers of blacks, often in larger numbers than the white population, combined action was a constant source of fear and a threat to "a way of life." The greater the proportion of bondsmen to whites, the more severe the punishments meted out for insurrection, real or suspected. Hysteria about possible involvement in rebellion led to execution of the "culprits" without benefit of clergy. Burning at the stake, slow death by strangulation, and allowing part or all of the corpse to rot above ground were accepted procedures in many areas. In seventeenth-century Virginia, before the plantation economy required large numbers of bondsmen, the threat of insurrection could be handled more "humanely." The archives of the county court of Westmoreland County described a punishment inflicted in 1688:

> Sam, a negro servant of Richard Metcalfe, has several times tried to start Negro insurrection in this colony. To deter him & others from the like practice, the sheriff of James City County or deputy [will administer a severe whipping to the slave pulled] behind a cart from prison around the town then

to the gallows & then to prison. Then sent to Westmoreland County where the sheriff will severely whip him at the next court. During that time he was to have a halter around [his] neck. The strong iron collar fixed to his neck with four spriggs [a wedge-shaped nail]. He wears this forever. He is never to leave [his] master's plantation. If he takes off [the] collar or leaves [the] plantation, he is hanged. [The sheriff was ordered to give him 29 lashes to the bare back.][26]

In the colonies north of Virginia, duties on imported slaves served two purposes: first, to raise money, and second, to prevent a large influx of blacks into the colony. The purpose of the duty laws in Virginia seemed to be only to raise money. Between 1699 and 1703, a duty of 15 shillings was placed on each imported servant. The revenue raised was used to rebuild government buildings in James City. The rate was 20 shillings on Negroes and "other slaves." In 1732 a similar duty was applied. Two years later, imported slaves were taxed to reduce the poll tax on the inhabitants; this, too, was re-enacted four years later. In 1740 5 percent was added to the 20 shillings to raise and transport troops. The tax was extended in 1742 to discharge the public debt. In 1745 a duty was placed "to support the public expense." In 1755, 1757, and 1759, the law was extended.[27] These duties became so onerous that plantation owners traveled to Maryland and North Carolina to get workers more cheaply. George Washington, who claimed to abhor the institution of slavery, was not above breaking Virginia law (as did many others) to get slaves for his plantations. Between the mid-1750s and 1770, he brought in slaves from Maryland. He gave the slave merchant John Carlyle £150 to pay for slaves; he later paid Carlyle £79 in gold for more blacks. Virginia tried to recoup its losses in revenue in 1759 and placed a 20 percent duty on imported slaves. This also forced the owner, if caught, to pay the Maryland or North Carolina duties as well as the Virginia tax. Washington was not above evading this additional expense. In 1761 Washington placed an ad in the *Maryland Gazette* for runaways purchased in 1759.[28] However, shipping records showed no slave ship docked on the southern shore of the Potomac that year. This implied that these slaves came into Virginia from out of the colony. Slaves purchased from other slaveowners were duty free. In 1759 Washington bought nine slaves from Colonel Henry Churchill for £406, and in 1761 he bought others from Thomson Mason. In an attempt to avoid evasion of the law, Virginia dropped its duty to 10 percent. In 1772 the 20 percent duty was reimposed and remained in effect until the outbreak of the Revolution.

There were a few small voices that opposed slavery and the slave trade in Virginia. Probably the first to raise his voice against the African slave trade, the Reverend Morgan Godwyn wrote a pamphlet entitled *The Negro's and Indian's Advocate*, published in London in 1680.[29] In 1772, Virginia passed 33 acts against the importation of slaves, but all were vetoed by the Crown.[30] At the Constitutional Convention (1787), George Mason, delegate from Virginia, opposed the extension of the slave trade for an additional 20 years.[31] He claimed that the 20-year extension would ensure the continuation of this terrible institution. He was voted down, however, by the Northern states, which were getting rich on the slave trade, and by the Southern states, which needed more slaves as they pushed farther south and west. Delegates from South Carolina and Georgia admonished other delegates, "No slave trade, no union." South Carolina's delegate, Butler, moved to insert in the Constitution this language: "If any person bound to serve or labor in any of the United States, shall escape into another state, he or she shall not be discharged from such service or labor in consequence of any regulations existing in the state to which they escape, but shall be delivered up to the person justly claiming their service of labor."[32] This fugitive slave article was a compromise for the eventual termination of the slave trade. Virginia, whose land was destroyed by tobacco agriculture, became a slave exporter to the Deep South, and it accepted this article despite the distaste of its delegates.

Maryland

Maryland was a royal grant made by Charles I to Lord Baltimore in 1632 to be a "haven for English Catholics." It was settled 25 years after Virginia and seemed to follow by a few years the larger colony in development, economy, and slave codes. Its early economy was based on the export of tobacco to England. This cash crop was grown by indentured servants and slaves in a large plantation system that developed toward the middle of the eighteenth century. Prior to this period, Maryland was occupied by small plantations and farms with very few, if any, slaves per family. Early in its history (1658), Maryland's slave population represented 3 percent of the total population; after the turn of the century, the slave population jumped to 24 percent. This growth was largely due to importation, predominantly from the West Indies before 1695, rather than from breeding. Imports reached 3,000 blacks per year.[33] Prior to the development of large plantations with many slaves, slaveowners could afford only few blacks, chiefly males. Female slaves represented about 40 percent of the black population. This limited any form of conjugal life among the new immigrants. The typical slave desired was "one man negroe aged between fifteen & five & twenty years. Cleere limbed free from all diseases. Soares pains aches or infirmityes in Sound & perfect health in body & mind."[34] The value of such a slave might be 8,000 pounds of tobacco, perhaps £53 sterling.[35] (Tobacco was the "coin of the realm" in Maryland.)

As in Virginia, slavery was accepted in Maryland for many years before it was enacted into law. One law in 1638 referred to all people, "slaves excepted," the first mention of slaves in Maryland statutes.[36] However, the terms *slaves* and *servants* were used interchangeably, and no hasty conclusions should be drawn about the existence of legal black slavery at this time. In 1644 a black African slave was sold in Maryland and listed as such. Examination of probated estates of the period listed the value of black and white indentured servants. Blacks were considerably more valuable, because they served for life rather than for a set period of years. Wills, related to indentures, listed the time yet to be served, but no time was listed for blacks.[37] The status of the blacks was settled by law in 1664. By a decree of the general assembly, "All negroes or other slaves in Maryland serve for life. Children born of slaves will be slaves like their fathers for life."[38] A white woman who married a black slave served his master for the duration of the slave's life. Children of this "shameful union" were to be slaves for life. Prior to 1664, however, the offspring of such unions served the master for 30 years. The laws prohibited white indentured women from forced marriages to black slaves by their owners. The woman was freed from her indenture contract if she could prove duress; also, her children were free. The master was fined 10,000 pounds of tobacco.[39] A minister who sanctified this marriage was fined a similar amount of tobacco. In rare cases, after the passage of this legislation, the courts protected the slaves: "Negro Thomas Hazleton petitioned for freedom from Major Thomas Truman. Negro belonged to Margery Duchesse who consigned him to Thomas Kemp to serve four years. It is now 12 months past four years." Thomas Hazleton brought suit for freedom, and the court declared him to be a free man (1676).[40] In 1681, the law was modified to change the status of the children: Negro children of white mothers and children of free Negro mothers were free. (The child now took the mother's status.)[41] This same year, the general assembly reasserted the statute of 1664, which stated unequivocally that all Negroes and other slaves imported and to be imported should serve *durante vita*, and their children should be slaves for the rest of their natural lives.[42] Some years earlier, a law denied baptism to Christianity as an open door to freedom. Slavery was thus set in stone and persisted for almost two centuries.

With this source of labor now firmly established, the wealthy whites could purchase more land and bodies to work it. A strong black couple was worth about £60. This was well beyond the means of most farmers. Probate of estates at the turn of the century showed most were evaluated at less than £49. In estates greater than £150, several slaves were part of the inheritance. On rare occasions, some estates were very great. For example, Richard Carter of Talbot County left an estate worth more than £4,126, including 56 negroes and 5 indentured servants.[43] The growth in the number of slaves led to the passage of a restraining "black code." G.W. Williams claimed that the Maryland state code was worse than any found in the other colonies.[44] He believed it was more cruel and inhumane. Review of the Maryland Archives did not corroborate this claim, however. Laws passed by the colonial assembly and judgments of the courts followed no particular pattern of cruel or inhumane treatment during the change from small ownership to the large plantations of the eighteenth century. Laws and rulings were no worse than those in other large slaveholding colonies. A provincial court tried the case of Symon Overzee, who chained his slave, Tony, for a misdemeanor (1658). Overzee then ordered Tony to work, but he refused. The master beat Tony with a twig of a pear tree, first with his shirt on, then on his bare back. The slave still refused to work, and the master poured melted lard on him. Tony still refused to work. Tony was then hanged from a ladder by his wrists, and he died after three hours. Symon was not found guilty of murder.[45] A case in 1665 concerned Jacob, a slave who assaulted his mistress, Mary Vyte, with a knife. She died four days after the assault. A jury of 12 men found Jacob guilty of petit treason (killing someone to whom a servant or slave owes fealty; grand treason is reserved for killing the king). Jacob was hanged.[46] It should be noted, though, that this was a jury trial, a right rarely enjoyed by slaves in other colonies. In 1784, Edward Morgan, white, was accused of assaulting a Negro woman. He failed to appear in court to answer the charges and was sent to jail.[47] In 1760 the Calvert County Court investigated the case of four blacks who claimed they were free men who were stolen from Africa by the captain of a trading vessel.[48] The governor of the province ordered the judge to review the case and take depositions from the officers of the ship to determine the guilt or innocence of the captain. If guilty, the captain was to be delivered to the court for trial. Statements indicated that one of the blacks named Captain Gray probably worked for someone on the coast of Guinea. He paddled a canoe that carried slaves from their pens to the ships. While on board the trading vessel, the brigantine *Edward*, helmed by Captain Cousin, he stole a scarlet jacket. Captain Cousins prevented Gray from going back to shore unless he received a slave in return. The shore personnel denied the request because "Gray was a scoundrel," and this was how they treated thieves. Captain Cousins was exonerated. From these cases cited, one can see that the slaves were "given their day in court." One might not agree with the decisions reached, but the courts did give them a hearing.

The laws pertaining to blacks resembled those of the other major slaveholding colonies. In laws of 1664 and 1681, slaves could not marry European women. Later laws prohibited freed blacks from marrying Europeans; freed blacks who disobeyed this law were sold back into slavery.[49] The statute of 1695 required slaves to have signed passes if they were off their plantation. The law recognized the "evil consequences of Negroes meeting on Sabbath & holy days." They would have the opportunity to embezzle and trade away their master's goods. They could also conspire to gain their freedom, which led to insurrection. Therefore, "no negro can travel from place to place or from plantation to plantation for visiting." Anyone picking up such a slave "may inflict corporal punishment as he sees fit," except not to life and limb or disabling the slave. The individual who inflicted this punishment was free from action by the slave's owner. The Negro could move around only with a pass from his owner or overseer. If the owner allowed free movement without a pass, he was fined 200 pounds of tobacco. If a Negro ran off into the woods and refused to surrender to his pursuers, those pursuers could kill the slave. This decree was posted in all churches four times a year. This decree allowing a pursuer to kill a resistant slave was strengthened by "a supplementary & explanatory act for the more effectual punishment of Negroes" in 1753.[50] With regard to any person prosecuted for killing a slave who resisted capture, "the public shall pay such person his costs & charges." Those who unlawfully "detained" a runaway were punished. In 1675, for example, Mark Cordeau detained a Negro belonging to another. A jury of 12 men ordered Cordeau to pay the owner 12,000 pounds of tobacco and court costs.[51] Anyone convicted of helping to transport a servant or slave out of the colony was fined triple damages. Those who brought runaways back to Maryland were rewarded by the owner with 400 pounds of tobacco and a casque or 40 shillings. If a slave was killed by his pursuers, his owner was recompensed for his value by the public treasury. Similarly, the owner of a slave who died in prison, who was executed for crimes, or who died while working for the county was paid his value by the colony. A decree in 1723 ordered the cropping of a slave's ears if he attacked a white person. A statute in 1729 stated that certain crimes were to be punished by hanging, quartering, and exposure of the remains to public view. Between 1752 and 1772, manumission was illegal. However, some laws protected the slave and demanded humane treatment by his owners. One master cut off a slave's ear to punish him for a misdeed, and the slave was freed by the province. Owners could be tried for murder if they killed a slave "without cause." In 1692 any slave who had been cauterized or dismembered was freed. Owners were "forced" to feed, clothe, and restrict the number of hours their slaves could work. Sundays and holidays were free days. Masters were fined the first and second time they broke this law; the third violation allowed the province to free the slave.

Commerce with slaves was illegal. In 1784, the notes of the Council of Maryland described Elizabeth Hope, who bought chickens from a Negro. This slave was later brought to court for stealing poultry, and was fined 2,000 pounds of tobacco.[52] To deny the black the knowledge of firearms, a law of 1756 punished any Negro or mulatto slave (except necessary attendants) found at the site of militia training. The slave was to be whipped up to 39 lashes, and the next offense would bring 49 lashes.[53] Sale of alcohol to a Negro was illegal. In 1758 William Jones of Ann Arundel County was fined £275 6 pence for selling rum to a slave.[54] (This was a great sum when compared with the total estate of many Marylanders.) In 1736, the assembly debated a statute to allow slaves a trial by jury rather than treatment in a "summary manner," this failed to pass into law.[55]

A freed slave had to carry a "Certificate of Freedom," which listed his age, name, physical characteristics, and the name of his previous owner. Freedmen could not sue whites or testify against them in court, and could not vote. They were also excluded from certain occupations.[56] Freed blacks could be sold back into slavery if they entered Maryland from another colony; to cover back taxes or fines; or if they could not "account for themselves."[57] Toward the end of the eighteenth century, Maryland suffered the same soil damage as did Virginia and so became a slave breeder and exporter. However, maintaining large numbers of slaves was not economically feasible. Many were hired out, sold, or manumitted. Some slaves bought their own freedom or ran away. Early in the nineteenth century, one-quarter of Maryland's blacks were free.[58] Maryland did not have a vociferous emancipation group; the state was active, however, in getting the freedmen back to Africa.

Duties on incoming blacks were passed to raise money, though there was no effort to use this power to keep out slaves. In 1695, to cover the cost of building a statehouse and other expenses, a duty of 2 shillings and 6 pence was placed on each servant. The duty on slaves was 10 shillings, with a fine of £5 for failure to pay; in 1716 this was raised to £4 per black.[59] Statutes for duties on slaves also covered alcohol and Irish papists. The duties on slaves and alcohol were revenue enhancers; the stated purpose of duties on Irish Catholics was to keep them out of a colony founded as a haven for English Catholics. A decree of 1736 placed an additional duty of 20 shillings on Irish and blacks.[60] The duty on blacks was levied to raise money to build public schools, and the money thus raised was considerable. In a letter to Lord Baltimore in May 1761, Governor Sharpe described a naval officer, Henry Darnall, who pocketed the money raised on slave importation: in nine months, Darnall stole between £300 and £400.[61] In 1763 £2 were added to the duty on slaves. Failure to report the new blacks led to a fine of £10 plus court costs.[62] This may have been an attempt to raise money to retire the debt incurred in the recent war with France. Other stated purposes of the duty included raising money to pay the lord proprietor of Maryland his quit rents,[64] to raise money to present a gift to the Indian Nations (to keep them peaceful),[64] and to raise £40,000 for the defense of the province.[65] The duty continued to rise until 1783, when the importation of blacks from overseas was prohibited.[66]

South Carolina

Carolina, the area south of Virginia and north of Florida, from the Atlantic to the Pacific, was given by Charles II in 1663 to eight strong supporters of the Restoration.[67] The northern part of the province was settled by people who drifted down from Virginia to the Albemarle Sound area in

1653. This land had been given by Charles I to Robert Heath in 1633. The area was not commercially viable, so many of its inhabitants gradually moved south to the Ashley River (Charleston). They were joined by a group from England who emigrated about 1670. A third group was composed of planters, with their slaves, from Barbados. The Barbadians carried their concepts of slavery to the Carolinas, and black slavery was recognized by the Carolina Grand Council in 1672, a short time after the settlement of the area.[68] In 1690 the first statute relating solely to slavery became part of the law of the land. This decree relegated the slaves' status to freehold property, except when slaves had to be used to pay their master's debts. Freehold was a higher form of property than chattel. Freehold property could not be moved; the holder could use it, but he did not have absolute ownership. The owner could use the slave's services rather than the slave himself. Chattels were the owner's personal belongings, which he used as he saw fit. Freehold status attached the slave to the land, like a serf. Chattel, by contrast, attached him to his master. This statute was disallowed in 1696, to be replaced by Carolina's first slave code, adopted from the Code of Barbados, passed in 1698. Negroes, mulattoes, and Indians, who were bought and sold, were slaves, and their children were slaves. In 1725 the governor proclaimed them to be chattel of their master.

In most of the other colonies, slavery grew slowly, usually as the need arose. In Carolina, the institution was almost a foregone conclusion. Four of the eight original proprietors were officials of the Royal Africa Company, the group that had the monopoly on acquiring and carrying slaves to the Western Hemisphere. Slavery represented a major source of their income. They reaped huge profits from carrying slaves from Africa, who could be used to work the land the proprietors had received. One of the proprietors, Sir John Colleton, was a Barbadian planter who used slaves to work his fields in the West Indies. In addition, Locke, the author of the Fundamental Constitution for Carolina, accepted the concept of slavery.[69] In seventeenth-century England, many philosophers and political scientists believed in Aristotle's ideas of slavery through conquest. Locke believed slavery was a continuation of the state of war: "If one has forfeited his life by an act deserving death, he may become subject to the person to whom he has forfeited it, who in turn may delay to take it, & make use of him to his own service, & he does him no injury by it." Locke believed slaves could only be taken in a just war. (See the Massachusetts section in chapter 5.) In diametrical opposition to this attitude, Locke also felt that man had "natural rights to the property of his own person": "Man has natural freedom ... since all share the same common nature, faculties & powers, all in nature free." (It was the latter concept that Jefferson adopted in the Declaration of Independence.) Locke accepted a form of white slavery as well, that of the "leet men" (estate men). The leet men were fixed to the land under the jurisdiction of the lord, without appeal.

The children of leet men were leet men for all generations (serfs).[70] This belief did not receive acceptance in Carolina. However, the tenth article of Locke's constitution was written into law: every free man had "absolute power & authority over his colored slaves, of whatever opinion or religion so ever." (Black Christians were slaves in Carolina from its beginning.) Finally, the environment made slavery a "necessity." The marshy land, along with the heat and humidity, made it impossible for white servants and Indian slaves to work the land. Blacks, though, were believed to be immune to the "ague" and could be used to produce rice, indigo, and tobacco, the cash crops of the colony.

Early in its history, Carolina tried to use Indians as agricultural slaves. These slaves were captured in repeated Indian wars on the frontier. The Tuscarora war, for example, produced 700 Native Americans for the market. Throughout Carolina's history, until the Revolution, militiamen were encouraged to capture Indian adversaries for their personal use. Early in the eighteenth century, one-fourth of the slaves in Carolina were Indians.[71] Because of the abundant pool of Indians, many were shipped out of the port of Charleston to New England and the West Indies. However, these slaves were recalcitrant, ran away at any opportunity, and were not productive. Between 1705 and 1715, Pennsylvania and the New England colonies prohibited the importation of Indians from Carolina. Those who remained in Carolina could be manumitted for "meritorious service" with permission of the county council. They then had to leave the province within six months or face re-enslavement.

In 1688, a law was passed to encourage immigration of white servants. This failed to attract white workers, however, and black men filled the void. Black slaves were first introduced in 1670 by Governor Yeaman. The number of blacks soon outdistanced that of their white owners and overseers. Early in the eighteenth century it was believed that there were three times as many blacks as whites in the province.[72] This large number of blacks was trouble to the white leaders for the remainder of the century. During the Revolution, South Carolina could not supply its required number of soldiers because they were needed at home to keep the restive blacks under control. The natural consequence of the rapid growth of the black population was a strict black code, which began in 1686. No white was permitted to trade with slaves. Blacks needed passes to leave the plantation. If slaves were found on another plantation on Sundays or holidays, even with a pass, they were whipped. The slave had no property; anything he owned could be seized and sold to benefit the poor of the parish. If more than seven slaves were found unaccompanied by a white, they could be seized and given 20 lashes. A master could hire out the services of a slave and keep his wages. Those who hired a slave without a certificate from his master were fined. A slave could not have access to a boat or canoe (Carolina shared a border with Spanish Florida). If a slave struck a white, he was whipped by the constable. A second offense led to a whipping, branding of his face, and slitting of his nose; a third offense brought the death penalty. Murder, burglary, arson, and repeated absence from the plantation were capital offenses. Stealing chickens or pigs was a misdemeanor and was punished by a brand to the right cheek. Recurrent commission of petty crimes and thievery could result in the death penalty. Slaves were not tried by juries. A slave accused of a crime was referred to the local justice of the peace, who jailed him; he was then tried by two justices and three freeholders. The testimony of other slaves was accepted for petty stealing of a value up to 40 shillings. In a trial for a capital offense the testimony of one Christian or two Negroes or slaves was required for conviction. Blacks who claimed that they were freedmen could present their case in a court of common pleas, a guardian of the black usually pleaded his case. The burden of proof was on the plaintiff. If he was judged free, he collected damages from the defendant. If the court found for the defendant, the slave received corporal punishment.[73]

Runaway slaves over 16 years of age, absent for more than 20 days, received up to 40 lashes. If the master did not carry out the sentence, the constable administered the whipping, and the owner paid him 20 shillings. A second escape resulted in an *R* being branded on his right cheek; the master was fined £10 if he failed to carry out this duty. The constable became his surrogate and was paid 30 shillings by the master. A third flight was punished by 40 lashes, and one of the slave's ears was cut off. The owner was fined £20, and he paid the constable 40 shillings for failure to carry out the sentence. A fourth escape resulted in castration. If the slave died from this operation, the owner received his assessed value from the public treasury. If the miscreant was female and she ran away a fourth time, she was whipped, branded with an *R* on her left cheek, and her left ear was cut off. If the owner did not carry out this punishment, he lost the slave, and the new owner carried out the punishment or paid a fine of £50. If the slave died as a result of this punishment, the new owner was not compensated. A fifth flight could bring the sentence of death or the Achilles tendon of one of his legs was cut. A free Negro believed to be involved in a slave's flight received 40 lashes and a brand on his forehead. If a slave was off the plantation and a white demanded to see his pass, the slave was forced to show it; failure to obey could result in beating, maiming, or death. The white was not prosecuted.[74]

The colonial legislature attempted to protect the slave from a cruel owner. By a decree in 1712, a master who killed his slave in a wanton manner paid the treasury a fine of £50. If he killed another man's slave, the fine again was £50 plus the value of the slave to his owner. If a white servant killed another person's slave, he served the slave's master five years after his indenture ended. In 1740 the law of 1712 was made more stringent. The wanton killer of one of his own slaves was fined £700, and he was barred from holding any office in the province. If he could not pay this fine, he was sentenced to a workhouse or a frontier garrison for seven years. The murder of another's slave resulted in the same punishment, but the murderer's salary from the workhouse or garrison went to the slave's owner. A white who killed a slave in "the heat of passion" was fined £350. A white owner who cut out a slave's tongue, gouged out an eye, castrated him, burned or scalded him, or cut off a limb was fined £100.[75]

The slave's workday was limited to 15 hours daily from March 25 to September 25, and to 14 hours during the shorter days of winter. The slave had to be fed properly and given clothes once a year. Failure to supply these needs properly led to a 50 shilling fine. Owners constantly feared "black powers with occult poisons," and therefore slaves were not employed in pharmacies and could not "practice medicine." They could not supply drugs to any white unless directed to do so by their owner.[76]

The limited number of whites of military age in a colony surrounded by Spaniards to the south and hostile Indians on the western frontier required arming of slaves in an emergency. A decree in 1704 urged commanders to appoint five freeholders to list the able-bodied slaves in the district. Their owners could appear before these freeholders to explain why their slaves should be exempt from military duty. Those slaves chosen for duty were armed by their owners and presented to the military leaders. The owner who refused service for his slave paid a £5 fine. If a slave was killed in action against the enemy, his owner was paid his value from the public treasury. If a slave was taken prisoner and escaped back to his own lines, he was emancipated. Freedom also followed the killing or capturing of an enemy. If the slave was wounded, he was set free and his owner was paid. If he deserted to the enemy, his owner was paid. If his master freed the slave for meritorious service, the new freedman had to leave the colony or face re-enslavement. The military training of slaves had its drawbacks. These "soldiers" knew how to use firearms and would steal and hide them whenever possible. Consequently, their huts were searched about every 14 days for contraband firearms as well as for stolen articles and runaways. Occasionally, masters permitted one black on the plantation to keep firearms; however, he had to show a permit from his master that was less than one month old.[77]

The increased severity of the slave code was usually a reaction to some event that the whites considered a threat to their existence or way of life. In 1738, the governor of Florida promised freedom to any slave who escaped to Florida. This resulted in tighter supervision of the slaves. The patrols, under the supervision of the militia, composed of poor whites who could not pay to be excused from duty, were urged to search carefully and punish any black who resisted their efforts. The Stono rebellion frightened the white legislators into passing a new code in 1740. Slaves were now considered chattel by law. (They were considered chattel by their owners for many years. Custom now became law.) Slaves were not permitted to assemble. They could not obtain alcohol, and they were denied training to read and write. They were not permitted to engage in trade.[78]

The freedmen represented an intrusion into white society. Free blacks were suspected of stealing, fencing stolen goods, teaching slaves to read and write, and fomenting rebellion. The number of free blacks could be controlled by making it almost impossible for a master to free a slave and forcing a freedman to leave the colony, usually within six months, or face re-enslavement. Freed blacks could remain in Carolina only by a special act of the assembly. Laws in 1800, as well as in 1820 and 1841, limited the right of a master to free a slave.[79] In 1760, a capitation tax of 35 shillings per head was placed on "all free negroes, mulattoes & mustizoes" between 10 and 60 years.[80] Whites were not subject to this tax, although a poll tax on white males had been in existence since 1737. The tax of 1760 was raised to 9 shillings 4 pence on all free "negroes, mulattoes & mustizoes." A poll tax on all free Negroes was added in 1789; this was set at 25 cents per head per year for ten years. The blacks petitioned the assembly to void these taxes because their ancestors were given freedom for "rendering some particular Services to their Country which the wisdom & goodness of Government thought just ... to reward their Fidelity with Emancipation." These petitions failed to move the legislature. The tax was raised to $2 per head in 1804, and raised again to $10 on free black mechanics and to a similar amount on each house occupied by blacks. This law followed the Vesey rebellion. An armed guard was developed to suppress the blacks, and the victims were taxed to support it.

Throughout the colonial period, there was a tug-of-war between the plantation owners and the government. The planters could develop large areas of the colony if they had enough laborers to perform the work. Very early in the province's history, importation of slaves was encouraged. Original settlers in the first year of settlement received 20 free acres for each black male imported and 10 acres for each female; this grant was lowered to 10 and 5 acres for the next five years.[81] The legislators feared an inundation of the province by blacks present against their will. In 1716, a statute was passed that required a planter to import one white servant for each ten slaves. He also received a bounty of £25 for each white imported. In 1719 a duty of £10 per head on blacks from Africa was imposed and £30 on blacks from the West Indies. (The differential resulted from the fear that intransigent slaves would be "dumped" on Carolina by the planters in the islands.) In 1722 a duty of £50 was placed on each black brought in from other colonies of coastal America, based on the same fear.[82] Following the excitement of the Revolution with its concepts of freedom, South Carolina in 1792 passed "an Act to prohibit the Importation of Slaves from Africa, or other places beyond the sea, into this state, for two years."[83] In 1800, no one could bring in slaves from offshore, and no one could bring in more than ten slaves from anywhere in the new nation.[84]

As was common in other plantation economies, the planters purchased more slaves than they needed, generally as a status symbol. These purchases were usually on credit, with interest sometimes as high as 25 percent per year. The planters were frequently forced to sell off the excess to avoid bankruptcy. This condition plus the prohibition on the import of foreign slaves led the local slave dealers to sell "country-born" rather than Africa-born blacks. A notice in the *City Gazette* of Charleston on March 10, 1796, advertised:

> 50 prime negroes for sale on Tuesday, March 15 near the exchange. Orderly negroes—fellows, wenches, girls, boys. They are prime, complete, & valuable. Country-born, young & able. Two can act as drivers, one a carpenter. Wenches are young & improving. Boys, Girls, children are smart, active, sensible. Some wenches fit for house or plantation. Boys & Girls for trade or waiting servants. Age & descriptions & qualifications available at office of subscribers, & at Brian Cape & Son, or Treasdale/or Kendall, merchants in Queen Street. They can give directions to where negroes can be seen. They are free of all encumbrances with warranted titles. They are sold because owner is getting out of planting. The owner selected them, at great expense over several years. They were purchased for stock & breeding. Any planter wanting them for breeding—they are choice & desirable. Anyone purchasing the whole group by private contract, apply to Brian Cape & Son. Terms, if sold together, will be convenient to purchasers & conditions of sale will be easy & will be declared on the day of sale.
>
> s/Colcock & Paterson[85]

North Carolina

The ministers of King George I recognized the dissension between the northern and southern parts of the Carolina province, and the two were separated in 1729. The southern colony was controlled financially and politically by the heirs and associates of the original proprietors, who were Anglicans and benefited from a plantation economy based on the backs of a large number of slaves. North Carolina was settled by farmers from Virginia who drifted down looking for cheap land. They were too poor to own more than an occasional slave, and large slave concentrations were too competitive for them. These farmers were probably servants who had completed their indenture contracts. The difference between these two areas increased during the eighteenth century. Quakers, who were generally opposed to the institution of slavery, also settled in North Carolina. They were joined by Scotch Presbyterians who had left Scotland after the disastrous defeats of the Jacobites. These supporters of the Stuart family opposed the Glorious Revolution that brought William and Mary (House of Orange) and the later Hanover monarchy; they were finally and totally defeated by the English at Culloden. Many of these Scotsmen emigrated and settled in western North Carolina. They were small farmers and tradesmen who had no prior experience with slavery.

Finally, North Carolina became a haven for splinter Protestant groups like the Moravians. This German group, followers of the martyred Jan Hus of Bohemia, purchased a tract of almost 100,000 acres in the Piedmont area, and developed their religious communities along the Yadkin River. This group had mixed feelings about slavery, though their bishop, Spangenberg, did not find the institution "unreasonable." They used bondsmen to do the heavy unskilled work of building their community and clearing the land. However, they were more interested in baptizing the blacks and bringing them into the congregation. Salem, their religious center, prohibited the presence of bondsmen within the community (although, they were present), and Moravian leaders discouraged their spread into the outlying areas. The requests for slaves by individuals were passed upon by the Board of Elders.[86] The board preferred that slaves be owned by the congregation rather than by individuals. The elders feared that slavery would damage the ethic of hard work that they were trying to teach to their children. They preferred keeping the number of slaves to a minimum, and pregnant black females were sold out of the community.[87] It was felt that a small slave group could lead to better integration into their church.

Large concentrations of slaves existed in the Cape Fear area along the Wilmington River. The land could support rice agriculture, and planters from South Carolina brought their slaves with them to create an aristocracy similar to what they left in the south. Overall, the slave population of North Carolina was limited and dispersed. In 1710 there were 800 blacks.[88] By 1729, the year of separation, there were 6,000 slaves diffusely scattered among 30,000 whites.[89] During the war with France, there were 15,000 bondsmen and 62,000 whites. Throughout the colonial period, the ratio of whites to blacks was approximately four to one. During this era, North Carolina had no concerted slave insurrection.[90] However, the legislature developed a strict slave code. Prior to 1729, laws passed in Charleston governed the entire area. In 1715 the concept of slavery for life was formally recognized.[91] A few years later the slave child was given his mother's status. Also in 1715 it was made difficult to hire out a slave's services.[92] If a slave committed a capital offense while hired out and he was executed, the owner did not receive compensation. Similarly, the owner of an unmanageable slave, sold from another province, was not compensated if his slave was punished for a crime in Carolina. A slave was routinely executed for rape or murder. Other capital crime convictions were treated by castration. Castration became the law specifically during the French and Indian War because the state treasury was bare due to the cost of the war and there was no money to pay owners for executed slaves. The sheriff performed the procedure and received 20 shillings for the "operation." He also received £3 to "cure" the patient. The concept of a slave court developed at this time. Prior to the court, the owner or overseers punished misdemeanors, while more serious crimes were adjudicated by a justice of the peace who had almost total power without restraints.[93] In slave courts, three justices of the peace and three freeholders, usually slaveholders, heard the case and a majority decided the guilt or innocence of the defendant. If the slave was executed, his owner received his value from a poll tax collected on all slaves. Although slaves could testify earlier, the slave court law of 1715 proclaimed that no Negro or mulatto, bound or free to the third generation, could be a witness, except against others of their kind.[94]

Laws were passed about whites in their relations with blacks. Whites could not harbor runaways; they were required to pay the slave's owner 10 shillings per day plus the cost of his loss of labor. More significantly, a white could be whipped for this offense. Trading with a slave resulted in a £10 fine. Owners of slaves had to feed and shelter their property properly. If a slave stole from another plantation to supplement his diet, the owner paid court costs and the value of the material stolen. Slaves could not build and use their own church on a plantation—the owner was fined £10 for this transgression. Instead, slaves were expected to worship with whites (and they could be watched while assembled). A white could not marry a black or mulatto. The participants and the minister who performed the ceremony were each fined £50, while the money was used to pay for bridges and courthouses. If a runaway absent for more than two months was killed during pursuit, his killer was free from prosecution if he took an oath stating that there was no other means of apprehension. The names of these runaways were posted on church doors.

Slaves, except personal servants or those in livery, could not leave the plantation without a pass. If they were picked up without a pass, the arresting white received 5 shillings plus 1 shilling per mile from the owner. If an owner could not be found within two months, the slave was hired out to pay his costs. He wore an iron collar and received 39 lashes from the constable for punishment. A master could not free a slave who had run away or was "unmanageable." A bondsman could be manumitted only for meritorious service, and he had to leave the colony or be sold back into service for five years. A statute in 1723 permitted the seizure of a previously emancipated slave to be sold back into bondage to satisfy the creditors of his former master.[95] If a freedman left and then returned to the province, he could be sold for seven years. He then had to leave the colony within six months, but if he returned, he could be sold once more for an additional seven years. Some freed slaves could remain in North Carolina as a result of a decree in 1740. If they performed a meritorious service, the court might give the master a license to manumit, and this permitted the freedmen's residence in North Carolina.

In 1729, a slave who passed from place to place had to stay on an accustomed route; if he was found on the road and on someone's property, that white could administer 40 lashes. If a white drank alcohol with a slave, the white could receive 40 lashes. Slaves could not travel at night or gather in white people's kitchens or in their own quarters; again, the punishment was 40 lashes and 20 for the white "host."[96] Slaves could hunt on the owner's property only when accompanied by a white. If they were found on another's property, the slave owner paid the landowner £1.

An all-encompassing slave code, "An Act Concerning Servants & Slaves," was passed in 1741.[97] This codified most of the previous laws and added other restrictions. In criminal cases, two justices of the peace and four slaveowners sat in judgment and decided punishment.[98] If three or more slaves conspired to rebel, the death sentence was mandatory. In conspiracy or lesser crimes, the court took testimony from slaves, freedmen, Indians, and whites. If a black gave false testimony, an ear was nailed to a pillory for one hour and then cut off. The second ear followed the first, as well as 39 lashes to his bare back. Blacks and Indians were not sworn in because they were not "Christian." However, they were charged to tell the truth or otherwise be punished by "God, the Revenger."

The majority of cases against blacks were for theft (57 percent), poisoning (21 percent) and murder (21 percent). The slave was pronounced guilty 93 percent of the time. Other charges included arson, rebellion, rape, assaulting the master, attacking another slave, and killing a horse. About 20 percent of those tried were executed, usually within three days; the usual method was by hanging. In rare cases, the miscreant was burned at the stake, and his fellows were forced to watch. If the slave was executed, his owner received up to £60, though this was changed in 1738. Rape and murder were still punished by the executioner's rope. All other capital crimes were punished by castration.[99]

A slave was not permitted to own property, particularly livestock—this could be seized and sold by the church warden. He could not carry arms without a certificate. If arms were seized, a justice of the peace ordered 20 lashes and his master paid court costs. One slave on a plantation could have a firearm certificate. He used the gun to hunt for his master's table and to protect the livestock. For this, he received a certificate from the chairman of the county court. A law of 1753 forced the owner to post a bond if his slave had a gun. If the slave injured someone, that person received the bond as well as a judgment against the master. A slave could not hunt with a dog. If caught, the dog was killed, and the slave received 30 lashes. A decree in 1766 permitted the slave to hunt on his master's or on the king's land, but he had to remain within five miles of his master's home; violation resulted in a £10 fine.[100]

If a freedman encouraged a slave to escape, he was fined 40 shillings, plus 5 shillings per 12 hours that the slave was absent. Failure to pay the fine resulted in the perpetrator's sale into servitude until the fine was paid. He also paid the slave's owner £25. If unable to pay, he served the owner for five years. If he shipped the slave out of the colony, he was prosecuted for a felony and jailed.[101]

There were laws to prohibit teaching of a slave to read and write.[102] The fear was that this ability would lead to reading abolitionist papers, forging passes, and dissatisfaction among slaves, that could lead to rebellion. Any white who taught slaves to read or gave or sold books to them was fined $100–$200, or was sent to prison. A free black who violated the law was given up to 39 lashes or imprisoned. Slave "teachers" who taught others to read received 39 lashes.[103]

The Revolution brought changes in the slave's existence.[104] Slaves received protection equal to that of whites in capital crimes. They received trial by jury if the punishment led to death or dismemberment. They could challenge jurors, had the right to counsel; the right to change of venue; and the right to appeal a verdict to the state supreme court. The slave court was replaced by county courts. If a white killed a slave in a wanton manner, he was tried as though he had killed a white; if guilty, he was fined $100 plus the slave's value. A second offense led to death without benefit of clergy.[105]

North Carolina received its separate status long after slavery was an established institution in colonial America. Manumission was very difficult early in its history, and the freedman was forced to leave after his emancipation. Therefore, there were few free blacks among the total number of blacks in the colony. However, the legislature restricted the activity of the free black. Free blacks could not associate with slaves. They could not marry a slave without the owner's written permission, with failure to obey resulting in one year of servitude. Free blacks could not form unions with white women. A child of such a union was bound out until the age of majority. The woman, if indentured, served one more year; if free, she was sold into servitude for two years.[106] The state constitution of 1776 gave the free black suffrage, but he could not vote for members of the assembly. This right to vote was removed later, following the counter-reaction to the liberties granted during the period of revolutionary fervor.

Georgia

The land between the Savannah and St. John's Rivers was separated from South Carolina and given in trusteeship for an additional colony in 1732.[107] The new colony served several purposes. Led by Lord Viscount John Percival, a group of English philanthropists saw it as a means of emptying out the poorhouses and jails of London to give the inmates "a second chance." Secondly, it would be a buffer between Spanish Florida and the rich colony of South Carolina. They envisioned a province filled with armed white farmers working their small plots of land. Finally, it fit in with the concept of mercantilism, held by most Europeans of the period. Silks and other exotic materials were imported from the Far East to satisfy the tastes of the newly rich

English gentry; these imports were paid for in specie. If silk, oil and dye production could be introduced in Georgia, England would not have to export gold. The aim of mercantilism was to create an independent, self-sustaining relationship between the mother country and her colonies. The newly developed factories produced goods for export as well as home use, and this brought in precious metals, the engine that drove mercantilism.[108]

Savannah became the first seat of white settlement in 1733 under the leadership of General James Oglethorpe, who helped pay the passage for some debtors in English prisons. The trustees were given control of the colony for 21 years; after this period, it would return to the king as a Crown colony (1753). The trustees formed a corporation to administer the colony, with General Oglethorpe as the military and civil affairs leader; they appointed the common council to govern and legislate for the province. This group was responsible to the corporation rather than to the colonists; a representative body responsible to the inhabitants was not permitted. A male settler received 50 acres of land. He could accumulate 500 acres if he brought in ten white servants who promised actively to defend the colony in a militia. The owner had to cultivate the land and pay quit rent to the trustees or return the land.[109]

The leaders opposed large land grants to avoid a plantation economy worked by slaves. Early in Georgia's history, slaves were prohibited, because white workers could not compete with slave labor and slaves could not be trusted in their midst. To prevent a slave influx, "an Act for Rendering the Colony of Georgia More Defensible by Prohibiting the Importation and Use of Black Slaves of Negroes Into the Same" was passed in 1734 and became effective in 1735.[110] White landowners who had slaves were fined £50, and the slaves were seized and sold by the authorities. Oglethorpe imported slaves to help build Savannah, but after the city's completion, they were returned to South Carolina. The law was unpopular, and the whites found ways to subvert the prohibition. Large landowners in south Georgia and around Augusta simply flouted the law, while colonial officials "looked the other way." Another technique called for renting blacks from South Carolina for 100 years.[111] The "rental" cost was paid in advance, and it usually equaled the perceived value of the slave. (There were probably about 350 black slaves in Georgia prior to the repeal of the prohibition.) Finally, the proslavery forces turned to petitions to the council in 1738 and 1741 to allow slavery. These were not approved. Finally, a petition in 1749 was approved, and slavery was legalized in 1750.[112] The petitions were supplemented by pamphlets. The pamphlets and petitions made other demands on the trustees.[113] The colonists wanted fee simple lands, abolition of quit rents, limited self-government, and the right to settle wherever they wished. (Fee simple land would allow the purchase and inheritance of land, which could lead to large plantations.) They argued that the climate of Georgia limited white men's ability to work: only slaves could be forced to work the land. Also, anything produced in Georgia could be produced more cheaply in South Carolina, because that state had slaves and Georgia simply could not compete. The "wisdom" of the "malcontents" became obvious to the trustees. Without slaves to work the land, the economy foundered and many whites emigrated to South Carolina. Added to the problems of the trustees was dissatisfaction in the English Parliament with their results in almost 20 years of running the colony. The hope of creating a silk industry was a failure. Occasional flash frosts, little knowledge, and little interest in growing silkworms killed the industry in its infancy. Finally, Parliament decreased and then ended the subsidy it had voted to sustain the young colony. In 1750 the Crown approved the repeal of the prohibition against slave importation, though there were limitations on the free import of blacks. For example, there had to be one white male immigrant between 16 and 60 years, able to bear arms, for every four blacks imported.

The early years following the repeal were not associated with a massive influx of slaves. The potential owners lacked capital to purchase slaves, let alone to outfit a ship to bring slaves directly from Africa. The early black immigrants came from South Carolina and the West Indies. No full-time slaver docked in Georgia ports, for Georgia could not absorb a shipful of slaves. Instead, commodity traders with a few slaves on board to fill empty spaces in the hold were more likely to get rid of their wares in Georgia. With the growth of a plantation system, particularly the right to fee simple land in 1751, the economy grew. The growth of plantations increased the demand for black labor, and by 1765 Georgia imported large numbers of bondsmen.[114] The white owners demanded and received slaves fresh from Africa rather than from the West Indies or other colonies; they, like their predecessors, feared sick or unmanageable slaves from the latter sources. To further decrease their source of supply, they placed a £10 duty on "seasoned" slaves (1761). Savannah became a major port for slavers directly from Africa, and the city "boasted" its own slave-trading firm, Cowper and Telfair. The slaves were paid for in produce as well as letters of credit payable with interest in 15 months. The numbers increased yearly so that 2,465 blacks were imported in 1774. Full cargoes of up to 340 slaves could be absorbed by Savannah at one time. This was the high point, because trouble with England curtailed the trade. In 1775 Georgia joined the other colonies in the Non-Importation Agreement, which included slaves. Prior to the Revolution, Georgia had 10,625 blacks in a total population of 23,375—a ratio of almost one to one. During and after the Revolution, Georgia lost large numbers of its bondsmen: some escaped to the deep forests, some formed marauding bands, and thousands left with the British in 1782. The war devastated Georgia's economy, and plantation owners were unable to meet the cost of new hands to replace the loss. It was ten years before they were able to start importing slaves from Africa (1792). The Haitian Rebellion put a damper on the desire for slaves, particularly those from the West Indies.

In 1755 Georgia adopted its first slave code. It was generally similar to South Carolina's code. In addition to the usual controls, new slaves had to be examined by health officers before coming on land.[115] Slave marriage was respected, and slaves were tried according to English law. A slave was tried before a single judge. In a capital case, when the slave was to be executed, the judge decided his worth and the treasury compensated his owner. No more than seven slaves were allowed off the plantation together unless accompanied by a white. Some slaves had gun permits, but they could not carry a firearm between Saturday night and Monday morning. They could not own canoes, horses, or cattle. There was a prohibition against teaching slaves to read and write. Slaves could not work more than 16 hours a day. They were allowed in the militia, usually to build fortifications. Slaves had to be agricultural workers; they could not learn a trade that would put them in competition with whites. There was one exception, however: slaves could learn to become coopers, and a cooper could take in a black as an apprentice.[116] The leaders of the colony realized that slave craftsmen would keep white immigrants from coming to Georgia.[117] A white who killed a slave while applying "moderate correction" could not be indicted for murder.

Georgia had just a few years with the "abominable institution" to develop any homegrown or imported emancipationists. The white leaders saw the economy grow after 1750, and they recognized that this followed the introduction of black slave labor. The ideas of freedom and equality, developed during the Revolution, seemed not to have gravitated that far south. Northern Georgia was occupied by the British. This occupation helped deplete the number of slaves, for those blacks who penetrated the British lines were taken with them when the British left. In many of the Southern states, religious groups like the Quakers tried to promote the concept of manumission. Again, Georgia was not included. Georgia was home to a group of Germans, the Salzburgers, who used slaves as early as 1734 to help clear the land and build the communities. Those who tried to escape received the same punishment from the Germans as they did from other owners. The Germans opposed general slavery, however, because of the danger of a "foreign element in their midst" and because "all blacks were thieves." Furthermore, the slaves could represent a "fifth column" to help the Spanish to the south. Their leader, the Reverend Johann Bolzius, agreed with the Georgia and South Carolina slave code.[118] He claimed slavery was permissible if the security of the community remained intact and the welfare of white labor preserved. He also looked for "enlargement of Christ's Kingdom" (conversion of the slaves to his sect).

Chapter 8

THE FREEDMEN

The national census of 1800 listed 1,002,037 blacks within the boundaries of the United States.[1] This represented 18.9 percent of the total population. Of this number, 893,602 were slaves and 108,435 were free. The number of freedmen had almost doubled from 59,000 ten years earlier. The greatest percentage of free blacks resulted from manumission, either of that individual or his ancestors. However, there were other means by which slaves became freedmen. A very small number were descended from people who had no slavery in their family tree—these were individuals who came voluntarily to America from Europe or Africa. Before the concept of black slavery became "written in stone" in the middle of the seventeenth century, blacks were indentured servants like many white Englishmen. When their contract of indenture ended, they received all of the rights and privileges given to freed white servants. The black Johnson family of Virginia and Maryland was a typical example, but not the only one, of this mechanism that produced free blacks. Future generations of these families had to avoid "slave catchers" and statutes to re-enslave blacks in order to retain their freedom. The ancestors of some blacks won their freedom from the courts. In the early colonial period, when there were few blacks, and they did not represent a threat to the white majority, slaves could petition the courts for their freedom. In some cases, this was granted. There was this case in 1692: "Okree, a Negro Man late slave to Mr. Jno. [Jonathon] Jones ... deced ... Jones in his last will and testament [gave Okree to his wife]. I give to her for no longer than she doth remaine a widdow, ... then the sd. old negro to be free & clear ... the sd. deced's widdow Beth lately intermarry'd with James Blaise who deteynes him as a slave. ...Wherefore he humbly prays this court ... grant him an order for his freedom. Whereupon this Court on due Consideration of the premises & perusal of the sd. deced's Will have adjudged the sd. Negro to be free & do accordingly grant him an order for his freedom."[2]

When the supply of warm white bodies dried up during the Revolution, black slaves were taken into the army to fill the ranks; these "volunteers" were promised their freedom if they survived. To some, it was bad enough to have to accept free blacks into the "colonial armies" early in the war, but the idea of arming slaves was abhorrent. However, necessity forced a revision of this thinking. Most of the black soldiers were from Northern states. South of Pennsylvania, and particularly in Georgia and South Carolina, the large numbers of blacks precluded arming them. The white owners of many bondsmen had a fear of rebellion, and many whites stayed out of the Revolutionary army to control the large black population in order to prevent this fear from becoming reality. Nevertheless, there were some Southern slaves in the service, particularly in the Virginia navy. In some areas of the South, after the end of hostilities, ... some masters tried to renege on the promise of freedom. Occasionally the legislature intervened to grant the veteran his promised reward.

In some Southern states, masters were prohibited from manumitting their chattel. Here, only the state legislature could grant freedom for "meritorious service." A common service was for a slave to expose a plan for rebellion on the part of his "brothers." The insurrection was usually put down before it started, often by the state militia, and the conspirators were executed or deported to the Deep South or the West Indies. The informer was freed. On rare occasions, the slave performed an important service to society. The incident of the slave who discovered the "cure" for yaws, cited earlier, was a case in point.

A substantial number of blacks gained their freedom by flight. These were usually young men who tried to find areas with large numbers of free blacks so that they could lose themselves in this pool of humanity. This meant locating in urban areas, particularly in the North. All newspapers carried advertisements from owners looking for their lost property. These notices described the individual, his scars (usually produced by punishment for previous attempts at freedom), his clothing, his ability to speak English or another European language, his musical ability, and his training as an artisan. The trained black cooper, bricklayer, brickmaker or tailor was usually the brightest, most costly, and most difficult slave to keep in subjugation. "Slave catching" became an important source of income for the poor whites of the South, for it was worth the cost to the plantation owner to send these individuals to Northern cities to bring back one or several valuable pieces of property. The activities of these catchers were protected by federal laws. As early as 1787, the Northwest Ordinance prohibited slavery in the area involved, but escaped slaves had to be returned to their rightful owners. During the nineteenth century, enforcement of fugitive slave laws resulted in riots and helped to polarize opinion preceding the Civil War.

Self-purchase and purchase of the freedman's relatives added to the pool of free blacks. Early colonial laws stated that the slave had no property of his own; his possessions belonged to his master. Some slaves worked Sundays and holidays, and their masters allowed them to keep the money they earned, in contravention of some states' laws. In states like Louisiana (1806), the law permitted the slave to keep the rewards of his Sunday labor.[3] Urban blacks and those on the frontiers, particularly those trained in a necessary skill, hired themselves from their owners. For a sum agreed upon, often between $80 and $100 per year, paid to the owner, the slave was then allowed to "sell his services" to others in the community; he could earn between 50 cents and $1 a day, depending on his skill and ability, and his savings could be used to purchase his freedom. Self-purchase was often written into the contract that allowed the slave to hire himself out from his master. The owner permitted such a contract for his most honest slaves who had performed meritorious service in the past. Occasionally the master broke the agreement by taking the money and then selling the slave away. To avoid this possibility, the slave used an intermediary. This individual received the slave's money, bought the slave from his owner, then freed his new property. The intermediary was usually a freedman who could be trusted.

On the frontiers, control of the slave was more relaxed if there was no place to which he could run. The bondsman could participate in the commercial life of these outlying communities, and some became craftsmen, tradesmen, and shopkeepers. Some, like Free Frank in Kentucky, were entrepreneurs. Frank was skilled in animal husbandry, housebuilding, and other requirements of frontier life, so he was too valuable simply to work the land. His owner earned more by allowing this slave to hire himself. Kentucky had laws that prohibited a slave from this practice, but these statutes were circumvented. If caught, the owner and slave were fined £10 each—financially, it was worth the risk to both participants. Frank developed a technique to produce saltpeter. (The demand for this product was always great. When added to sulphur and charcoal, the end product was gunpowder.) Frank dredged crude nitrate from limestone caves; the salt was extracted by soaking it in hot water. Boiling left a concentrated solution that was crystallized by leeching it through wood ashes. The slave bartered his product with peddlers, and he sold the material he received in trade. Frank also produced whiskey, because he had a still used for lead production. (One wonders what happened to the nervous systems of his whiskey customers.) He also produced salt from the evaporation of water from a salty creek. The slave's original owner died, and his heirs allowed Frank to buy the farm and his other enterprises; they agreed to a price of $500 for his freedom. He purchased his own freedom, and two years later he purchased his wife, who was owned by another family. She too was skilled—Lucy could weave cloth, and she was also an able candlemaker. With their combined capital, Frank speculated in land, and he saved enough to purchase his children. The family left the area to relocate in Illinois, but not before Frank obtained a "Certificate of Good Character" signed by 19 prominent men of the community. He started farming in his new location and earned enough to buy 16 family members out of slavery for $15,000 over a period of 40 years.[4] The story of Frank and Lucy demonstrated a common obstacle to slave marriage. When a bondsman married a bondswoman who belonged to another family, her children belonged to her master. As was the case with their mother, their freedom had to be purchased individually from her owner.

Many bondsmen were freed in the last will and testament of their owners. George Washington's will was a case in point. He ordered that his slaves were to be freed after his wife's death. In some situations, however, this benevolence went awry. Jefferson planned to manumit his slaves in his will, but his estate was in arrears, and so his creditors seized his valuable chattel property to satisfy his debts. His slave Lucy, believed to be his concubine after his wife's death, and the mother of his children, was sold away from the plantation by these creditors.

In the North, many blacks were freed by state constitutions and state laws. The New Hampshire Constitution prohibited slavery. This had very little significance, though, because there were few blacks in that state, either slave or free. The Massachusetts Constitution declared that all men were born free and equal; state leaders accepted this proposition literally. The other New England states generally followed Massachusetts's lead. The Middle Atlantic states freed their slaves by law, often over a period of years in order to give them a "breaking-in" period during which to prepare for freedom.

In the colonial period, private property was almost sacred. Many of the rights and privileges of citizenship depended on the ownership of property. Yet the voluntary manumission of chattel property, very costly to the owner, resulted in the largest number of freedmen. The legal right of manumission evolved from the inherent right of a property owner to abandon title to his property. This right existed without the sanction of law but could be restricted by legislative action. There were three avenues by which the state could restrain the individual. First, laws could be passed that required the owner to post a security bond, so the new freedman would not become a public charge. This mechanism prevented manumission of a sick or old slave who was a drain on his owner. Decrees of this kind were passed in New Jersey, Pennsylvania, Delaware, Massachusetts, Connecticut, New York, Rhode Island, Maryland, North Carolina, Tennessee, and Mississippi. Toward the end of the colonial and federal periods, these laws were modified. New York in 1785 declared that a bond was not needed if the slave was under 50. New Jersey (1786) required no security for slaves between ages 21 and 35; 12 years later, the age was raised to 40. Second, the state could issue a decree forcing freedmen to leave the state. As early as 1691, Virginia ordered the owner to pay the cost of transporting his ex-slave out of the colony; the owner was fined £10 if the slave remained in the colony after six months. Virginia in 1806 could sell a freed black back into slavery if he was still in the state 12 months after manumission.[5] Third, the state could prohibit manumission entirely. In Virginia in 1723, the slave could be freed only for meritorious service. During the excitement of the Revolution, Virginia in 1782 removed restrictions on manumission. However, the fervor lasted just five years and the restrictions were repealed. In 1775 North Carolina prohibited manumission not approved by a county court. This decree was frequently disregarded, however. In 1778 North Carolina posted a reward for the capture of an illegally freed black; the prisoner was then sold back into bondage. A slave owner in Georgia had to receive permission from the legislature to dispose of his chattel (1801); the master was fined $200 if he failed to receive this permit. To avoid the restrictions placed on manumission, the master could sell the slave to himself for a nominal sum. Robert Pleasant in 1772 sold his slave in this manner to circumvent the law in Virginia.

> I Robert Pleasant of Henrico County in the Colony of Virginia Merch. Send Greetings, Know ye that I the said Robert Pleasant for divers and good Causes and valuable Considerations ... thereunto ... & more especially for & in consideration of the sum of five shillings lawful money of the Said Colony to me in hand paid by my Negro Slave Boy James, the Receipt whereof I do hereby acknowledge Have Manumitted remised & released, and by these presents Do manumit, remise & release unto the said Negro Boy James all his servitude from hence forth to accrue, all my Estate Right, Title & Interest whatsoever of in & to the said Negro Boy; but I do declare that it shall not be lawful for either my self, my heirs Exects, administrs. or assigns or any other person or persons whatsoever to deprive the Said Negro Boy of the full free & uninterrupted enjoyment of his liberty, but that he shall possess & enjoy the same as full as any other person who hath never been in Bondage. Witness my hand & Seal this 8th day of October 1772. Sealed & deliver'd in presence of Robt. Pleasant.[6]

In states that permitted voluntary manumission, the road to freedom still had some minor detours. In addition to the manumission certificate, other legal papers were required. In New York, Henry Rutgers freed his slaves.

> Know all Men by these presents, that I Henry Rutgers do, by these presents, for good & valuable considerations, fully and absolutely manumit, make Free, & set at Liberty, one slave, named Thomas Boston hereby willing and declaring that the said Thomas Boston shall & may, at all times hereafter, exercise, hold, and enjoy, all & singular, liberties, rights, privileges, & immunities of a free man fully to all intents & purposes, as if he had been born free. And I do hereby, for my executors, administrators, & Assigns, absolutely relinquish & release all my right, title, & property whatsoever, in & to the Said Thomas Boston as my slave. In Testimony whereof, I have hereunto set my hand & seal, the twelfth day of June one thousand eight hundred & seventeen. Sealed & delivered in the presence of R. Riker. Henry Rutgers.[7]

The manumission statement was then recorded by the Recorder of the City of New York: "On the twelfth day of June 1817, Henry Rutgers, Esqr., appeared before me and acknowledged that he executed the above instrument, as his voluntary act & deed for the purposes herein mentioned. I allow it to be recorded. s/R. Riker, Recorder of the City of New York." Then the slave had to be examined to check his employability:

By Jacob Radcliff, Mayor, & Richard Riker, Recorder of the City of New York. It is hereby certified, that pursuant to the Statute in such case made & provided, we have this day examined one certain male Negro Slave named Thomas Boston, the property of Henry Rutgers, which slave is about to be manumitted, & he appearing to us to be under 45 years of age, & of sufficient ability to provide for himself, we have granted this certificate, this twelfth day of June in the year of our Lord, one thousand eight hundred & seventeen. s/Jacob Radcliff, R. Riker[8]

Henry Rutgers obtained the necessary certificate from the mayor and recorder. According to the statute of 1785, other officials were empowered to give the certificate; including the overseers of the poor plus five justices of the peace or two aldermen. If the certificate was denied, the master could appeal to the court of general sessions. Children could be freed if the master received a certificate stating that the parents would provide for them; the certificate cost 50 cents.

The freedman was always treated differently from other free citizens in the colonies. In Virginia (1670), "no negro or Indian baptized & free shall be capable of any purchase of a Christian [this meant white], but not prevented from buying any of their own nation." This law was revised later and stated that a Christian white servant purchased by a free Negro or mulatto was immediately free.[9] In Maryland (1664) a law on the books stated that all blacks were slaves forever. Examination of recent court records of the period described many free blacks involved in court cases. In 1690 a free black, Richard Butchery, was fined 500 pounds of tobacco for fathering a bastard with a white servant girl; he also had to compensate her master with 800 pounds of tobacco.[10] If he had committed this offense two years later, however, he could have been sold into slavery; this was then reduced to seven years of servitude in 1699. In 1678 all blacks and mulattoes were "exempt" from militia service. (It is important to understand that militia service was largely a social rather than a military obligation. Furthermore, the movement to political office was often through the militia.)

In the eighteenth century, the number of blacks increased, and the degradation and adverse statutes increased proportionately. In the census of 1790, there were almost 60,000 free blacks.[11] About two-thirds of them lived in New England and the Middle Atlantic states. Between 1780 and 1790, the black population of Philadelphia increased 176 percent. At the end of the century, New York and Philadelphia had the largest free black populations. Free blacks settled in close-knit communities where businessmen, mechanics, and entrepreneurs could develop to serve their own people. The free black had more security in the North, but on rare occasions he could be claimed as an escaped slave, kidnapped, and sent to the Southern states. He had to carry proof of his free status at all times. The freedman had this certificate, but his children, if born free, did not. It cost as much as a week's shelter for a family to obtain a certificate.

Living conditions for blacks were abysmal. Their "colonies" often occupied the worst slums of the city. In Philadelphia, they lived in cellars described as wretchedly dark, damp, and dirty; these rented for 12½ cents per night, and were usually occupied by several families. In the winter there might be as many as 20 lodgers each night. Blacks also occupied small wooden buildings behind the main house. These were about six feet square without windows or fireplaces. Near the door was a hole about one foot square to let fresh air and light in and foul air and smoke out. The roof leaked. The floors were at ground level, so water in the yard moved into the house in rainy weather. There was no room for bedding, and a box was the only furniture. The inhabitants reached their "homes" through narrow alleys between rows of shanties. Some of these huts were two stories high, and their inhabitants reached them on inclined boards extended from ground level. These "pens" covered a backyard, and light could never reach the ground floor. Each floor was occupied by one or two families without privacy or comfort. These huts rented for 10 cents per night. There were usually no children in these huts because they did not survive infancy. The owner of the land could build a double row of shelters with 20 "apartments" for $100; at ten cents per night, he could gross over $1,600 per year. The more prosperous families could rent a single room in the main house for $1 per week. Here, there was better sanitation and protection from the elements. Occasionally a sickly child might be found in these rooms, because he had survived infancy. The breadwinner in the family earned 50–75 cents per day if he found work.[12] These slums bred crime and violence, but the police feared going among large groups of blacks, and most crimes went unpunished or were settled locally. If a freedman was arrested for a crime, his sentence was more severe than that of a white man who had committed a similar transgression. These conditions supplied the fuel for the Southern apologists of slavery. Robert Hayne, a senator from South Carolina, declared in Congress that blacks were treated as outcasts and assigned to "the dark and narrow lanes, and obscure recesses" of the cities: "There does not exist on the face of the earth, a population so poor, so wretched, so vile, so loathsome, so utterly destitute of all the comforts, conveniences, and decencies of life, as the unfortunate blacks of Philadelphia & Boston."[13]

Blacks in northern cities could obtain only menial jobs such as a domestic work or physical labor. They had to compete with the new white immigrants for these means of livelihood.[14] Whites refused to accept them as fellow workers or as apprentices. A black with a skill was not hired, because white workers would leave the factory or shop. When craftsmen joined to form "unions," blacks were not accepted. A black with business ability could not get credit from a bank to start or expand a growing business, because he was a "poor credit risk." Even in death, the black remained isolated: he could not be buried in a white cemetery.

In the early nineteenth century, a foreign visitor described the blacks in Philadelphia, and his picture was not as bleak as those of others who visited America.[15] Free blacks were lackey coachmen, and many owned their own carriages, which were the best maintained. Whites preferred to hire them, because the driver would not assume equality with the passenger, and the occupants could order them in the "tone of masters, and it might be thought they were in their own carriages." Barbers were almost entirely black, for it was believed that whites were too proud or lazy to shave themselves. The barber shop was a lounging place and reading room; conversations made the operators aware of daily happenings in the community. The freedmen contributed more to the poor fund than they received. Blacks made up more than 8 percent of Philadelphia's population, but only 4 percent were paupers. They paid more than $100,000 in rents each year, and they supported their churches, valued at more than $1 million. They supported their own Sunday schools, tract societies, Bible societies, temperance societies, and more than 50 beneficent societies, which spent more than $7,000 yearly to relieve sickness and distress. No member of these groups was ever convicted of a crime.

In smaller communities, particularly in New England, freedmen could rise above the usual menial condition, becoming small businessmen and mechanics who filled necessary niches in society. The blacks were basket makers, shoemakers, fortune-tellers, undertakers for their community, musicians (some of whom composed music and opened music schools), bakers, physicians, lawyers, caterers, restaurateurs, and farmers.[16]

In addition to financial obstacles, black men in the North faced legal hindrances. In five Northern states, they could not testify against whites and were ineligible for jury duty except in Massachusetts. Whites feared the black vote, because they believed blacks might vote as a bloc and elect freedmen to local and state offices. There was a property requirement for suffrage which most blacks could not accumulate. This denial was not directed specifically against blacks but rather against giving the poor a voice in government. However, in New York the estate requirement for the vote was lowered for white men only. In much of New England, freedmen had voting rights approximately equal to those of other citizens if the mobs allowed them to get to the polls. State constitutions written in the fervor of the Revolution granted suffrage to black men, but these rights were gradually eroded by amendments and new laws. Pennsylvania, New York, Delaware, New Jersey, and some of the newer states like Ohio restricted black suffrage in this way. Many Northern states restricted their immigration, and some tried to force blacks to return to their original counties. Some required blacks to post a bond to guarantee good conduct and to avoid their becoming a public charge.[17]

The federal government considered the United States a white man's country. The first naturalization law passed in 1790 granted the rights of citizenship to all free white aliens who resided in the United States for two years.

The militia law (1792) restricted service to whites.[18] Congress restricted suffrage to "free white male inhabitants" when the District of Columbia was incorporated (1802). Territorial governments, which would in the future become states, restricted the vote to white males, and the United States Congress accepted this restriction in their constitutions. Only a white male could carry the United States mail. On the face of it, this seemed a minor restriction. However, white officials believed that keeping blacks out of the postal service prevented them from spreading insurrectionary ideas. It also kept them in the dark about "natural rights": blacks might learn that a man's rights did not depend on his color. Blacks were not eligible for passports because they were not citizens under the Constitution. The State Department granted them certificates to travel, which stated that they were born in the United States, were free, and that it was the government's duty to protect them if they were wronged by a foreign government while in its jurisdiction for a legal and proper purpose. In the early years of the nineteenth century, while the North controlled finances and manufacturing, the South controlled much of national policy formulated by Congress. This might explain the bizarre conclusions reached in the sixth national census, which listed numbers of insane and idiots by section and state.[19] There were 11 times as many insane and idiot free blacks as slaves. In the South, 1 in 1,558 blacks suffered from this handicap; in the North, it was 1 in 1,445. Geographically, as one proceeded South, the incidence decreased. In Maine, 1 in 14 Negroes was insane or an idiot; in Massachusetts, 1 in 43; in New York, 1 in 257; in Virginia, 1 in 1,299; and in Louisiana, 1 in 4,310. These figures represented further evidence that "darkies were better off in slavery in the south."

Freedmen were feared and unwanted in the South.[20] The white power structure feared their criminality, believing that they sold liquor to slaves and incited them to riot. Free blacks were thought to be congenitally delinquent and likely to become public charges. The whites attempted to control this group by forcing a black to carry a Certificate of Freedom, which listed his name, stature, complexion, and the way his freedom was obtained. Any white could ask a black to show it. If he failed to produce the card, the black was treated as a runaway slave and hired out or sold back into slavery. The certificate was purchased for $1, and it was renewed yearly if the holder lived in the city, or every five years if the black lived in the country. The freedman could be forced back into servitude if he did not have the money to pay debts, taxes, court fees, or fines. A freedman could not vote or hold legal office. In the excitement following the Revolution, blacks were given suffrage in every state except Georgia and South Carolina; this privilege was gradually removed with time. Surprisingly, free blacks could vote in North Carolina until 1835.[21] Freedmen could not testify against whites or purchase firearms without a permit. If a black obtained a gun without this permit, both he and the seller were fined. He could not purchase alcohol without the recommendation of a reputable white. There were also curfew laws that restricted his right of assembly. In some areas, a reputable white had to be present at black church services to monitor activities and sermons. Freedmen were segregated in public accommodations, in public activities, and in education. They did not have the freedom to move from place to place. If blacks left their county for more than 60 days, they could not return. In Delaware, attendance by a black at a political meeting was a misdemeanor that carried a $20 fine. In Georgia and Florida, the black man had to have a "white guardian" to whom he had to report regularly.[22]

The freedman could support his family in agricultural work in return for wages or goods.[23] Some became tenant farmers, and some could own land. As in the North, they did menial work as laborers and domestics in urban areas. A few lucky ones had salable skills they had learned in slavery. The developing tobacco and iron manufacturing industries employed blacks in the dirty jobs. A fortunate few became businessmen with substantial estates. Overall, their blacks' wages were lower, and their work was more strenuous and dirty—jobs that white workers refused. Added to this, some states put restrictions on their capacity to earn a living. Maryland in 1805 prohibited freedmen from selling corn, wheat, and tobacco without a license. A black seaman had to stay on board his ship when docked in Southern ports; if he was picked up off the ship, he was taken to jail and had to pay for his upkeep while in jail. Failure to pay could lead to his sale back into slavery. There were certain occupations prohibited to freedmen. In Georgia, they could not be typesetters, for obvious reasons. In other areas they could not be clerks or peddlers without a license.[24] (A peddler could safely move from one plantation to another.) Perhaps the most serious restriction on the freedman, second only to his ability to support his family, was the right to remain in the state where he was born. After emancipation, he had to leave the state within a set period of time or face re-enslavement. Virginia (1806) gave him 12 months in which to move.[25] The problem with this statute was that other states prohibited the blacks from moving into their territories; the prohibition might be a security bond against becoming a public charge or outright prevention at the border crossing. Virginia in 1793 forbade free blacks to enter the state, and other states followed.

Even in the face of these restrictions, a few blacks were able to survive and prosper. Some became wealthy traders and businessmen. Others were able to own large tracts of land. Unhappily, some of these freedmen forgot the hopelessness of slavery and bought and used slaves as did their white neighbors. For instance, in 1654 a Virginia court upheld the claim of Anthony Johnson (a black freedman) for the "perpetual service" of John Casor (a black). Review of other early Virginia records showed deeds of sale and transfer of slaves between free blacks, and the mention of slaves in wills, and suits by slaves for freedom from their black masters. In Henrico County, Virginia, in

1795, George Radford, black, paid £33 for Aggy, a Negro woman. Mary Quickly, a black, was sued for freedom by Sarah.[26] Cyprian Ricard of Louisiana had 91 slaves controlled by white overseers.[27] The largest black slave owner started life as a slave: John Carruthers Stanly was the offspring of an Ebo woman and her owner, John Wright Stanly. The child was taught the barbering trade. While still a slave, he opened a barber shop in New Bern, North Carolina, where he could earn as much as £10 per month. He was freed by his new owners, the Stewarts, after they petitioned the Craven County Court. Stanly, for himself, petitioned the North Carolina legislature for his freedom as further security against slave catchers. He then bought his wife and two boys and successfully petitioned for their freedom. The new freedman then purchased two slaves, taught them barbering, and they took over his shop. Over the years, he acquired wealth, land, and slaves—he had 32 slaves in New Bern and more than 100 on his plantations. Stanly hired slaves from their masters to maintain his property and to build cabins for his own chattel property, and he employed three white overseers (Benjamin Miller controlled 87 slaves, Amos Hadles supervised 25, and John Mills 19). Around 1830 he owned 163 slaves and was one of the largest slaveholders in North Carolina, owning more than twice as many slaves as the next largest black owner. His treatment of his chattel property was no better or worse than that of his white contemporaries: he did not concern himself with family ties among slave families and broke up these families if it was financially beneficial. His property in slaves, before business reverses, was valued at $12,850.[28]

Blacks owned blacks in Boston early in the eighteenth century. Court records showed similar cases in Connecticut, Alabama, and Maryland later in that century. Early in the nineteenth century, 21 percent of free blacks in Petersburg, Virginia, owned slaves. At this time, 3,775 black men owned 12,760 slaves.[29] A free black in the South could elevate his social position by owning slaves; he tended to oppose universal emancipation, because this would submerge him into a large group of freedmen. Some blacks sold their own families. In Kentucky, for example, a man sold his son and daughter for $2,200. A Georgia woman sold her husband "because he opposed her." A son sold his father to a trader "to teach him some manners."

In many instances, the purchase of blacks by blacks was altruistic, not financial in motivation. Some rich blacks purchased slaves to free them. Often, the new freedman paid his benefactor his "price" from his future earnings. In other cases, blacks purchased families out of slavery. Many states had forced emigration policies for newly freed slaves. This statute was contravened by the new "owner," who kept the blacks in bondage in order to keep the family together in the county in which they lived and had been born. There was a serious drawback to this scheme, however. Freedmen rarely made wills and were intestate when they died, so the state could re-enslave their families and sell them away.

The newly found freedom could not be handled by some blacks. They could not work and support their families under the restrictions placed upon them by a white society that wished to remove this new "nucleus of insurrection." Some petitioned their masters to take them back into service under any condition stipulated by the white man. Others, like Jupiter, a slave freed by Robert Henly, were without skills. Jupiter indentured himself to one white master after another, and between times, he was picked up for stealing hogs. He became a regular in the courts, either defending himself against indictments for law breaking or suing his earlier contractual partners.[30]

Most freedmen recognized early that they had to depend upon themselves and join together to make a place in a society despite repression by whites. They petitioned legislatures and state courts, with limited success, to redress their grievances. A group of free blacks in South Carolina sent a memorial to the legislature:

> An act of assembly ... in the year 1740 commonly called the Negro Act ... Your memorialists are deprived of the Rights & Privileges of citizens by not having it in their power to give Testimony on Oath ... nor can they give Testimony in recovering Debts due to them or in establishing agreements ... except in cases where Persons of Colour are concerned ... Trial without the benefit of a jury & subject to Prosecution by Testimony of slaves without oath ... do now contribute to the support of the Government by cheerfully paying their taxes.... They are ready & willing to take & subscribe to such an oath of allegiance to the states as shall be prescribed by this Honorable House, & are willing to take upon them any duty for the preservation of the Peace in the City. ...Your memorialists do not presume to hope they shall be put on an equal footing with the Free white citizens of the State. ...They only humbly solicit ... this Honorable House shall dictate in their favor by repealing the clauses ... substituting such a clause as will effectually Redress the grievances.... Signed 1st July 1791, rejected 13 July.[31]

The action on this petition and many others was usual and expected. In rare cases, particularly in the North, groups of blacks sued for and received their freedom, as well as rights and privileges of free citizens. In Dartmouth, Massachusetts, free blacks petitioned the legislature to be given the vote because they were taxed without being represented; in 1783 black taxpayers were given the vote. In Boston (1787) taxpaying blacks wanted their children to attend public schools; this was denied.[32]

Petitions to Congress were usually rejected as well. For example, a group of blacks petitioned Congress to redress a wrong committed by North Carolina.[33] In 1775 North Carolina passed a law that prohibited manumission. White owners often disregarded the statute, and North Carolina in 1778 decreed that a reward would be paid for the capture and resale of illegally freed blacks. In 1797 four blacks who had escaped capture petitioned Congress for protection and freedom for their relatives who had been freed, then captured and resold. Jupiter Nicholson described the North Carolina law and how freedmen were hunted down by men with dogs. His mother, father, and brother were victims of the 1778 statute. Another writer, Job Albert, described being put in prison, and how he escaped and traveled by night to Virginia; his mother and sister were not so lucky. Thomas Pritchett was freed and given land by his ex-master. He had to leave this all behind because he feared the loss of his freedom. He went to Virginia, then to New York. Later he returned to Virginia to see his wife and children. To his dismay, he was listed as a runaway in local newspapers, and he fled to Philadelphia. The writers also described a freedman in a Philadelphia prison in accordance with the Fugitive Slave Act. He was manumitted in North Carolina, retaken, and sold back into slavery; he then escaped to Philadelphia, where he married and lived in freedom with his wife and family for 11 years. This unfortunate was imprisoned when an agent of a North Carolina "claimer" demanded his return. The petitioners begged the government to give them the rights of all free men and to use its constitutional powers to provide relief for blacks. "We can not have representation in your councils, but we address you as men to do right & justice & to encourage innocent & put down evil-doers. Blacks have affections, sensibilities, family ties. They look for a remedy of this evil law from the Legislative body of an enlightened people." No action was taken.

Far more beneficial than the generally ineffectual attempts at legal redress were the black organizations and churches developed for self-help. On April 12, 1787, Richard Allen and Absolam Jones formed the Free African Society in Philadelphia "without regard to religious tenets, provided the persons lived an orderly & sober life."[34] The society provided benefits for the sick, widows, and orphans. Its members maintained correspondence with freedmen in other cities and worked with the Philadelphia Abolition Society to achieve the latter group's aims. Members paid one shilling each month, used to provide funds for the needy who did not cause this poverty by improper behavior. Members who were drunk and disorderly were suspended, as were delinquent associates. The group provided schooling and apprenticeship for the children of dead members. It also raised money to purchase a site for a black church, and petitioned the city for a portion of land in Potter's Field to bury black members. By 1790 the society had an account at the Bank of North America for £42.[35] Early in the next century, Philadelphia's blacks formed insurance companies with black administrators, benevolent societies, female benevolent societies, and churches.

Similar societies developed in other urban centers. The African Society of Boston in 1796 described its goals for its white neighbors to see.[36] The society was formed for its members' mutual benefit. Members proclaimed themselves as citizens of the commonwealth, and they would take no one into the society who broke the laws of the country. To join, one had to apply at a monthly meeting and be supported by three members. If accepted one month later, the applicant had to read the rules of the organization (or have them read to him). Upon admission, he paid 25 cents to the treasurer and a similar sum each month. The new member was entitled to benefits one year after admission. Dues had to be paid at the monthly meeting by the member or by his proxy. Those discharged by the society received their dues minus the cost of discharging them. Absence from meetings for one year led to discharge. A sick visiting committee, in office for three months, attended the sick and provided what the society could supply. The sick visiting group could call an emergency meeting. If a family was destitute and could not pay sick costs, the society covered them. The Society would bury the dead if the family lacked funds, though if death was due to intemperance or other similar causes, benefits were denied. The legal widow and children, with evidence of a legal marriage document, would be cared for by the society for as long as the widow behaved decently and remained a widow. Children were placed in foster homes so they could learn to care for themselves. Members were to "watch over each other so they can grow in grace & be aware of the Lord, Jesus Christ, & live soberly, righteously and Godly so we can live together in the hereafter." Those members who had to travel long distances from home left a will with their legal wives or with the society. If they failed to return, the society ensured that their estate would go to the rightful heir.

Some freedmen caught the virus of color consciousness, with its associated bigotry. In Charleston, South Carolina, the free blacks classified themselves into strata: there were children of free colored parents, mulattoes of free colored mothers, children of free Negro and Indian parentage, and, finally, manumitted slaves. A group of free artisans of light color joined to form the Brown Fellowship Society (1790). They emphasized mixed blood, light skin, free ancestry, economic position and devotion to the concept of slavery.[37] They educated their children, married within their class and kept slaves. The light skinned blacks felt they had more in common with the whites than with their darker neighbors. A membership fee of $50 kept out the "lower classes."[38] Like other fraternal societies, they stressed education, assistance to widows and children, cemetery plots, and the ability to maintain a private meeting place. In 1791, perhaps to mimic their lighter brothers, darker blacks formed the Free Dark Men, which later became the Humane Brotherhood; this group's professed goals were similar to those of the earlier organization.[39]

In the colonial days and in the fledgling republic, white international fraternal organizations grew and prospered. Freedmen, like other citizens, wanted acceptance to these clubs. Prince Hall, a veteran of the Revolution who had lived in Massachusetts since 1765 and was a Methodist minister in Cambridge, applied to the American Masons to form a black lodge. He did not attempt to join any of the all-white lodges, but even this small request was denied.[40] Hall had been one of 15 blacks initiated into the Masons by the British Army Lodge of Freemasons in Boston (1775). When the British army left Boston, it left the blacks a license to meet as a lodge according to

Masonic usage; the army lodge permit was intended for use until a full warranty could be obtained from the Grand Lodge of London. When his request was denied in the United States, Hall made a similar request to the London lodge, which granted a charter to Hall, Boston Smith, Thomas Sanderson, and "several other brethren." Three years later, African Lodge 459 was established in Boston, with Hall as its grand master, Smith as senior warden, and Sanderson as junior warden.[41]

In his address to the African lodge, the master Mason explained his beliefs as a mason and a Christian. He urged his listeners to sympathize with their fellow men and with their families if death intervened. Hall attacked the concept of slavery and the trade that tore African families asunder, and he urged sympathy toward those who had fallen in battle to maintain their freedom. Members were reminded that they enjoyed health, family, and freedom, but that this could change suddenly. As a Christian minister, Hall turned to God and the Bible. Moses was advised by his father-in-law, Jethro the Ethiopian, to choose leaders who were men of God and truthful. He urged his listeners to pray to God for patience and strength to bear their troubles. Patience was needed to withstand the insults and mob attacks on the streets of Boston. It was better to be wronged than to do wrong, and Hall urged blacks to refrain from their own mob violence in retaliation. The minister told his listeners that though they were deprived of education they had minds, reasoning, and ability to think. He urged the new Masons "not to fear men but to fear God ... Respect for those that God put in places of power. Do just to those who hire you. Treat them with respect but not worship. God will defend us against our enemies. Live, act and die as Masons. Put not your hand to Masons of any color." Following Prince Hall's lead in Boston, a new black lodge of Masons was started in Philadelphia (1797), with Absolam Jones as its master and Richard Allen as its treasurer. The same year, Hiram Lodge number 3 was founded in Rhode Island for members of the Boston lodge who lived in Providence.[42] The Masons were pioneers, and other black fraternal organizations followed. The Odd Fellows, like the Masons, had to receive their charter from England.

Black churches were vital parts of the freedman's world. They were used for worship and as social centers, meeting places, school houses, and temporary hiding places for escaped slaves. When colonial laws assured slave owners that baptism of their slaves did not bring freedom, they accepted Christianity for their bondsmen. Large plantations had black churches with slave or itinerant and black preachers. These churches served the master's purposes, because slaves could be taught subservience and honor to those that "God placed over them." Services were supervised by a white, usually the overseer, to stop the propagation of unwanted ideas. Generally, these congregations accepted the religion of their owners, usually Anglican, later Episcopalian. However, the Baptist church made inroads, particularly during the

Revolution.[43] George Liele founded the Baptist church of Savannah in 1779. Liele was a Loyalist and fled to Jamaica after the war, and so his authority was shifted to Andrew Bryan's shoulders. Under Bryan's leadership, the Savannah church became the nucleus of the Negro Baptist churches of Georgia. This branch of Protestantism spread to the larger cities of Virginia and South Carolina during and after the Revolution and eventually to the North.

In the North, blacks could pray in white churches, but they were kept isolated from the other parishioners. The first all-black church in the North was founded by Absolam Jones, and it was an outgrowth of the Free African Society of Philadelphia. The society raised funds from its members and from sympathetic whites (Benjamin Rush, Ben Franklin, George Washington, and Thomas Jefferson). The required amount of money was reached in two years, and the Saint Thomas Protestant Episcopal Church of Philadelphia was completed in 1791. The African Methodist Episcopal Church (Bethel), founded by Richard Allen, was established following an insult to black worshippers at the Saint George Methodist Episcopal Church in Philadelphia.[44] While on their knees, the blacks were lifted bodily from the "white area." They left the church, and in 1786 they started a black church that was completed in 1799. African Methodist Episcopal churches were then started in Baltimore and Wilmington, and in communities in Pennsylvania and New Jersey. By 1816, these churches were bound into a formal organization with a black bishop (Daniel Coker followed by Allen). Four years later, Philadelphia could claim 7,000 black communicants in the African Methodist Episcopal Church. The blacks in New York followed their Philadelphia counterparts and withdrew from the white Saint John Methodist Church to establish the African Methodist Episcopal Zion church (1796).

Most black parents recognized the importance of education to carry them to a higher socioeconomic level. Their access to education, however, was severely restricted. There were almost no public schools open to black children in the eighteenth century.[45] In Maine black pupils could attend public schools. They were excluded, though, in Connecticut. Massachusetts permitted each community to regulate the presence of black children in its schools. In Boston, black children left integrated schools because of abuse. In 1787 and again in 1796 black parents, under Prince Hall's leadership, petitioned the legislature and the Boston selectmen for black schools, but this was denied. So the freedmen formed the Africa School in 1798 in the home of Primus Hall. The children were taught by two Harvard students hired by the families. Some years later, Elisha Sylvester, a white, taught classes in the basement of the African Baptist Church. This school received a grant in a will left by Abiel Smith (white), and it became the Smith School. Later, the school received $200 annually from the city, and each parent paid 12½ cents per week per child.[46] In 1820 Boston opened the first all-black primary public school.

In Philadelphia, prior to public education, poor children attended private schools and were reimbursed from funds taken from the school tax. Black children did not attend these schools, however. The Quakers started a school for black children in 1774. After the war, the movement grew with bequests from philanthropists, and before the end of the century, there were seven such black schools. Philadelphia opened public schools for poor white children in 1818; four years later, black children were afforded this opportunity. In New York State, black parents refused to send their children to mixed schools because of the abuse heaped on the children. The New York Society for Promoting Manumission of Slaves established the African Free School in 1787. The school was initially supported by the parent society plus student fees. These failed to cover expenses, and so in 1813 the state ordered that the school receive funds from public school taxes. Seven years later the school could boast an enrollment of more than 500 black pupils. There was private schooling available to black children in New Jersey in 1777. Burlington, Salem, and Trenton had such schools taught by Quakers. The Abolition Society of Wilmington held school for black children the first day of each week; later, a true school, a library, a black teacher, and a black women's academy were added. Education for blacks in the South was limited to a few larger urban areas. However, the slave rebellion of 1800 stopped most education for black children.[47] The ability to gain an education in the north could produce a John Russwurm—the first black college graduate (Bowdoin, Maine, 1826). Russwirm went on to greater things. With Samuel Cornish, he established *Freedom's Journal*, the first black newspaper, in 1827. He later went to Liberia and became governor of the Maryland colony.[48]

Until the recent past, a minority group in a country strove for acceptance by the majority; they had to show the "others" that they were worthwhile members of society. The Herculean work performed by the blacks of Philadelphia during the yellow fever epidemic of 1793 was a case in point. The disease ravaged society. President Washington and the federal government, the state, and most city officials left the stricken community. Those who could afford it used any means of conveyance to leave death behind. When the sickness struck a household, husbands left wives, wives left husbands, parents left children, and children left parents to die without the basics of civilized care. Those who became sick on the road were left to die where they fell. Banks were left untended, and city services ground to a halt. This was probably similar to what happened to society during the bubonic plague of the Middle Ages. It was believed, thanks to Dr. Benjamin Rush and other medical luminaries, that blacks were immune to the disease. (Blacks who grew up in Africa developed a mild illness as children, which gave them lifelong immunity. Those born in the United States were as susceptible to the disease as anyone else.) The black inhabitants of the city, for the most part too poor to leave, did the work that a civilized society expects of its citizens.

They charged for their services and were taken to task by Matthew Carey. Absolam Jones and Richard Allen, leaders of the black community, refuted his attack. They claimed that the blacks were solicited by the newspapers to act as nurses and to work in burial details because they were "immune" to this disease. Blacks joined in groups to visit the sick. Delegations met with the mayor, one of the few officials who stayed in Philadelphia, to determine how best to be of service. Blacks advertised in newspapers that they would bury the dead and procure nurses for the sick. Originally they asked no pay, but the work soon became arduous. Two-thirds of the volunteers at the Bush Hill Hospital were black. Others became "doctors"; under Dr. Rush's tutelage, they learned where to get medicine and how and when to deliver it. They also learned to bleed patients, the foundation of Dr. Rush's therapy. Those who removed the dead left their remuneration to the bereft family. Often they paid out of pocket for coffins. The writers, Absolam Jones and Richard Allen, believed that the black community paid out £177 more than it received; they also lost daily wages for 70 days without recompense.[49]

Black people buried several hundred poor as well as strangers. Black leaders hired others to work as nurses and paid them $6 a week from their own funds. Many of these nurses were hired away for $2 to $4 per day. The organizers had no control over this group. White workers extorted higher wages from the victims than did the blacks. There were only two black women attendants at the Bush Hill Hospital during the period when patients were not cared for, and nurses used the provisions for themselves. When this condition was ameliorated, those black women were kept on, but the whites were discharged. Poor blacks showed more humanity than did poor whites. Some blacks rendered service until they fell sick and died. Those they served did not look after the families these nurses left behind. There were as many whites as blacks who pilfered, but black nurses outnumbered whites by 20 to 1. Blacks were accused of poor nursing, but they were pushed to care for patients night and day without rest and were not able to provide proper care in all cases. When black nurses became sick, they frequently were turned out of the house where they had served. Blacks were believed not to contract the disease, but bills of mortality showed that black deaths were proportionate to their numbers in the population. In 1792, before the epidemic, 67 blacks died; in 1793, the year of the epidemic, 305 died. Blacks bled 800 people during the epidemic, but they did not receive the usual fee of $1.50. They cared for orphans and carried them to orphanages. Rumors spread that blacks stole between 100 and 200 beds from houses of the dead. Anyone who witnessed this outrage was asked to bring the guilty party in for punishment so the innocent would be cleared. As expected, the rebuttal of Jones and Allen to Matthew Carey fell on deaf ears. In their refutation of the charges, the authors showed that they accepted the racist concept that black was bad: "We wish not to offend, but where an unprovoked attempt is made to make us blacker than we are...."[50]

Throughout history there have been individuals who rose above all manner of repression to reach a pinnacle. These individuals became beacons to others of their group. In colonial America, many blacks, often born into slavery, could be elected into this group. In the Southern colonies, laws prohibited slaves from learning to read and write. Some masters disregarded these statutes, however, and they surreptitiously taught their favorites the basics. It was in the more lenient North that blacks could learn to read and write and express themselves in literature. Jupiter Harmon, a slave in a Long Island family, produced poetry of a religious nature. In 1761 he published "An Evening Thought Salvation by Christ with Penitential Cries." He also wrote a later poem to Phyllis Wheatley (1778).[51] Unhappily, he also preached the master's belief that blacks had to bear slavery until they were freed in heaven.

Phyllis Wheatley was taken as a child from Africa. She was a slave of the Wheatleys of Boston, who gave her a liberal education followed by manumission. Phyllis was sent to London for her health, and there she published *Poems on Various Subjects, Religious and Moral* in 1773. The book was reviewed in England, and all reviewers were positive in their critiques. They were impressed with her knowledge of mythology and literature as well as her piety, with some writing that there was a need for new views about blacks' mental ability. The book was not considered a work of genius, but they were impressed that Phyllis had been introduced to the English language only 16 months earlier. It was a belief commonly held in England that "people born closer to the sun" were dull compared with those raised in cooler climates. Wheatley's work caused many Englishmen to take a second look at Africans. After her return to America, Phyllis produced "His Excellency, General Washington," "Liberty and Peace," and other poems.[52]

Gustavus Vassa, taken from Africa at 11 years of age, was a slave in Virginia, then belonged to a British naval officer, and finally to a Philadelphia merchant from whom he bought his freedom. In the safe haven provided by a more accepting England, he attacked Christians for enslaving blacks in *The Interesting Narrative of the Life of Oboudah Equiano or Gustavus Vassa.*[53]

In a period when blacks were thought not to have the capacity for higher math (Jefferson), Benjamin Banneker was accepted as an eminent mathematician and astronomer. He was born free and learned to read from the Bible through the help of his grandmother, Mollee Welch. He received more formal training in a mixed school in Maryland taught by a white teacher. Early in life, Banneker developed a keen interest in math, and his ability in this field was recognized by many scholars. At age 30, he built a clock, parts of which were wood and were carved with a penknife. This attracted the attention of George Elliott, a Quaker, who was a mathematician and astronomer; he loaned instruments and books on astronomy to his new friend. The science of astronomy found an eager student in Banneker, and he was able to predict a solar eclipse in 1789. At the age of 61, in 1792, he produced his first almanac, which was published in Baltimore. Banneker, like many liberated blacks, smarted under the assumption that blacks were inferior to whites in the arts and sciences. He sent a copy of his work to Thomas Jefferson, secretary of state to George Washington. Jefferson responded to this communication with his own letter, which stated that he was pleased that nature had endowed blacks with talents equal to those of others; this appearance of lack of talent was due to the degraded condition in which they were kept in Africa and America. As a result of Jefferson's urgings, Banneker was appointed a member of the group led by Major Pierre Charles L'Enfant, the French architect and engineer who laid out Washington, D.C. After completing this work, he returned home to work on his almanacs. It was said that the only serious mistake he made in mathematics was the prediction of the time of his death: he lived eight years longer than his calculations had suggested and died in 1806.[54]

Despite the achievements of people like Banneker, many whites, often with superior educations, could not give up their ingrained attitudes about black inferiority. Sir Augustus John Foster, in his *Notes on the United States, 1804–1812*, discussed Banneker's abilities to solve difficult mathematical problems and produce an almanac, but in other respects he "appeared to little advantage"; his letters were "childish and trivial." Blacks had little foresight. Their mental qualities were "as inferior to the rest of mankind as a mule to a horse." He thought that little good could come from their emancipation.[55]

Paul Cuffee of Massachusetts could have been a model for Horatio Alger.[56] He was the free son of an African native who had bought his own freedom and married an Indian girl. He had no formal education, but he taught himself arithmetic and navigation at home. Cuffee developed enough skill in navigation to plot trips to England, Russia, and Africa later in life. At 16, he signed on with a whaler as a common seaman. During one voyage, while hostilities with England were high, his ship was captured by the British. Cuffee was freed after three months, however, and returned to farming. He also built an open boat to trade with the shoreline communities in Connecticut, but this venture was a failure. His second boat was seized by pirates. Cuffee then joined his brother in a boat-building venture, which was successful after the Revolution ended. The brothers continued to build larger boats, and Cuffee took one on a whaling expedition. The oil and bones were sold in Philadelphia, and the profit was used for building larger ships. In 1795 the brothers built the 69-ton *Ranger*, then the 162-ton *Hero* (1800), and the *Alpha* of 268 tons (1806). At this time, Paul Cuffee owned one ship, two brigs, several smaller vessels, and property in houses and land. Like his father, Paul married an Indian girl and raised a family in Westport, Connecticut. The community had no school, and Cuffee tried, with no success, to get his neighbors to build one. He then built a school on his own property at his own expense and offered it to the community. Cuffee was instrumental in establishing, and was also a major contributor to, a Quaker meeting house in 1813. The entrepreneur was active politically as well. In 1780 he and a group of freedmen petitioned the General Court of Massachusetts (the legislature), claiming that, as taxpayers, they should have the right to vote. This petition was acted upon favorably by the next meeting of the legislature.

Cuffee is remembered primarily for his involvement in colonization.[57] He learned about the Sierra Leone colony and sailed there with a cargo of material he believed the settlers could use. With firsthand information about the potential of the colony, he returned to the United States in 1812. War with England had broken out, and he carried a British cargo. His ship, *The Traveller*, was confiscated, but it was returned after a direct appeal to President James Madison. After the war, Cuffee carried 38 passengers along with a cargo of tobacco, soap, candles, flour, iron for a sawmill, a wagon to be used to carry material overland (rather than on people's heads), grindstones, nails, glass, and a plow. Cuffee's personal expense for carrying the passengers was more than $4,000. He returned to the United States in 1816, just before the organization of the American Colonization Society, which turned to him for advice on encouraging American blacks to return to Africa. He spoke to conferences of black and white audiences in the larger cities of the country. The society distributed propaganda supposedly by American blacks in Sierra Leone. It was "a land of Canaan, abounding in honey and fruits, fish and oysters, wild fowl and wild pigs. The only thing that Africa wants is the knowledge of God—fear not to come, if the Lord will." Cuffee died on July 27, 1817, before he could carry other emigrants to Africa.

The organization and growth of black churches produced a group of ministers who became leaders of their people. Prince Hall, the Mason, was the minister of an African Methodist Episcopal Church in Cambridge. Lemuel Haynes, the offspring of an interracial couple, received formal and informal training in theology. As a Congregational minister, he had white congregations in Connecticut and Vermont. Richard Allen was born a slave in Philadelphia and was sold to a family in Delaware. In 1777 he had a "religious conversion" perhaps related to the breakup of his family when they were sold away to satisfy his owner's debts; he joined the "Methodist Society." Allen and his brother bought themselves out of slavery for £60 in gold and silver. The debt was finally paid in 1783. After the war, he preached in New Jersey, Pennsylvania, Delaware, and Maryland for three years. He eventually moved to Philadelphia, where he founded and became bishop of the African Methodist Episcopal Church.[58] Absolam Jones, born in Delaware, was founder of the Negro Protestant Episcopal Churches. George Liele, Andrew Bryan, Morris Brown, James Vareck, Daniel Coker, and John Chavis were other leaders of the independent black church movement.[59]

When given a reasonably "flat playing field," many blacks were able to strike out in several directions, and some warrant mention. Jean Baptiste

Pointe Sable, an explorer, built a trading post in 1765 which grew into the city of Chicago.[60] James Derbon, born a slave, was sold to several physicians and finally ended as a slave to a New Orleans physician. His owner taught him French and Spanish and how to prepare drugs. He also assisted the physician and learned the trade (the most common way of training doctors at the time). Derbon bought his freedom and set up a practice in New Orleans that produced about $3,000 per year. He received a "stamp of approval" from Benjamin Rush, who interviewed him and found him to be "very knowledgeable." Finally, in the business world there was James Forten, born free in Philadelphia. He served in the navy during the Revolution and was captured and then exchanged by the British. After the war, he was apprenticed as a sailmaker. Forten eventually owned his own sailmaking loft and left an estate valued at $100,000.[61]

Chapter 9

COLONIZATION

Colonization, even when seen as a great humanitarian effort, was racist. The Southerners who backed the idea were more honest than their Northern countrymen—they wanted to get rid of their free blacks. In their eyes, this group represented a nucleus of conspirators ready to inflame their slaves to rebellion. Freedmen were also seen as thieves, receivers of stolen property, "shiftless and no-account," and a burden to the economy. In the North, its supporters saw colonization as a way to "separate the races." The belief in colonization started early in the colonial period, but most of the active work occurred in the nineteenth century. As late as December 3, 1861, President Abraham Lincoln proposed, in his first annual address, that Congress adopt a plan for colonization. He thought suitable places might be the isthmus between the Americas, the Isla à Vache, Haiti, "somewhere in Texas, or a negro asylum in Florida."[1]

In 1714 a "Native American" (not an Indian) in New Jersey proposed sending blacks back to Africa; he would have been satisfied to send them "to some territory beyond the limits of continental America or to an unsettled area of our public lands."[2] The supporters of deportation worked for a century to gain support without too much success. They looked for support from religious groups, humanitarian societies, and state and federal governments. Most whites in continental North America abhorred the idea of racial integration; they worried about a "mongrelization of the white race."[3] The abolitionists looked to colonization as a means to avoid miscegenation. A newspaper in Philadelphia, the heart of abolitionist sentiment, urged Negro colonization. Anthony Bezenet, the Quaker abolitionist and teacher of blacks, wanted them colonized "west of the Allegheny Mountains along the Mississippi River." Thomas Jefferson urged removal to prevent the black "staining the blood of his master." In 1777 he urged freedom for newborn blacks, training them in a trade, and then shipping them out; they would remain under white protection until they could care for themselves. Jefferson suggested the West Indies as a place for blacks, under governments of their own color. Jefferson's protégé, James Madison, urged blacks' removal to Africa, for he believed that they could not live with whites. They could not be sent to the

West because "the savages" would destroy them; if they were settled too near to whites, a racial war would erupt. Madison, in his early thinking, urged emancipation and forced deportation. As he mellowed with age, he still urged colonization but without force.

The slave rebellion in 1800 gave greater impetus to the movement to get blacks out. Governor James Monroe of Virginia, in a letter to President Jefferson, urged the removal of "black conspirators"; he later included all freedmen. After leaving the presidency, Jefferson felt that colonization was "the most desirable measure which could be adopted for drawing off the black population. Nothing is more to be wished than that the United States should themselves undertake to make such an establishment on the coast of Africa." In his later years, Jefferson believed that Sierra Leone was the best place for blacks. He urged the U.S. minister to Great Britain to discuss the idea with the English government. Sierra Leone, however, was not willing to accept U.S. "conspirators," who were seen as troublemakers, so Jefferson turned to Santo Domingo and finally to the Louisiana territory. The Virginia assembly urged its representatives in Congress to push for "a black state in Louisiana." In 1787 the Negro Union of Newport, Rhode Island, suggested a return to Africa.[4] An anonymous writer in New Hampshire (1795), where slavery was prohibited in the state constitution, urged emancipation and dependence on whites until blacks could govern themselves; then they could be sent to Africa or the West. Eventually blacks could develop a state that would have a voice in Congress. In 1805 Thomas Branagan, a Quaker and ex-slavetrader, urged a separate black state in the Louisiana territory, "someplace 2000 miles away" from white America. Other abolitionists believed deportation could be used for financial gain. Francis Blair of Missouri preferred Central America, because blacks could "civilize" the area and develop commerce within the United States. Many, like Dr. Delany, feared that the advancing frontier and the expected annexation of Canada precluded settling blacks in the West or in Canada.[5] Churchmen like Samuel Hopkins, an early leader in the abolitionist movement, wanted to send blacks to Africa to Christianize that continent (1793).

After the dissipation of the terror inspired by the slave rebellion of 1800, the urge to get the blacks out was put on the back burner. Abolitionist activity subsided, while growing animosity toward England prevented joining that nation in a common venture; the Southern states also made manumission more difficult, which effectively dried up the pool of freedmen in the South. The idea did not die, however; it simmered quietly. The Union Humane Society of Ohio urged that the state of the Negro race be eased and that Negroes be removed beyond the reach of the white man.[6] The Kentucky Colonization Society petitioned Congress for a suitable territory to "be laid off as an asylum for all those negroes & mulattoes who have been, & those who may hereafter be, emancipated in the United States." The money to carry and support them would come from the federal government. Charles Fenten

Mercer introduced a bill in the Virginia legislature to ask the national government to find a territory in the north Pacific or Africa in which to settle free blacks and those afterward emancipated in Virginia. Samuel Mills, a missionary, stated, "We must save the negroes, or the negroes will ruin us." If Negroes could be removed, slaveholders would free their slaves. He believed an area could be set aside in Ohio, Indiana, or Illinois which blacks could colonize. Here they could be tested, and they could develop leaders; then they could be shipped to the far West or to Africa. The far West was cheaper, but Africa was better. Ships of war could be used to transport them, and they could provide protection for the new settlers. The deportees could start trade with the interior and make up the initial costs through this activity.[7]

Following the end of hostilities with England in the War of 1812, the idea of colonization began to percolate again. The western territorial boundaries of the rapidly expanding nation were settled, and Americans moved west. This removed the area as a potential resettlement site for freedmen, and so all eyes turned southeast. The leaders of the movement looked for guidance to Great Britain. After the American Revolution, England and its territory in Nova Scotia felt themselves "inundated" by American slaves. Those who successfully escaped into the British lines were taken with the British army when it evacuated the United States. In addition, Great Britain had a good number of black freedmen. Lord Chief Justice Holt decided that "as soon as a slave enters England, he becomes free." In the court case of *Somerset v. Stewart*, Lord Mansfield proclaimed, "The air of England has long been too pure for a slave and every man is free who breathes it." The case involved James Somerset, a slave of Charles Stewart of Jamaica. Stewart brought Somerset to England as his body servant. When it was time to return, the slave refused. He was put in chains on the *Ann and Mary*. Lord Mansfield granted a writ of *habeas corpus*, which forced the captain of the ship to produce Somerset. Mansfield referred the matter to the Full Court of the King's Bench on June 22, 1772; that court found for the black. The ruling was applied only to Great Britain and not to the Sugar Islands, a source of great wealth to the mother country.[8] The freedmen were not trained to earn a living in industrialized England, however, and they wandered the streets of the English cities begging and committing crimes in an attempt to support themselves. Whether English racism was reactivated by the sight of so many black faces on the streets, or whether a humanitarian movement started by Granville Sharp, Thomas Clarkson, William Wilberforce and Dr. Smeathman was responsible, the idea of resettlement in Africa surfaced.[9] The British government purchased two square miles from Naimbanne, king of Sierra Leone, in 1787. Four hundred blacks and 60 whites (predominantly prostitutes) were taken on the *Nautilus* to Sierra Leone on May 9, 1787. However, disease, indolence, and attacks by the natives killed off all but 64 of the pioneers. In 1791 the Sierra Leone Company raised £1.25 million for colonization. The following year, 100 Europeans, followed by 1,131 blacks, left for the colony. Again, disease and feuds decimated the population. Adding to their troubles, ships of the French navy attacked the colony in 1794. The population was later expanded by a shipment of 550 maroons from Jamaica and ex-slaves from Nova Scotia. (Maroons, short for *cimaroons*, were outlaw blacks who escaped their slave status on plantations in Jamaica. They eventually "formed a nation" in the mountains and attacked the English plantations. Great Britain was forced to sign a treaty of peace with them, and many volunteered to return to Africa.) By 1800 the funds that had been raised were almost gone, and there was nothing to show for the money. In 1807 Sierra Leone was formally annexed to Great Britain. The population was supplemented by slaves taken off trading vessels by the British navy after the trade was outlawed. With sanitation, order, and education, Sierra Leone became productive, and the population grew. Missionaries from the Anglican and Methodist churches brought Christianity to the inhabitants. By 1811 there were 1917 inhabitants, including white Europeans, blacks from Nova Scotia and Jamaica, and African natives. The land was fertile and produced sugar, coffee, cotton, indigo, rice, and Indian corn.[10]

Sierra Leone could also claim a few American freedmen among its citizenry, courtesy of Paul Cuffee of Massachusetts. As was discussed earlier, Cuffee was the Quaker son of an Indian mother and a slave father who had purchased his freedom. He was a sailor, a navigator, a very successful shipbuilder, and a tradesman.[11] Cuffee founded the Friendly Society of Sierra Leone to "open a channel of intercourse between Negro Americans and Sierra Leone" after his visit to Europe and Africa.[12] With his own funds, Cuffee made a second trip to Sierra Leone with 38 black passengers in several family groups, and he reported his observations on the new colony to the newly formed American Colonization Society. The black entrepreneur died before he could lead any more blacks to Africa.

The major players in the movement to remove blacks were initially in New Jersey and Virginia. The Reverend Robert Finley of the Princeton Theological Seminary and trustee of Princeton University activated the New Jersey Colonization Society. The New Jersey law of 1804 promised eventual freedom to black slaves in the state.[13] White New Jerseyans, however, felt they would be "swamped" by free blacks; they anticipated 20,000 new freedmen in their midst, and this gave impetus to colonization. The New Jersey Colonization Society faltered early in its life, but it was reorganized by Commodore Robert Stockton in 1824 with help from Theodore and John Frelinghuysen and Samuel Bayard. They received financial support from the Presbyterian and Dutch Reformed churches. Stockton acquired Cape Monseurado in Africa for their expected emigrants. There was no government financial support, though, and philanthropic donations dried up. The organization revived in 1838 under William Halsey.[14] At their meeting, members pledged between $1 and $50. The New Jersey legislature appropriated $1,000 for each of two years and $4,000 in 1855. With private pledges, the society was able to purchase the *Saluda* for transport, plus 160,000 acres of land in Africa. Between 1820 and 1853, 24 blacks volunteered to leave. The status of blacks in the North deteriorated by midcentury, and a group of 78 emigrated after 1853.

Virginia too had large numbers of free blacks. Following the Revolution, the spirit of universal liberty led some masters to free their bondsmen. However, the main source of new freedmen was the worn-out land. Landowners found slave labor to be unprofitable, and many freed their slaves. (Between 1800 and 1810, the number emancipated approached 30,000.) In 1800, 1808, 1811, 1813, and 1816, the Virginia legislature asked the governor to petition the president to find a place in Africa for this "deluge." In Richmond, Virginia in 1816 the American Society for Colonizing the Free People of Color of the United States was founded.[15] Bushrod Washington, a nephew of the first president and a Supreme Court justice, was elected president of the society. Henry Clay of Kentucky was one of its strongest organizers.[16] The goal of the organization was "to promote a plan for colonizing with the consent of the free people of color residing in our country, in Africa, or such other places, as congress shall deem most expedient. To effect this object, in cooperation with the federal government and such states as may adopt regulations upon the subject." The organization would have a president, 13 vice presidents, a secretary, a treasurer, a recorder, and a board of managers. Samuel Mills and Ebenezer Burgess were appointed to find a proper location for the deportees. The financial support of the organization came from private donations, particularly the churches—special services were held around July 4, 1817, to collect funds from their parishioners. The leaders of the organization believed that blacks could not achieve their fullest potential in the United States because of prejudice. The society would cause the gradual elimination of slavery, because the owner could manumit his slaves and send them out of the state. Other stated purposes included ridding the country of undesirable and dangerous blacks (those conspirators who precipitated slave revolts), Christianizing and "civilizing" Africa, and opening Africa to American trade, with Liberia as a commercial station to the interior. The group also wished to undermine the transatlantic slave trade, which still persisted.[17] These ideas were supported by every Protestant denomination in America. They were equally approved by the legislatures of Virginia, Maryland, Tennessee, Ohio, New Jersey, Connecticut, Rhode Island, Indiana, Vermont, Pennsylvania, Massachusetts, New York, and Delaware. Private and public figures supported the society's aims, and donations poured in.

The first meeting was held in Washington, D.C. Elias Caldwell was the principal speaker. He made the following statements: that free blacks had a demoralizing influence on civil institutions; that they could never be equal to whites in America; that they would be happy only in a district by themselves; that they could not be settled in America, because they would make common cause with the Indians and the border nations and give refuge to escaped slaves; that the climate of Africa was suitable to them and they could live more cheaply there; that they could spread Christianity; that they would stop the slave trade and deter slaveholders from purchasing more slaves.[18] The speaker urged the federal government as well as private philanthropists to support the organization's aims. With free passage and a homestead, no black would refuse to go. The society opened its doors to all citizens at a cost of $1 per year or $30 for life. (There were no black voices raised at the meetings, and there were few takers of this "beneficence" from their white countrymen.)

The Society of Free Men in Philadelphia met that year and condemned the project. Richard Allen and James Forten of Philadelphia protested the scheme as an outrage to the freedmen.[19] They saw it as a benefit to the slaveholders of the country. Free blacks would never leave, because the move would remove all hope of freedom for the slaves. Most blacks had no sympathy for the colonization society and no confidence in its leaders; it was considered the worst enemy against which the blacks had to contend. Freedmen believed that they should be raised to equal status with the whites of the country. Black leaders advised blacks to pray to God to go to heaven, but they could not wait for God to raise their status in this life—they had to do it themselves. All leaders saw education as the one true equalizing force in America. Other blacks refused to go because they considered themselves the first successful cultivators of the wilds of America. Colonization represented a return to perpetual bondage. Most blacks looked upon the society as racist and that its aims were to degrade and isolate them. However, some black leaders saw colonization as an opportunity to escape the repression of white America. Daniel Coker, who helped organize the African Methodist Episcopal Church, Lott Cary, a Baptist minister, and William Cornish, the minister of Bethel Church in Baltimore, favored the move early. John Russwirm, an educated black, initially opposed the idea, but he reconsidered and became a successful leader in Liberia.[20] Other educated blacks who recognized their second-class position in America decided to try for a new life. Abraham Camp in the Illinois territory wrote on July 13, 1818:

> I am a free man of colour, have a family and a large connection of free people of colour residing on the Wabash, who are all willing to leave America whenever the way shall be opened. We love this country & its liberties, if we could share an equal right in them; but our freedom is partial, & we have no hope that it will be otherwise here; therefore we had rather be gone, though we should suffer hunger and nakedness for years. Your honour may be assured that nothing shall be lacking on our part in complying with whatever provision shall be made by the United States, whether it be to go to Africa or some other place; we shall hold ourselves in readiness, praying that God (who made

men free in the beginning, and by his kind providence, has broken the yoke from every white American would inspire the heart of every fine son of liberty with zeal & pity, to open the door of freedom for us also).[21]

During the nineteenth century, there was considerable white migration from Europe to America. These newcomers, often well-trained artisans, displaced blacks in housing and jobs, and so more blacks opted to go. The Nat Turner rebellion brought more repression on blacks, and more begged to leave. The *James Perkins* carried 339 blacks from the county of Southampton, Virginia. In 1832 six vessels of emigrants left the United States. Maryland voted $200,000 to export blacks; Kentucky voted a substantial amount for the same purpose. Between 1820 and 1830, 1,430 emigrated. In 1832, 1,037 left.

Samuel Mills and Ebenezer Burgess in 1818 found a "favorable" site in Africa. In 1820 the *Elizabeth* carried two agents of the Colonization Society, two government representatives, and a small group of blacks to Sherbro Island. Fever caused them to abandon this site, though. In 1821 a group led by Eli Ayers (from the society) and Captain R.F. Stockton (representing the navy) went to Sierra Leone to await the purchase of a site for settlement. They purchased Montserada, between the Montserada and Junk Rivers south of Sierra Leone.[22] But the local tribes refused to acknowledge their possession, and the settlers were taken to Perseverance Island while a new contract was made with King George (an African). Section 4 of the land contract stated:

> The American Colonization Society shall have the right, in consideration of 500 bars of tobacco, three barrels of rum, five casks of gun powder, five pieces of long heft, five boxes of pipes, 10 guns, five umbrellas, 10 iron pots & 10 pairs of shoes, the immediate possession of the tract of unoccupied lands bounded toward the west by Stockton Creek & on the north by St. Paul's River.[23]

This same year saw the founding of Monrovia, the capital of the colony. An additional tract, the Sester Territory, was perpetually leased to the society on October 27, 1825, by King Freeman for one hogshead of tobacco, one puncheon (a large cask) of rum, and six boxes of pipes, to be paid for and delivered annually.

The original group of colonists were followed by a large number from Maryland under the Reverend Yehudi Ashmun. They built houses and forts, and they were able to control the local tribes. After external forces were controlled, internal quarrels developed. These too were settled. During this period of early settlement, the Colonization Society in the United States trained future settlers in government participation, so that they could take responsibility rapidly. A constitution, written by Professor Greenleaf of Harvard in 1824, called for one white man, the agent, to be administrator. The blacks would vote for their potential leaders, and from this pool, the agent would choose men who would become their actual leaders. Ultimate control would still reside with the board of managers in the United States. It was expected that the colonists would gradually assume complete control of their own affairs. In 1829 male suffrage elected the officers, but the agent still had veto power. A legislature, formed in 1832, could override the agent's veto. Twenty-three years after the first constitution was adopted, constitution for the independent Republic of Liberia was ratified. It called for separation of church and state, and prohibition of slavery, stating that only Negroes could be citizens, and that no citizen could be involved in slave trading inside or outside of the state.[24] The U.S. government paid part of the agent's salary, supplied arms, underwrote the cost of fortifications, and hired and paid for a physician. With the development of a stable government and society, there was some prosperity, and trade increased.

In its formative years, the colony could not support itself, and more funds were required to keep it functioning. Membership dues, which came from America, France, and England, and from private philanthropists, legacies, and state appropriations, were never enough. The federal government, while interested in the concept, did not adequately support the colony financially in its early years. Henry Clay believed that it would cost $1,040,000 plus 65,000 tons of shipping to send adequate numbers of colonists and support them until they became self-sufficient.[25] He introduced a bill in Congress in 1833 to raise funds from the sale of public lands, with the money being turned over to the states. These funds would be used for education and internal improvements and to help the states to encourage emigration. The bill was vetoed, however, by President Andrew Jackson. The expenses of the society continued to mount, and it found itself in deep debt. The society tried to cover the costs of a physician, the agent, treatment of the settlers for new diseases in their new country, support of colonists who waited on docks for shipping, as well as the cost of shipping, support of public schools in Africa, maintenance of roads and buildings, presents to the native kings, fortifications; purchase of more land for the expected influx of freedmen; and the building of courthouses and jails. In the United States, the agents who scoured the country looking for money had to be supported as well (annual salaries were between $250 and $350). A new family in Africa received a comfortable cottage similar to native structures, plus $50 to sustain itself until it was self-sufficient. After 12 months, the emigrant was expected to help newcomers with house building. Material was purchased from local traders for which drafts on the society were signed. Other expenses included teaching young people to become the colony's doctors and dentists, freight haulers, and the charter of additional vessels. To these expenses was added the cost of buying food after the first rice crop failed—the local merchants were willing to sell food but at inflated prices. Food was also sent from America, but much of it was consumed on the long voyage by passengers, crew, and vermin. Between 1817 and 1836, 3,415 emigrants were settled at a cost of $332,586.28.

The financial structure of the colonization society called for the core group in Washington to handle administration and direct activities of the settlers while the auxiliaries in the states supplied the funds. But local auxiliaries expressed their discomfort with this concept and took independent action. Maryland, where 25 percent of the blacks were free, became the leader in the independent movement. Its lead was followed by New York, Pennsylvania, Mississippi, and Louisiana. The Maryland auxiliaries formed an independent group, and in 1827 they successfully lobbied the state legislature to raise $1,000 per year to transport Maryland blacks. The state rescinded this allotment in 1829, because only 12 blacks were settled in 1828. The local auxiliaries then joined formally and became the Maryland State Colonization Society in 1831 in Baltimore. They believed they could raise more money in Maryland if they could show potential philanthropists that their money would only be used for the transport of Maryland blacks. Before founding its own colony, the national organization accepted Maryland blacks for $20 per head to cover their expenses in the settlement. Paid agents of the Maryland Society raised funds, addressed meetings of blacks to encourage emigration, hired places on vessels and formed colonies for their new life in Africa. Thirty-one blacks left on the Orion; most of them were rural people who had not been exposed to their own leaders.

In 1831 the state legislature passed a statute to finance colonization — this was probably a result of Nat Turner's revolt in neighboring Virginia. The state pledged $20,000 the first year and $10,000 for each subsequent year. The board of managers of the fund was notified when a slave was manumitted: the new freedman was contacted and urged to emigrate. If he refused this "beneficence," the board notified the county sheriff, who arrested him and forcibly sent him out of Maryland. In 1832, 144 left Maryland for Liberia. The emigrants sent reports back about improper treatment at the site of the national group, however, and so the society decided to set up a new colony for Marylanders.

In 1833 Cape Palmas was chosen as the site of settlement, which was 300 miles south of Monrovia. The colony was initially 20 square miles in area. In two years, the society held deeds for 800 square miles in the domains of nine kings. The Maryland Society sent its first group to the new colony with a prepared constitution and bill of rights. All males declared their support for the document and swore off alcohol. No slavery was permitted. A governor was appointed by the Maryland Society, but other officials were elected locally. The colony was to be predominantly agricultural. Dr. James Hall, the first governor, along with his assistant, the Reverend John Herseltz, and 19 emigrants, sailed on the Ann in 1833. They tried to entice Marylanders in Liberia to join the new colony, and 34 came over. Land was purchased from African kings for the site. In 1837 there were 200 settlers with a black governor, John Brown Russwirm. Russwirm was also publisher of the Liberia Herald, founded in 1830.[26]

Lack of funds forced the Maryland Society to send agents to the Northern states to raise additional money. This source was limited, because Northern abolitionists scorned the Maryland Society as a tool of slaveholders. In addition, they had their own blacks who could be shipped out. Maryland agreed to accept out-of-state freedmen if they were paid for by donations from these areas (115 emigrants were supplied by Virginia and Georgia). New emigrants received furniture, tools, and six months of support until they were acclimated. A male received five acres of land within the town limits and as much land out of town as he could cultivate. In 1858, 1,250 blacks left for the colony. Many slaves in Maryland were promised manumission if they left; they refused, though, because they believed it was a ploy to sell them to Georgia. In the years of its greatest activity (1831–59), the society raised $45,385 from private donations and $255,703 from the state. After 1858 Maryland lowered its support to $5,000 per year. In 1854 Maryland in Liberia was proclaimed an independent nation. A war with the natives broke out two years later. The Republic of Liberia sent help, and they defeated the local tribes. The Maryland nation then joined Liberia as the Maryland county of the Republic of Liberia.[27]

Maryland's lead was followed by the New York Colonization Society, joined by the Young Men's Colonization Society of Pennsylvania. They set up a combined Quaker temperance colony at Bossa Cove along the Saint John's River in 1835. Twenty-six black artisans emigrated, and eventually a total of 126 were sent. All of these separate areas would later form the nation of Liberia. They were attacked by native chiefs, but true to their Quaker beliefs, they refused to fight. Eighteen were killed, and all the houses were destroyed; the survivors fled the colony.[28] The Mississippi Society formed the colony of Mississippi in Liberia 130 miles southeast of Monrovia. The town of New Georgia was founded five miles south of Monrovia; its citizens were slaves taken off captured slavers. This became an agricultural area. The community accepted Christianity brought by Methodists and Baptists.[29] North Carolina supplied 1,200 ex-slaves. Many of these were recruited when North Carolina changed its strict laws against manumission—slaves could now be freed in a last will of their master.[30] These ex-slaves were hired out to raise money for their transportation and were then shipped to Liberia. The colonies sponsored by the national and state associations eventually controlled 300 miles along the west coast of Africa, from Cape Palmas to Cape Mount. It was composed of six groups: Cape Palmas, Cape Mesurado, Cape Mount, River Junk, Bossa, and Sinon.[31] In 1847 Liberia became an independent unified republic, with Joseph Roberts its first president. As an independent entity, Liberia received more emigrants. The Fugitive Slave Act of 1850 prompted more emigration, which persisted until the Civil War.

What of the life and day-to-day activities of these deportees? Individual letters by the literate freedmen gave some insight into their problems and accomplishments. One ex-slave, Henry Harmon, aged 30, was emancipated by the Dorsey family of Anne Arundel County, Maryland. He left the United States in 1837 but maintained a relationship with this family by mail. In one letter, the freedman assured the white family that his health was good except for colds due to weather changes. There were five deaths in the Maryland Colony within one year; this was therefore not a "sickly place." They were at peace with the natives. Several of the original groups returned to America because they could not survive in Africa. Harmon believed that they could not survive because they would not work. All of Dorsey's ex-slaves were doing well, and they sent their love. Nicholas Jackson was a constable, and his son, Nicholas, had his own farm. Richard Donalson was a carpenter and was doing well. John Jackson was living with Governor Russwirm; his boys were apprenticed to a cabinetmaker.[32]

In a letter written two months later, Harmon described a change in his life that had brought on a bout of depression and homesickness. He asked all the members of the Dorsey family to write to him. Harmon asked for "meat of any kind, bacon, pork and fish." They had no "silver money" and could not purchase supplies from the ships in the harbor. He also requested wood planking for a floor in his house, which should cost $7 for 100 board feet, and a few pounds of nails. Harmon asked his Maryland correspondent to advise Harmon's family in Maryland that he was well and looked forward to their emigration that fall. In a letter in 1843, Harmon described how he had become a teacher at the Tubman school, at a settlement in the wilderness away from Cape Palmas. In addition to his teaching duties, he was also a justice of the peace and a captain of the Howard Volunteers (a militia of 60 men). Harmon also worked in a supply store. After eight years, things improved. He had a good supply of meat and bread, and he planned to build a larger house. Harmon never expected to see America again, because he enjoyed "perfect liberty" in Liberia. Other ex-slaves of the Dorseys were also prospering. Nicholas Jackson, Sr., had a store. Nicholas Jr. managed a store. Jonathan and Nelson Jackson were doing well as carpenters, but Richard Jackson failed in all of his undertakings. Jonathan was married and had his own home. The colony did not produce wheat, and they used rice to make their bread. Harmon described the process to his correspondents: "When we want bread, we beat rice in a mortar, sift it to produce a white flour, knead it and treat it like other bread. ... We have wild deer, hogs, goats and other animals to supply meat which we can get most, but not all the time." The Maryland family sent shoes, but Harmon asked them not to send larger coarse shoes, because it was too warm: "They burn and draw the feet." Harmon's wife requested some silk to make a dress. He did not know the cost of this item, so he would wait for the bill before sending the money. His wife wanted a blue or purple or any dark color but not black. Harmon acknowledged receipt of eight barrels of soap, but five went for the cost of shipping. He also received a barrel of pork and one of flour for the five in his family. Harmon requested that the Dorseys send him various garden seeds so that he could see which would grow in Africa. He also requested trading goods like tobacco and calico and particularly tin cups, which the natives desired most. He assured them that the new Liberians were at peace with the natives. Harmon was mentioned in a census of Liberians in 1852. He still taught school, had four children, and lived on a one-acre plot, where they raised potatoes, coffee, cotton, and fruit trees.[33]

The Liberian colonization concept was a failure if one considers the numbers of those who went compared with the available pool. From 1820 to 1833, 2,885 went to Africa. Of these, more than 2,700 were from the slave states, and two-thirds were manumitted to emigrate. From the beginning until 1852, 7,836 left America. Of these, 1,720 were born free, 204 purchased their own freedom, 3,868 were freed to leave for Liberia, and 1,044 were freed and sent by the federal government. Precise numbers of those who left American shores were not available. However, by midcentury, there were 434,495 freedmen and a total of about 2 million blacks in America; of these, fewer than 15,000 emigrated to Africa.[34] The Liberian colony received the most financial backing and caused the most interest in the white population. It was not the only place, though, to receive these deportees. There were four colonies in upper Canada for freedmen, supported by white philanthropists (Elgin, Wilberforce, Dawn, and Port Royal). There was a settlement in Mercer County, Ohio (Wattles). Except for Elgin, these colonies were not successful, because the leaders were dishonest and incompetent. The inhabitants feuded with each other, and the planners had grandiose schemes that could not be realized. Elgin, by contrast, had a competent leader in William King. The inhabitants considered these communities temporary. They looked south to avoid the Canadian winters, and they hoped to return when all blacks were emancipated in the United States.[35] Other blacks went to Haiti following an invitation from President Jean Pierre Boyer of that country. The British outlawed slavery in the West Indies in 1835, and the ex-slaves left the plantations. Free laborers were needed, and some American blacks emigrated to these islands, particularly Trinidad, which accepted several hundred in 1839 and 1840.

Chapter 10

OPPOSITION TO SLAVERY IN COLONIAL AMERICA

The movement to free slaves in colonial America was different from the activity in the decades before the Civil War. If one discounts the actions of the slaves themselves, there was little violent activity on the part of whites to bring about liberty and freedom for blacks. Colonial America did not produce a John Brown. The emancipation movement worked largely by pamphlet and petition. The incident closest to "taking the law into their own hands" involved the case of John Davis. Davis lived in an area that was claimed by Pennsylvania and Virginia. The Pennsylvania Gradual Emancipation Act of 1780 called for freedom of black children born after 1780, following a period of indenture. Slave owners were forced to register their slaves with the court clerk at $2 per head; if not registered, they were free. The dispute between Virginia and Pennsylvania was settled, and Pennsylvania gave slave owners in the disputed area an extension for registration until January 1, 1783. Davis lived in this area, but he did not register his slaves. He took his slave, John, to Virginia and hired him out to a Mr. Miller. Members of the Pennsylvania Abolition Society went to Virginia, found John, and brought him to Pennsylvania. Miller then hired three men to retrieve John. They were successful in 1788, and the slave was sold to a Virginian. Pennsylvania indicted the three men for kidnapping. Governor Thomas Mifflin of Pennsylvania wrote to Governor Beverley Randolph of Virginia to extradite the men; Randolph refused. The case reached President George Washington, who involved the attorney general and Congress. This resulted in a congressional statute in 1793 covering the extradition of fugitives and the rendition of slaves to their rightful owners. The case had an unhappy ending, though, for the three Virginians were not extradited, and John remained a slave and was lost to history.[1]

The people of the eighteenth century still respected private property. They knew that at some time in the past someone had paid for these unhappy humans. While they encouraged manumission as done freely by the owner, they also believed owners should be paid for their private property if they were less generous. There was no real "underground railway" to spirit private property away from the rightful owners. Finally, American scientific thinkers, like many of their European counterparts, believed that blacks were probably a lower subgroup of humans, and that they did not have the mental capacity to compete with whites in a free society. The solution to this problem was to ship freed blacks someplace else—the colonization concept.

It is universally accepted that the Quakers were in the forefront of the freedom movement, with the Methodists in second place. However, the Puritan ministers of New England early voiced their opposition to this inhumanity, and they stimulated others of the same mind to fight the institution. Throughout the eighteenth century preachers published pamphlets and letters and preached to their congregations on the inhumanity of slavery. Their actions were not completely altruistic, however. The economic foundation of the province of Massachusetts depended upon white indentured servants who would eventually become freeholders; the presence of black slaves would prevent white Englishmen from migrating. Also, there was the fear of miscegenation if there were not enough white men to "marry our daughters." Samuel Sewall, a merchant, churchman, magistrate, and judge, published *The Selling of Joseph* on June 24, 1700. Sewall was concerned about the growth of slavery in New England. At the time, most Puritans believed that blacks bore the "curse of Cain," and that slavery was their atonement. Sewall pointed out that liberty was second only to life. No one could deprive others of this God-given right. All men were the sons of Adam and had an equal right to liberty and the comforts of life. All people were the offspring of God and were of one blood. It was better for the welfare of the province to have white servants for a number of years than to have black servants for life. Blacks made unwilling servants because they desired liberty. They were so different from whites that "they can not embody with us. They can not remain in our body politic." Black men took up space and replaced white men who could marry the whites' daughters. Masters were tempted to fornicate with slaves rather than find white wives. The removal of slaves from Africa separated families that God had joined, and slave ships caused many deaths. Sewall denied that blacks were the posterity of Cain. He also denied that preaching the Gospel of Christ to them redeemed the concept of slavery. Evil could not be perpetrated to achieve good. Finally, Sewall placed his readers in the slave's situation. How would we feel if we were captured and made slaves?[2] (This condition developed later in the century when Barbary pirates made slaves of captured Christians.)

In 1716 a pamphlet of financial interest appeared in Boston entitled *Some Considerations Upon the Several Sorts of Banks Proposed as a Medium of Trade.* The author believed that slaves were a hindrance to populating and improving the country. Those who bought slaves were as guilty as those who stole them in Africa. He urged the passage of a law that would end slavery within 20 years. The pamphleteer also urged the political and financial leaders actively to bring white servants; they were to be given homes as well as 50–60 acres of land after completing their indenture. In 1733 the Reverend Elihu Coleman printed *Testimony Against the Anti-Christian Practice of Making Slaves of Men*.[3] The title adequately explained the text.

Samuel Hopkins was pastor of the First Congregational Church of Newport, Rhode Island, between 1770 and 1803. At this time, Newport was a major center of the slave trade. Hopkins witnessed the misery of blacks chained together and disembarking from the vile-smelling slave ships, and so he used his pulpit to attack the slave trade, as early as 1771. Within a year, he included the evil of slavery itself in his sermons. He also went from house to house to urge masters to liberate their slaves. Unhappily, he did not reach the rich traders and owners; his congregation was very poor, and it is unlikely that any of his parishioners owned slaves.[4] Hopkins had the opportunity to address the Continental Congress in Philadelphia in 1774. He reminded these leaders that the blacks "have an equal right to freedom." His text urged the members to secure "universal liberty to white and black." Blacks were "our brethren who have as good a right to liberty as ourselves, and to whom it is as sweet as it is to us, and the contrary as dreadful." Hopkins then urged the members to prohibit the slave trade and boycott all merchants who defied the order. The preacher went one step further in 1776, calling in his *Dialogue Concerning the Slavery of Africans*, for the abolition of slavery. He attacked the concept of black inferiority. Slavery was a transgression against Divine Law, and Americans were being punished for this by the British oppression. Hopkins tried to organize the clergy of New England against slavery. In 1784 his church was closed to slave owners, and in 1787 published in the *Providence Gazette* an essay against slavery. He warned against scourges descending on America if slavery continued. The Rhode Island Assembly, under Hopkins's influence, outlawed the slave trade by any of its citizens in 1787. Heavy fines accompanied this interdiction. Slave traders were fined £100 per slave and up to £1,000 for each ship in this nefarious trade. Rhode Island's slavers then moved to Connecticut, with Hopkins in hot pursuit. He urged Connecticut's clergy to petition their assembly to follow Rhode Island's lead. Toward the end of his life, Hopkins in 1801 formed the Missionary Society of Rhode Island to teach the Christian gospel to Africans in that state.[5]

Sewall and Hopkins were joined by other Congregational ministers who preached to their congregations about the barbarity of the slave trade and of slavery. The Reverend Isaac Stellman published *Beauties of Liberty* in 1772 in Boston, calling for the immediate abolition of slavery.[6] Harvard College, still predominantly a training school for Puritan ministers, questioned the legality of slavery at its commencement exercise in 1773.

The Germantown Quakers' protest against slavery in 1688 is credited as the start of open public protest against slavery in America. However, it was preceded by emancipation activity in both England and America. In 1657 George Fox, founder of the Society of Friends, asked American slave owners not to deny Africans the benefits of religious instruction. He journeyed to America and urged slave owners to free their bondsmen after a period of service; they were not to turn them out empty-handed at the completion of their servitude.[7] Fox was followed by a Philadelphia Quaker, George Finley, who urged William Penn to end slavery in the province. In 1682 Penn decreed that no slave could be sold or transported away after he had worked satisfactorily for one master for 14 years.

The Germantown protest, attributed to the Quakers, was actually produced by the Mennonites of that community.[8] A missive (1688) was sent to the yearly meeting of the Philadelphia Society of Friends. Francis Daniel Pastorius, its author, asked those attending the meeting if any of them would wish to be handled the way slaves were—sold as slaves for the rest of their lives. He compared the slave trade to that of the Turks, who captured Christians and sold them into slavery in Turkey. However, Americans were worse, because they were Christians. Blacks were captured and transported here against their will. One should do to others what one would have done to oneself. Those who bought men were the equal of those who stole them. There had to be liberty of body as well as of conscience. Slave owners committed adultery with their slaves and tore families apart by selling husband away from wife and children away from their parents. Christians in Europe would not wish to come to America if they knew of the involvement in slavery. (Some Quakers were involved in the slave trade at this time.) Stealing was wrong, and bringing stolen material (human bodies) to America was wrong. It was a duty to deliver the people out of the hands of these robbers. Slaves had as much right to fight for their freedom as whites had to keep them as slaves. Those who thought it was a good thing to handle slaves this way should let others know. Americans would let their brethren in their native countries learn of this attitude. Pastorius's ringing words retain their clarity over three centuries: "Here [in America] is liberty of conscience, which is right and reasonable here ought to be likewise liberty of the body.... Pray what thing in the world can be done worse towards us, that if men should rob or steal us away and sell us for slaves to strange countries, separating husbands from their wives and children."[9]

The activity started by Pastorius was continued by George Keith, who, in 1693 published *An Exhortation and Caution to Friends Concerning Buying or Keeping of Negroes.* The yearly meeting in 1696 advised Friends not to buy slaves except to free them. The Pennsylvania and New Jersey Quakers urged members not to import slaves and to introduce blacks to the Friends' religion by bringing them to meetings. In 1696 the yearly meeting in Philadelphia acted favorably on the Germantown protest. This action was followed two years later by Robert Pyle's address to the congregation:

> Sum time past theyre was sum inclination upon my mind to buy a negro, or negroes, by reason of my English servents being out of their times and having a great familie of small children, might be an help unto mee being for a tearm of life that I and my children might have ye more liberty, etc; but theyr arose a question in mee, ye lawfulness theyr of under ye Gospel minis-tration remembering the comment of Christ Jesus, Do unto all men as ye would have all men doe unto you; and we would not willingly be slaves tearm for life; also considering yet Christ divine for all mankind, they being a part, though yet ungathered. I also had heard that they, in theyr own country, did make war one with another, and sold one another for slaves, the sum being stolen from their country. Now, whether our buying of them do not encurredg rather than discurredg them in that wicked work/ I considered, also, that if all friends that are of ability should buy of them that is in this province, they being a people not subject to ye truth, nor yet likely so to bee; they might rise in rebellion and doe as much mischief; except we keep a malisha; which is against our principles, and if they should bee permitted to doe us harm, whether our blood will cry inocent whether it will not be said you might be left alone ... but if it bee not lawfull for to buy negroes for turm of life in this gospel time, what shall be done with these yet friends have already; whether they ought not to be larned to read english and to put them forward to goe to meetings, and endevors used to convinced them yet ye witness god might be reached in them, and whether every quarterly meeting should not have full powr to see yet Christian endevors bee used toward them that if possible they might bee prevailed upon, and if it should please ye lord to open theyr under-standing and bring them measurably to bee obedient to his hevenly Requir-ing why should not ye quarterly meetings bee proper judges in setting them free, provided ye marster bee not too much loss and ye servent have not been time enogh to answer his marster they be quarterly meeting may determine ye time wt. might be thought fit, that no loss might bee on neyther hand.[10]
>
> [Note: In Quaker religious services, there was no minister nor prepared pro-gram. The congregants sat quietly. If a congregant had a "visitation" that com-pelled him to address the assembly, he arose and spoke as the words came to him.]

Early in the eighteenth century, the fight was taken up by William Southeby, who denounced slavery and petitioned the Pennsylvania Assem-bly to end lifelong bondage. He published a vigorous antislavery pamphlet (1715) that was too strong for the staid Quaker leaders, and he was upbraided for his actions.[11] John Fanner, one year later, demanded complete liberation of slaves, and he was disowned by the Newport Friends. A significant mile-post in the battle of the Friends against slavery came with the work of John Woolman.[12] In 1743 he had to write a bill of sale for the purchase of a slave in New Jersey. This started him thinking about the evils of slavery, and he authored two pamphlets. In the first, in 1754, *Some Considerations on the Keep-ing of Negroes*, he claimed:

> All nations are one blood. We all spend a short time on earth & we are all subject to the same illnesses, infirmities, frailties, temptations, & death

judgment before God. We are all brothers. We sometimes get the feeling we are superior in mind & knowledge, then there is danger in our conduct toward them. They are of the same species. We are in a higher station with gifts from God. These gifts must be used to help the weak. If not, this shows ingratitude to God for these favors. God's love is universal, so man must open his heart to others. If we were in their place for generations, without the benefits of civilization, wouldn't we be like them? Constant oppression affects their behavior. If our property is taken from us, we can only love our oppressors through Divine Influence. There are differences in customs & manners among different peoples. This doesn't permit violence toward others. Missionaries to bring them knowledge of God is good, but taking them from their own land for profit is evil. If men are biased by narrow self love absolute power over others is unfit for them. Men govern other men & try to make them happier. Absolute command can only be in the hands of the perfect. Weak men who think they are perfect are unfit to govern. Calling someone a slave & keeping him in low estate, fixes the notion that they are lower than we. Then we lose our capacity to judge & govern. When we demand hard labor from others without pay, we become severe in our judgments of them & we brutalize them for criminal behavior. One evil leads to others & true Friends will feel concern on this account.[13]

Woolman's second pamphlet, written in 1762, claimed that the Scriptures called for manumission. Negroes were not inferior to whites; with education they could be equal to others. Labor was good if not performed to excess; slaves denied their masters the benefit of work. Woolman also discussed the racial nature of slavery. Most people associated blackness with slavery and whiteness with liberty. Woolman's writings had a strong effect on his coreligionists as well as on others, and his influence and ideas spread beyond the borders of New Jersey.

The Friends slowly moved from pamphlets to action. The yearly meetings actively opposed the slave trade. In 1761 the London yearly meeting disowned all members in the slave trade. The New York yearly meeting followed the London lead seven years later, and in 1770 they disowned all holders of slaves.[14] In 1769 the Rhode Island yearly meeting opposed slavery, and four years later they disowned slaveholders. By the end of the Revolution, no member above the Mason-Dixon line held slaves. By the end of the century, Southern meetings also voted to excommunicate all slaveholders.

Quakers are usually associated with Philadelphia; however, the tenets of their religion found fertile ground in the other areas as well. They preached the importance of an inner light, the minor importance of dogma and creed, the brotherhood of man, and belief in the possibility of completely cleansing oneself of sin. During the period of religious upheaval in America, many joined the Society of Friends, and meeting halls were founded in New England, the Mid-Atlantic colonies and parts of the South. An occasional hanging in Massachusetts may have hampered their spread temporarily, but Rhode Island, which early granted religious toleration, had active congregations. As early as 1717, a meeting in Rhode Island denounced the slave trade. After 1760, New England Quakers could not import slaves. In 1783, Friend Moses Brown of Providence petitioned the general assembly to abolish slavery and prohibit Rhode Islanders from participating in the slave trade. West New Jersey was an appendage of Philadelphia and generally followed Quaker rulings in that city. John Woolman influenced the Maryland Quakers with his pamphlets. The Maryland Quakers at their general meeting at Third Haven (1762) stated, "Friends should not in any way encourage the importation of negroes by buying or selling them, or other slaves." That year too the Friends at West River, Maryland, declared, "No member of our society should be concerned in importing or buying of negroes, nor selling any without the consent & approbation of the monthly meeting they belong to." The yearly meeting disowned slave owners in 1768. They also decided against passivity about this issue: one could not be appointed to the Station of Elders unless he actively spoke out against the institution. In 1773 the yearly meeting made itself responsible for the emancipation of all Quaker-owned slaves. The monthly meeting was to appoint a committee to speak to slave owners to urge them to manumit their bondsmen. Finally, in 1778, the yearly meeting called for the expulsion of all slave owners. Quakers could not hire slaves or work as overseers where slaves were employed. By 1790 there were no Quaker slave owners in Maryland.[15]

Delaware gave birth to the Nicholites, or "New Quakers." Joseph Nichols, a farmer near Dover, Delaware, began his ministry in the 1760s, before Woolman's influence spread to the region. Like the Quakers, the Nicholites had no paid ministers and no programmed worship service—they sat silently "until called upon to speak." They rejected war, oaths, and capital punishment. (In these ways they were almost identical to the Friends.) They also adopted the Quaker "monthly meeting for business" of church affairs. Nicholites preached against slavery, disowned members with slaves, refused to stay in houses where slave labor was used, and refused to hire slaves; some would not eat at the same table with slaveholders. They refused to purchase goods where slave labor was used. Nicholites refused to wear dyed garments, because slaves were used in the production of dyes. Blacks were accepted into the new religion, and a basic rule of the group was to help the freedman in his new life. The religion spread as far south as North Carolina before Nichols died. Following his demise, most Nicholites drifted back into the Quaker fold.[16]

The Friends did not make major inroads into Virginia, the center of Anglicanism in North America. South Carolina, and later Georgia, needed slaves to maintain the economy, so their inhabitants were not interested in manumitting their private property. North Carolina, with its diverse population, had active Quaker meeting houses. North Carolina also had strict laws against emancipation. However, the North Carolina yearly meeting in 1774 allowed and urged its members to free their slaves. They had to notify the monthly meeting beforehand, so that the slave's ability to earn a living as a freedman could be determined. No one was permitted to buy or sell a black without the consent of the monthly meeting. A year later, all Quakers were advised to free their slaves. Committees were organized to visit Quaker slave owners to help them "cleanse their hands." In 1777 the North Carolina Legislature repassed the 1741 law against manumission; sheriffs captured the freedmen and sold them at auction. To circumvent this edict, the Quakers kept ownership of their slaves but let them live as free men and benefit from their labor. In 1796 North Carolina passed a statute that allowed religious societies to appoint trustees to receive gifts on their behalf. Quakers "gave" their slaves to trustees appointed by the yearly meeting. These trustees hired the "slaves" out and distributed the money to them except for an amount to care for the young, old, and sick.[17] The year 1796 was important in the history of the North Carolina Quakers in their relationships with blacks: the yearly meeting declared that "blacks were completely equal to whites in the eyes of God, & all nations of men were of one blood." Early in the nineteenth century, Friends developed a kind of "underground railway": they smuggled illegally made freedmen to the new states of the Northwest Territory, where slavery was forbidden. The Quakers were very active in the colonization societies, and North Carolina Friends were able to send a group to Haiti. The Haitian president, Jean Pierre Boyer, promised American blacks that they would receive land, tools, provisions, and part of the cost of transportation. The Quakers sent 119 to Haiti, but many returned, for they could not be assimilated into a new culture and religion, and the work required to get started was excessive. Friends also sent freedmen to Canada and Africa. They were met with opposition when they tried to send some to Philadelphia—Philadelphia Quakers felt that there were already too many freedmen there.

The Friends did not believe emancipation was enough. They knew that these people who had been treated little better than farm animals could not function in a white society, and so they urged their members to prepare the potential freedmen with education and religious training. They pursued the belief in education after the slaves were freed. Anthony Bezenet established a Negro school in Philadelphia in 1759.[19] A free school for black children was proposed in Virginia in 1782 to "make them worthy capable citizens." Philadelphia Quakers formed the Philadelphia Society for Free Instruction of Colored People. Similar societies were formed in Baltimore, Providence, Newport, and Burlington, New Jersey.

After they had cleansed their coreligionists of the stain of slavery, the Quakers had to spread the word of freedom to other groups; they also had to attack the institution by legal means. The two-pronged attack was carried out by abolition societies, which propagandized their neighbors, and by petitions to legislatures to try to erode this evil practice. As early as 1700, the Friends in

Pennsylvania urged the legislature to stop the importation of slaves. The assembly placed a small duty on imported slaves, which was repealed by England. In 1712 a duty of £20 per black was passed in Pennsylvania, but this was lowered to £2 in 1729.[20] When free of English rule in 1780, the assembly abolished the importation of slaves and called for the gradual abolition of slavery in the state. The preamble to this statute stated, "It is the duty of Pennsylvanians to give substantial proof of their gratitude for deliverance from the oppression of Great Britain by extending freedom to those of a different color but the work of the same Almighty hand."[21] After the Revolution, many Northern states followed Pennsylvania's lead, pushed by the Friends and other sympathetic groups. In 1783 the Quakers of Rhode Island petitioned the general assembly to abolish slavery and prohibit Rhode Islanders from engaging in the trade. The assembly passed a mild bill that called for the gradual abolition of slavery. Rhode Islanders were permitted to remain in the trade provided they did not bring their black cargo to Rhode Island ports. The statute stated in part, "Those who are struggling for the preservation of their rights and liberties among which that of personal freedom is greatest must be willing to extend a like liberty to others."[22] Massachusetts's new constitution claimed that "all men are born free and equal." Unlike the Declaration of Independence, this document included blacks.[23] New Hampshire then followed Massachusetts's lead. New York State passed a manumission act in 1785, followed by New Jersey in 1786. New Jersey also forbade the importation of slaves that year. Connecticut and Rhode Island called for gradual abolition. In 1788 New York permitted masters to free slaves under the age of 50 without assuming financial responsibility for the new freedmen. Virginia in 1782 allowed masters to free slaves without the consent of the legislature. The Deep South refused to follow its Northern neighbors during this post–Revolutionary War spirit of general freedom and liberty, however. Quakers were advised to leave the Deep South or suffer the fate of whites in Santo Domingo (Haiti).[24] This warning, along with their distress about the immorality, illiteracy, irreligion, cruelty of slavery, violence, terrorism, and the militarism needed to keep blacks subjugated, forced many Quakers to give up this area as a lost cause.

The first of many manumission societies was founded in 1775 in Philadelphia. The Society for the Relief of Free Negroes Unlawfully Held in Bondage had its activities curtailed by the British occupation of the city, but it was revived in 1784. The Pennsylvania society encouraged the formation of other societies; sent petitions to Congress; publicized state laws concerning free blacks and slavery; printed and distributed antislavery literature; corresponded with emancipationists in England and France; and helped freedmen get started in their new life.[25] The preamble to the group's constitution (1787) stated its aims:

> All men are the same, made by God. We must promote each others happiness no matter how different we appear. Those who acknowledge the obligations of Christianity, have the greatest duty to use all means to bring

freedom to all members of the human race & especially to those who are entitled to freedom by any other constitutions of the United States, but are in
bondage, by fraud or violence. The members believe in the truth of these principles, desire to spread them, under favor of God, the group formed the Pennsylvania Society for Promoting the Abolition of Slavery, Relief of Free Negroes
Unlawfully Held in Bondage. s/Ben Franklin, President; James Pemberton
and Jonathan Penrose, Vice Presidents; Benjamin Rush, Treasurer[26]

New York followed Pennsylvania and formed the New York Society for
Promoting the Manumission of Slaves, with John Jay as its president. New
Jersey then followed New York. By 1790 Delaware, Connecticut, and Rhode
Island had similar societies. Maryland had three societies: the Maryland Society, the Chestertown Society, and the Choptank Society. The Maryland Society for the Abolition of Slavery in 1789 was largely organized by Maryland
Quakers.[27] They also organized the African Academy in Baltimore to teach
blacks to take their place in society. They faced ridicule, ostracism, and bodily harm in a slave-supported agrarian society. The Maryland Abolition Society successfully petitioned the state legislature to pass easier manumission
laws.[28] Slave owners could manumit slaves in their last will and testament. If
an estate was not in debt, the owner could free slaves below 50 years of age.
Free blacks or those about to be freed could not be shipped out of Maryland.
Masters were forced to care for sick and old slaves. The law also ended the
required 31 years of servitude for children of mixed marriages originally passed
in 1715 and 1728. The society urged the legislature to grant rights to free
blacks which were promised to Americans in the Declaration of Independence; here, the group was less successful. It filed lawsuits on behalf of blacks
for freedom, claiming to have been successful in obtaining freedom for 138
blacks. The group's constitution required members to "bear testimony against
slavery," spread truth abroad, and assist fellow abolitionists. No slaveholder
could be a member, although slave holders with "legal knowledge" could be
honorary counselors. Under the society's influence, the Maryland legislature
(1796) prohibited the import of slaves or the export of free blacks. However,
this same statute severely restricted blacks. They could not testify against
whites in freedom suits. Free blacks without a means of support had to provide security for their behavior or leave Maryland or be sold into servitude
for a set period. Free blacks could be prosecuted for lending slaves their freedom certificates. After ten years of good work, the society died suddenly in
1798.

The Choptank Society was organized in 1790 by Quakers, Nicholites,
and Methodists.[29] Like other groups, it petitioned Congress to abolish the
slave trade, and hired lawyers to threaten slave owners with legal action to
force them to free their bondsmen. These actions were based on the investigation of records to show that there was a free person in the slave's family
tree. The society taught blacks how to behave in white society, including the

attendance of worship services. Children were taught useful trades. Freedmen were urged to be truthful in their dealings; to refrain from alcohol, frolicking, or amusements; to observe the sacrament of legal marriage; to record births and deaths; to save some of their earnings; and to learn reading, writing, and arithmetic. The group also urged slave owners to free their property. The Chesterton Society had aims and projects similar to those of the Choptank Society, but both died out by the end of the century. Other societies formed and disintegrated early in the nineteenth century with goals of trying to correct perceived wrongs against blacks, whether free or slave.

By 1792 there were state and local antislavery societies from Massachusetts to Virginia. The first national convention met in Philadelphia in 1794. The convention urged the abolition of the slave trade and the purchase of slaves by philanthropists to free them; guaranteed to support the freedman if he became a charge of society; refused to buy material manufactured by slave labor; found jobs for freedmen; made certain employers did not take advantage of their black workers; and opened schools to educate black children and adults.[30] The delegates recognized the necessity for gradual abolition and published a plan to carry it out:

> The plan must ameliorate the condition of the master and the slave. The plan must allow the slave to rise in the scale of moral and intellectual improvement to lead to eventual enfranchisement. How to end slavery with the safety of the master and happiness of the slave? Immediate universal emancipation is not the answer. It would produce as much evil as it cures. The slave has been kept degraded and like a machine. To suddenly free him would be dangerous to him and to society. Emancipation must be gradual. He must first pass a state of pupillage which would lead to the enjoyment of liberty. The slave must be attached to the soil—give them an interest in the land they cultivate. Children of slaves must get schooling. Arbitrary punishment must be abolished. Prohibit the transport of a slave from one state to another. No slave is to be sold out of the county or town without his consent. Each slave with a family is to have his own hut and land to cultivate. He would pay the landlord rent. He is to be paid for each day he works for the master who subtracts what he provides in maintenance. The time a slave spends on his ground is deducted from his pay. There must be laws for their government. They would develop diligence and fidelity which would be rewarded, and negligence and crime would be chastised. This plan was tried by Joshua Steele in Barbados with excellent results. Three hundred debased negro men were advanced to honest industrious servants without the use of the whip and he tripled his income in a few years.[31]

Despite the fine plans of most of the societies, they gradually ossified, decayed, and fell apart.

The Methodists joined the Quakers in their opposition to slavery shortly before the Revolution. Methodist churchmen, with the exception of George Whitefield, opposed the institution. John Wesley, the founder of the denomination, in Thoughts of Slavery (1774) vigorously opposed lifetime bondage.[32]

In 1780 a conference in Baltimore took a strong antislavery position. Traveling preachers were forced to free their slaves. Three years later this order was extended to ministers with stable congregations; they had to obey or face suspension. Lay Methodists were prohibited from holding, using, or selling slaves or would face suspension. In 1784 all Methodist slave owners had to agree to free their slaves within one year. This edict created hostility in Virginia and the Deep South, and the ruling was rescinded for ten years. Methodist ministers like James Meacham referred to blacks as their brothers. James O'Kelly blamed black "shortcomings in character" on their environment, lack of training, and inability to enjoy the fruits of their labor.[33] Methodists tried to divest themselves of English racist attitudes toward blacks. They believed blacks could be taught to become proper members of society, and early in their history, blacks were welcomed into their congregations. In 1796 the Methodist General Conference decided that those with an official position in the church had to attend a lecture against slavery by their minister. Members were permitted to buy slaves if they agreed to free them and their offspring within a limited period of time. Those in the slave trade were excommunicated. The attitude of the church was expressed in 1800 in "The Address of the General Conference of the Methodist Episcopal Church to all their Brethren & Friends in the United States." It was signed by Bishops Coke, Asbury, and Whatcoat. The address "talked of the great national evil of negro slavery as being repugnant to the rights of mankind ... and to the spirit of the Christian religion ... that so large a proportion of the inhabitants of this country, who so truly boast of the liberty they enjoy, ... should continue to deprive of every trace of liberty so many of their fellow creatures equally capable with themselves of every social blessing & of external happiness."[34]

The bishops further urged each annual conference of the church to petition its state legislature on behalf of emancipation.

The Methodists were a splinter off the Anglican, later Episcopal Church. As such, they were English, and they looked for converts among the Anglicans, who were well entrenched in the South. It took courage to preach against slavery in the "birthplace of slavery," where society was supported by permanent bondage. Their efforts were sometimes met with stoning, as occurred in Charleston in 1788.[35] After the turn of the nineteenth century, Methodists, like the Quakers and other abolitionist groups, emigrated from the South, leaving only a few proponents of emancipation.

Revolutionary ardor encouraged ministers and laymen of other sects to voice their opposition to permanent bondage. The New England Congregationalists (Puritans) were joined by Presbyterians, Baptists, and Dunkers in condemning the institution. Preachers sermonized to their flocks claiming that the oppression visited on them by the English was in retribution for holding blacks in lifetime servitude.

The Quakers, of all the sects in America, were first and foremost in their opposition to slavery. Why are there not more African-American Quakers than the predominant Methodists and Baptists? Was it because Friends' services or meetings were quiet and plain and held in unadorned meeting houses (as were those of Congregationalists)? Was it a lack of structure in their meetings? Perhaps, but a more logical explanation was that the Quakers did not welcome black converts and tried to discourage them from applying for membership. Applicants who were "almost white" received more consideration for membership. In 1783 at a yearly meeting members decided that a monthly meeting might consider the application of a woman of white, Indian, and Negro origin "on the same ground in common with other applications for admission to membership." Far more explicit was Joseph Drinker's 1795 letter to his congregation in Philadelphia:

> Let prejudices prevail with them. So far on account of externals, & outward circumstances as to plead against those people being admitted into church fellowship with us, upon any terms whatever in direct opposition to our Fundamental Principles, viz—that God is no respecter of persons.... Christ died for all men.... He did not say there should be one fold for Black sheep & another fold for White sheep.... Now if we say one thing & practice another, shall we not be charged with hypocrisy.... Let us examine our own hearts & see if Pride is not the Bottom of those Prejudices so that some are ready to say to those poor despised Blacks, Stand off. I am more holy than thou art. There is no People in the World that I ever heard of who hold forth such Liberal Universal Principles as the People called Quakers, & yet to my astonishment they are the only People I know who make any objections to the Blacks or People of Color joining them in Church Fellowship.... All people should come & partake with us, that they might sit in Heavenly Places in Christ-Jesus.... This is ... the sincere desire of an obscure brother known by the name of Joseph Drinker. Philadelphia, 1st month 1795[36]

The Quakers, Methodists, Baptists, and Congregationalists attacked slavery because it was against God's laws. By searching the Bible, they could find material they could interpret to further their arguments (as could the proslavery Christians). However, there were men and women in America who attacked the institution because of conscience. Of the first four presidents, three were Virginian slaveholders, but all opposed slavery. Early in his life, George Washington would probably have been considered "upper middle class." He inherited some slaves from his half-brother, but he became rich following his marriage to Martha Custis. By law, all her property, inherited from her first husband, went to George, her second husband. Washington managed several plantations with more than 200 slaves. Early in his career, he was businesslike in his relations with his property, animate and inanimate. His slaves were cared for medically but not indulged. No slave was excused from work unless he had a fever. With the help of books, home remedies, and an overseer, he cared for routine illnesses. In the event of a medical problem beyond his ability, he called the physician who cared for his own family. When one of his retainers was bitten by a rabid dog, he sent the slave to a Pennsylvania physician for "definitive" care. This same Washington, however, bought and sold slaves and tried to recapture runaways. There were ads placed in local newspapers in no way different from others of those in his class trying to reclaim their property. He was not averse to selling recalcitrant slaves to the West Indies, where they were frequently worked to death. In a 1766 letter, Washington asked Captain John Thompson "to sell the negro Tom in any of the West Indies islands for what he will fetch. Bring in return one hogshead of molasses, one hogshead of rum, one barrel of limes if they are good & cheap, one 10 pound pot of tamarinds, two pots of mixed sweetmeats each five pounds. Anything left in 'good old spirits.' Tom is a rogue & a runaway. He is healthy, strong, & good at the hoe. He will sell well if kept clean & trimmed up a little before sale. You will get the regular commission. Keep him handcuffed till you are at sea."[37]

His will, probated in 1799, showed a completely different Washington. He stipulated that all of his slaves were to be freed after Martha's death. The old, young, and infirm were to be clothed and fed by his heirs for as long as they lived. Those who had no parents, or parents who did not wish to care for them, were to be bound by a court until they were 25; they were to be taught to read and write and to learn a useful occupation. None of his slaves, at the time of his death, were to be transported or sold out of Virginia. Washington gave immediate freedom to the mulatto William Lee, unless he preferred his present status (William was lame and incapable of employment). Lee, who served Washington during the Revolution, was given an annuity for life of $30, as well as food and clothes.[38]

What created this change in Washington during the 30 years between the letter and the will? Could it have been the Fairfax Resolves (Virginia 1774), which Washington had a hand in writing? The seventeenth resolution stated: "Resolved, that it is the opinion of this meeting, that during our present difficulties & distress, no slave ought to be imported into any British Colonies on this Continent; & we take this opportunity to declare our most earnest wishes to see an entire stop forever to such a wicked, cruel, & unnatural trade."[39] Could his motivation have been the very strong abolitionist sentiments of his "adopted" son, Lafayette? Or could it have been financial? Like most Southern planters, Washington was on the edge of bankruptcy. Most owed large sums to London merchants and slave traders. In the worn-out land of Virginia, slave labor was not financially successful. In a letter to Robert Lewis (1779), Washington claimed that he would not sell his supply of slaves because he opposed the sale of humans.[40] He also opposed hiring them out, because it would split up families. Washington claimed he was losing money, and the sale of land for $50,000 still would not keep him afloat.

During the Revolution, Lafayette, who replaced Benedict Arnold in Washington's affection, suggested to Washington that an area be purchased and slaves freed—they would become tenants on the land. Washington thought it was a "kind idea." After the successful conclusion of the war, Lafayette again discussed it with Washington (1783): "Let us unite in purchasing a small estate where we may try the experiment to free the negroes & use them only as tenants ... and if we succeed in America, I will cheerfully devote a part of my time to render the method fashionable in the West Indies. If it be a wild scheme, I had rather be mad in this way than to be thought wise in the other task." Washington never followed up on this idea. In a letter to Lafayette on May 10, 1786, he stated: "Would to God that a like spirit might diffuse itself generally in the minds of the people of this country. But I despair of seeing it. Some petitions were presented to the assembly, at its last session, for the abolition of slavery; but they could scarcely gain a reading. To set the slaves afloat at once would, I really believe, be productive of much meanness & mischief; but by degrees it certainly might, & most assuredly ought to be affected, & that, too, by legislative authority."[41]

In addition to manumission by legislative authority, Washington wished to see blacks trained for freedom:

> Slavery is neither a crime nor an absurdity. When we propose as our fundamental principle, that liberty is the most inalienable right of every man, we do not include madmen or idiots; liberty in their hands would become a scourge. Till the mind of the slave has become educated to perceive what are the obligations of a state of freedom, & not confound a man's with a treatise. The gift would ensure its abuse. We might as well be asked to pull down our old warehouses before trade has increased to demand enlarged new ones. Both horses & slaves are bequeathed to us by Europeans & time alone can change them; an event, which you may believe me, no man desires more heartily than I do. I pray for it on the score of human dignity but I can clearly foresee that nothing but the rooting out of slavery can perpetuate the existence of our Union by consolidating it in a common bond of principle.[42]

A letter from Washington to Robert Morris of Philadelphia (1786) described his attitudes toward the institution. He opposed slavery but respected the right to private property, and he condemned those who took private property without recompense:

> *Dear Sir:*
>
> *I give you the trouble of this letter at the instance of Mr. Dalby of Alexandria, who is called to Philadelphia to attend what he conceives to be a vexatious lawsuit respecting a slave of his, whom a Society of Quakers in the city (formed for such purposes) have attempted to liberate ... & if the practice of this Society of which Mr. Dalby speaks, is not discountenanced, none of those whose misfortune it is to have slaves as attendants will visit the city if they can possibly avoid it; because by so doing they hazard their property; or they must be at expense. This will not always succeed of providing servants of another description for the trip.*

I hope it will not be conceived from these observations, that it is my wish to
hold the unhappy people, who are subject of this letter, in slavery. I can only say
that there is not a man living who wishes more sincerely than I do, to see a plan
adopted for the abolition of it, but there is only one proper & effectual mode by
which it can be accomplished & that is by Legislative Authority, & this, as far as
my suffrage will go, shall never be wanting. But when slaves are happy & con-
tented with their present masters, are tampered with & seduced to leave; when a
conduct of this sort begets discontent on one side & resentment on the other, &
when it happens to fall on a man whose purse will not measure with that of the
Society, & he loses his property for want of means to defend it; it is oppression in
the latter case & not humanity in any, because it introduces more evils than it
can cure.[43]

John Adams, the second president, was a native of Massachusetts. By the
time he assumed his position, Massachusetts had eliminated the institution
of slavery within its boundaries. His wife, Abigail, had long held antislavery
sentiments, and one wonders if she was not the force behind this president.[44]
Before and during the Revolution, she wrote to John about these feelings: "It
appeared a most ubiquitous scheme to me to fight ourselves for what we are
daily robbing & plundering from those who have as good a right to freedom
as we have. ...I have been sometimes ready to think that the passion for liberty cannot be equally strong in the breasts of those who have been accustomed to deprive their fellow creatures of theirs."[45] John Adams despised the
concept of slavery, but he feared the consequences of free blacks in the midst
of a white culture. This attitude is borne out by his letter to Robert Evans:

Every measure of prudence therefore, ought to be assured for the eventual
extirpation of slavery from the United States. I have through my whole life,
held the practice of slavery in such abhorrence that I have never owned a
negro or any other slave though I have lived for many years in times when
the practice was not disgraceful; when the best men in my community thought
it not inconsistent with their character; and when it has cost me thousands
of dollars for the labor & sustenance of my free men, which I might have saved
by the purchase of negroes at times when they were very cheap.[46]

Adams worried for and about the blacks. He believed there would be
"insurrections of the Blacks against the Whites." Military forces would be
called to suppress these disorders, and whites would be driven by madness to
exterminate the blacks. Adams looked forward to the "total extirpation of slavery, but not with precipitate action. The country could not force unwelcome
action on the south. Emancipation had to come slowly & carefully. If congress suddenly freed them, 99% would ask their masters to care for them
again. Many would become criminals roaming the countryside. Only a few
would seek subsistence by their own labor. Provisions would have to be made
to furnish Negroes with the necessities of life."[47] He hoped colonization might
work, but he doubted the success of such a venture. Adams threw his hands
up and admitted he did not know what should be done with blacks.

Thomas Jefferson was a complex man. He was a reader, writer, statesman, inventor, scientist, and planter. Like his predecessors, he hated the institution of slavery, but, like many learned men of his time, he believed blacks
were a lower variety of the species of man. As such, they could not function
in competition with whites and should be removed for their own protection.
As early as 1769, while a member of the Virginia House of Burgesses, he tried
to change the laws against emancipation to make it easier to manumit slaves,
but he failed. In "A Summary View of the Rights of British-Americans,"
Jefferson opposed domestic slavery and the slave trade, stating, "The abolition of domestic slavery is the great object of desire in those colonies, where
it was unhappily introduced in their infant state."[48] In 1774 he submitted the
Fairfax Resolutions to the Continental Congress. The first step needed to
destroy this "political & moral evil" was to stop the slave trade, which he later
attacked in the Declaration of Independence. With the supply cut off, white
citizens could prepare for the gradual emancipation of their slaves. The freed
slaves would then work for themselves on foreign soil. They could not be left
in America, a country controlled by the white man, because they could not
be assimilated. He believed black children should be raised by their parents
until a certain age, and then they should be brought up at public expense and
taught a craft. Women at age 18 and men at 21 were then to be colonized
where proper. They would be supplied with arms, household implements,
seeds, and animals. The United States would give them protection in an
alliance until they were strong enough to care for themselves. Ships used to
send them out would carry back white workers. Jefferson believed that blacks
had to be removed to prevent a mixture with whites. Africa was the best place
to send them, because they could bring the blessings of civilization to Africa.
Other suggested sites were Portuguese possessions in Brazil or the island of
Santo Domingo. Money for the project could come from the sale of lands in
the territories.[49]

Jefferson had a low opinion of blacks' abilities, as noted earlier. He
believed they were inferior to Indians and lacked literary ability. Blacks had
an aptitude for music, but they were physically and mentally inferior to whites.
Jefferson claimed they needed less sleep (he observed their festivities' running well into the night before a workday). Negroes were as brave as whites
and more adventuresome. Africans lacked thought about the future. They
were not ardent, and their grief over a loss of a loved one was transient. They
were ruled by sensation rather than reflection. Their memory was as good as
that of whites, but they were inferior in reason. Blacks could never understand Euclid's geometry. In imagination, they were dull, tasteless, and unable
to produce great thoughts, painting, or sculpture. When introduced to the
poetry of Phyllis Wheatley (a freed slave born in Africa), Jefferson thought
it was second rate. Blacks were inferior to whites in body and mind as endowed
by nature. Their moral sense was equal to that of whites, and they stole

because they had no protection under the laws of property. Whites were subtler and more delicate in passions while blacks were crude. Blacks were more animal in their lovemaking, with less sentiment. Blacks secreted more bodily wastes through the skin than the kidneys, which produced their disagreeable odor. They were more tolerant of heat and less of cold.[50]

Despite their "inferior nature," Jefferson still opposed enslaving them.

> The institution damaged both master & slave. It created despotism in the master & degrading submission in the slave. White children exposed to their treatment imitated the ways of their elders & learned the techniques of tyranny. Those who allowed it to exist made despots of whites & enemies of blacks. The end result was the destruction of morale in the master & loss of love of country by the slave. Slaves preferred another country to the place they were forced to labor. Could liberty be secure in this type of nation when liberty was a gift of God. God could intervene because He was just & turn things around. God did not have to take the white side in a battle. The slave was growing & preparing for emancipation which hopefully would come with the consent of masters.[51]

Jefferson's apologists saw a change of heart, however, in his attitudes toward blacks at the end of his life. He read Benjamin Banneker's almanac and marveled at his ability to solve complex problems in Euclidean geometry. In a letter to the Marquis de Condorcet, Jefferson wrote, "The lack of talents seen in negroes might be due to their degraded condition and not proceeding from any difference in the structures of the parts on which intellect depends."[52] A correspondent, Henri Gregoire, sent Jefferson a copy of *Littérature des Nègres*. In a letter to Gregoire, Jefferson admitted to the mistakes of his earlier beliefs about their inferiority. Jefferson explained this away by his observations in his own state where their opportunities were so limited:

> My doubts were the result of personal observation on the limited sphere of my own state. Where the opportunities for the development of their genius were not favorable, & those of exercising it still less so. I expressed them, therefore, with great hesitation; but whatever be their degree of talent, it is no measure of their rights. Because Sir Isaac Newton was superior to others in understanding, he was not therefore, lord of the persons or property of others. On this subject they are gaining daily in the opinion of nations & hopeful advances are making towards their re-establishment on an equal footing with other colors of the human family. I pray you, therefore, to accept my thanks for the many instances you have enabled me to observe of respectable intelligence in that race of men, which cannot fail to have effect in hastening the day of their relief.[53]

Nevertheless, he still had doubts about blacks' intellectual ability. In a letter to Joel Barlow, Jefferson questioned Banneker's ability, hinting that Banneker might have turned to Elliott, a white neighbor and mentor, for help in solving mathematical problems.

Like Washington, Thomas Jefferson believed emancipation had to come gradually through legislation. At the Revolutionary Convention in Virginia

(1776), Jefferson submitted a bill calling for emancipation. After the war, he again introduced a statute to the Virginia legislature. During the Confederation period, he pushed for the termination of slavery in the Northwest Territory after 1806, but he remained a strong proponent of colonization to Africa in his final years.

James Madison, a slave owner, also opposed the institution of slavery. He described it as a "portentous evil that was a moral, political, & economical blot on our free country." Unlike his predecessors, he stressed the financial shortcomings of slavery. Slaves were unskilled and could not be taught the skills required for a diversified industrial economy. Madison called for gradual emancipation and deportation, initially to the West: "However, our frontier was advanced so rapidly, it would soon impinge on their lands." He then advised resettlement in Africa. In a letter to Robert Evans (June 15, 1819), he stated that he believed general emancipation had to be gradual, equitable to the master, and consistent with the prejudices of the nation:

> To make it equitable, it required the consent of the master & slave. The master required compensation, the slave had to find freedom preferable to his present state. To satisfy the prejudices, the freedman was removed from areas of white population. The blacks were strongly marked by physical peculiarities. They would become dissatisfied if left among the whites & would rebel against the ruling class without the control of moral & respectable conduct. They would bring the benefits of religion & civilization to Africa. Since the nation as a whole would benefit, the nation should support this concept. The money would come from the sale of western lands. It would cost $600,000,000 to underwrite the project. We could sell 200,000,000 acres at $3 per acre or 300,000,000 at $2 per acre. This represented only one-third of our western lands.[54]

Madison expressed these same beliefs to Lafayette in 1821: "The repugnance of whites to their continuance among them is founded on prejudices, themselves founded on physical distinctions which are not likely soon, if ever, to be eradicated." Madison was stung by the criticisms of Europeans about American maintenance of this institution. To Lafayette, he wrote, "Most taunts come from the quarter most lavish of them, the quarter which obtruded the evil, & which has but lately become a penitent, under suspicious appearance [England]." In this letter, he described another plan for gradual abolition. All female slaves were to be purchased at birth for $100 each. They would remain with their master to receive a proper education and would then be let go. In a letter to Thomas Drew (1833), Madison again advanced emancipation and deportation. The costs would be subsidized by grants of the federal and state legislatures, legacies, emancipations without recompense, and the sale of public lands. The United States had enough ships to send them to Africa or to Caribbean islands under black domination. Removal of blacks would encourage white immigration from abroad.[55]

Ben Franklin, with a mind probably as keen as Jefferson's, was a strong opponent of slavery, and he used his acerbic wit to attack the institution. After many years of service to the young country, Franklin was elected president of the Pennsylvania Society for Promoting the Abolition of Slavery, the Relief of Negroes Unlawfully Held in Bondage, and for Improving the Condition of the African Race (1787). As president, he addressed the people of Philadelphia on the evils of slavery:

> Slavery is such an atrocious debasement of human nature, that its very extirpation, if not performed with solicitous care, may sometimes open a source of serious evils.... The unhappy man who has long been treated as a brute animal, too frequently sinks beneath the common standard of the human species ... he has not the power of choice; & reason & conscience have but little influence on his conduct, because he is chiefly governed by the passion of fear.... To instruct, to advise, to qualify those who have been restored to freedom, for the exercise & enjoyment of civil liberty; to promote in them habits of industry; to furnish them with employment suitable to their age, sex, talents, & other circumstances; & to procure their children an education.[56]

In his speech, there was no talk of colonization, for Franklin believed that freedmen could be absorbed into a white culture. Franklin also composed a memorial from the society in which he urged Congress to "promote the abolition of slavery, & for the relief of those unlawfully held in bondage." He urged Congress to stop the traffic in "human species."

In an essay, he attacked slavery in financial terms. Franklin believed that the "labor of slaves can never be so cheap here as the labor of working men in Britain." Money loaned out (to purchase a slave) brought 6–10 percent per year. A slave cost about £30 sterling. He added the yearly interest this money could bring. Franklin factored in the risk to the slave's life, his clothing, diet, expenses of sickness and loss of time, loss by his neglect of business (neglect was natural to one who did not benefit from his own diligence), the expense of a driver to keep him at work, and his pilfering (every slave is a thief by nature). He urged the reader to compare this to the image of a man working in iron or wool manufacture in England. The cost of labor in England was much cheaper than slave labor in America. Franklin also discussed slave labor in the sugar islands, which deprived whites of employment and prevented white immigration. Those who lived off slave labor wasted money that could maintain 100 individuals. Slaves worked too hard and were fed poorly; this resulted in more deaths than births. Consequently, more had to be imported from Africa, which kept the abominable slave trade in business.[57]

In 1790 Franklin, using the name "Historicus," published in the *Federal Gazette* a parody on a speech given by Mr. Jackson of Georgia, who extolled the benefits of slavery to the slaves. At this time, the Barbary pirates attacked ships and sold their crews and passengers into slavery in the Islamic world.

Franklin wrote as though he were a Muslim, using the usual arguments of proslavery Americans: We needed the Christian slaves to do common labor in hot climates. The supply was decreasing, so we had to take more. How would we pay slave owners to free their property? What would we do with freed slaves in our midst? Weren't they slaves in· their own country? Here, they learned the true doctrine of Islam. If sent back, they would be sent from light to darkness. Should they be planted in the wilderness? As slaves of Islam, they did not have to fight and kill other Christians. Slavery was approved in the Koran. Freeing them would depreciate our lands and homes, create discontent, and start insurrection.[58]

Two Europeans who came to American shores to help in the war for independence rank high in the pantheon of emancipationists, even using their fortunes to advance their beliefs. Tadeusz Kosciuszko of Poland stated in his last will:

> I hereby authorize my friend, Thomas Jefferson, to employ the whole thereof [of money he left in the United States] in the purchase of negroes from among his own or any others, & give them liberty in my name, in giving them an education, in trade & otherwise, & in leaving them instructed for their new condition in the duties of morality, which may make them good neighbors, good fathers or mothers, husbands or wives, & in their duties as Citizens, teaching them to be defenders of their Liberty & Country & of the good order of society, & in whatever will make them Happy & Useful. I make the said Thomas Jefferson, my executor of this. 5th of May, 1798[59]

Lafayette, the scion of a noble family in autocratic France, put his beliefs into practice during his lifetime. It has been said that this nobleman developed his ideas while convalescing from a wound suffered at the Battle of Brandywine. He lived among Moravians and Quakers in Pennsylvania. Perhaps too his Catholicism played an important part. (The Catholics treated their slaves and freedmen differently from the Protestant English.) Catholics believed that slavery was an accident of being that did not affect personality. The religion taught its communicants that the slave was equal in the essentials of manhood in the sight of God. Slavery was an opportunity to Christianize the blacks. Catholics believed slavery was accidental and temporary and that it did not abolish the inherent rights of men. All men were brought together in the bond of faith, and all were children of one God.[60]

As mentioned earlier, Lafayette communicated with Washington about his beliefs on emancipation. At one point he told Washington, "I would never have drawn my sword in the cause of America if I could have discerned that thereby I was founding a land of slavery." The young Frenchman believed that slaves should be educated and prepared for the responsibilities of citizenship and then manumitted. To put his ideas into operation, he bought an estate in Cayenne, French Guiana, for 120,000 livres; then he purchased slaves and brought them to the area. Lafayette called for gradual emancipation following education and discipline to train them to act for themselves. His overseers brought the slaves together and burned all the whips and other instruments of discipline. The slaves learned that crimes committed by blacks or whites would be treated identically. Many of the local planters as well as the king's plantations showed interest in following Lafayette's lead. As was common among politicians with grandiose ideas, the day-to-day control of the plantation fell to Lafayette's, and she had priests from the seminary of Saint Esprit send a missionary to teach religion and morality. Unhappily, the project withered and died. Lafayette fled the excesses of the French Revolution, and his property was confiscated. His plantation in Cayenne was awarded to more active supporters of the Revolution, who sold the black workers back into slavery. Despite the sad ending of this project, Lafayette still kept up his activities to end slavery. He was a member of the Society of Friends of the Blacks in Paris, which was associated with similar groups in England. Their aim was to abolish the slave trade. He was also a member of the New York Emancipation Society and the Manumission Society.[61]

A list of the opponents of slavery of this period would resemble a list of American heroes of the pre- and post–Revolutionary eras. John Jay, who would become the first chief justice of the United States Supreme Court, believed, "It is much wished that slavery may be abolished. The honor of the States, as well as justice & humanity, in my opinion loudly call upon them to emancipate these unhappy people. To contend for our part liberty, & to deny that blessing to others, involves an inconsistency not to be excused."[62] Gouverneur Morris, whose input into the drafting of the United States Constitution is recognized, stated, "It was a nefarious institution. It was the curse of heaven on the states where it prevailed." Thomas Paine, whose pamphlet Common Sense helped ignite the Revolution, added, "Consider what consistency or decency they complained so loudly at attempts to enslave them, while they held so many hundred thousands in slavery & annually enslaved more without any pretence of authority, or claims upon them. Slavery was no less immoral than murder, robbery, lewdness and barbarity. Americans must discontinue and renounce it, with grief & abhorrence."[63] Patrick Henry, governor of Virginia, who bequeathed his immortal words to generations of young orators, stated: "I will not, I cannot justify it [slavery]."[64] Arthur Lee, one of the American ministers to France during the Revolution, declared slavery "shocking to humanity & abhorrent to the Christian Religion. It depraved free men as well as slaves."[65] Benjamin Rush, the leading physician of the period and a signer of the Declaration of Independence, said, "Slave keepers were hardened monsters & violators of the eighth commandment. The slave was a victim of lawless power & injustice."[66] (Rush, without medical experimentation, "thought out" the explanation of many illnesses. He believed that many of the physical traits of the black were similar to the results of leprosy, and that therefore, black skin and facial features were due to disease.[67]) To this list of emancipationists could be added Alexander Hamilton, James Otis, Henry Laurens, and John Dickinson.

The greatest opponents of slavery, but those with the weakest voices, were the blacks. In the states south of New Jersey and Pennsylvania, the slave could do nothing to change his status except to revolt, and in continental America, no slave revolt was successful. The freedman was little better off. He was barely tolerated, and he tried to keep a low profile. The freedman had churches and organizations to teach other blacks how to behave in public to set a proper example for their white neighbors. In the North, slaves sometimes joined together and obtained white lawyers to petition for their freedom. There were four types of cases that reached the courts. First, some Northern states had gradual abolition laws that gave freedom to slave children after they finished an indenture period to their owner. The owner occasionally refused to grant their freedom or tried to sell the child to a neighboring slave state. Secondly, gradual abolition laws called for the registration of all slaves. Failure to register the slaves meant they were free. Third, most states had laws against the importation of slaves. Therefore, imported slaves were free. Fourth, some masters manumitted slaves in their wills. If the heirs refused to give up this property, the cases ended in court.[68] As early as 1701, Abda, a slave in Connecticut, filed a suit against his master for trespass. Unfortunately, the court found for his owner, and he remained a slave.[69] It was during and after the Revolution that slaves in the North besieged the courts with petitions for freedom. In Massachusetts they petitioned to earn money for their labor with the intent to purchase their freedom, to grant freedom, and to receive land for past work, and they petitioned the Committee of Correspondence for its help in gaining their freedom.[70] In New Hampshire, they claimed a natural right to freedom. Similar pleas were sent in Rhode Island, Connecticut, and New Jersey.

Occasionally a black man reached a level of eminence where he could freely express his attitudes about the situation that so many of his brothers and sisters had to endure. Lemuel Haynes, the child of a mixed marriage, was a minister to a white congregation in Connecticut. He preached that God made blacks no different from other men, but that as a result of slavery they viewed themselves as below others. They were despised, ignorant, and licentious. Perhaps in fear for his livelihood, Haynes did not attack slavery overtly in his sermons. However, in an early monograph, written during the Revolution, he declared that liberty was a natural right of men, a divine gift, a jewel handed down from heaven. Just as an Englishman had a right to liberty, so did an African slave. Slaves were not blessed by the gifts of Christianity. If given the opportunity, blacks could achieve the same heights as whites.[71]

Blacks could and did speak their minds anonymously. In an essay entitled "Othello," the author, reputedly Benjamin Banneker, castigated whites:

"In you [whites] the superiority of power produces nothing but a superiority of brutality and barbarism. Weakness, which calls for protection, appears to provide your inhumanity. Your fine political systems are sullied by the outrages committed against human nature and divine majesty. When America opposed the pretensions of England, she declared that all men have the same rights. After having manifested her hatred against tyrants, ought she to have abandoned her principles?"[72]

Chapter 11

MISCEGENATION

During the colonial era, three "races" occupied the Western Hemisphere: the Native Americans, the blacks, and the whites. Early in the seventeenth century, the English carried some racial baggage about cohabiting with "inferior races"; this attitude grew as the century matured. More important than racial attitudes was the presence of white women in the colony. The Puritans in New England and the Anglicans in Virginia brought their wives and daughters to the New World, and therefore, there was little mixture of the races. By contrast, the early English who went to the West Indies were single adventurers. They hoped to earn a quick fortune by pushing slaves in the cane and tobacco fields. If they survived disease and small wars with the Spanish and French, they hoped to return home to England, marry, and live the life of a gentleman. While in the Indies, they took black concubines whom they planned to leave behind with their mixed families. The influx of white women resulted in more permanent communities. The French and the Dutch, like the early English in the West Indies, left their women in Europe and took "wives" from among the Indian women. They too planned to leave their native families when they returned to Europe. The Spanish and Portuguese were largely "color blind." Their early expeditions too were made up largely of men who needed local (Indian) or imported (black) females. In addition, the Iberians had had a longer and more intimate exposure to the Africans than had people of other Christian European nations. Before the European discovery of America, Portuguese expeditions brought Africans to Portugal and Spain, where they intermarried with the white inhabitants.

The early Puritans looked upon the Indians as a blight that had to be overcome in order to create their theocratic paradise. The natives were killed off by disease (a sign that God was on the Puritans' side) and war. Many became slaves of the new rulers in New England. In Virginia there were some unions between the English men and the Croatian women. The men preferred the lifestyle of the natives and went to live among them. They were severely punished, however, often with death, if captured by the white authorities. John Rolfe, one of the colony's most eligible widowers, married Pocahontas, a daughter of Chief Powhatan. This might have been a "dynastic union" to maintain the safety of the English colony at Jamestown. However, following the marriage, there were deliberations in council to determine whether Rolfe should be tried for treason.[1] (It is possible that this may have been for an unrelated offense.) The inquiry ended after some external problems intervened in the fragile colony. As a result of the deliberations and punishments, English and Croat unions ended.

The introduction of blacks in 1619 brought new problems for the authorities. The English considered the blacks an inferior subspecies of man, and they frowned on any form of liaison, temporary or permanent. In 1630 Hugh Davis was denounced for defiling his body by "lying with a Negro woman." The authorities called this an "abuse to the dishonor of God and the shame of Christians." He was whipped publicly to punish him for the offense. The sting of the whip was forgotten in time, however, because ten years later he was caught repeating this "perfidious" act. Davis did penance in church for his sins, but his black consort was whipped.[2]

During the century, colonies passed laws against fornication, and interracial marriage was forbidden. However, sexual appetites and the desire to experiment resulted in frequent court appearances. In Massachusetts, early court records indicated that Christopher Mason was convicted of getting Mr. Rock's Negro maid with child. He was punished with 20 lashes; he paid court fees and prison fees; and he posted a bond of £20 for good behavior (1672). Several months later, Mr. Rock was in court again. His Negro maid, Bess had committed fornication and had had an illegitimate child. She received 20 lashes, and her owner paid court fees. Mr. Warren's Negro, Joan, committed fornication with Indian Jasper to produce a bastard. She was given a choice of punishment, either 15 lashes or a fine of 40 shillings to the county; she was also responsible for court costs. John Pinchon's Negro servant (slave), Miriam, committed fornication and gave birth to a bastard; she named Mr. Cornish, an Englishman, as the father. She received 10 lashes and paid a fine of 40 shillings to the county plus court costs; Mr. Cornish was not tried for his involvement in the affair.[3] In Massachusetts, fornication was a serious offense, and interracial fornication was doubly serious. A black or mulatto man who slept with a "Christian white woman" was expelled from the province. A white man who slept with a black woman was whipped, and she was expelled from the province (1705). The threat of severe punishment, however, failed to keep "lovers" apart. In 1758 Nathaniel Perley brought action against Flora, "a Negress," in Essex County Court in Massachusetts, charging that she had published "Lies & False Reports." She claimed "he had to do with her" on several occasions. Flora was brought before the justice of the peace, where she admitted saying these things "because she says they are true." This brought the case to a close.[4] (Perley probably had a reputation for interracial dallying.)

The South was not immune to the crossing of racial lines. In Virginia fornication was a misdemeanor punished with a fine; fornication with a black resulted in double fine (1662). Court and parish records in North Carolina revealed that fornication was one of the most prevalent crimes in the colony. Church wardens often received more in fines from fornicators, many of them women, than from any other source. A goodly number of these illegal acts produced children of mixed racial lines. Most illegal liaisons occurred among the servants, who were thrown together with the slaves and endured a similar lifestyle. However, many in the highest socioeconomic class were also involved. For instance, the daughter of North Carolina's highest-ranking Revolutionary general, Robert Howe, gave birth to two sons whose father was a black slave.[5] Often these women, whose husbands took their pleasures in the slave quarters, had similar liaisons with male slaves. In many cases, they also resorted to infanticide to maintain their social status and marriage. In South Carolina, a white man could be sold into servitude for a period of years for fathering a child with a black woman.

Interracial marriage was not completely unacceptable in early seventeenth-century Virginia. Toward the end of the century, however, racial antipathy, particularly against blacks, became the norm.[6] Accompanying the growth of the doctrine of racial inferiority, laws against intermarriage were passed by provincial legislatures. In Maryland in 1661 a white woman who married a black slave became the servant of his owner during his lifetime; her children were slaves as well. Such a marriage was considered "a disgrace to many Christian nations." Prior to the passage of this statute, the offspring of these unions were servants until their thirtieth birthday. If it was discovered that the master had forced a union between his white female servant and his black male slave in order to increase his slave population, the woman and her children were freed, while the master and the minister who had performed the marriage were fined. In 1681 Maryland reduced the status of any free white, male or female, to that of an indentured servant for seven years for cohabiting with a black; the black partner became a slave for life, and the progeny served for 31 years.[7] In 1715 and 1717 Virginia passed laws against intermarriage that were equally strong. In 1691 intermarriage led to expulsion from the colony for the white woman because of the fear of "spurious issue"—that is, mulattoes. (The term *mulatto* was taken from the Spanish word meaning young mule. This made reference to the product of "two species." The term *mulatto* was also defined by the state. In Virginia having only one black great-grandparent made one a mulatto; in North Carolina, it was one black great-great-grandparent.) The Virginia law of 1691 was re-enacted in 1705 with stronger penalties. In 1753 Virginia declared that an English woman with a mulatto child would be fined £75, paid to the church wardens. If she could not pay the fine, the wardens could sell her into servitude for five years. The wardens then paid her fine, equally divided among the king, the parish, and the informer. The child was indentured until his or her thirtieth birthday. A free white who married a black or mulatto was fined £10 plus six months in jail, while the minister who performed the rite was fined 10,000 pounds of tobacco.[8]

Six colonies had strict specific laws against intermarriage by 1725. Massachusetts, like its sister colony Virginia, feared "spurious issue" and made intermarriage illegal in 1705. Pennsylvania followed suit in 1725, fining the minister involved £100. A free black man or woman who married a white person could be sold into slavery. If they committed fornication only, the black partner could be sold into servitude for seven years; the white was punished according to the laws of adultery and fornication. The Pennsylvania law was ineffective, not enforced, and eventually repealed.[9] Mixed couples were not uncommon on the streets of Philadelphia. New York lagged behind. In the statute that called for gradual emancipation of slaves (1785), blacks and whites were forbidden to marry. However, this stricture was deleted from the final version.[10] Later in the century, Massachusetts simply voided the marriages (1786), as did Rhode Island in 1798.[11]

The worst scenario was forced union. The term *rape* could not be used to cover all cases, because a white man could not be accused of rape when he had forced sex with a female slave. Generally, when a white owner went to the slave quarters, the woman he chose received special advantages. Her children ate better and were clothed better. She could look forward to a less onerous lifestyle with easier work. Occasionally the owner felt paternal affection for his offspring, particularly if his marriage was barren, and he educated the child and sometimes sent him out of the country. The female recipient of this largesse frequently was "married" to a male slave, but he could not interfere. Slaves could not sign contracts, and marriage was a contract. Therefore, they could only accept the situation. There were cases of forced sex with a female slave, but the "recipient of this attention" had no recourse to the law. If a white male raped another man's slave, he could be charged with trespass against that individual's property.[12] Rape of a free black female must have occurred during this period, but no references to this situation could be found. Perhaps this was due to the inability of a black to testify against a white in a court of law.

The attempt to rape or the actual act by a black man against a white woman had dire consequences for the rapist, particularly as the number of blacks increased in the county. In Suffolk County, Connecticut, in 1679 John Negro pulled Sarah Phillips off her horse and "attempted to ravish her." He received 30 lashes and paid the victim £5 as well as the charge for the prosecutor and court costs; his owner had to expel him from the county (probably the colony).[13] During the eighteenth century, the punishment for attempted or actual rape was execution by burning or hanging, and castration of the black assailant was written into several colonial criminal codes. As a punishment, castration was strictly an American concept (the English had no punishment of this nature). It probably developed from a fear of the "lower species in their midst." In the early eighteenth century, New Jersey and Pennsylvania ordered castration for a black who had raped a white woman; this statute was disallowed by the mother country. Of interest, Pennsylvania decreed castration for whites as a replacement for execution in capital offenses, including sodomy, bestiality, a second rape, and incest.[14] The law was never used against whites, though Virginia allowed castration of blacks for rape in 1769. The decree was repealed in 1805.

The most "celebrated" case of miscegenation was that of Thomas Jefferson and Sally Hemings. People of the period, particularly Jefferson's political adversaries, accepted this as fact and proclaimed it in newspapers. Sally was the slave daughter of Betty Hemings, born in 1773. Her father was John Wayles of Charles City County. Betty was the slave child of a white father and slave mother; therefore, Sally had only one black grandparent. John Wayles was also the father of Martha, who married Thomas Jefferson, (Sally was Martha's sister). When John Wayles died, his slaves went to Martha, and her marriage to Jefferson brought the slaves, including Sally, to Jefferson's estate. Martha Jefferson was sickly and almost a total invalid at the end of her life. Betty Hemings nursed Martha until her death in 1782. Sally, like her mother, was raised to be a "house slave." They were taught the management and care of the main house and its inhabitants. Jefferson had three daughters with Martha: Lucy, who died as an infant; Martha, who accompanied her father to France after her mother's death; and Polly, who followed her father and sister to France, accompanied by Sally Hemings, now aged 14. Sally looked more like a white adolescent than a black slave. Polly and Sally made a detour on their trip to Paris with a stop in London. Abigail Adams, the wife of the minister to England and the second president-to-be, took them under her wing. It should be remembered that Abigail, from an old Massachusetts family, opposed slavery. She must have taken a special interest in this slave child uprooted from her family in Virginia. After London, the girls journeyed to Paris to join Jefferson, who was minister to the Court of Louis XVI. After two years in Paris, the family returned, and Sally may have had an infant son. She became a house slave at Monticello. During the following 20 years, Jefferson was occupied with state and national affairs, and he returned to Monticello at irregular intervals. It was believed that he had liaisons with his slave during these interludes. In 1809 he left the presidency and returned home. Sally had given birth to several children who resembled Jefferson, according to his political enemies. The newspapers condemned Jefferson, and a song made the rounds of the taverns of the country:

> *Of all the damsels on the green,*
> *On mountain or in valley,*
> *A lass so luscious ne'er was seen*
> *As Monticello Sally.*
> *Yankee Doodle, who's the noodle?*
> *What wife was half so handy?*
> *To breed a flock of slaves for stock,*
> *A blackamoor's a dandy.*

It was believed that Sally gave birth to four (or six) of Jefferson's children: Beverly, in 1798; Harriet, in 1801; Madison, in 1805; and Eston, in 1808. There was also Tom, Sally's oldest son, born in Paris. According to French law, anyone born in France was free, and Tom was able to leave Virginia when he came of age. Beverly escaped to freedom. Madison and Eston were apprenticed to Sally's brother, John, a carpenter. Harriet became a house slave. Thomas Jefferson died on July 4, 1826. His will manumitted Madison, Eston, and John, and their carpenter uncle who was named guardian of the boys. In the will, Jefferson entreated the Virginia House of Burgesses to spare these future freedmen from deportation (which was a Virginia statute at the time). Jefferson thought that they would not become public charges, because they were employed in building the University of Virginia. Sally and Harriet were to remain as slaves to his daughter, Martha, whom he entrusted with their care. However, Jefferson died in debt, and the female slaves, along with Monticello, were sold to pay his debts. Harriet eventually became free, married, and spent her days in Albemarle County, Virginia. Sally was sold away, probably to the Deep South.[15]

Aside from the Rolfe-Pocahontas union and the early English liaisons with the Croat Indians, the mixture of the English with the Native Americans was not great; however, it did exist. The term *mustee* (also *mastee* and *mestizo*) was applied to the offspring of a white and an Indian, as well as to that of a black and an Indian. If such children remained in a white environment, their progeny would become indistinguishable from the whites within one or two generations. If taken to their Indian parent's tribe, their offspring would resemble others in the tribe within the same period of time.

Historians have written differing accounts of early black–Indian relations. Some described Indian raids on white settlements that spared the black slaves.[16] In the 1622 Virginia massacre, 347 whites were killed, but no black casualties were mentioned (this was before blacks were relegated to slave status); this may have been because blacks hid. Indians tortured white captive men but not black prisoners. They regarded whites as warriors, and torture was a mark of respect for their vanquished adversaries. Other writers, by contrast claimed that the Indians saw the blacks as allies of the whites, who took their hunting grounds away and converted them to farms and plantations. The Indians knew about slavery before the arrival of the whites and held slaves in low esteem, not worth their attention. Finally, the Indians had to recover from their awe and fear of black skin. They believed these newcomers were devils ("abimacho" in New England, "manitto" in Virginia). Indians and blacks were first thrown together in the West Indies. Indians captured in the Pequot and King Philip's Wars were made slaves by their Puritan captors. They did not perform well in forced servitude, though, and many were shipped to the sugar islands. They were replaced by black slaves, so the two groups of slaves mingled in the West Indies and later in continental America.[17] This mixing increased after the middle of the seventeenth century.[18] As the black population grew in America, the Indians of the East Coast were almost entirely absorbed by the blacks. In newspaper ads for runaways, the owner frequently described the escapee as being of mixed Indian-black ancestry. This mixed ancestry, particularly if the maternal side was Indian, was used by black slaves to prove they were free through the maternal line. The whites used this union to steal Indian land. The progeny of these unions were "not Indian anymore," and the land was "a convenient asylum for an idle set of free blacks." The first legal marriage between an Indian and a black took place in Massachusetts in 1764. Today, many of the remaining small tribes in the Northeast retain a large amount of black genetic input.

Blacks tried to escape from their white owners by fleeing to Indian lands. Their treatment by the Native Americans varied. Some were killed outright, which was rare. Some were returned to their white masters according to treaties signed by their chiefs and colonial governors, which also was uncommon. Although most tribes disregarded these treaties, the whites in South Carolina were able to convey their distaste for blacks to the local tribes. These Indians became trackers of the escapees and returned the blacks to their owners for the reward.[19] A fair number of runaways became "slaves" of the Indians (this was a rather "benign" state). Early in the nineteenth century, the Cherokees of North Carolina owned more than 1,000 slaves. Many were adopted by the tribe and grew in stature among the Indians.[20] James Beckworth, a black trapper, became a chief of the Crows. Jim Boy was a chief of the Creeks, John Horse was a Seminole leader, and Absolam was a Seminole counselor.[21] The border between Georgia and Florida was a route of escape for black slaves, who were welcomed by the Spanish and the Seminole Indians, an offshoot of the Creeks. These blacks intermarried with the Seminoles. Black women took Seminole men and produced mustees, who were slaves through the maternal line, according to slave catchers. It is believed that one of the causes of the Seminole War of 1836–37, after Florida was annexed to the United States, was the fear of Seminole fathers that their "slave" children would be seized.

Chapter 12

SLAVE REBELLION
AND BLACK CODES

The African slave did not receive the fruits of his labor. After years of 14- to 18-hour days, beatings by overseers, destruction of family ties, and poor food and shelter, many bondsmen rebelled. This rebellion could take the form of malingering; self-mutilation; suicide; destruction of his owner's crops, tools, and livestock; running away; or criminal activity like stealing and violent insurrection. Using a knowledge of plants and their side effects, the slave could temporarily make himself truly sick, or he could feign illness. The overseer or owner developed criteria for the diagnosis of true versus sham illnesses. Slaves were bled and given remedies from a medicine chest for real illnesses, and they were forced into the field for simulated problems. (Washington's slaves were considered sick only if they had a fever.) Self-mutilation could consist of cutting off one or several fingers, a hand, or toes, or irritating an inflamed area to produce an infection. Suicide was the ultimate form of self-mutilation, usually accomplished by drowning or hanging. Suicide deprived the master of his labor, and it was a means of getting "home." Many believed they would return to Africa after self-destruction. In some areas suicide reached such major proportions that the owner threatened to commit suicide to follow them and bring them back. The "carelessness" of the slave who caused the loss of his owner's property, if done in a well-reasoned way, brought minimal physical punishment. It was this "carelessness" that was cited to prove that the black was an inferior, nonthinking being.

Running away was a major form of rebellion, and it created a very expensive problem for the owner. He paid for newspaper advertisements, bribed informers among the slaves, and paid the cost of the slave catcher, who at times was sent out of his province. If the slave was recaptured, the owner paid for his food and lodging while in the county jail. He also paid the sheriff's fee, as well as that of the individual who returned him to the plantation. This last cost was paid on a mileage basis.[1] The ad for a runaway was the most common notice in North Carolina newspapers.[2] Like advertising today, it was a vital source of revenue for struggling newspapers. The runaway in 89

189

percent of the cases was a male who ran away by himself; he was usually between 20 and 35 years of age and seldom more than 50 years old.[3] Frequently the runaway tried to find his wife and family who had been sold away. Males knew the countryside, because many were hired out to work on other plantations. They also knew the urban areas, roads, and waterways where boats were stored, and there were ferrymen who would take them without too many questions asked. They often had job skills and could pass as free blacks in urban areas. Field hands and house workers ran away less frequently. Artisans, river workers, and African-born slaves ran away in greater numbers. The artisan and the boatman ran away singly to towns a good distance from home. They usually spoke English well enough to be understood. Africans left in small groups, and few spoke understandable English, so they were apprehended more easily. Those who ran away in larger numbers were usually family groups. In 70 percent of the cases, the group was composed of two slaves. Larger groups ran into an increased risk incidence of betrayal, detection, and capture. In urban areas, slaves working in a shop or in a home departed in a group. Early in the colonial period, black slaves left with white indentured servants with whom they had more in common than either group did with the master.[4]

The actual act was rarely spontaneous, but rather was a well-planned operation. The slaves hid money, food, and clothing on boats until the opportune time. Horses were also hidden for future transportation. Many left the area, but some remained in the neighborhood to be near their families; they were helped and sustained by other slaves. This was a dangerous practice, because they could be declared outlaws. The owner received a Declaration of Outlawry from two justices of the peace, and as an outlaw, the slave could be shot on sight without retribution befalling his executioner.[5] The most popular time to escape was in the harvest season, between September and November, followed by the spring planting season, between February and April. A fair number also escaped between May and August. The coldest season, between December and January, found them close to the hearth. The harvest season was favored because fruits and vegetables were ripe and could sustain them. Also, hay provided shelter for sleeping. Generally, 48 percent were killed or recaptured, and some committed suicide. Africans, because of their lack of familiarity with the English language, were captured 73 percent of the time. Some individuals left for a short period to obtain respite from the harshness of slave life; they returned voluntarily after a short period of freedom. On occasion, runaways were able to join others to form bands. These groups, called "maroons" frequently inhabited the swamplands. (The term maroon was derived from the Spanish *cimarrones*, meaning outlaws or runaways.) There were probably 50 distinct maroon communities in the continental United States in the two centuries preceding the Civil War. They were usually located in the Southern provinces, where the people hid in mountain caves and forests as well as in the swamps. Some were settled communities where the inhabitants grew food, raised livestock, and built reasonably substantial habitations. The largest was probably in the Dismal Swamp between Virginia and North Carolina, which was said to contain 2,000 escaped slaves. Many raided neighboring plantations for sustenance. As early as 1672, Virginia offered rewards for hunting and killing these outlaws. In 1733, the governor of South Carolina offered a reward of £20 if one was brought in alive, and £10 if brought in dead. State militias were trained to attack and destroy these colonies, and full-scale military expeditions were required to destroy the larger communities. During the Revolution, these bands sided with the British, who armed them. After the British defeat, these "soldiers" fled with their arms and carried on a guerrilla war against the Americans. Whites joined the Catawba Indians to form companies to hunt down the blacks for the bounty on their heads; they supplied proof of the destruction of these maroons by bringing in black scalps. The families of men who were killed fighting these outlaws received aid from the states. Slaves who helped whites recapture other slaves were sometimes given their freedom. Some of the maroon groups joined the Spanish in the south or the Indians on the frontier to fight the common enemy. The Americans sent military expeditions against these groups in Florida until east and west Florida were annexed to an expanding United States.[6]

To retrieve his valuable property, the slave owner used all the forces of law, from the county sheriff to the federal government. In addition, he had private resources. He could hire professional slave catchers armed with "nigger hounds," who could detect "nigger smell." The owner could also advertise in local newspapers as well as in those out of state. The Annapolis, Maryland, *Gazette* of August 20, 1761, received an ad from Fairfax, Virginia, on August 11, 1761, reading:

> Ran away from Plantation of the Subscribers, on Dogue-Run in Fairfax, on Sunday the 9th instant, the following Negroes, viz. Peres 35 or 40 years of age, a well-set Fellow of about 5 feet 8 inches high, yellowish Complexion with a very full round Face and full black Beard, his speech is something slow & broken, but not in so great a Degree as to render him remarkable. He had on when he went away a dark colour'd Cloth Coat, a white Linen Waist-Coat, white Breeches & white Stockings. Jack [with a description], Neptune [with a description], Cupid [with a description]. The two last of these Negroes were bought from an African Ship in August 1759 & talk very broken & unintelligible English; the second one, Jack, is Countryman to these, and speaks pretty good English, having been several years in the Country.
>
> The other, Peres, speaks much better than either, indeed has little of his Country Dialect left, and is esteemed a sensible judicious Negro.
>
> As they went off without the least Suspicion, Provocation, or Difference with any Body, or the least angry word or abuse from their Overseers, 'tis supposed they will hardly lurk about in the neighborhood, but steer some direct course (which cannot even be guessed at) in Hopes of an Escape: Or,

perhaps, as the Negro Peres has lived many years around Williamsburg, & King William County & Jack in Middlesex, they may possibly bend their Course to one of those Places.

Whoever apprehends the said Negroes, so that the Subscriber may readily get them, shall have, if taken up in this county, Forty Shillings Reward, beside what the law allows: & if at any greater Distance, or out of the Colony, a proportionable Recompense, paid them, by

George Washington

N.B. If they should be taken separately, the Reward will be proportional.[7]

A similar notice ran in the *Virginia Gazette* on September 21, 1769:

RUNaway from subscriber in Albemarle, a Mulatto slave called Sandy, about 35 years of age, his stature is rather low, inclining to corpulence, & his complexion light; he is a shoe-maker by trade, in which he uses his left hand principally, can do coarse carpenter's work, & is something of a horse-jockey; he is greately addicted to drink, & when drunk is insolent & disorderly, in his conversation he swears much, & in his behaviour is artful & knavish. He took with him a white horse, much scarred with traces, of which it is expected he will probably endeavor to dispose; he also carried his shoemaker's tools, & will probably endeavor to get employment that way. Whoever conveys the said slave to me, in Albemarle, shall have 40S reward, if taken up within the county, 46 if elsewhere within the colony, & 101 if in any other colony, from

Thomas Jefferson[8]

Notices for runaways were not limited to the *Maryland Gazette*, the *Virginia Gazette*, the *South Carolina Gazette & Advertiser*, and the *South Carolina Weekly Advertiser*. The *Boston Evening Post*, the *New York Gazette*, the *Pennsylvania Gazette* and the *American Weekly Mercury* (Philadelphia) carried evidence that the more benign North had its fair share of fugitives. All offered rewards, but in many cases the amount was not mentioned: "Whoever brings him to his said master ... shall be satisfied for their Pains, by me.... Philadelphia, January 31, 1721." The name of the escapee, his description, and his training were always included: "Prince had Guinea Country marks on his face"; "Leonard was 40, 5 feet 10 inches [much above normal height for a slave] ... can Read & Write ... can bleed & draw teeth —£3 reward"; "He is a blacksmith; has drove a carriage, can shave & dress hair, & is a cobbling shoemaker"; "Speaks Swede & English well"; "Negro Woman 28. She can cord, spin, & knit & milk, & any other country work"; "Bricklayer & Plasterer"; "Taylor"; "Sawyer." "He is a Methodist Preacher, called Preaching Dick. He is in company with a white woman named Mary, who is supposed now goes for his wife. He went off in company with a white Servant Man named John." Occasionally the owner expected his runaway to return voluntarily: "Or if the said Negro will return to me, at my House in St. Mary's County, he shall be kindly served, & escape all punishment for his offense." The ads occasionally offered rewards for the capture of those who helped runaways escape (this was a serious crime, and some states ordered the death penalty for this offense): "Total $500 reward. One Hundred Dollars paid on conviction of white person taking or having taken off Tom's irons & $20 if by a negro. Also $50 will be paid on delivery of him to the master of the work house. $50 for Cyrus, $100 for Hercules & a further reward of $200 to be paid on conviction of them being harbored by a white man." The *City Gazette & Advertiser* of March 5, 1800, printed this notice: "Sam was enticed away by one Isaac Randall an apprentice of Thomas Merriott."[9]

Also in these classifieds, the strange names given to the slaves should be noted. Their names fell into four categories: classical, Hebrew, Christian (English), and African. The owners gave them English names like Dick, Nanny, Bill, Jack, and Frank. Occasionally they used Latin and Greek names, perhaps in ridicule; Cato (a Roman statesman) was heard commonly, as were Pompei, Caesar, Titus (the emperor), Neptune and Sylvia (gods of mythology), Primus, Felix, and Prince (the last was very common). Hebrew names included Sarah, Jonathan, Shubal, and Moses. Finally, there were African names like Quam, Coffe and Bandung. (These might have been the sound of their native names to English ears.) The slaves were rarely given surnames and commonly used their owner's family name.[10]

In addition to private resources, the owner could depend on legal authorities to help him regain his property. As early as 1629, the Dutch West India Company promised to do all in its power to return to their masters any slaves or colonists fleeing from service. This ruling was actually a propaganda ploy to entice the Dutch in the home country to emigrate to New Netherlands; it showed them that private property would be protected if they came. In 1636 the English and Dutch agreed to return each other's slaves if they fled and successfully crossed the border. The New England Confederation, composed of Plymouth, Massachusetts, Connecticut, and New Haven (1643), protected private property. If a servant ran away to any part of the confederation, a magistrate's certificate from his home area called for his return to his rightful owner by all inhabitants of this union.[11] New Jersey in 1686 had a fugitive slave law that awarded 20 shillings for the return of a fugitive. Rhode Island (1714) fined a ferryman for taking a slave across a waterway without a certificate from his owner, and all citizens were called upon to retrieve fugitives (although Rhode Island had an earlier statute that outlawed involuntary servitude). The Northwest Ordinance and the Federal Constitution called for the return of escaped slaves (they were not referred to as slaves). Congress in 1793 proclaimed that a person held in service in one state who escaped to another could be seized by his owner, or by the owner's agent or lawyer. The escapee was brought before a federal judge or any magistrate of the city, town, or county where the arrest was made. If the magistrate was satisfied by affidavit or oral statement of the fugitive's status, he granted a warrant to return the runaway to his state of origin. Anyone who obstructed the seizure or hid the runaway paid the claimant $500 if convicted. Many in the North defied federal and state laws to protect the escapee. In Boston, for example, a runaway named Josiah Quincy was saved when a mob beat a marshal trying to do his duty. Some slave owners defied the laws for their own pecuniary gain. They placed very general ads in the newspapers about having caught a black fugitive. These were not usually checked into by the original owners, because they would have had to send slave catchers at their own expense, and so the fugitive joined the other slaves on the plantation at minimal cost to his new owner.[12]

The Indians living in areas bordering the American colonies were urged to catch fugitives. In 1699 Maryland offered a "match coat" (a mantle made of fur) to any Indian who returned a fugitive.[13] Virginia offered financial rewards for the return of this form of property. In the South, blacks ran away and joined the Creek settlements. The governors of Virginia, North Carolina, South Carolina, and Georgia signed a treaty with the Creeks in 1763, according to which, for each slave they returned, the Creeks would receive £5. The Indians preferred to keep the blacks, however, because they were superior to the Indians in agriculture. The blacks were kept in a benign form of slavery, paying their new owners a portion of the crops they raised. Georgia then increased the reward to 50 pounds of leather per slave or 60 pounds if the slave was brought to Savannah. The Spanish in Florida, by contrast, welcomed runaways and gave them freedom. The former slaves frequently became members of their armed forces and were able to supply information about English forces to their new friends. New York's Governor Crosby met with the Sachems of the Six Nations on September 8, 1723, to urge them to return fugitives. The reward was a substantial one, including a rifle and two blankets per runaway. Other similar treaties were signed in 1765 by New York and its Indians.[14]

Runaway slaves who were caught were treated severely. If a group ran away, its leader was frequently executed. Often he was "whipped and pickled" before execution (the whipper rubbed salt or vinegar into the whip's wounds). Others were "gibbeted" (hanged on an upright post with a projecting arm, so they slowly strangled rather than having their necks broken from a scaffold). The gibbet was also used if the slave tried to kill his master in his escape attempt. Some were burned at the stake. "Lesser" punishments were meted out to the followers or to those who ran away individually. A first attempt led to up to 40 lashes; an *R* was branded on the right cheek for a second offense; an ear was cut off plus 40 lashes for a third attempt; castration was performed if the slave tried a fourth time (a female fourth-time offender had her left ear cut off and an *R* branded on her left cheek); and a fifth offense resulted in execution or incision of the Achilles tendon. Imprisonment was rare, because it deprived the owner of the slave's labor. The scars left by these punishments were used to describe the fugitives in newspapers: such descriptions as "Signs of Correction," "left ear cropped," or "scars of previous whippings" were included in ads without feelings of guilt by the owners. The great expense incurred by the owners for repeat offenders often led them to add "dead or alive" to the notice. Owners preferred the recalcitrant slave dead because the state frequently reimbursed them for the value of the slaves who were killed. "Bring me his head" in an ad meant that proof of the slave's death was required.[15] Those who helped slaves escape or harbored them temporarily were punished by the law. In Maryland, the conspirator paid the owner the full value of the slave, or he spent a year in prison. A white servant who helped a slave escape had to work four years for the master after his term of indenture ended, or he paid the value of the slave.[16] The sheriff was forced to read these statutes aloud at each of the county courts once a year. Failure to perform this duty brought a £5 fine.

The slave committed many crimes short of rebellion; the law saw these as either major or minor. Most minor crimes included stealing and striking a white person. In the slave's mind, stealing was not a crime—he was simply taking what he needed to sustain himself. Pilfering, petty larceny, perjury, and striking a white were punished by whipping, but a second offense of striking a white could lead to execution. In South Carolina the punishment was loss of an ear, a brand on the cheek, and slitting of the nose. Often the owner handled petty crimes without legal intervention. However, there were courts to try these offenses if they were reported. A justice of the peace or a county court could pass judgment. Capital offenses included murder, insurrection, "petty treason" (killing someone in authority of lower stature than the king, which was "grand treason"; in the colonies, all whites were "in authority"), rebellion, arson, attempted or actual poisoning (most slaves used arsenic, strychnine, corrosive sublimate, or laudanum rather than "plant poisons," with which they were supposed to be familiar), burglary (stealing in a house), rape or attempted rape of a white woman, killing or stealing cattle, and buggery (homosexual practices).[17]

As the number of slaves in a state increased in proportion to the white population, the punishment meted out for major crimes became more severe. In New York (1698), Jack was sentenced to death for burglary. The sentence was not carried out, but it frightened him enough so that he never appeared in court again.[18] In many similar cases, the sentence was not carried out, because the property was too valuable. Densworth, a black, was found guilty of burglary. He was imprisoned for one month and burned on his face (1704, New York). In Maryland the punishment for petty treason was to cut off the slave's right hand, and he was then hanged. The corpse was decapitated and quartered, and the parts were placed on display to terrify other blacks.[19] In major offenses, the bondsman was tried in a slave court composed of three justices of the peace and four slaveholders.[20] This court meted out justice promptly and severely. In Virginia, "if any slave resist his master [or other by his master's order correcting him] and by the extremity of coercion could chance to die, that his death shall not be accounted felony, but the master [or that other person, etc.] be acquitted for molestation, since it cannot be presumed that prepensed malice [which alone makes murder a felony] should induce any man to destroy his own estate."[21]

In North Carolina a law of 1758 permitted the court to pronounce a verdict of execution for murder or rape. Other felonies could be punished by castration. The law on castration was repealed in 1764, but in the six years of its existence, about one dozen were performed. Execution was usually by hanging, but burning at the stake for particularly heinous crimes did occur. In some instances, the hanged corpse was burned after its head was cut off and placed on a pole. Slaves were brought to watch the execution, and on occasion an arrogant slave was forced to cut the head off. In some trials, the punishment by burning was passed if the criminal burned a house *(lex talionis*—an eye for an eye).[22] In South Carolina in 1769 Dolly was burned for poisoning an infant in her care and trying to poison its father. In the same province in 1772, the punishment for murdering Captain Lazarus Brown by his slave was burning. South Carolina continued to burn slave transgressors until 1830. Jerry was the last black so executed. Jerry raped and attempted to murder his owner's wife. After his execution, Jerry's owner petitioned the legislature for $400, his appraised value. The legislature voted $122.45, one-half to the owner, the other half to the victim. (In common law, a man could be burned only for heresy, a woman for petty treason. In the colonies, English common law was stretched to cover a new set of circumstances not appreciated in the mother country.)[23] In 1830 hanging became the only means of execution for blacks.

Georgia prescribed the death penalty for many crimes by slaves. These included carrying poison to others who administered it or teaching others how to make it. Rape or attempted rape of a white woman received the same penalty as did burglary and the destruction of a white's house. In addition to the usual minor crimes prosecuted in most states, Georgia added the possession of arms and ammunition, drunkenness, absence from the plantation, and working in Savannah without a proper badge. The miscreant was brought to trial rapidly, and the punishment was carried out with equal speed. The owner could appeal for clemency in capital cases. In this circumstance, the governor became the final court of appeal. If a slave was sentenced to death, the court decided the means of execution, either hanging or burning. Statutes demanded that punishment of a slave for a felony or misdemeanor be carried out publicly to deter other slaves from similar transgressions. An owner who punished a slave privately was fined. If the court was not certain of a slave's guilt in a major case, he was deported. This prevented him from bragging to other slaves that he "beat the system."[24]

The greatest fear of whites living among large concentrations of blacks was insurrection. Whites expected uprisings at any time, and in many places the plantation resembled an armed camp. The whites had hiding places they could reach in an emergency. Many kept clothes packed and ready for instant evacuation. The master kept the best firearms available to put down any slave activity. Most whites belonged to militia companies, which represented their best chance to survive a revolt. During the Revolution, many Southern whites refused to join the federal army, because this would take them away and leave their families unprotected.

Most laws regarding blacks were passed to prevent revolts, or were passed in response to past rebellions. It is claimed that there were 250 uprisings during the period that slavery existed in the United States.[25] However, one wonders how many smaller uprisings were not reported in order to prevent other slaves from "getting ideas." When one thinks of uprisings, one imagines the slaves on a plantation rising suddenly against their masters. However, blacks did not wait until they arrived on land—many attacked the crews of ships taking them to America. There were 55 documented insurrections on board ships in 150 years, and there may have been 200 more minor skirmishes. Most revolts occurred within sight of the coast of West Africa. The Coromantee blacks were the most difficult to control and the most likely to revolt; the slaves from Benin and Angola were more docile. There were reported outbreaks on the *Albion* (1699), the *Tyger*, the *Eagle*, the *Ann*, the *Robert*, and the *Henry*. The ship owner could take out insurance to cover loss of his cargo due to insurrection. With this coverage, a captain would throw sick blacks overboard and collect on his insurance, claiming they were killed in a mutiny. Crew members on slave ships kept small arms on their persons at all times, and the ships were searched daily for iron, wood, and knives, which could be used to fashion weapons by the slaves. Crewmen were stationed at all openings. The captain learned from past experience that he could expect a revolt when the incidence of suicide increased. Women had more freedom on deck, and they smuggled material used for weapons to the men. When a rebellion was put down, the punishment was savage. One Captain Harding forced the insurrectionists to eat the heart and liver of a sailor they had killed. A woman leader was hanged by her thumbs and whipped, then slashed with knives.[26] In a particularly violent revolt on board the *Kentucky*, 47 blacks were executed by strangulation with a rope slowly pulled up over a yardarm. They were then shot in the chest and thrown overboard. To save the chains they carried, their legs were hacked off.[27]

Investigators of slave revolts agreed that economic problems precipitated most revolts on land. During the almost cyclically recurring depressions, the overseer was forced to get more work out of each "unit," and there was an associated skimping on food and clothing. Perhaps the most serious consequence of an economic downturn was the sale of part of the slave population to keep the mortgaged plantation afloat. Black families were broken up to receive the best price for an individual. Other causes of insurrection included rumors, misinformation, and foreign intervention.[28] In 1730 Virginia was to receive a new governor. It was rumored that Christian slaves would be freed upon his arrival, but this anticipated emancipation failed to materialize. During the period encompassing the Revolution, talk of liberty and equality filtered down to the slave quarters. While some bondsmen were freed during this period, most slaves could look forward only to a life of subjugation— their freedom came only with the grave. During the post–Revolutionary period (1785–1805), religious changes were developing. The growth of the Methodist Church with its egalitarian views led many to believe freedom was at hand. War with a foreign power kept the whites busy with problems created by their enemies, and there was less supervision of the slave population. The Spaniards were notorious for fomenting rebellion among the slaves in the Deep South. Their ability to cause trouble extended as far north as Maryland.[29] During the War of Jenkin's Ear (1740), the assembly of that province accused the Spanish of being in collusion with the Roman Catholic clergy of Maryland to instigate rebellion among the slaves. Word of successful revolts in other places like Haiti eventually reached the slaves of the United States, and many hoped that they could duplicate the results achieved in Haiti. (It should be mentioned that no American slave revolt was ever successful.) Finally, the growth of urban communities where slaves worked next to freedmen led to plots against the white establishment. It was almost impossible to supervise these groups. Taverns became important sites for groups to congregate.[30] Freedmen and bondsmen could meet; white servants and blacks found taverns that welcomed them; blacks, free or slave, with silver in their pockets, found white prostitutes in saloons who were "color blind." State and local governments recognized the dangerous potential of these inns and decreed them off-limits to both blacks and Indians. The Dutch were the first to restrict taverns to whites only. In Albany (1702) the constable could forcibly remove blacks and Indians on the Sabbath; the tavern owner was fined 6 pence per individual removed. In 1778 a saloon keeper could lose his license for three years for serving these groups in Albany. It was believed that the uprisings in New York City in 1712 and 1742 had developed in taverns.

Slave uprisings occurred in the North and in the South during the colonial era. During the Revolution, and until the turn of the nineteenth century, uprisings were only a Southern problem. Writers have tried to classify uprisings, but their boundaries were not clearly delineated. Uprisings were described as systematic and rational, unsystematic and vandalistic, and, lastly, opportunistic.[31] The revolts led by Gabriel Prosser and Denmark Vesey were categorized rational uprisings. These leaders wanted to overthrow the slave system and create a black state. Intense planning was required to bring about this end. The conspirators planned to take over a city and extend outward. Recruitment from these surrounding areas was vital for success. This rebellion was associated with armed conflict and bloodshed. The revolt led by Nat Turner was considered vandalistic and unsystematic. Its driving force was opposition to the slave system, with destruction of the slaveholder. This second type lacked preparation and was born completely formed. It occurred in a rural area, usually in one county, and it lacked definite goals. Finally, the third type sought escape from servitude. It was conceived and planned rationally, but its flashpoint was spontaneous. Virginia was the site of most uprisings (25 percent), followed by Louisiana (15 percent) and South Carolina (15 percent). The uprisings in these areas were largely in agricultural counties (tobacco counties in Virginia, rice counties in South Carolina, and sugar areas in Louisiana). The match that started the conflagration was usually a charismatic, literate, aware individual, free or slave. He frequently believed he was divinely inspired and had a personal destiny to lead his people. The first and second types of uprisings caused panic among the local whites, with revenge taken against the revolutionaries as well as innocent blacks, white moderates, and strangers. The third type resulted in reprisals only against the offenders.

The overall result of uprisings was greater oppression of all blacks. Legislatures passed stricter laws concerning blacks, and the patrol system developed for close supervision of all blacks in the colony. South Carolina passed a patrol act in 1737, which was strengthened and enforced after the Stono Rebellion. All whites were forced to give a certain amount of time to work in patrols to oversee and discipline the blacks in their area. The period of service ranged from one to six months in different counties. The work of the patrol was supervised and supported by the militia. The wealthy slave owner rarely joined the patrols used to protect his property; he could afford the fine for failure to do his duty. Consequently, the duty fell on the poor white, who received no stipend for his time. The poor white was taught by his minister, the newspapers, and the government that the black was inferior to him. He could accept the government controlled by a small aristocracy, because it supplied a group upon which he could look down. He also saw the slave as a threat to his own capacity to earn a living. The white patrolman suffered no financial loss if he killed a slave. The end result was that these "pattyrollers" (local patrolmen) became lynching parties.[32] The patrols could ride into slave quarters at any time to search for arms and other instruments of rebellion. They could break into any assemblage of blacks to investigate for conspiracies. A law in North Carolina (1794) gave justices of the court of pleas and of quarter sessions power to appoint six men from each militia company to the patrol. They made rounds at least every two weeks, and they could whip any black found to be off his plantation without a pass. These poor whites supplied their own arms and horses during this period of duty, and they were prohibited from consuming alcohol during this time.[33]

Little will be gained from listing all the uprisings during this era. Often these involved a few slaves who were rapidly put down and executed or deported. The larger uprisings involved many slaves as well as freedmen, white servants, and white sympathizers. These revolts resulted in serious consequences to all blacks as well as to society in general. The insurrections in New York City of 1712 and 1741 fit all the criteria for a major rebellion. New York had more slaves than any Northern province. New York City was a large urban center where blacks could congregate. The slave code of that state was harsher than that any other in the North. Problems developed with this "foreign population" gradually over several years. In 1696, a slave "assaulted the mayor on his face" after he told a group to disperse. The slave was tied behind a cart and pulled around the community; he received 11 lashes at each corner. In 1708 a black woman and an Indian man were burned for murdering their master, mistress, and five children.[34] The revolt of 1712 was started by a group of blacks who vowed to meet in Mr. Crook's orchard in the middle of town. At midnight on April 6, 23 blacks came together armed with firearms, hatchets, and swords. A slave who belonged to Mr. Vantelburgh set fire to the outhouse (or a barn), and the fire spread. When whites gathered to contain the blaze, the slaves shot into the crowd. Nine whites died, and six were wounded. The blacks fled into the woods, but they were soon captured by a detachment of soldiers ordered from the fort by Governor Robert Hunter, joined by militia units from New York and Westchester. Of 27 slaves captured, 6 committed suicide and 21 were executed. The executions of the ringleaders were extremely harsh; the followers were hanged. The governor reprieved Mars, Tom, Coffee, Husea, and John, with the latter two claiming they were free men and subjects of the Spanish king. The owners of the executed slaves were paid their value from provincial funds.[35]

The result of the uprising was the passage of stringent antislave laws, which were added to over a 30-year period. A master was permitted to punish his slave at his discretion but not to cause loss of life or limb. No more than three blacks could congregate at one place; those who defied this law received 40 lashes. A black who struck a Christian could be punished in any way short of loss of life or limb. No one was permitted to harbor slaves. Manumission was not permitted unless the master posted a £200 bond, which could be doled out to the freedman at £20 per year if he fell on hard times. Any slave involved in a conspiracy to kill, rape, or commit arson or who killed another slave was executed. "An Act Suppressing & Punishing the Conspiracy & Insurrection of negroes and other slaves" dispensed with the requirement of a grand jury for an indictment; the black could be tried outright before any court of Oyer & Terminer, which was a court to try major crimes.[36] No slave was to handle any firearms; the punishment for so doing was 20 lashes. A law of 1722 prohibited gambling. Those caught so engaged were whipped publicly. (The authorities believed that gambling led to stealing.) To avoid conspiracy among groups of blacks, a dead slave had to be buried in daylight. Nine years later, the number of mourners was restricted to 12 plus the gravediggers and pallbearers. Following the revolt, New York and other colonies placed duties on imported slaves to keep their numbers down. However, those tariffs were vetoed by the mother country.

The attempts to reduce the black population were failures. At the time of the second uprising in 1741, there were 2,000 blacks in a population of 20,000. It was impossible to supervise them adequately and keep them from congregating. The second rebellion started on February 28 when the home of James Hogg was robbed of linen and other belongings worth £60. John Hughson was apprehended, and he admitted to receiving stolen goods from two blacks, Caesar and Prince. On March 8, Fort George was burned to the ground. One week later, the roof of a house caught fire. On April 1, a storehouse burned to the ground. In the next four days, the city was the scene of four additional fires. The white population started to panic, and many left the city. The colonial government, in the person of Lieutenant Governor George Clarke, issued a proclamation of reward and pardon to anyone who would reveal the culprit. The city council offered a reward for the names of conspirators: £100 for white men, £45 for blacks, mulattoes and Indians, plus £20 and freedom to any slave who turned a conspirator over to the authorities. Mary Burton, Hughson's white indentured servant, was questioned about the robbery and fires. She described a conspiracy to burn down the city and kill the whites. Mary named Caesar, Prince, and Peggy Kerry, a prostitute who lodged at Hughson's house. She had had a child with one of the black conspirators. The mastermind of the plot was John Hughson, who would become king of New York. Caesar was to be appointed governor. With each retelling, her tale became grander and more vile. The number of involved whites grew. All of those accused were tried before the New York Supreme Court. On May 10, the court ordered that two slaves be hanged, although they denied any knowledge of the conspiracy. On June 12, Hughson and his wife were executed. They too proclaimed their innocence. Initially, Peggy Kerry denied knowledge of the plot, but she later admitted complicity in order to earn the governor's pardon. She claimed that the plot was hatched at John Romme's tavern. She later recanted the Romme story and was rewarded with the noose. Other slaves were implicated in two fires that broke out near the house of a man who had purchased two Spanish slaves. (These purchased bondsmen claimed they were free men.) Witnesses testified that they saw a black man fleeing from one of the burning buildings. These fires resulted in the mass arrest of many slaves. One slave, Quack, caught in the roundup, admitted that he had burned Fort George. This information was tainted, through, by the way in which it was extracted.[37]

On June 19, Clarke promised pardons and transportation out of the colony for slaves who confessed to their involvement within a specified period. Sixty-seven slaves confessed and implicated others. These confessions frequently contradicted others obtained at the same time from other detainees. However, judges believed what they wanted to believe despite the contradictions. The story accepted by most was that each slave was to burn his master's house, kill the nearest whites, and take over the city. Mary Burton and others confessed to their involvement when faced with death. Quack and Coffee confessed when the wood piled around their stakes was ignited. Two slaves, Sarah and Jack, implicated anyone they could think of when faced with execution; Jack was freed.[38] The violence and excitement increased when Clarke received a communication from General James Oglethorpe of Georgia, claiming that Spanish and Roman Catholic priests were going to burn English cities. These priests would go through the English colonies pretending to be physicians, dancing instructors, and members of other trusted occupations. Then they would gain the confidence of the families and use them as bases for carrying out their planned acts of arson.[39] Further proof of this plan was found in a Spanish vessel manned partly by Spanish blacks. One was suspected of involvement in the conspiracy, and all were seized and sold into slavery. Suspicion also fell on John Ury, a Latin teacher, who was suspected of being a disguised priest and the mastermind. Mary Burton corroborated this belief. At Ury's trial, Mary Burton, John Hughson's daughter Sarah, and William Kane, a soldier, testified that Ury gave absolution to slaves when they pillaged. The witnesses gave this testimony when they were threatened with death by the tribunal. Ury was sentenced to death by resurrecting an old law that imposed severe penalties on Roman Catholic priests in New York. Ury became the focus for anti–Catholic feelings, and he was executed in September. Mary Burton then started to incriminate some of the wealthy and influential citizens in New York. This brought the "reign of terror" to a halt, and the trials ended. The slaves who survived returned to their masters. The Rommes and several members of the Hughson family left the colony. Mary Burton was rewarded for her help, and she disappeared from the pages of history.

The conspiracy theory consumed the citizens as the fires did the houses. Perhaps it started with the need for a scapegoat. The winter was unusually severe, and fuel was low. The Hudson River froze, and ships carrying food and grain from upstate could not deliver to meet the city's needs, so perhaps the inhabitants needed someone to blame for their misery. Added to this was the fear of a French or a Spanish invasion (the War of Jenkins' Ear). Finally, robbery and fencing of stolen goods may have been a cause of the fires—fires were set to allow the perpetrators to run into the houses to "save the treasures from the fire." The conspiracy theory was not limited to the lower socioeconomic class of the city. A letter from Daniel Horsmarden to Calwallader Colden of August 7, 1741, demonstrates his complete acceptance of the generally held belief:

> It was discovered that popery was at the bottom. The priest Ury was convicted as one of the principal conspirators & is to be hanged. If providence had not interfered, the inhabitants would have been butchered by their slaves and the City in ashes. This was to have been carried out under an Oath of Obligation administered to the conspirators by Jonathan Hughson & Ury the

priest. Ury baptized them into the Roman Catholic faith & told them all sins would be forgiven if they destroyed the heretics. They would be doing God's service. They brought to light 90 negroes & about 12 whites. Thirty negroes & four whites (including the priest) were executed. Many among us tried to discredit Mary Burton the Original witness. Her testimony was corroborated by negroes who were about to be burned at the stake. Everything Mary Burton said has been confirmed.[40]

Unlike the uprising of 1712, no new antiblack laws were passed. However, the revolt took its toll. Arrests and punishments occupied the inhabitants for one year. One hundred fifty slaves and 25 whites were imprisoned. Eighteen slaves and four whites were hanged. Thirteen slaves were burned at the stake, and more than 70 blacks were deported to the West Indies.

The Stono (Cato) Rebellion in 1739 was the explosion that had been building up in South Carolina for decades. Four proprietors of the colony were members of the Royal Africa Company, so there was unlimited import of blacks into the colony. Very early in the colony's history, the number of blacks exceeded that of the white's. (In 1724 there were three times as many blacks as whites in the colony.) Uprisings or rumors of rebellion brought severe penalties due to the fears of the small white ruling aristocracy. In 1720 several slaves were burned at the stake because of a rumor of a revolt outside of Charleston. In 1730 a small uprising in this area was easily put down. There were three uprisings in 1739. The most serious occurred at Stono, 20 miles west of Charleston. An eyewitness described the uprising:

> A number of negroes having assembled together at Stono, first surprised & killed two young men in a weare-house, & then plundered it of guns & ammunition. Being thus provided with arms, they elected one of their number as Captain, & agreed to follow him marching toward the south-west, with colours flying & drums beating, like a disciplined company.... They plundered & burnt every house, killing every white person they found in them, & compelling the Negroes to join them.
>
> Governor Bull returning from Charleston from the southward, met them & observing them armed, spread the alarm, which soon reached the Presbyterian Church at Walton.... By a law of the province, all Planters were obliged to carry their arms to church, which at this critical juncture proved a very useful & necessary regulation. The women were left in church trembling with fear, while the militia, under the command of Captain Bee, marched in quest of the negroes, who by this time had become formidable, from the number [of slaves] that joined them.
>
> They had marched about 12 miles, & spread desolation through all the plantations in their way. They halted in an open field & began to sing & dance, by way of triumph. During these rejoicings, the militia discovered them.... One party advanced into the open field & attacked them, &, having killed some negroes, the remainder took to the woods & dispersed. Many ran back to their masters; but the great part were taken & tried. Such as had been compelled to join them, contrary to their inclination, were pardoned, but all of the chosen leaders & first insurgents suffered death.[41]

A little fleshing out of this account is needed for completeness. The governor of Florida (which was Spanish) prepared for war with England, and he offered freedom to all English slaves who successfully reached St. Augustine.[42] On September 9, 1739, a group of South Carolina blacks, originally from Angola and under the leadership of "Captain Tommy," broke into a fort and obtained firearms and alcohol. They marched south and attacked plantation homes along their route of march. The white occupants were killed outright, and the slaves were encouraged or forced to join their army. They stopped to celebrate their victory with alcohol, dancing and singing. The South Carolina militia caught them and killed 40, while the rest fled back to their plantations. Almost two dozen whites were killed in the violence.

There were additional uprisings in 1740. Fires broke out in several sections of Charleston; it was estimated that these fires caused £250,000 in damages. One slave admitted his involvement, and two blacks were hanged. During that same year, a plot involving 200 slaves was discovered. One hundred fifty slaves were taken, and ten were hanged daily to suppress the black population.[43]

The result of these uprisings was very stringent laws to control blacks, as well as rules to ameliorate their degraded condition. In addition, attempts were made to increase the white Protestant population. The patrol system was more strictly enforced, and the duties of the militia were increased. The militia supervised the patrol system. Slaves were defined as personal chattel. Decrees prevented the assemblage of blacks, the use of liquor by slaves, and the teaching of blacks to read and write, except under the aegis of the Society for the Propagation of the Gospels in Foreign Ports (SPG). This group, an offshoot of the Anglican Church, was permitted to start schools to train blacks in the tenets of the Christian religion, and it trained blacks to become teachers of other black and Indian children. A school was built in Charleston, and the £400 required for its construction was subsidized by 16 white Charlestonians. To ease the slaves' life, owners could not work them on Sundays. They were required to supply their chattel with adequate clothing. The number of hours of work permitted per day was listed. The slaves worked longer days in the summer than in the winter, when daylight hours were shorter. To decrease the number of slaves entering the colony, duties were raised. This accomplished little or nothing, though, because land was being brought under cultivation in the West, and the demand for slave labor increased. In 1741 the duty was £100 per head, which was ten times the previous duty. Slave owners tried to divide their slave population by enlisting slave informers, who were rewarded handsomely for their fidelity to their masters during uprisings. Slaves received money, fancy clothes, and sometimes freedom for siding with their masters. This technique bore fruit. For instance, an insurrection planned for 1740 in St. John's Parish was revealed by Peter, a slave belonging to Major Condes. Under the guise of a "dancing bout" in

Charleston, the slaves were to gather and start their revolt; the uprising was to spread to the plantations around Charleston. In 1743 Sabrina betrayed a group planning to escape to Florida. Some slaves went one step further and became slave hunters to gain better treatment for themselves and their families.[44]

In an attempt to destroy the Spanish influence in Florida, the South Carolina General Assembly assisted General Oglethorpe of Georgia in his invasion of Florida, provided 500 troops, 500 Indians, supplies, and a promise of £40,000 in currency. The invasion failed, as did the regulations imposed on the blacks. Blacks continued to congregate. They bought and sold openly in the markets of Charleston. Many whites assisted the blacks in their purchases for their own personal gain. Slaves were admitted to taverns and could consume all the alcohol their funds covered. Slaves were able to hire themselves out without their master's knowledge. After the duty act that was enforced until 1744 ended, the influx of blacks increased. By 1752 approximately 1,000 blacks were sold in South Carolina each year. In 1760 the number reached 3,600. Prior to the Revolution, there were one and a half times as many blacks as whites in South Carolina.

Gabriel Prosser and his two brothers, Solomon and Martin, were slaves on a tobacco plantation six miles outside of Richmond, Virginia. Gabriel was trained as a blacksmith, and he could read and write. The blacksmith was taller than six feet and a little wild.[45] One year prior to his uprising, he came to the attention of the law when he and Solomon had a fight with a neighboring planter, Absolam Johnson. Solomon was tried and acquitted of threatening bodily harm, but Gabriel was convicted of biting off most of Johnson's left ear. Maiming was a felony with a death penalty for a slave (a white could serve two to five years in jail for this crime). However, Gabriel was let off with a T brand on the base of his left thumb. His owner also posted a bond of $1,000 in goods and chattel to ensure his good behavior.[46]

Gabriel prepared carefully for this rebellion; planning it for August 20, 1800. At this time the fields would be ready for harvest and the livestock fattened for slaughter. He believed his followers could live off the land until they achieved their goals. It has been claimed that he could count on 1,000 slaves from Henrico County as well as Carolina County, Goochland, and Petersburg. His lieutenants believed that 50,000 slaves would join them after their initial success. Several of his followers had fought in the Revolution, and they became group leaders. Prosser planned to recruit the Catawba Indians but decided against it at the last minute. The leader planned to have the coconspirators meet on Prosser's land and march to Richmond in three groups. One would attack the capital, another the magazine for arms, and the third the penitentiary. Prosser kept a supply of swords, bayonets attached to sticks, and 500 bullets to be used when necessary. The slaves would capture and fortify Richmond and wait for news of other cities being taken or that an army of slaves was marching to Richmond to give them support. The outlying slaves were to kill all the whites and establish a black monarchy with Gabriel Prosser as king. If this plan failed, they would march to the mountains and defend themselves. During the spring before the uprising, Prosser brought other slaves into his conspiracy; most were city slaves who lived away from their plantations. He suspected that house slaves were allied to their masters, and he did not take any of them into his confidence. Prosser had several trusted lieutenants. Reuben Byrd, a freedman, controlled the blacks in Petersburg, 25 miles south of Richmond. Sam Byrd, Sr., was a free mulatto who controlled the blacks in Hanover. Men were enlisted from as far away as Charlottesville, 65 miles northwest of Richmond. News was spread by a black mail carrier along the small towns on his route. A bondsman on the James River spread the news to Norfolk and Suffolk. They were all to wait until violence erupted in Richmond before moving. Prosser tried to get rural slaves to join him, but he was less successful despite revealing his plan to them.

According to the plan, he would kill his owner, Thomas Henry Prosser. Conspirators would meet at Brooks Bridge. One hundred men would be left to guard the bridge, while another 100 would go with Prosser to storm the capital. They would march under a banner proclaiming "Liberty or Death." Robert Cowley, a free black doorkeeper (at the magazine), would supply them with arms. Fifty men would start a fire at Rockett's tobacco inspection station, in the warehouse section, as a diversion. Prosser planned to take Governor Monroe as a hostage. At this period in history, there was a division in Virginia over the coming election between the Federalists, whose strongholds were in the cities, and the Republicans, whose support was rural. Prosser assumed that rural whites would not come to the aid of the city whites. He planned to spare Methodists and Quakers because of their efforts to end slavery. Frenchmen would be saved because France was in a "small" war with the United States. Poor women without slaves would also be spared. Prosser expected poor white laborers and Frenchmen to join him. (Charles Querrey and Alexander Bettenhurst were claimed as supporters by Prosser.)[47]

The uprising was pushed back to August 30. However, an unusually heavy rainstorm drenched the area that night and carried away bridges and other means of communication. Prosser tried to get word out to postpone the attack for one night. Meanwhile, two slaves, Pharaoh and Tom, who belonged to Mosby Sheppard, told their master of the plot. Sheppard spread the alarm and went to Governor James Monroe to advise him to prepare the state. In Petersburg, another slave told his master, Benjamin Harrison, about the uprising. The militia was called out. Units guarded the capital, the penitentiary, and the arsenal, and others patrolled the countryside to pick up suspected slaves. Martial law was declared, and militia units hanged slaves they picked up on the roads. Prosser escaped. Monroe established a board of inquiry composed of magistrates Miles Seldan and Gervas Storrs and the Henrico County

Court of Oyer & Terminer. An attorney, James Rind, was appointed to defend the conspirators. A black, Ben Woolfolk, was caught in the net; to save his life, he named Prosser as leader as well as other Richmond blacks. Other surrounding communities hunted for their own conspirators. The authorities were able to find lists of insurgents written by literate slaves. At the end of September, Prosser was betrayed by a black named Billy, who received a reward. The leader was on board the schooner *Mary*, which sailed between Richmond and Norfolk; he was returned to Richmond and held in solitary confinement. Gabriel, Solomon, and Martin, along with their confederates, were tried and hanged in October 1800. Approximately 35 blacks were executed.[48] Monroe found the names of the Frenchmen who supported Prosser, but he kept them secret for political reasons. The Republicans were pro-French, and Monroe feared that this knowledge would drive many into the Federalist camp.

The results of this uprising, like the others, were strict antiblack laws and more intense patrol activity, and it is said that this uprising was one of the factors in the formation of the American Colonization Society.

The uprisings of Denmark Vesey and Nat Turner (while really beyond the time frame of this chapter) involved significant numbers, an unusual amount of planning, and consequences for both blacks and whites.

Denmark Vesey was a slave of Joseph Vesey, a ship's captain, and so the bondsman traveled around the world with his master. Joseph Vesey eventually gave up the sea and settled in Charleston, South Carolina, as a slave trader. At the age of 33, Denmark Vesey won $1,500 in the East Bay Street lottery. He paid the captain $600 for his freedom in 1800 and worked as a carpenter to support himself; he was eventually able to accumulate a modest estate. As a freedman, he had more freedom of movement, and he was able to hold meetings in his house as well as to deliver talks at black religious meetings. Denmark knew the Bible and quoted from the Scriptures to inflame his audiences against their white oppressors. Denmark compared his listeners to the Israelites, who gained their freedom from the Egyptians. He found passages from the Bible to demonstrate the sins of slavery, and he quoted from speeches delivered in Congress against the institution.[49] He repeated the words of Congressman King, who believed that slavery was "a great disgrace to the country."[50] Vesey referred frequently to the success of the revolt in Haiti. He had no interest in the American Colonization Society, because in his view blacks had opened the country with their labor and it belonged to them. Vesey planned a violent uprising for Sunday, July 14, 1822. This would be the darkest night of the month, and it celebrated the start of the French Revolution. This time was chosen because many whites had left Charleston to avoid the summer heat with its attendant miasmas (malaria and yellow fever), and the slaves would be reasonably free of restraints in the city. The leaders feared, however, that their plans had been leaked to the authorities, so they moved up the date one month to June. It is difficult to ascertain when the plan evolved in his mind, but Vesey planned extensively; chose his lieutenants carefully; did not take any "house slaves" into his confidence, because they were too close to their white masters; drew up a battle plan; and stored weapons, including 250 pike heads, bayonets, and 300 daggers. His aides were Rolla, Peter Poyas, and Monday Gill. He and two appointed agents traveled in and around Charleston and enlisted many blacks, perhaps as many as 9,000. Vesey had a blacksmith, Tom Russel, as his armorer, and Lot Forrester as his courier. Denmark's overall plan was to kill all the whites; burn down Charleston; take money from the banks and supplies from the stores; seize the vessels in port and kill the crews except the captains; and then sail to Santo Domingo. Peter Poyas and his followers, joined by a group from James Island, were to seize the arsenal and guardhouse and cut off the whites. Ned Bennett and his group were to assemble on the Neck and seize the arsenal. Rolla and his soldiers were to assemble at Governor Bennett's Mills, kill the governor, and proceed to Cannons Bridge to prevent the whites from Cannonsborough from going to Charleston. A fourth group was to take the guardhouse at Gadsden's Wharf. Another group was to seize a powder magazine at Bulkley's Farm. A group commanded by Gullah Jack, an African-born witch doctor, who, it was believed, could make his followers invulnerable to enemy arms, was to disarm the militia at the Neck and obtain arms from Duquerron's shop. Naval stores on Meig's Wharf were to be seized. A company of black cavalry would patrol the streets to prevent whites from congregating to form effective fighting units. Finally, a group was to be kept around Vesey to carry out any new orders needed as the revolt progressed. Bacchus Hammett would seize unguarded arms on the Neck. The shops of gunsmiths in Charleston were noted for seizure during the uprising. Vesey also enlisted black barbers to make wigs and whiskers for disguise if that became necessary. He expected all blacks he encountered to join his army; those who refused were to be killed. The surprising part of these preparations was that this black had the freedom of the city. He could scout out gunsmiths, arsenals, guardhouses, and other important areas to be seized at the start of the uprising.[51]

Unfortunately for the group, an informer learned of the plot. John C. Prioleau's slave, Devany, heard of the plan from William, a slave of the Paul family—a Vesey lieutenant had tried to enlist William, a house slave. Devany reported this knowledge to George Pencil, a free black, who urged him to tell his master. Devany told Prioleau's son (or wife), who told the master, Colonel John Prioleau, about the information he received on May 30. The city council and the governor were informed, and a meeting was held with Devany, who repeated the information he had received from William. William denied all knowledge of the uprising and was thrown into solitary confinement. The following day, William admitted to his knowledge of the plan to

Captain Dove, the warden. He implicated Mingo Harth and Peter Poyas, who were arrested. They were able to talk their way out of their captors' hands. William (or another slave) was able to advise the authorities that the uprising was scheduled on June 16 or July 2 at midnight. Troops were ordered out. Captain Cattell's corps of hussars, Captain Miller's light infantry, Captain Martindale's Neck Rangers, the Charleston Riflemen, and city guardsmen were all under the command of Colonel Robert Y. Hayne. The city was on guard, and the rebels did not attack. On June 17 the city council sent out letters to get potential jurors for the expected trials. The slaves would be tried under an old law dating to 1740. On the night of June 17, an investigation into the information was started, and ten slaves were immediately arrested. Vesey was arrested on June 22 and tried on June 27; he and his lieutenants were sentenced and hanged on July 2. Other trials lasted until August 13. A total of 131 blacks were arrested. Thirty-five were hanged, 43 banished, and 53 exonerated. Whites were implicated, and four were arrested and fined for the misdemeanor of inciting slaves to insurrection. The whites probably joined the conspiracy against the white authorities because the slaves competed with their ability to earn a living, and the authorities were major slaveholders. The cost of the aborted uprisings was itemized. The investigation, construction of gallows, the executioner, and the £200 to the black who supplied the information came to a grand total of $2,284.84¼. The city of Charleston tried to get reimbursed for its expense from the state.

After the blacks received their punishment and the excitement subsided, many questioned whether a conspiracy had really existed.[52] There was no network in the countryside, and no activity was seen in rural areas. No cache of arms was discovered, no definite date for the uprising was known, and no underground apparatus came to light. William Johnson, a judge, and the brother-in-law of the governor, believed it was a case of mass hysteria. Governor Thomas Bennett questioned the legality of the proceedings: specifically, a trial closed to the public; tainted testimony to gain immunity; and freedom given from the noose for those who implicated others. These "nonbelievers" thought the plot started with loose talk. A black uprising in Charleston was almost impossible. The city police were well organized, and the urban slaves had more freedom and affluence than their country kin. Black superiority in numbers was only slightly greater than that of whites.

The end result of this "uprising" was more stringent statutes.[53] No free blacks were permitted to enter the state. If a free black native left South Carolina, he could not return. Free blacks were taxed and forced to have white guardians to guarantee their proper behavior. No slave was permitted to hire himself out. Slaves purchased from the West Indies, Mexico, South America, Europe, or states north of Maryland were prohibited from entering the state—the slaves, particularly from the North, might carry abolitionist ideas.[54] The Negro Seamen's Act was passed to keep free black sailors on their ships while in port.

The Nat Turner Rebellion was responsible for more white deaths than any uprising before or since.[55] It created fear among whites all over the South. Nat was born a slave in 1800. He learned to read, write, and study from the Bible, becoming a "preacher" and a "prophet of God" and conducting services somewhat resembling those of the Baptists.[56] He was probably schizophrenic and believed that God had chosen him to do some great work because he was an "instrument of God." He saw visions of black angels fighting white angels in heaven.[57] He saw private messages on leaves written in blood. Nat saw a kingdom of liberty for blacks, with white slave owners as the enemy. In 1828 he was visited by a spirit who told him that "the serpent is loose." He was urged to take up the yoke laid down by Jesus and fight that serpent. Turner received a "sign from God" in the form of a solar eclipse on February 12, 1831, and he actively began to plan the uprising. He made four slaves his lieutenants. They decided to "strike for liberty" on July 4, but Turner fell sick and the revolt was canceled. The second sign came on August 13, when Turner saw a greenish blue color in the sun for three days and "blood on the moon" for three nights. Nat addressed a religious meeting of the slaves, and they showed acceptance of his plan by wearing a red bandanna on their necks. The plotters met on the afternoon of August 21 to rise up that night. Six slaves started the rebellion by murdering Joseph Turner and his family at Cross Keys, ten miles from Jerusalem, Virginia. Arms and horses were taken from the dead family. Other slaves joined them, and in 24 hours they had 70 adherents.[58] By August 23, 57 whites had been killed. Turner ordered them not to kill women, children, and men who did not resist. The group set out for Jerusalem, the county seat of Southampton County, to gather more arms. They approached the house belonging to the Parker family, and a part of the band went in to enlist the Parker slaves, but they found liquor and became drunk. Turner and a group remained outside the gate until Turner went inside to see what was delaying the others. The remaining group, left at the gate, was attacked by whites who had heard the alarm. Turner and those in the house came outside and forced the whites to retreat. A company of militia appeared, and the slaves fled. The mayor of Norfolk, Virginia, asked Colonel Eustis from Fort Monroe to help put down the rebellion. On August 24, three companies of artillery with one cannon and spare arms were mustered; they were joined by detachments from the warships *Warren* and *Natchez*. The growing army received reinforcements from soldiers, other militias, and volunteers from Virginia and North Carolina. A massacre followed, with the killing of blacks, those involved along with those who were innocent. One white man was found dead among the conspirators; his face had been blackened with ash as a disguise. Some of the conspirators were decapitated "as a lesson."[59]

Turner escaped this maelstrom, but he was captured on October 30 by Benjamin Phipps. He was brought to trial and pleaded not guilty, because he was following God's command. Judge Jeremiah Cobb pronounced the sentence of death on November 5, and Turner was hanged on November 11. More than 180 blacks were executed without trial. The massacre would have continued unabated but for General Eppes's threat to impose martial law. Thirteen slaves and three free blacks were hanged legally after a trial. Whites asked each other with perplexity why the slaves had revolted—they were reasonably treated by Virginia standards. The consensus was reached that outsiders had incited them. The "Walker Pamphlet" had been discovered some weeks earlier and most pointed to *The Liberator* as the source. The newspaper had passed from hand to hand in the slave quarters throughout Virginia. Southern newspaper editors called upon the mayor of Boston to suppress this source of revolution. William Lloyd Garrison, its editor, continued to publish the paper, however. In absentia, he was indicted in Raleigh and New Bern for inciting to rebellion.[60]

As occurred following the other uprisings, laws against free blacks became more restrictive. Police codes were strengthened. Attempts at education of blacks were suppressed. The Virginia business as a breeding ground and supplier of blacks to the Deep South was ruined, for the states south of Virginia passed laws prohibiting all importation of slaves from Virginia. They feared that Virginia would send the most rebellious slaves to get them out of the state. The governor of Louisiana called the legislature into session: "In all probability attempts will be made to introduce to Louisiana slaves of vicious habits ... participants in the late horrible scenes at Southampton."[61]

The results of these insurrections have been described in relation to the individual revolts. The black codes, increased patrol activities, and increased duties to try to keep black numbers down have been cited. There were several overall consequences, however, that developed secondary to these uprisings. The South became a white armed camp. Every white had a gun and was a soldier in the army formed to keep the black man "in his place." The Quakers, and to some degree the Methodists, left the South; they were considered abolitionists who put improper thoughts into "childish black heads." The Quakers were followed by many nonslaveholders because of fear; in addition, they could not compete with slave labor. When fear for their lives became part of the equation, many felt there was little to hold them in the South. The South was not depopulated by this exodus, though and those who remained could add to their finances as overseers, slave catchers, and substitute patrol members. Many blacks were executed after uprisings, and their masters were compensated from provincial financial funds that were collected from slaveholders and nonslaveholders. The poor white had little for which to be taxed, but several states had poll taxes that affected everyone. The South remained an agricultural area with very little large-scale manufacturing. The moneyed class had its wealth tied up in slaves and land, with little left over for machinery and factories. Northern investors preferred the relative safety of the North. This fear was encouraged by newspapers in the North, which carried stories about the revolts in graphic terms accompanied by lists of white deaths. Furthermore, a large factory in the South could bring many blacks together where they could plan further rebellion. Laws were passed by the federal and state governments to restrict the slave trade, but these were poorly enforced because of a lack of resources, as well as the need for more slaves to work new land opened in the West. Also, many of these laws were on state books for a specified short period of time. In the North, at the turn of the century, laws for gradual emancipation became commonplace. In the South, emancipation became more difficult and in some places was impossible. The concept of colonization smoldered in the eighteenth century, but it became a conflagration in the nineteenth. To quote John Randolph (1816), colonization would "secure the property of every master in his slaves by removing free Negroes who excited discontent among slaves."[62]

Much has been written about slave codes, and at this point it would be proper to describe the basic provisions of all codes. Blacks were believed to be barbarous, wild, and savage, and could not be ruled by the laws that governed the remainder of the population. Special laws had to be passed to govern this undesirable but needed class of laborers in the middle of a white society. These statutes were passed to prevent disorder, rape, and inhumanity to which they were prone, and to protect white citizens. Laws pertaining to these unwelcome laborers were passed over the years in response to some infraction committed by these people. Many laws duplicated previous laws, and others contradicted them. Codifications, related to blacks, were required to bring order out of this chaos. The code in South Carolina in 1712 was a model for other codes in the South. It stated that all Negroes, mulattoes, mestizos, and Indians who were sold for slaves would remain slaves, as would their children. They would remain slaves for life unless they performed some meritorious deed; they would be freed if they could prove they had been free men in the past. This last condition was adjudicated by the governor's council. No master was to give a slave a pass for Sunday, a holy day, or other time. The only slaves allowed off the plantation were those who were body servants or who were wearing livery. Slaves caught off the plantations were to be whipped by any white man who found them; whites who did not carry out this rule were fined 20 shillings, half to the poor through the church warden and the other half to the informer. A ticket that allowed a slave to leave a plantation temporarily bore the slave's name, the place to which he was sent, and the time he was expected to return. Anyone who gave a ticket in his master's name was fined 20 shillings. Any white could check a black's ticket. If the bondsman refused to present it, the white could beat, maim or kill the slave.[63]

Masters or their overseers were required to search the slaves' quarters every 14 days to check for runaways, guns, swords, and clubs; these were removed and secured. Also, they searched for clothes not given to the slave by his master; these were considered stolen and were taken into custody. The discovered material was described in writing, and this written description was given to the provost marshal or clerk of the parish. The description was then posted on the church door. and in other public places. Any white who recognized the material as stolen and could identify it as belonging to him paid 12 pence and was sent where the material was stored; he then received the items he identified. Anyone who neglected this duty to the rightful owner was fined 20 shillings. A white man suspected of trading with slaves for stolen goods was to appear at the next general sessions by order of any justice of the peace. The accused miscreant had to prove that he had obtained the material legally. If he failed to do so, the goods were forfeited. No black or slave could carry a firearm off the plantation without a certificate from his master or when accompanied by his master. A white who apprehended a black could seize the firearm unless the master redeemed it within three months' time and paid him 20 shillings. The master kept all firearms in a unfrequented room or he was fined £3. Slaves who went to Charleston on Sundays or holidays to drink, fight, curse, carry clubs, or otherwise profane the Sabbath were in a position to perform wicked designs against the inhabitants. Town constables were empowered to impress any white into a posse to search for slaves in houses in or around Charleston. Those caught were publicly whipped and bound over to the marshal. The marshal paid the constable 5 shillings per slave. The marshall was reimbursed this 5 shillings and any other expense he incurred while holding the slave. The marshal treated the slave as a common runaway with the same penalties. If a white refused to join a posse, he was fined 80 shillings, and if the constable failed to cooperate with the marshal, he too was fined 20 shillings. The master was not permitted to give his slave a pass to Charleston or other plantations on Sundays or holidays unless some function had to be performed; the nature of the business was described on the ticket. Failure to obey this rule led to a 10 shilling fine.[64]

If a complaint was made to a justice of the peace that the slave committed a felony (killing, burglary, burning a house), the justice of the peace issued a warrant to apprehend the offender and for all to give evidence of the crimes if they had any knowledge. If the slave appeared guilty, he was sent to prison or put on trial immediately. The justice of the peace called another justice plus three freeholders (slaveholders). (This kept Quakers off the court, because they had no slaves.) The "judges" and those to give testimony were advised when and where to appear; the freeholders were sworn in. If the slave was found guilty of murder or other heinous crimes, he received the death sentence, which was carried out almost immediately. The means of execution was carried out by the court's judgment. If the crime did not deserve death, the court prescribed any punishment that was not disabling unless a law specifically called for it (for example, cutting the Achilles tendon). This too was carried out promptly. If a slave stole or destroyed property not belonging to his master and of less than 12 pence in value, he was taken to the justice of the peace. If found guilty, he was publicly whipped up to 40 lashes. For a second offense, one ear was cut off, or he was branded on his forehead. For a third offense, his nose was slit. For a fourth offense, he was tried as a burglar or murderer; if found guilty, he was executed or received any judgment deemed proper by the judges. If the justices or the freeholders refused to do this duty, they were fined £25.[65]

If a slave killed a slave who belonged to another master, and his master sent him out of the province, his master paid the other owner the value of his lost slave. If the slave killed a white, and the owner sent him out of the province, the fine was £500. The case was adjudicated by the court of common pleas of the province within one year. Any slave meeting or preparation for a slave meeting (to plan an uprising) was tried by two justices of the peace and three freeholders. If found guilty, the perpetrators were executed. If someone carried the slaves away or failed to present the suspected offenders to the court, he was fined £50 per slave. If more than one slave was involved, the governor and council could order death to the leader; the rest of the slaves were returned to their owners. The freeholders of the county paid the cost of the executed slave proportional to the number of slaves they owned. If a freeholder refused to pay his assessed cost, the justices and the freeholders issued warrants on the goods and chattel of the owner; these were sold at auction to pay the assessed cost. Anything above the value was returned to the owner. The part paid by the individual had to be less than one-sixth the value of his slaves. If the money raised did not cover the cost of the executed slaves, the provincial treasury made up the difference.[66]

The South Carolina code of 1712 was not "written in stone." Different problems arose, and different laws and codes had to be fashioned for the 150 years that slavery persisted in the United States after this date. Many new laws and regulations followed black rebellion. Others were written to cover contingencies that were specific to one state or community. Georgia, only four years after slavery was legalized, developed a strict code to control the influx of blacks. In this area, as in many of its statutes, Georgia copied almost verbatim the laws of its "older sister to the north." The code in Georgia recognized every slave as a potential danger to whites. Acts of violence to people or property were treated as capital offenses. In the codes of 1765 and 1770, any slave who carried poison to someone who planned to administer it or who taught others how to use poison was deemed as guilty as the users and was executed. Rape or attempted rape, burglary, or destruction of a white's house merited the death penalty. The court could decide on the means of execution. Execution was carried out in public, and the miscreant's head was cut off and placed on a pole at the site of the crime.[67]

North Carolina had fewer slaves in proportion to the whites than any of the Southern states. Much of its code was copied from Virginia's, but the slave's existence was easier than in other states. The code of 1715 reduced blacks' mobility, and discouraged commercial and social relations between the races. Some trusted slaves requested and received more liberty; they could rent houses and other lodging in town, and they could engage in commercial activity. Slaves were permitted to hire themselves out, and if they had free time they were permitted to entertain themselves with horse racing and other amusements. After dark, more stringent rules were enforced on their activity. After the Stono Rebellion, laws were more strict and enforced to the letter.[68]

Finally, death was pronounced by the judge more commonly following rebellions. Intervention by the slave's master was not countenanced. Also, the mode of execution took more time to achieve its goal so that the accused could contemplate his misdeeds. It was hoped that other slaves, who were forced to attend the execution would have second thoughts about rebellion. After the New York Uprising of 1741 the judge intoned, "[As to slaves Tom and Furniss] ... these to be burned with fire and to continue in the fire till they be consumed to ashes; [as to Robin] ... to be hung in chains alive and so to continue without any Sustenance until he be dead; [as to Clause] ... broke upon a wheel and so to continue languishing until he be dead, his head and quarters to be at the Queen's Disposal."[69]

Chapter 13

BLACKS AND CHRISTIANITY

For generations Africans followed a religion that satisfied their needs. Some blacks were introduced to Christianity by the Portuguese who explored the west coast of Africa. Africans taken to the Iberian Peninsula were accepted by the Catholics there and became new communicants to that religion. A smaller number reached northern, Protestant Europe and were baptized. In the New World, in the colonies of Spain and Portugal, Catholic priests welcomed the slaves into their religion, as had their predecessors in Europe. However, the English in North America were more grudging in their conversion of slaves to Protestantism. English common law prohibited a Christian Englishman from keeping another Christian as a slave; therefore, slaves were denied the sacraments of their masters' religion. This attitude refuted one of the arguments used in favor of slavery—namely, that the heathen would be converted to the one true religion and their souls would find eternal salvation. To bring order out of these conflicting concepts, colonial legislatures passed laws that denied freedom to the newly converted black Christians.

Virginia stated in 1667 that "baptism doth not alter the condition of the person as to his bondage or freedom in order that diverse masters freed from this doubt may more carefully endeavor the propagation of Christianity." John Locke's *Treatise on Government*, adopted by South Carolina as its constitution, claimed that all men could worship as they pleased, but spiritual freedom did not affect the status of the slave. Every free man in Carolina had "absolute authority and power over his negro slaves of what opinion of religion soever."[1] Maryland's act of assembly (June 4, 1692) stated, "Many have been discouraged from importing slaves. Those with slaves have prevented their receiving the Holy Sacrament of Baptism for fear they would automatically be freed with their children. It was enacted by the General Assembly with the support of King and Queen that no slave becomes free on becoming Christian."[2] Virginia, in 1705, repealed an earlier law (1682) that freed blacks born of Christian parents in England, and Christians from Spanish colonies, English colonies, and other Christian lands. New York, to encourage baptism of Indians, Negroes, and mulattoes, ruled in 1706 that this conversion would not free them.[3] Therefore, the acceptance of Christ did not change the social (and particularly financial) status of the blacks.

There were other obstacles to bringing the slaves into the "protection of Christianity." Most colonies had laws against teaching blacks to read and write, because then they could read and disseminate propaganda against the institution of slavery. Therefore, Christianity had to be learned by rote. Also, there was the unspoken fear of slave revolts. Bringing slaves together for services could lead to secret schemes for insurrection. Furthermore, most slaves worked all day. After sundown they had to prepare and eat their main meal as well as prepare food for the next morning. They worked seven days a week until colonial legislatures enforced Sunday rest. Many used this day to raise food on their "own" plots to supplement the meager provisions supplied by their masters. One needed a reasonably full belly and a little spare time to accept spiritual concepts. Finally, one needed clerics with time and desire to minister to this group. Many in white society questioned the presence of a soul in these "subhuman brutes." Bishop Berkeley in England believed that blacks were "creatures of another species who had no rights to be included or admitted to the sacraments."[4]

The slaves seemed to have an "underground telegraph system" so they could keep in contact with slaves of other plantations and even receive news from the colonial capital. The statutes passed to deny freedom with baptism failed to impress the blacks, and for decades they accepted the premise of freedom and Christianity. Letters by James Blair of Virginia to his supervisor in England (1729, 1731) described slave attitudes:

> And the Negroes themselves in our neighbourhood are very desirous to become Christians, and in order to it come and give an account of the Lord's Prayer and the Creed, and Ten Commandments, and so are baptized and frequent the church, and the Negro children are now commonly baptized. I doubt not some of the Negroes are sincere converts; but the far greater part of them little mind the serious part, only are in hope that they shall meet with so much the more respect and that some time or other Christianity will help them to their freedom.
>
> But it is certain that notwithstanding all the precaution we Ministers took to assure them that Baptism altered nothing as to their servitude ... yet they were willing to feed themselves with a secret fancy that it did and that the King designed that all Christians should be free ... There was a general rumour among them that they were to be set free. And when they saw nothing came of it, they grew angry and saucy, and met in the night time in great numbers and talked of rising ... There were four of the Ringleaders hanged.[5]

In New England, the Puritans wrestled with the concepts of slavery and Christianity. Many opposed the conversion of slaves, because this "might give them notions of social equality" (social here meant their status as free or slave). Others believed they had a soul that had to be saved. In 1674 John

Elliot urged masters to send slaves to him once a week for religious instruction. Ezra Stiles, minister of the Second Congregational Church in Newport, Rhode Island, gave special instructions in Christianity to black communicants. There were approximately 1,200 blacks in Newport during his ministry; of these, 30 were Christian and members of the various Protestant congregations.[6] The Mather family urged the introduction of Christ to the slaves. Increase Mather preached obedience by the slaves to their masters with fear and trembling, because that was God's word.[7] Cotton Mather urged teaching the gospel to slaves. He founded a school for slaves in 1717, and he urged masters to help convert the "most brutish of creatures upon Earth": "Will you do nothing to pluck them out of the Jaws of Satan the Devourer? ... [Save] your servants, for being made Christian Servants." In his treatise "The Negro Christianized," Mather stated, "The baptized then are not thereby entitled into their liberties." In another work, "Rules for the Society of Negroes" (1693), Mather urged that those who were disobedient and unfaithful to their masters must be "rebuked" and denied attendance at church meetings. Runaways must be brought back and punished. However, he insisted that masters treat slaves "according to the rules of humanity, as persons with immortal souls in them ... not mere beasts of burden." Mather urged that slaves were to rest on the Sabbath. He formed a society to instruct blacks in Christianity, and he conducted slave marriages according to Christian ritual.[8] Converted slaves were accepted into the Puritan religion and were not exempt from the problems of the period. They were accused and were the accusers during the witchcraft scare at the end of the seventeenth century. In Salem, Candy, a slave, was accused of bewitching Ann Putnam. He was tried before a white judge and jury like whites accused of this felony. Candy was pronounced innocent.[9]

Earlier, the work of the Quakers in helping to abolish the slave trade and slavery itself was chronicled, as was their failure to attract many black communicants to their religion. As early as 1671, George Fox and William Edmundson urged religious training for slaves.[10] Shortly after the settling of Pennsylvania, Friends meetings were open to blacks. In 1698 masters were urged to bring their slaves to meetings. William Penn instituted regular meetings for blacks in Philadelphia. In 1756 Quarterly Meetings were started for blacks, which continued for 50 years. Other sites for black meetings were started in Flushing, Long Island, and Burlington, New Jersey. The Quaker influence on blacks in Christianity was surpassed by other important activities, such as opening schools for black children and adults. Anthony Bezenet's school in Philadelphia could point to graduates like Richard Allen and Absolam Jones, who became leaders in the large black community of the city. Although they were not Quakers, these black leaders inserted into the Charter of the Free African Society that the clerk and treasurer of the organization were to be Quakers "in perpetuity." Black marriage certificates resembled those of the

Quakers. Individual Friends heeded George Fox's request that they make land available to blacks for cemeteries. In Burlington, New Jersey, a few blacks were buried in white Quaker cemeteries.[11]

The Quakers were not a proselytizing religion in general, and specifically not to the blacks. The Philadelphia Meetings of Quakers in 1796 proclaimed that meetings (congregations) were at liberty to accept persons into membership without reference to nationality or color. Rejection of membership was rarely made overtly because of color. However, black applicants were discouraged privately. If this failed, their applications were locked up in committee for years.

The Anglicans made few converts among the slaves, but not for their failure to proselytize. In the seventeenth century, the king urged his colonial governors to force plantation owners to bring their chattel to Christ. Dr. Thomas Bray was appointed commissary to Maryland by the bishop of London. (A commissary was a deputy of the bishop appointed to supervise far-flung areas of the diocese.) Dr. Bray sent clergy and books to develop parochial libraries, and he later visited Maryland to determine what progress had been made. Upon his return to England, he petitioned the king for a charter for a missionary society. In 1701 King William III issued a charter to the Reverend Bray and Associates to form the Society for the Propagation of the Gospel in Foreign Parts.[12] The charter members were actually participants in the Society for the Promotion of Christian Knowledge founded four years earlier. Their purpose was to collect funds to maintain "orthodox" clergy and propagate the gospel. Originally they were to send gospel messengers to offer worship and education to His Majesty's subjects in the British Empire. Basically, the Church hierarchy in England felt the need to get Anglican missionaries to the distant corners of the British Empire to minister to Anglo-Saxons who became lost to the faith because of the distance from England as well as the sparsity of settlement. These missionaries soon recognized a need to minister to the Indians and blacks whose souls were going to hell. The missionaries were reasonably successful south of New England. The Puritans did not oppose conversion, but they did oppose the intrusion of the Church of England.[13]

In New York, Elias Neau was a prime mover to carry out the responsibilities of the Anglican mission. While his duties called for work with Indians and blacks, he preferred the blacks because they were more numerous and were readier for instruction. He was successful despite the attitudes of the white masters. By 1707 he could point proudly to 75 blacks in classes one to three times a week. He taught Church catechism, the Ten Commandments, and the Lord's Prayer. He wished to baptize his students, but their owners feared that conversion meant freedom. Neau turned for support to the governor, who sponsored the act stating that baptism did not affect the civil position of the slaves. After this statute was on the books, owners were more cooperative and more baptisms followed.[14]

Elias Neau was a pious man, and, as is rarely the case, he was the right man at the right time. The Reverend John Sharpe described Mr. Neau to his supervisors in England. The Society had "tender concerns for the souls of the Indians and Negroes who are slaves at New York ... to instruct them in the knowledge of Jesus Christ and Salvation through Him. He is a person of great humility which is the foundation of all virtue. He can condescend familiarly to discuss with these poor slaves, who are put to the vilest drudgeries and consequently esteemed the scum and offscourges of men. He can take pains to accommodate his discourse to their capacities whilst he inculcates the great truths of the Gospel."[15] Neau's work was set back by the slave revolt in 1712. Whites believed that Neau's school was a place of conspiracy and that instructing blacks made them cunning and insolent. The organization's leaders believed that none who attended catechism school were involved. However, two were accused. One of them had been baptized and he died protesting his innocence. One who had not yet been converted was hanged in chains; after five days of torture he still protested his innocence.[16]

Attendance at Neau's school was further jeopardized by a statute passed by the New York legislature after the revolt. No black was allowed on the streets after dark without a lantern. If his master refused to supply the lantern, the slave was forced to remain in his quarters. Neau's classes were held in his house at night. Neau's work was continued by others after he died, and by 1750 slave owners in New York were more disposed to have their slaves taught and baptized. Members of the Anglican hierarchy who visited New York were impressed with the spiritual advances and piety of the slaves.[17]

Pennsylvania and New Jersey, largely Quaker strongholds, showed little response to Anglican missionaries. Dr. Bray's Associates developed a school for blacks in Philadelphia in 1759. This organization was founded in London in 1724 for the purpose of funding clerical libraries and schools to bring the sacraments to the slaves.[18] The Anglican Church was the state church in most of the southern colonies, and it was in the South that the Society for the Propagation of the Gospel made some advances. Maryland and Virginia, the oldest colonies in the South, had an adequate supply of clergymen, so there was little need for the missionary activities of the S.P.G. Furthermore, Maryland had a large Catholic population. Before the founding of the S.P.G. Anglican priests had recognized their duty to the heathen. The Reverend James Blair in 1699 developed a plan to bring Anglican Christianity to the blacks and Indians. He urged the clergy to spend more time with the heathen, and to gain the cooperation of the masters, he offered a financial reward. Every Indian, mulatto, and black child was to be taught and baptized before the age of 14. These new Christians had to learn the Apostle's Creed, the Lord's Prayer, and the Ten Commandments. If the master concurred with the plan, he received a certificate that exempted him from paying a levy on his slaves until they were 18. Those without the certificate started payment of the levy when the slave reached 14.[19] Plans like Blair's, as well as the efforts of the S.P.G., bore little fruit. The early plantation owners opposed educating and Christianizing their slaves. These wealthy planters who controlled the colonial governments protected their property by the law of 1705, which prevented emancipation by baptism. However, they worried that the slaves would see themselves as their masters' equal, at least in the eyes of God. The failure of the S.P.G. and the Anglican clergy to make any progress led the bishop of London to write a pastoral letter to all the clergy and the heads of households to encourage the teaching of Christian principles to the slaves. But 3,000 miles was a long distance, and the bishop of London's communications had little effect. Masters retained the nagging feeling that Christianity would make the slaves more difficult to control. However, the S.P.G. could point with some pride to schools for blacks in Fredericksburg and Williamsburg.[20]

The movement to Christianity among Virginia's slaves started with the Great Awakening (1740–90), and particularly after the Revolution.[21] Prior to this period, the Anglican hierarchy realized, most slaves "lived and died strangers to Christianity."

Definite strides were made in South Carolina. Before the founding of the S.P.G., Anglican clerics tried to bring Christianity to the blacks. The Reverend Samuel Thomas of Goose Creek Parish in South Carolina became an active schoolmaster to the blacks (1695). After ten years, he could point to 20 blacks who understood English and could read and write. Thomas believed he had "related" to 1,000 blacks during his ministry.[22] In 1706, Dr. Le Jan became a missionary to the Carolinas. He tried to get masters to allow their slaves to come to his classes. The missionary met the same obstacles as had his predecessors. The masters believed that Indians and blacks were no better than animals and cared nothing about their immorality. The missionary tried to prevent polygamy among the slaves, but his success was limited. He baptized a few blacks, and by 1712 he had "40 to 50" students in his school.[23] In 1743 the Reverend Alex Garden, a commissary of the S.P.G., opened a school for black children and boasted an enrollment of 36. The society purchased two young baptized slaves, Harry (or Henry) and Andrew, for £56, 9s. 3½d.; these slaves were 14 and 15 at the time. They were to learn the principles of Christianity and receive a simple, basic, secular education. In turn, they would act as teachers to black adults in an evening school and to children in day classes.[24] A schoolhouse was built for them in Charleston at a cost of £308, and in 1744 they had 60 students.[25] The school's purpose was to turn out 30–40 students trained in the Bible who would carry this knowledge to other slaves. However, the virus of learning had to be destroyed, and the legislature in 1740 prohibited all teaching of slaves. After this law was passed, only free blacks could become students. In 1764 the school was closed, for unknown reasons.

North Carolina proved to be infertile ground for the propagation of Anglicanism. The colony had suffered in Indian wars and political wars, settlements were small and scattered, and the inhabitants refused to cooperate. Few missionaries were sent; those who did arrive were spread so thinly that they could only be itinerant rather than stationary. Moving frequently from place to place, they had little time to devote to the blacks. By 1757 there were a few permanently established missionaries who could carry on the work of the organization.[26]

Georgia did not formally permit slavery until 1750. However, the society felt that it had to bring white Englishmen back to the fold, and missions were established in Savannah and Frederica in 1744. After the introduction of slavery, Dr. Bray's Associates placed a schoolmaster in Georgia, in 1751.[27]

The work of the Anglican societies ended with the American Revolution. The titular head of the Anglican Church was the king of England. All services began with a prayer for the health of the king, and naturally this did not sit well with the rebels. The societies were then forced to move their activities to Canada, Bermuda, the West Indies, and Africa.

The two Protestant groups that made the greatest inroads among the Africans were the Baptists and the Methodists. Their activities were closely interwoven with the Great Awakening, the religious revival that started in the colonies about 1740. George Whitefield, an itinerant Methodist preacher, was probably the spark that ignited the conflagration. Methodism was founded by John Wesley in 1739; it was originally a group within the English church, but it separated in 1795. John and his brother attracted the poor city workers and agricultural laborers who had fallen away from the conservatism of Anglicanism. Their church was built on emotionalism, the conversion experience, and piety, rather than on training in biblical concepts. The Wesleys went to the colonies to preach in 1735 and gained many converts, particularly among the blacks. Methodism was spread to the slaves by the evangelical preaching of George Whitefield. He urged education and conversion of slaves along with more humane treatment. He believed that slaves had little time for education and Christianity because they worked seven days a week. In his letter "To the Inhabitants of Maryland, Virginia, North and South Carolina Concerning the Negroes," he condemned brutality and urged Christianization. The writer claimed that slaves worked harder than horses and were treated no better than dogs; they were "cut with knives." Whitefield felt most slaves would be better off dead and was surprised that more did not commit suicide. It was sinful to buy them "as though they were Brutes." They deserved a larger share of "the fruit of their labors." God had punished South Carolina for its treatment of the slaves; these punishments included the small-pox epidemic, the failure of the invasion of St. Augustine, Florida, and the slave uprising. Whitefield prayed that the slaves would never get the upper hand, but if such a thing was permitted by Providence, the "Judgment would be just." He also preached that slavery was the root cause of degeneracy in South Carolina, including fancy balls, fancy dress, drinking, and dancing.[28]

When a "have not" becomes a "have," however, his opinions are often altered. In 1740 Whitefield acquired a slave plantation. He then decided that Georgia could not flourish without slaves. He rationalized his change of attitude toward slavery by stating that it was a Christian duty "to make [the slaves'] lives comfortable and lay a foundation for building up their posterity."[29]

The Methodist Church had great appeal to the slaves. Beyond its original tenet of opposition "to the great evil of slavery," it excluded from its ministry those who held slaves in colonies where they could be freed: "Slavery was contrary to the laws of God and man, and wrong and hurtful to society." All buying and selling of slaves was forbidden. It was this belief that led to the fracture into Northern and Southern Methodists in 1844. The Southerners felt that slavery was sanctioned by the Holy Scriptures and was therefore no sin. Slavery was a matter of the states' concern and none of the church's business.[30] Of some importance to the slave was the concept that piety was more significant than learning—a black could become a preacher with credentials that came "directly from God." Many black Methodist preachers purchased their freedom and became itinerant ministers to bring hope and salvation to their pagan brothers. Others, like Allen and Jones, founded churches in more tolerant Philadelphia. In some ways, Methodism resembled the ancient African religion. The potential convert sat on a "mourner's bench" surrounded by singing dancers. He prayed continually until he was convinced of his perfect relief from damnation. When this feeling gripped him, he leaped from his seat and ran to proclaim "the joyous news," accompanied by a shout. The shout became an indispensable part of slave religious worship.[31]

The church was formally inaugurated in America in 1784, although Wesley had baptized several slaves in 1758, and a Methodist congregation of five members, one of whom was black, existed in New York in 1766. In 1786 Bishop Francis Asbury organized the first Sunday school in the United States, in Maryland, where blacks and whites attended together. In 1800 blacks could be ordained by the church. Blacks and whites attended the same church. Where black membership was large, blacks were encouraged to form their own congregation, leading to "less opportunity for friction," and giving the blacks "better opportunities for self-development." That the Methodists were successful in America could be seen by their numbers. At the end of the Revolution there were 15,000 members, with 84 preachers. In 1816 there were 214,235 communicants, and of these, 42,304 were black.[32]

The Baptists, like the Methodists, were dissenters from the Church of England, and like the Methodists they received communicants during the Great Awakening. The Baptists in America were largely a Southern religion, but the North could boast a few congregations. Providence, Rhode Island, had a black congregation without a church building in 1774. Boston had the First African Baptist Church in 1805, New York had an Abyssinian Baptist Congregation in 1808, and Philadelphia followed in 1809. The early black Baptist leaders in the South tied their fortunes to the invading British. The first Southern black Baptist church was started in 1773 on the estate of a Mr. Galpen in Silver Bluffs. His mill was used as the church, and the millstream was used to baptize new communicants. When Savannah, Georgia, fell to the invading British, the Reverend David George and 40 slave communicants escaped to that city to find freedom under the British. George and his followers then went to South Carolina with the victorious British. The British were finally forced out of the South in 1782, and so the congregation traveled to Nova Scotia and then to Sierra Leone.[33] The church at Silver Bluffs reopened after the war under the leadership of Jesse Peter, a slave. The congregation moved to the First African Baptist Church in Augusta in 1793. There was probably an earlier Baptist church in Augusta, led in 1779 by George Liele. Liele was baptized and converted to the Baptist faith; he then set out to instruct his people. White ministers ordained him a minister of the Church. While still a slave, he founded a church near Savannah. He was later freed by his master, a Tory, who was killed in action. Liele indentured himself to Colonel Kirkland of the British army. He followed his master to Jamaica after the war where he started preaching in 1784. His ministry was always to slave congregations, so he had to earn a living as a farmer. Liele left an acolyte in America to continue his work. Andrew Bryan, his successor, was ordained. His preaching went against the attitudes held by the white controlling class; he was imprisoned twice and whipped. Finally, Chief Justice Henry Osborne gave him liberty to preach what he felt in his heart. During this period, Andrew was still a slave of Jonathan Bryan. After his master's death, Andrew purchased his freedom for £50. He then developed a Baptist church with 700 slave members. He later divided the congregation and developed the Second Baptist Church. Some years later, with continued growth, a third church was started.[34]

Presbyterianism made few inroads into slave culture. It was predominantly a religion of the Scots, who were not usually slaveholders. Furthermore, the Scots came to America in large numbers in the mid–eighteenth century and were able to obtain only cheaper land away from the tidewater plantations. So the Scots were farmers with little need for slaves. The Presbyterians were able to make some converts during the Great Awakening, though, when a few of their ministers went out to save some souls.

Continental America was largely a Protestant enclave, but Catholics made some inroads, particularly in Louisiana and Maryland. The lands under French control obeyed the "Code Noir," according to which masters were forced to teach their slaves to read so they could study the Bible.[35] The Spanish did not have a black code, but they had no objection to their slaves' learning to read and welcomed the slaves into the "true religion." Maryland was originally settled as a haven for English Catholics. However, the Protestant leaders feared Catholic preaching to slaves and indentured servants. Thomas Greaves, in a sworn deposition, stated that the priests in St. Mary's County tried to convert Protestants and the slaves of Protestants.[36] The priests warned them of permanent damnation if they did not follow Roman Catholic doctrine. The clergy of the Anglican Church complained to the administrative authorities that there was a "great growth of Popery which was notorious," and that priests with their preaching were subverting Protestants. The Jesuits "endeavor to subvert servants and negroes of protestants and keep them under their authority. In the event of an insurrection, they will be dangerous."[37] According to Booker T. Washington, the Catholic Church was the first to send missionaries to Africa, and it was the first Church into which blacks were received as members.[38] The slaves could not become Catholic priests because of the requirement of celibacy in a society where slaves were encouraged to breed. A priest required extensive training, and he "could not get his credentials from heaven." However, the Catholics did make inroads among the blacks, and it may have been this activity that goaded the Protestant sects to send missionaries to teach their branch of Christianity and start schools.

What were the benefits of conversion to Christianity to the slaves and their masters? The blacks received little relief or benefit from Christianity. They had had their own religion for ages in Africa. It satisfied their needs, and it was a more gentle religion when compared with that of Native Americans or the white transplants. The Africans did not kill millions of people over different interpretations of "the Book" or how to cross oneself. One might argue that Christianity salvaged black souls and gave them a life with God in the hereafter. If this situation truly existed, it was worth their trials on earth. If nothing else, it gave blacks hope for a better life in heaven after death. Heaven was a beautiful, comfortable place beyond the sky. It had golden streets and a sea of glass on which angels danced and sang in praise of God on his golden throne. There was no sun to burn them in that bright land of never-ending sabbath. Friends and relatives would be reunited. The slave in heaven would be rich and free to sing, shout, walk, and fly about. He would not experience the fears and sorrows of parting. He would have rest from toil and care in the companionship of heavenly groups. The slave knew he would meet the children torn away from him for sale on earth.[39]

Once the white master was reassured that he would not lose his slave through baptism, he "had all the aces." Through the white minister, whose salary he paid, he used religion to keep the black "in his place." Thomas Bacon, in a sermon to a black congregation in Maryland, demonstrated this control. The slave was to do all services for them [whites], as if you did it for God himself.

... Your masters and mistresses are God's overseers ... if you are faulty toward them, God himself will punish you severely for it in the next world.

If overseers punish you unjustly, accept it. However, in the next world, he will deal with them severely and God will make amends for it in heaven.[40]

The rules of duty to the master were spelled out minutely. Slaves should be obedient and subject to the master in all things; they should not be "eye-servants" (those who work only when they feel they are being watched); they should be faithful and honest to their masters and mistresses—not purloining or wasting their goods or substance, but showing all good fidelity in all things; and they should serve their masters with cheerfulness, reverence, and humility.

Other white ministers preached to their black congregations that they were inferior and cursed by God to be slaves of the whites: they suffered the "Curse of Ham." They were advised to respect all whites and to keep their hats off and their eyes downcast when talking with any white. Black ministers, free or slave, had to "toe the line" drawn by whites.[41] Often they were subsidized by the white master to keep their brothers in their place. In most cases, black preachers held midweekly meetings in the slave quarters, and they preached openly to the slaves in the master's church on Sundays. A white observer was present during the service, and he could stop the meeting if he believed the message was improper. Black preachers were safe as long as they preached the "slave catechism" that blacks had to be obedient and patient, and accept conditions on earth with their rewards to come later in heaven.[42] In some communities, blacks were permitted to attend services with whites— of course, they were isolated in the corner or the gallery of the church. Here too they learned of the divine right of white masters and the superiority of the white race. Different sermons were preached, but most boiled down to the same concept, "servants, obey your masters."[43] It must also be remembered that the white ministers were often the sons of the large plantation owners. They grew up in a slave society and accepted the concepts they preached.

Many blacks accepted the Christianity that was spoon-fed to them by white and black preachers. Others rejected the religion of their white masters, which preached their enslavement and inferiority. In some congregations, they modified this Christianity by adding African beliefs (spirit possession and the "call and response" form of gospel singing). Often, they kept their owners and overseers in the dark about their hybrid religion and had religious meetings in their quarters away from the view of the whites. Slaves believed there was a "God's Bible" different from the one used by their white masters. The Old Testament story of Moses who led his people out of slavery in Egypt was probably the most significant part of God's Bible.[44]

Chapter 14

BLACKS IN WAR

Blacks in colonial America fought in all of the colonial wars, the great majority against their will, although they had no stake in who won or lost. The American Revolution was the most significant war of the period, and it has been estimated that 5,000 blacks saw service. The numbers are unreliable, because black soldiers' names were used infrequently. A soldier might be listed as a Negro or a mulatto, or only a first name was used. Prior to the Revolution, blacks, both free and slave, were mentioned in militia laws in the individual colonies. They were armed in emergencies despite a nagging fear of insurrection. English law required every community to have a militia force of able-bodied men, usually between 16 and 50 years of age. With the introduction of blacks into continental America, laws were needed to govern their service. Even in New England, where their numbers were limited, regulations existed. As early as 1645, Absolam Pearse who was black, was listed as capable of bearing arms in the Plymouth Colony. Seven years later, there were enough blacks in Massachusetts so that a militia law required all "Negroes, Indians, and Scotsmen" between 16 and 60 to join in militia training. This rule was short-lived, however. Massachusetts and most New England colonies, by general agreement, later prohibited blacks from joining militia companies. Free blacks in these areas were required to work on public projects for as many days as the whites were engaged in training.[1] In 1656 Massachusetts excluded blacks and Indians from the militia by legislative order. Massachusetts reversed itself in 1707 when it called upon "free negroes, mulattoes and Indians" 16 years and older to appear with militia companies and remain in service until the company was discharged. Failure to report resulted in a 20 shilling fine or eight days of labor.

Connecticut prohibited arming blacks in 1661. This statute followed the uprising of Indians and blacks in Hartford. New Netherlands, never a populous colony, recruited black slaves and armed them with tomahawks and half pikes to fight the Indians. Blacks were also used to build fortifications and breastworks around New Amsterdam. In 1746 New Jersey recruited a regiment of free blacks and Indians 21 years and older to fight in Canada. They were to be combat soldiers and some could become sergeants and corporals as well as drummers. They would receive £6 above their pay for enlisting.[2]

In the South, white leaders faced a dilemma. As the black population increased, and in some colonies surpassed the number of whites, the fear of a black armed revolt had to be measured against the need to use the blacks against the Indians, French, and Spaniards on the borders. The Deep South buffered Virginia and Maryland from these dangers. In 1639 Virginia excluded all blacks from receiving arms and ammunition. North Carolina in 1715 required all free men, 16–60, whatever their color, to join the militia and attend at muster.[3] In 1746 servants were expected to join the militia, but slaves were excluded. Instead, slaves between 16 and 60 worked up to 12 days each year on road service. They worked alongside white and black servants. This system of mandatory road-work ended in the 1770s when it was replaced by a poll tax on all males to pay for private companies that performed roadwork. In outbreaks of Indian war-fare, all able-bodied men, free and slave, had to serve. Blacks fought in the Tus-carora Indian wars of 1711 and 1715; 400 blacks joined 600 whites to defeat the Indians in the Yamassee war. Before the settlement of Georgia, South Carolina was the colony closest to Spanish Florida. A statute in 1708 required each mili-tia captain to enlist, train, and bring to the field one slave armed with a gun or lance for each white man in his unit.[4] These were usually the most trustwor-thy slaves, and they apparently enjoyed this duty. Benefits included temporary freedom from field work, a sense of importance when chosen; the possibility of adventure, and the ability to obtain alcohol. In the Yamassee war, the slaves fought as soldiers in mixed units. But the danger of equal numbers of armed blacks in militia units was addressed in 1747 with a law requiring that slaves in a unit not exceed one-third of the whites and that no more than one-half of the male slaves in the colony be enlisted.[5] In time of danger, the slave received a gun, a hatchet, a powder horn, and a shot pouch with 20 lead balls and 6 spare flints. Any slave who killed or captured an enemy soldier received his freedom. Too many qualified for this bonus, however, and the ruling was changed to give slaves £10 in cash.[6] In 1747 South Carolina thanked its black militiamen who "behaved themselves with great faithfulness and courage in repelling the attacks of His Majesty's enemies." In the war against the Cherokees (1760) 200 blacks were used as wagon drivers and pioneers (laborers). An attempt to arm 500 slaves for combat was defeated in the legislature. Georgia formally permitted slavery in 1750, and in 1772 a slave enlistment law was passed for protection against the Indians, French and Spaniards.[7] Any slave who showed courage in battle received a livery coat, red cloth breeches, a hat, stockings, a shirt and shoes and was free from work on the anniversary of the battle.

Blacks fought in King Williams' War (1689–97), Queen Anne's War (1702–13), King George's War (1744–48), and the French and Indian War (1754–63).[8] In the French and Indian War, blacks were combatants, scouts, wagoners, and laborers. They served in mixed militia units from Massachu-setts, New York, New Jersey, Pennsylvania, Virginia, and South Carolina. Blacks won honors at Fort Duquesne, Fort Cumberland, and the Plains of

Abraham (Quebec). Blacks also served as privateers and on warships as marines, able-seamen, and cooks. They received the same pay as their white comrades, though unhappily, much of this went to their masters if they were slaves.

Historians have dated the start of the American Revolution from the founding of Jamestown; from the development of colonial legislatures; and from the attempts to prevent British parliamentary laws from being enforced in America. The "shot heard 'round the world" was fired in Lexington. The events preceding the British attempt to seize Sam Adams and other revolutionaries, as well as a cache of ordnance in Concord, all started in the Bay State. Prior to the actions at Lexington and Concord, Boston was a hotbed of revolutionary activity. The Stamp Act, quartering of troops to protect tax commissioners, and unemployment, which white laborers attributed to British soldiers who took civilian jobs at half pay when off-duty, resulted in repeated skirmishes between the British and local "toughs."[9] On the night of August 28, 1765, "boys and negroes began to build bonfires on King Street and blow the dreaded whistle and horn that sent Boston mobs swarming out of taverns, houses and garrets." A Boston newspaper described another event: "In the morning, nine or ten soldiers of Colonel Carr's Regiment were severely whipped on the commons. To behold Britons scourged by Negro drummers was a new and very disagreeable spectacle." Another incident involved three soldiers in a fight with ropemakers. The soldiers were driven off, but they returned with reinforcements. A black man led the civilians and was upbraided by a citizen, "You black rascal, what have you to do with white people's quarrels?"[10]

The leader in the Boston Massacre was Crispus Attucks, an escaped slave of mixed black and Natick Indian ancestry ("attucks" meant deer in the Natick tongue). Twenty years earlier, Attucks had been described in the *Boston Gazette* (Tuesday, October 2, 1750):

> Ran away from his master William Brown of Framingham, on the 30th of September last, a Mulatto Fellow, about 27 years of age named Crispus, 6 feet 2 inches high, short curl'd hair, his knees nearer together than common, had on a light colour'd beaver skin coat; plain brown Fustain jacket, or brown all-wool one, new Buckskin breeches, blue Yarn stockings, and a checked woolen shirt, "Whoever shall take up said run-away and convey him to his abovesaid master, shall have ten pounds, old Tenor Reward, and all necessary charges paid. And all Masters of Vessels and others, are hereby cautioned against concealing or carrying off said Servant on Penalty of the law."[11] [Old Tenor was paper currency in Massachusetts and Rhode Island.]

Attucks probably blended in with the blacks of Boston (10 percent of the total population of 16,000), where he supported himself for 20 years as a cattle dealer and on ships out of Boston Harbor. Attucks marched into history on March 5, 1770. Whig patriots claimed that the action started when soldiers of the Twenty-ninth Regiment became abusive to civilians; striking unarmed citizens with the broad side of their cutlasses. Several boys armed with sticks met three soldiers with drawn cutlasses. They scuffled and one boy was cut on his arm after he made insults against a British officer. Ten or 12 comrades joined the three soldiers with cutlasses out of their scabbards. Some bystanders rang the fire bell, and many civilians gathered. The soldiers withdrew. They were followed to the Custom House on King Street where the mob taunted the lone sentry with iced snowballs; he called for help. Captain Thomas Preston and a squad of eight ran to help. A group, including Attucks, came to the scene from Jackson's Corner.[12] Crispus led a charge on the soldiers with a shout, "The way to get rid of these soldiers is to attack the main guard; strike at the roots: this is the nest." Attucks grasped a soldier's bayonet and threw him to the ground. He yelled, "Kill the dogs, knock them over." The crowd pushed into the soldiers. A soldier believed he had heard an order to fire, and he shot and killed Attucks. Other soldiers fired, and 11 civilians were hit. Samuel Gray, Samuel Manerich, James Caldwell, and Patrick Carr either died immediately or somewhat later of mortal wounds. Attucks and Caldwell lay in state at Faneuil Hall. Three days later, all five were buried in a common grave in the Granary Burying Ground, with approximately 10,000 mourners attending the funeral. The stone over their grave was inscribed:

> Long as in Freedom's cause the wise contend,
> Dear to your country shall your fame extend;
> While to the world the letters stone shall fill
> Where Caldwell, Attucks, Gray and Manerick fell.[13]

The soldiers were tried for the catastrophe, with John Adams (the future second president) acting as their defense attorney. He referred to their attackers as "a motley rabble of saucy boys, negroes, and mulattoes, Irish Teagues, and Jack Tars."[14] Adams claimed that Attucks tried to be the hero of the night: he led his army, formed them, and marched them to King Street armed with clubs; he urged his followers not to be afraid of the soldiers. The defense attorney described him as a short mulatto fellow whose very looks were enough to terrify any person. He had hardiness to fall in on them. He grabbed a bayonet in one hand and knocked the man down with the other.[15] Adams called as a witness a slave named Andrew, who testified that Attucks had a long cordwood stick and that he struck at Captain Preston and at Hugh Montgomery, a grenadier. The soldiers were exonerated, but the defense lawyer had second thoughts after the trial. In a letter he wrote: "This was the declaration of war, and was fulfilled. The world had heard from him, and more, the English-speaking world will never forget the noble daring, the excusable rashness of Attucks in the holy cause of liberty. Eighteen centuries before he was saluted by death and kissed by immortality, another Negro bore the cross of Christ to Calvary for him. When the colonies were struggling wearily under their cross of woe, a Negro came to the front and bore that cross to the victory of glorious martyrdom."[16]

After the Boston Massacre, relations between the colonies and Great Britain deteriorated at a rapid rate. The Tea Party led to the Intolerable Acts against Massachusetts, and finally the rebellion started. Blacks were among the Minutemen at Lexington and Concord; behind the walls and trees from which a withering fire destroyed many retreating British soldiers; at Menotomy (under the leadership of David Lawson, a black veteran of the French and Indian War), where they captured the British supply wagons; at Fort Ticonderoga; at Breeds' and Bunker Hills, where Peter Salem killed Mayor John Pitcairn and Salem Poor was mentioned for conspicuous bravery.

After the initial excitement, white leaders re-evaluated the situation in relation to their black countrymen. Many thought that the black was still a savage, too stupid to be employed in fighting the battles of free men, and they objected to enlisting blacks. Some believed that employing "uncivilized" people to fight the British would provide an excuse for the British to use blacks and Indians against Americans. There was always the anxiety over arming slaves, "lest they become our masters." Whites also feared that the army would become a haven for runaway slaves. Despite slaves' involvement in the earlier battles, Massachusetts took an official stand against enlisting slaves. The Committee of Safety reported to the Provincial Congress in May 1775 that this was a contest between Great Britain and the colonies, and it involved the liberties and privileges of the latter. Admission of any persons but free men as soldiers would be inconsistent with principles being supported and would reflect dishonor on the colony. This report in the *Provincial Journal of Massachusetts* did not refer to free blacks. However, when George Washington was given command of the troops around Boston, he issued orders to recruiting officers that prohibited enlistment of any Negro or any person not native to the country unless he had a wife and family and was a settled resident. In the Continental Congress in September 1775, Edward Rutledge of South Carolina demanded that Washington discharge all blacks from the service, but he failed to receive the necessary votes from the other representatives. On October 8, 1775, a council that included Washington, Ward, Lee, Putnam, Thomas, Spencer, Heath, Sullivan, Greene, and Gates debated the advisability of enlisting blacks into the service. They were unanimous in their rejection of slaves, and a majority was against free blacks. A committee composed of Benjamin Franklin, Benjamin Harrison, Thomas Lynch, and the deputy governors of Connecticut and Rhode Island, and the Committee Council of Massachusetts Bay agreed that all blacks were to be rejected. This was followed by Washington's general order of November 12, 1775, which declared that neither Negroes, boys unable to bear arms, and old men unfit to endure the fatigue of campaign were to be enlisted.[17]

This high-handed failure to use black manpower was changed by British action. To buy an army (Hessians) or impress an army from the streets of British cities, pack the soldiers into disease–ridden ships, and turn them loose in a place whose extreme climate would contribute to the decimation of the Europeans was too expensive for Parliament to undertake. Instead, the British could enlist the white Loyalists who were about equal in number to the patriots, as well as the blacks, who represented 20 percent of the total population. General Thomas Gage in June 1775 suggested that the British use Negro slaves to increase their army and decrease the rebel army and its support by black laborers.[18] British ships (*Mercury* and *Otter*) in the Norfolk area took defecting slaves on board as early as July 1775.[19] John Murray, earl of Dunmore, governor of Virginia, considered enlisting slaves over a period of months before his proclamation of November 7, 1775. He believed that the rebellious Virginia planters would be deprived of their workers and would be forced to return home to protect their families and property. Also, slaves would be excellent laborers for the British army. Finally, Dunmore realized he could not expect any help from British headquarters in Boston to keep Virginia loyal. In a letter to the earl of Dartmouth, he stated that if he received arms and ammunition, he would develop a force of Indians, Negroes, and others to hold Virginia. On June 8, 1775, Dunmore left Williamsburg, the capital, and boarded the man–of–war *Fowey* in Norfolk harbor; he then patrolled Virginia's waters and attacked, plundered, and carried off slaves from plantations without adequate defense.[20] After a victory by British foes at Kemp's Landing, with the help of some black troops against the Virginia militia, Dunmore, now on board the *William*, made his famous proclamation:

> ... and I do hereby further declare all indentured servants, negroes, and others, (appertaining to Rebels) free, that are able and willing to bear arms, they joining his Majesty's troops, as soon as may be, for the more speedily reducing this Colony to a proper sense of their duty to his Majesty's Crown and dignity ... all his Majesty's liege subjects to retain their quit-rents, or any other taxes due, or that become due, in their own custody, till such time as peace may again be restored to this at present most unhappy country ...
>
> Dunmore
>
> God Save the King![21]

Dunmore hoped to enlist 10,000 slaves under white officers. Each slave would receive one cow, one guinea, and his freedom; Loyalist owners would receive a receipt bearing 6 percent interest for each slave enlisted. Virginia's House of Burgesses reacted promptly to this proclamation: local patriots in the countryside were doubled, highways were guarded, and owners of small craft increased their vigilance. The activities of the patriots were described in a letter to Major General Charles Lee of Virginia from Colonel Isaac Read (April 7, 1776): "The Negroes in this part of the Country, stole the Boats lying in the Rivers and Creeks, and made their escape to Lord Dunmore in the Night, I detach'd twenty-five men with orders to examine the different landings and coves on the Western branch of the Nansemord River and Chuckatuck, to remove all the small craft they could find, ... to destroy all such boats as the owners thereof should refuse to aid in removing."[22]

Virginians also resorted to "psychological warfare" against their slaves, who were told that the English were responsible for the slave trade; that slaves who defected would be sold to the West Indies; that Dunmore treated his own slaves badly; and that Dunmore would take only those who could bear arms—"Wives, children, the old and infirm would be left behind to suffer their master's wrath." Also, the slaves were told that they were better off under Virginians than among the English. The Virginia Convention on December 13 promised all runaways that they would be pardoned if they returned within ten days; otherwise they would be punished. Any slaves found with arms would be sold to the West Indies. Runaway slaves picked up before they reached the British would be imprisoned; then they would be returned to their masters who would send them inland, away from the lure of British ships. Slaves of British sympathizers were sent to lead mines in the West. Occasionally slaves were tried and executed as "an example to others." The masters were particularly harsh toward slaves recaptured from the British in combat. The owners of these executed slaves were not pleased with the loss of their valuable property, because they could not be replaced easily. Some of these recaptured slaves were auctioned off, and the money received, minus expenses, went to the masters. Attempts at keeping the slaves loyal to their patriot masters were not effective.[23]

The first week after the proclamation, 300 slaves reached Dunmore. The "governor" had no Virginia dry land that he controlled, and so the blacks had to reach his armada for safety. Those who reached his ships were formed into fighting units. Earlier black defectors fought successfully at Kemp's Landing, but they were soundly defeated at Great Bridge.[24] In this latter engagement, half of Dunmore's 600 troops were black. The uniforms of these black troops were inscribed *Liberty to Slaves* and they were referred to as "Lord Dunmore's Ethiopian Regiment" under the command of white Major Bird. The escapees were also used as pilots on small British craft to plunder shoreline plantations and to act as foragers for the navy. Some became "batmen" (body servants) to British officers. (General Charles Cornwallis allowed each officer two personal servants.) Patriots claimed that Dunmore used the blacks to spread smallpox: two were supposedly infected with the disease and sent to Norfolk to infect the inhabitants of that important seaport.[25]

The blacks were packed on the British ships, and they suffered epidemic diseases that killed many. By June 1776 there were barely 150 able-bodied blacks on board. On August 6 of that year, the British ended their depredations and sailed for Sandy Hook, Bermuda, and St. Augustine. Of a total of 800 slaves who reached the fleet, 300 remained alive in weakened condition.

About 500 blacks died during a brief occupation by the British of Gwynn's Island. Dunmore, to the very end, claimed his plan could have been success-ful. He could have had 2,000 blacks under arms; these plus the Loyalists would have subdued the rebellious colony. However, "a malignant fever has carried off an incredible number of our people, especially the blacks. Had it not been for this terrible disorder ... I had no doubt of penetrating to the heart of the enemy."[26]

Despite Dunmore's failure to use escaped slaves successfully, the British high command still believed that the slaves of patriots were an important resource that could be tapped. In England, where the war was not popular, people were appalled at the idea of inciting slaves to insurrection against their "American Brethren." British officers had to obtain slaves surreptitiously, because they needed soldiers and laborers, color notwithstanding. As the war passed to the South, the issue of blacks became more significant, particularly in areas where they outnumbered the whites. On June 30, 1779, Comman-der-in-Chief Henry Clinton proclaimed that a captured armed American black soldier would be purchased at a set price from his captor. No Briton was permitted to capture a slave who sought refuge with the British army. This slave would receive security behind British lines and could perform any occupation he believed himself capable of doing. In the Southern theater, the British took many blacks, sometimes raiding for this purpose alone, the idea being to deplete the South of its labor force. At the approach of British forces, Patriots sent their slaves to the interior to avoid their loss. The British fre-quently forced recalcitrant slaves in occupied areas to build forts and to per-form other labor. If the slaves belonged to a Tory, the master paid for their service, at 2 shillings per worker per day. Slaves of patriots were promised freedom if they crossed Cornwallis's lines. The British issued guidelines for the use of slaves, because there was a great demand for them by competing units. Heads of departments turned in lists of slaves to the paymaster; they had to distinguish between Loyalist and patriot slaves. Wages were set at 8 pence per day for common laborers, 18 pence per day for craftsman, with two women considered equal to one man. The heads of departments turned in money to the paymaster, who would pay Loyalists for their slaves. These department heads gave vouchers to Loyalists which could be used to clothe slaves. Slaves received identification tickets from the paymaster, and failure to have a ticket resulted in arrest (presumably to prevent spying).[27]

The British rented several thousand Hessians and paid their costs in America. Like their British allies, the Hessians recruited blacks. Most drum-mers recruited by the Hessians were blacks from South Carolina—28 of 47 were from Charleston. Virginia supplied 14, and New York 11. Most of these recruits were in their teens or early twenties, though one was 52 years old. Some were runaway slaves, but most of these were reclaimed by their Loy-alist masters. A few were permitted to carry muskets, and two became grenadiers. Other blacks were teamsters, laborers, or servants to the officers. Of the group, one was wounded in action, but none was killed. Some were lost from illness, while others were captured by the patriots. Most were lost by desertion, particularly as the war seemed to be ending. If caught by the Hessians, they were forced to "run the gauntlet" but were then taken back into service.[28] The Hessians seemed to show no racial prejudice toward the black soldiers, and their pay was high. One wonders how they treated these men, the likes of whom they had never seen before. Did they treat them like pets, children, or equals? Lieutenant John Charles von Krafft of the Hessian army claimed, "I had to examine a negro drummer for theft, and because he denied it, had him spanked."[29] When the Hessians left America, 31 blacks joined them. Many of them died of tuberculosis in Europe, though one married and raised a family. One reached the anatomy laboratory after death, where the prosecutor showed his audience that the black man was like a white man under his black skin.

Britain's early use of blacks was not lost on George Washington. Following Dunmore's proclamation, the American commander on December 30, 1775, gave "leave to Recruiting Officers to entertain them" (blacks) to try to prevent free blacks from joining the British armies. The following day, Washington wrote to the president of Congress in Philadelphia that he was allowing free Negroes to enlist because they "are very much dissatisfied at being discarded. As it is to be apprehended, that they may seek employ in the ministerial army." If Congress disapproved his action, he would rescind it. Congress replied in January 1776 "that the free negroes who have served faithfully in the army at Cambridge may re-enlist there, but no others." Slaves were excluded.[30]

Although Washington was aware of the need to use black resources, many of the colonies still refused to "mongrelize" their units with blacks. Massachusetts did not allow slaves to enlist, and a majority of a convention in Massachusetts refused all Negro enlistments.[31] That same year, the Bay State again excluded nonwhites and prohibited whites from sending blacks in their place. Other New England states followed this lead. Pennsylvania (April 1776) excluded blacks from participating in military training. In New York, no "bought servants" were to be part of any company. Shrewsbury, New Jersey, ordered blacks to turn in their weapons until the "present troubles" were settled. Virginia permitted free blacks to enlist, but no other Southern state followed its lead.

The horrible loss of manpower in army hospitals, desertions, and battle forced the new country to turn to a largely untapped source of cannon fodder, the 500,000 blacks in a population of 2½ million. Many leaders urged the use of blacks in war. General John Thomas in a 1775 letter to John Adams favored black enlistment. Samuel Hopkins (1776) thought that slaves could be prevented from going to the British if they were set free and encouraged to labor and fight for America. Alexander Hamilton urged emancipation. The new freedmen were to be given swords to secure their fidelity, animate their courage, and influence those in bondage by opening a door to their emancipation. James Madison wanted to free and arm the slaves. These new freedmen would be placed in mixed units commanded by white officers. They would not be dangerous, for, Madison predicted, they would lose sympathy and attachment to the slaves left behind. General Nathaniel Greene of Rhode Island, the commander in the South, urged the governors of South Carolina and Georgia to enlist blacks—all to no avail. In a letter to Governor John Rutledge of South Carolina, he stated that he thought they could raise enough black and white troops to force the British out of Charleston. He wanted to raise four regiments, two for the Continental Line and two to defend the state. Greene also suggested a corps of pioneers and craftsmen, each of 80 men; the slaves would be freed and treated like white soldiers.[32] The state legislature turned the general down, however; its members had a better use for the slaves: each white who enlisted would receive a slave from the state.

Perhaps the strongest supporters of enlisting slaves were the Laurenses of South Carolina. They were probably the largest slaveholders in the state. John Laurens, in a letter to his father, Henry, of January 14, 1778, wrote, "Cede me a number of your able-bodied slaves to turn into soldiers." Slaves were conditioned to the "habit of subordination," which was one of the chief qualifications for an excellent soldier. John believed he could form a corps of well-trained ex-slaves ready to fight. This would also prepare them for eventual freedom, which he and his father both desired. Henry believed it would be proper to set them free first and ask them to enlist. He believed not 10 percent would enlist. However, Henry gave his son permission to come to South Carolina to try to advance his idea. John had second thoughts, though, and abandoned the plan temporarily.[33] Later that year, with the Palmetto State besieged by the British, Tories, and Indians, John gave his original plan further thought. He and Alexander Hamilton, both aides to General Washington, urged John Jay, president of the Continental Congress, to accept black troops.[34] The aides requested two to four black battalions. The slave owners would supply men proportional to the number they owned; they would be paid by the Continental Congress for the men enlisted. It was believed that blacks would make excellent soldiers under John Laurens's command. Supporters of the plan denied the commonly held notion that blacks were too stupid to be soldiers, but stupid men under good officers made good soldiers. Slaves were not stupid. Their natural abilities were equal to those of the whites; it was simply a lack of training that made them appear this way. Their lifetime of servitude and subordination would make them soldiers more quickly than whites. Their officers were to be men of good sense and sentiment. Many would object from prejudice and self-interest. Whites were taught contempt of blacks which was unfounded by experience. If Americans did not use them, the enemy would. The patriots should offer them their free-dom with their guns; this would result in fidelity and courage and would have a good influence on those left behind. The circumstance the country was in and the dictates of humanity called for the acceptance of this project.

In March 1779 John Laurens laid his plan before Congress. Henry Laurens wrote Washington, asking him "to give his blessing" to this endeavor. Washington was opposed to the idea, however, believing it would stimulate the British to arm more slaves and cause restlessness among the slaves left in bondage. On March 29, 1779, Congress suggested that South Carolina and Georgia raise 3,000 blacks, joined into two corps, commanded by white officers appointed by the states. The owners of the slaves would receive up to $1,000 from the national treasury for each slave accepted. The slaves accepted into service would not receive a bounty, but they were to be fed and clothed by the national government; after the war, they would be freed and given $50. The plan had to be approved by the two states involved. John Laurens was sent down to try to persuade them to accept the enterprise. He failed, but the concept developed a life of its own. General Benjamin Lincoln, appointed in 1778 to lead the Southern armies, petitioned Governor Rutledge for black soldiers. In 1780 the legislature ordered 1,000 slaves enrolled as pioneers, oars-men, and mariners. Congress tried to get these states to raise 1,000 black combatants rather than auxiliaries, but failed. The idea was presented repeatedly by John Laurens (until he was killed in action), and by General Nathaniel Greene until the end of the war—without success.[35]

The army continued to shrink. (In December 1776 Washington had only 3,000 troops, and of these, only 1,400 were fit for duty.) Congress and the states had to take another look at the slave potential. Congress ordered the states to raise 88 battalions on September 16, 1776. The numbers were apportioned according to population. Massachusetts and Virginia had to raise 15 each, Delaware 1. But the states failed to reach their quotas, and Congress called for a draft in January 1777. By the summer of that year, Northern states were enlisting free blacks with a bounty, as well as slaves. New Hampshire had a bounty for slaves if they served three years; the bounty was turned over to their master as the price of the slave. In return, the master issued a bill of sale and a certificate of freedom. New Hampshire was able to raise a regiment of slaves, with white officers. For the most part, this ended slavery in New Hampshire, which was relatively uncommon there to begin with (there were only 629 slaves in the state at the outbreak of the Revolution).

The Massachusetts Assembly, to meet its quota, called for a draft of every seventh man, excluding Quakers. There was no mention of the exclusion of blacks. Thomas Kinch, in an artillery regiment at Castle Point, in a letter to the General Assembly claimed that the Massachusetts army was depleted by sickness, death, and desertion. He believed new attacks by the British would be launched in the spring, but 200 or 300 blacks could be raised in a separate unit with himself as the commanding officer. He believed that keeping blacks separate would increase their esprit de corps. The suggestion stimulated considerable debate, but no action was taken. Later, a company of 100 blacks was formed, with three black sergeants, four black corporals, three black drummers, and two black fifers. They would serve until the end of the war and would then be free. In April 1778 blacks were enlisted in integrated units, and slaves were accepted. Massachusetts raised several black companies, one under Major Samuel Lawrence, a second under a black named Middleton, called the Bucks of America, and the third the Massasoit Guards, named after the Indian friendly to the early settlers in Massachusetts. The state enlisted 572 blacks into service out of a population of about 3,500 slaves.[36]

The Joint Legislative Committee of the Bay State recommended on April 18, 1778, the creation of a black regiment. It would have the same number of soldiers as a white regiment, with white officers and one white sergeant in each company. The enlisted men would be blacks, mulattoes, and Indians who were able-bodied. Any servants or "others" needed permission from their masters and would receive all bounties, wages, and encouragement allowed by Congress to other soldiers. If a slave was admitted, he became a free man. If disabled in the war, he would be supported by the state, not his ex-master. The master was to receive recompense for his property from the state, depending on the assessed value. The plan was vetoed, though, by the council. The general court of the state could see the light at the end of the tunnel (the end of the war), and on March 3, 1781, a militia act was passed that banned blacks because there was no further need for warm bodies.[37] The militia was called the Training Band. It was composed of all able-bodied men 16–50, except for blacks, mulattoes, and Indians. Any male, 16 to 65, not included in the Training Band was on an alarm list, excluding blacks and mulattoes. This exemption probably reflected the increasing social and political role of the militia.

The story of the Massachusetts Bucks is hidden in controversy. It may not have been a military unit. Instead, it was a group of "Protectors" who guarded the property of Boston merchants against Tory sabotage. Governor John Hancock made their leader, Middleton, a "colonel," and the unit received a banner from the governor for "courage and devotion."[38]

Connecticut, with a slave population of about 5,000, was unable to encourage many to enlist. There was a sprinkling of blacks in mixed units, but of the nonwhites, Indians were the largest group to enlist. Blacks in the Sixth Connecticut Battalion, originally dispersed among the companies, were brought together into one black company (the Colonials) or the Sixth Company. There were three white officers (Captain David Humphrey was the commanding officer) and 56 black enlisted personnel. They remained together until November 1782 when the company was disbanded and spread throughout the battalion. After the draft law of 1777, a committee advised the Connecticut legislature that any able-bodied slave should be encouraged to enlist in the Continental Battalion being raised in the state. The state paid the owner, and the slave who enlisted was freed. His ex-master was not responsible for him if he became disabled in the war. The master received his bounty and one-half of his wages. However, if he received the slave's value from the state, the ex-slave received all of his wages. The statute was rejected by the upper house of the legislature. Connecticut then enacted a strange scheme to get warm bodies. All able-bodied men in a community were divided into classes. Each class supplied one or more men to fill the town's quota. Two men could substitute an able-bodied recruit who enlisted and freed them from the draft. The man secured was not questioned as to color or civil status.[39]

Of the states in New England, only Rhode Island had a slave economy resembling that of the South. As was described earlier, the Narragansett area (North and South Kingston and Cranston) had plantations with large numbers of slaves. (About one-third of the population was black.) This small state with a relatively small white population had 4,373 slaves. As the Revolution progressed, much of the state was occupied by the British, but the legislature was able to raise the two regiments requested by Congress. The regiments were decimated, and at the Valley Forge encampment (the winter of 1777–78) there were barely enough effectives to form one regiment. General James Varnum on January 2, 1778, sent a letter to George Washington:

> The two battalions from the state of Rhode Island being small, and there being a necessity of the state's furnishing an additional number to make up their proportion in the Continental army; the field officers have represented to me the propriety of making one temporary battalion from the two, so that one entire corps of officers may repair to Rhode Island, in order to receive and prepare the recruits from the freed. It is imagined that a battalion of negroes can be easily raised there. Should that measure be adopted or recruits obtained from any other principle the service will be advanced. The field officers who go upon this command are Colonel Greene, Lieutenant Colonel Olney, and Major Ward; seven captains, 12 lieutenants, six ensigns, one paymaster, one surgeon and mates, one adjutant, and one chaplain.[40]

In February 1778 the Rhode Island legislature decreed that "every able-bodied Negro, Mulatto, and Indian may enlist into the two battalions to serve during the war with Great Britain. The slave received all bounties and wages given by the Continental Congress to other soldiers. Slaves who passed muster before Colonel Christopher Greene were free as though they never were slaves." Those who became sick or injured by service would be supported by the state. The owner would receive up to £120 per slave (about $400 in Continental paper). The owner had to send the slave's clothes with him, or he would not receive the money. To determine the value of a slave, a committee of five was appointed, one from each county, and three made a quorum. They examined the slave and determined his worth to his master. The officer who enlisted the slave gave him a certificate that relieved him of service to his master. The master received a certification of the value of the slave from the committee. The treasurer of the state gave the owner a promissory note payable on demand with interest of 6 percent per year. The money came from Congress to the state, but first the money borrowed out of the treasury was repaid. To justify the act, the assembly stated, "The whole powers of government are required to recruit Continental Battalions. General Washington sent the proposal to Governor Cooke sent to him by General Varnum to enlist slaves. History shows that the bravest, truest nations in the past liberated their slaves to fight for them. The capital and a large part of the state are occupied by the enemy, therefore it cannot raise the required two battalions from free men only." The legislature further decreed that the enlistment of blacks to obtain freedom would end after June 10, 1779, when the act reached its termination date.[41]

There was considerable opposition in the state to the plan. Opponents claimed that there were not enough blacks in the state who would enlist to form a regiment. Raising several companies of blacks would not answer the purpose and would be a useless expense to the state. The idea would be looked down upon by other nations. The other states would feel that the blacks were not equal to their troops, and therefore Rhode Island would not get the same credit as for white troops. The enemy would think that the colonials could not raise enough troops to fight them and would mock the patriots Dunmore was mocked when he raised his black regiment. The British might raise more black regiments against the colonials. The cost of raising this regiment would be much higher than raising a regiment of whites and would not produce the same good effect. There would be great difficulties in purchasing slaves from masters, and masters would not be satisfied with the price allowed. The enemy would treat these soldiers with contempt, and therefore it would be impossible to get equal exchange of prisoners.[42]

Slaves were propagandized by the opponents. They were told that they would be in the most dangerous places and would be used as shock troops. If taken prisoner, they would not be treated as prisoners of war but instead would be shipped to the West Indies and sold into slavery. Despite this activity, as well as obstacles put in their way by owners and traders, many enlisted.[43]

After the statute was passed, blacks joined the service as soon as they received their masters' permission. The name Cuff Greene comes down to us as that of the first slave to enlist. The total number of black enlistees is not known. Generally a battalion was composed of four companies of 34 men each, or 136 troops, so probably 225–250 enlisted. Most owners allowed only one of their bondsmen to enlist. Most slaves went to the Continental Line, and the Continental Congress was expected to pay the costs. However, Congress had no money, and the state treasury was expected to pay. This was given in Continental Loan Office Certificates. The total sum was £10,437,

6 shillings, 7 pennies for all the slaves, and eventually the state made good on these notes. Colonial records of August 1, 1782, showed that the assembly listed the number of individual slaves recruited, and that masters were paid in silver money.[44]

Congressman William Eustis, an army surgeon during the war, praised the soldiering of the black troops: "In Rhode Island, where their numbers were more considerable, they were formed, under the same considerations, into a regiment commanded by white officers, and it is required, in justice to them, to add, that they discharged their duty with zeal and fidelity. The gallant defense of Red Bank, in which this black regiment bore a part, is among the proofs of their valor."[45] Colonel Greene was mortally wounded at Points Bridge, New York, in May 1781, and his black bodyguards surrounded him. All were killed by the British, who then reached Greene and killed him too. Greene was succeeded by Jeremiah Olney until the regiment was disbanded at Saratoga, New York, on June 13, 1783. The black troops fought at the battles of Rhode Island, Red Bank, Points Bridge, Yorktown, and Fort Oswego. The Fort Oswego campaign resulted in a sad ending for many blacks. On the road from Saratoga to Fort Oswego, the army was led off course; many blacks froze to death as a result of this error.

After the war, Rhode Island kept its promise to the black enlistees. The legislature in June 1784 appointed a committee to inquire into the circumstance of ex-slaves who enlisted and were now unable to support themselves. The committee determined the amount of money they were to receive. In February 1785 the committee was charged to draft an act for the support of the blacks who were now chargeable.[46]

New York City was taken by the British early in the war and was occupied until 1783. Although there were approximately 15,000 slaves in the state in 1775, little could be done with them to advance the patriots' cause. In 1776 the New York legislature permitted substitutes, white or black. Slave substitutes were promised their freedom. The legislature in March 1781 authorized the enlistment of slaves into the Continental Line to be used for the defense of the northern frontier; it called for two regiments of blacks. Slaves who served satisfactorily for three years or until discharged were freed, and their owners were paid in land grants for their freedom. If an owner delivered up his slaves, he would be free of their care forever.[47]

New Jersey's Militia Act of 1777 ordered all effective men between 15 and 50 to join militia units. The law was amended the following year to exclude slaves. An act of 1779 restricted the militia to free white males. Finally, another act called for "all able-bodied effective recruits" (servants, minors, and apprentices were exempt), but slaves were permitted to join. The statute of 1781 called for "all men 16 to 50," but it was amended the following year to "such inhabitants that are desirous of joining."[48] Part of New Jersey was occupied by British forces, and its proximity to occupied New York allowed the slaves who deserted to reach British lines. In a letter to C. Cuyler (May 25, 1780) Major General James Pattison complained that the Negroes in New Jersey had taken advantage of a British post there to escape from their masters; from this post, they went to New York City. If this continued, it would be a burden to New York, and they should be prevented from crossing the North River.[49] Of New Jersey's 7,600 slaves, few went into the Continental service.

Pennsylvania, like Virginia, was expected to raise 12 regiments. Between Continental soldiers and militia, 33,000 men from the Keystone State saw service. How many were black, free, or slave is not known. Pennsylvania, the leader in the emancipation movement, still had about 10,000 slaves at the start of fighting. In addition to Philadelphia's occupation, there was a large Tory influence. Also, the Quakers who controlled the legislature maintained neutrality in the war; consequently, there was no activity to emancipate slaves to join the Continental army. Delaware, after its separation from Pennsylvania, counted itself a Southern state. There were 9,000 slaves in Delaware, and the state put approximately 2,700 men in uniform. As in the states of the Deep South, many slave owners in Delaware felt they were needed at home to protect their families from the slaves in their midst. The Continental Congress requested one regiment from the state. ("Request" was an apt term. Congress could not demand compliance by the states with its directives.)

Maryland, with 80,000 slaves, was not as concerned about slave insurrection and arming blacks as were its sister states in the South. A greater threat to slave owners was the possibility of escape to British ships in the Atlantic Ocean and Chesapeake Bay, as well as raids by escaped blacks on shoreline plantations. Correspondence between community leaders and Governor Thomas S. Lee described local actions taken against these attempts by their ex-bondsmen. James McHenry of Baltimore described the purchase of two "look-out boats" to keep Negroes from deserting to the enemy.[50] Richard Barnes kept 60 men patrolling the area to prevent blacks from going over to the enemy. Correspondence of the state council (1780) described a raid on Viana from an offshore boat. The raiding party included 12 whites and 21 blacks. They burned vessels, took away other blacks, broke glass, and destroyed stills. The area may have had a large Tory population, because "many local whites favored them and they had difficulty raising a militia of 30 men." If the incursions were not stopped, "our most valuable negroes will run away."[51]

Early in its history (1715) Maryland exempted all blacks and slaves from militia training or other military service, but the exigencies of the Revolution changed this prohibition. In 1777 the state encouraged free blacks to enlist.[52] This was the year when Congress called for a draft, and the state looked the other way when slaves were substituted for their masters. Three years later, the state developed an unusual draft plan. The state was divided by property. Each area with a combined value of £16,000 had to furnish one recruit, free or slave.[53] That same year, Maryland allowed slaves to enlist; it was the only Southern state to take this action. Any able-bodied slave between 16 and 40 who enlisted with his master's approval was accepted. However, there was no promise of emancipation with the service. In 1781 Maryland drafted free blacks and mulattoes. In the middle of the year, Maryland was expected to raise two battalions of militia (1,340 men).[54] At this time too Lafayette suggested to the assembly that Maryland should raise a regiment of blacks under a Major McPherson. The suggestion was disapproved, but the state resolved to raise 750 blacks to be incorporated into other units; it failed completely in this endeavor. There were probably 95 blacks from Maryland in service among 18,000 whites who served in some form in the war.

Virginia's colonial history was closely intertwined with that of its black population almost from the time of its founding. Early, the colony had to deal with its Indian neighbors. Later, the enemies were the French and Spanish. When the colony was 30 years old, the house of burgesses passed its first statute related to its blacks: on January 16, 1639, slaves were expected to help in invasions.[55] If a slave killed or took an enemy prisoner, observed by a white Virginian, he was freed, and his master was paid out of public funds. If the slave was killed in combat, his master was similarly recompensed. A slave who was disabled and could not work for his master was freed and supported with public funds. If a master believed his slave was trustworthy, he could arm him during an invasion to the same degree as a white Virginian.

The number of free blacks increased during the seventeenth century, and the legislature recognized their presence in a statute of May 9, 1723. In an invasion, all free Negroes, mulattoes, and Indians who were capable had to join the military, where they were used as drummers, fifers, and pioneers (laborers). In 1775 Virginia was the site of battles between Tories and patriots. The Virginia Convention ordered all males, hired servants, and apprentices between 16 and 50 to be enlisted in the militia.[56] Blacks were frequently apprenticed by their masters until they were 31. Some masters refused to allow them to go, and several were seized forcibly. The use of blacks as noncombatants was stopped by a militia act of 1776. One year later, free black men were drafted, because "they could best be spared." Some free men enlisted, but they had to show a certificate from a justice of the peace to prove their free status. Slaves were used as substitutes for their masters, although this was not legal until a statute passed in 1783. The Virginia legislature granted freedom to all slaves who served. Some slaves, perhaps fearful that freedom would not be granted for service, ran away and joined the American force as opposed to Virginia's forces. Virginia had a respite from the war until 1779 when the British returned. At this point, Virginia drafted free blacks and slaves. Virginia was second to the New England states in the number of blacks supplied to the army: about 500 free blacks and a small number of slaves. These soldiers served in mixed units, usually as auxiliaries. Occasionally they were combatants.

The rivers of Virginia and its coast served as a means of escape by the slaves to the occupying British. Thomas Jefferson believed that 30,000 escaped to the British in 1778.[57] (Lord Tarleton "appropriated" 30 of Jefferson's bondsmen.) Of this large number, 27,000 were said to have died of typhus and smallpox. The fear of losing valuable property, and the use of this property against their previous owners, led to calls for Northern soldiers to suppress the flight. Major General Charles Lee "Light-horse Harry" in a letter to Robert Morris (April 16, 1776) feared "an insurrection of negroes, we must apply for some battalions to your middle colonies." With 165,000 slaves in their midst, Virginia's leaders had to give serious consideration to this potential internal enemy. In letters to colonels William Peachy and John Mercer (April 2, 1776) Lee said, "If the British landed with considerable force, they would take Williamsburg and York. Possession of these places would give an air of superiority and dignity to their arms, which in these slave counties is a matter of infinite importance." A similar letter was sent to Edward Rutledge of South Carolina (April 3, 1776), as well as to Richard Henry Lee. This same anxiety was seen in orders to Brigadier General John Armstrong (April 10, 1776): "As in Slave counties so much depends on opinion, and the opinion which the Slaves will entertain of our superiority or inferiority, will naturally keep pace, with our maintaining or giving ground." Lee also urged that slaves be moved to the interior of the state. In a letter to Colonel John Muhlenberg (April 23, 1776), Lee ordered him to "procure the best intelligence what men are on board Lord Dunmore's fleet, who have families at Portsmouth." Their families were to be sent to Suffolk.[58] "All the negroes capable of bearing arms to be secured immediately, and sent up to Suffolk."

As described earlier, North Carolina was not a major slaveholding state when it separated from South Carolina. However, by the outbreak of the Revolution, there were about 75,000 slaves within its borders. Much of its white male population was occupied keeping the slaves under control, because the state supplied only about 7,200 men to the Continental Line. There was little legislation that encouraged slaves to enlist. In 1778 any slave who enlisted in a branch of the service would be freed, and these free men would forever be exempt from the fugitive slave laws.[59] The state had a use, however, for blacks who did not enlist. A statute gave one "negro man slave" to any militiaman who was hurt or maimed in service and could not afford medical care—the slave would be his pension. The wife and family of a militiaman killed in action would receive similar compensation.[60]

The most trustworthy slaves in South Carolina were armed against inroads by the Indians and Spaniards after the colony was settled. The profits generated by large plantations using many slaves, particularly in rice and indigo, resulted in the demand for and importation of more blacks. In 1775 South Carolina had 110,000 slaves. In Charleston, and on the large plantations, slaves outnumbered whites three to one. The legislators of South

Carolina (the plantation owners) were initially loyal to Great Britain, but they turned to the patriot cause following rumors of a slave conspiracy and rebellion armed and instigated by the British. The Provincial Congress authorized raising three regiments to protect the colony from the British externally and from the slaves internally. The royal governor (Lord Campbell) was believed to be involved in the conspiracy. Suspicions were intensified after Lord Dunmore's proclamation in Virginia. The legislators accused the governor of bringing in arms for slaves on the ship that brought him to Charleston. Like Dunmore, Campbell left South Carolina for the safety of a British ship, *Tamar*.[61] At this time too many slaves left South Carolina for the British fleet in Carolina waters.

The Provincial Congress on November 20, 1775, "resolved, that the Colonels of several regiments of militia throughout the Colony have leave to enroll such a number of able male slaves, to be employed as pioneers and laborers, as public exigencies may require, and that a daily pay of seven shillings, six pence be allowed by the service of each such a slave while actually employed."[62] (The money was paid to the owner.) It would have been a bonanza if the owners received the money in specie. John Sansun received £204 for his slaves in an artillery brigade. John Keating received £366 for public works performed for the Continental Army. David Hórry received £1 for his slave killed at Savannah in 1779. South Carolinians earned a few extra pounds from selling provisions to the Royal Navy, which blockaded the state.[63] However, the council prohibited this sale to ships whose officers took escaped slaves on board (December 1775). This source of income disappeared after militia troops captured Sullivan's Island in Charleston harbor; it was fortified and defended with the famous palmetto logs. British ships were then not able to pass its batteries to attack Charleston proper. The fleet finally left South Carolina's waters after the defeat of its navy under Sir Peter Parker on June 28, 1776.

South Carolina was expected to raise several regiments for the Continental Army under the draft law passed in Philadelphia. The state was unable to meet its quota, however, because of the fear that large numbers of slaves would rise up if whites left the state. So the legislature attempted to raise troops with an offer of an able-bodied slave to every white who enlisted for ten months, the bounty being taken from plantations of Loyalists. The state raised 6,413 troops for the Continental Army, but it had 56,163 in its militia units who did not leave their respective counties.

The war returned to the Deep South in 1779. In March of that year, Colonel Isaac Huger was sent to the Continental Congress by South Carolina to appeal for troops from the North, for there were not enough whites to keep the slaves under control and fight the British.[64] Congress suggested that they could raise a force of Negroes (3,000–4,000 troops in three regiments from South Carolina and Georgia). The blacks were disciplined and would be a formidable force against the enemy; this approach would also lessen the danger to the state by removing the most vigorous and enterprising of the slaves (Laurens's plan). The troops would have white commissioned and non-commissioned officers. Congress would pay their owners up to $1,000 per slave under 35 years of age. If the slave served well, despite lack of pay and bounty, and returned his arms, he would receive $50 plus his freedom ("Freedom with their muskets," according to Alexander Hamilton).[65] This time, Governor John Rutledge of South Carolina approved of the idea, but it was vetoed by both state legislatures (Washington commiserated with Laurens, but covertly he opposed the plan).

The British occupied Georgia, Charleston, and a large part of South Carolina in 1780. General Lincoln urged Rutledge to raise a battalion of 1,000 blacks to do "fatigue duties for the garrison" in artillery; he was refused. Lincoln was replaced by Gates, and he in turn was replaced by Nathaniel Greene, who was treated similarly. After the defeat of Cornwallis, the Deep South still remained insecure, believing that the British would try to conquer and retain South Carolina and Georgia with 3,000 troops sent from New York. To counter this threat, an attempt was made to raise a corps of blacks, but this idea was rejected. The "prejudices against the measure are so prevailing, that no consideration could induce them to accept it. Pioneers, artificers, wagoners, servants to the officers are talked of." Overall, the attempts by South Carolina to keep its slaves out of British hands was reasonably successful. Between 1775 and 1783, the state lost 25,000 slaves of a population of 110,000 (either killed by medical diseases introduced by the British army or carried away, with them at the end of the war).[66]

Georgia's place in the Revolution resembled that of South Carolina, on a smaller scale. In the 25 years during which slavery was legal in Georgia before the outbreak of the Revolution, the state accumulated about 16,000 slaves. The number of slaves in relation to the white population was too high to allow whites to join the Continental Army, and Georgia raised about 2,600 men for the American line. Rather than supplying troops, Georgia requested soldiers to protect its population from the internal danger of slave insurrection, and from the external danger of the British and Indians on its borders. In a request to the Continental Congress, its deputies claimed Georgia was surrounded by enemies.[67] It provided livestock (cattle), had excellent harbors and rivers, and had inhabitants loyal to America. On its coast, British ships ravaged the land—"their negroes are daily inveigled and carried away from their Plantations." The British took cattle from the offshore islands. East Florida, to the south, made inroads into Georgia, which was a buffer for South Carolina. South Georgia had cattle and rice in danger from the British. To the west, 15,000 Indian warriors were ready to attack. "Add to all these considerations the vast Numbers of Negroes we have, perhaps of themselves Sufficient to subdue us in Point of Numbers the Blacks exceed the Whites; and the ready Channel of Supply and secure retreat which St. Augustine affords renders them much to be dreaded." It was believed that at least six battalions were needed to defend Georgia. If they could not be raised in Georgia, the other states were to send regiments taken from the Continental Line. Georgia's leaders requested funds from Congress to build fortifications to protect the state from incursions by Indians from Florida: a fortified state would be able to protect South Carolina, North Carolina, and Virginia. The state also requested money to buy 5,000 head of cattle as a bribe to the Indians to remain neutral. General Lee, in a letter to Richard Peters (August 2, 1776), and then in a meeting with the Council of Safety (August 19, 1776), urged the invasion and capture of St. Augustine in East Florida. He was certain that Great Britain was bribing the Indians to side with them against the patriots. The Indians made incursions into Georgia and carried off many blacks and about 2,000 head of cattle. The British also built a fort on the St. Mary's River which afforded asylum to "Negro Deserters." Georgia favored his plan: "It will be a means of preventing the loss of Negroes, either by desertion or otherwise by land."[68]

Georgia was included in the call to South Carolina to raise 3,000 black soldiers, and like its northern neighbor, Georgia refused. However, slaves were permitted to enlist as substitutes for their masters in return for a promise of freedom. Austin Dabney, an enlisted slave, served with heroism in Colonel Elijah Charles's Artillery Corps, suffering a broken thigh at the Battle of Kettle Creek (1779). Forty years later, the state gave him 112 acres of land, as a reward and pension.[69] Approximately 200 slaves, taken from confiscated Loyalist estates, were permitted to join the Continental Line as pioneers in the hope of taking East Florida. There may have been 100 slaves in state militia units.[70] Rather than join the army for freedom, however, other slaves escaped to the British lines and to the fleet in Georgia's waters. To prevent this loss of valuable property, the Georgia legislature ordered one-third of each county's militia to be left behind to patrol their areas in order to prevent insurrection and flight of slaves.[71] Some of these runaways were caught and hanged. Despite these attempts at control, three-fourths to seven-eighths of Georgia's slaves were able to flee. Many left with the British when they evacuated Savannah. Far more escaped to East Florida. Some stayed behind to fight their former masters, calling themselves the "King of England's Soldiers." This group ravaged the shores along the Savannah River and into South Carolina. They remained a threat until May 1786 when the combined militia forces of Georgia and South Carolina destroyed their swamp fortress. Many were taken or killed, but some escaped deeper into the swamps; others occupied Bellisle Island in the Savannah River. Eventually all were routed out.[72]

There was less uneasiness about the blacks, free or slave, in the navy. Perhaps they were outnumbered by the white crew, but most likely they were not armed in a place where they could become centers of insurrection to other slaves. Before the war, blacks served onboard ships. Runaway slaves were accepted for long voyages without questioning their status too closely. Royal Navy press gangs were "color blind," and many blacks were taken off the streets for service. Following the outbreak of hostilities, a Continental Navy, state navies, and privateers needed warm bodies—the need for seamen was greater than the supply, particularly on Continental ships where the crew's share of prize money was less. These vacancies were filled by blacks. (A recruiting poster in Newport, Rhode Island, in 1775 called for able-bodied recruits, black or white, for naval service.)[73] Onboard ships, blacks were able seamen, "powder-boys," servants to the officers, and pilots of ships, particularly in the Chesapeake Bay and the rivers that emptied into it. They had been experienced sailors in these waters before the war. Blacks served in crews under John Paul Jones, David Porter, James Barry, and others.[74] The state navies of Massachusetts, Connecticut, and Pennsylvania had black marines. In one episode of the war, a black was captain of the schooner *Cheerfully*.[75] The Maryland Council wanted a ship to take Maryland soldiers from *Head of the Bay*. Stephen Steward, who described the incident to the council, could not find any white volunteers to sail such a rescue mission in the face of British ships patrolling the area, but a black skipper was found. Steward's ship was sent off with "a valubell Negro."

The British used escaped slaves in their navy. These men performed the same duties as blacks in the American navy. They served one added function when they knew the area: they were part of marauding parties that went ashore to destroy patriots' property and to bring back slaves for British service. If a black on an American ship was taken by British privateers, he was often returned to his master, if the master was a Loyalist. More commonly he was sold to increase the value of the prize. The British also used these seamen in prisoner exchanges.[76]

Several thousand slaves gained their freedom through service in the navy, particularly those from the northeast. The promise of freedom was less often honored in the South. At times the state intervened to emancipate a slave. Caesar, a bondsman from Virginia, pilot of the schooner *Patriot*, captured the British brig *Fanny*. After the war, though, Mary Tarrant, his owner, returned him to slavery. The leader of the state legislature appointed a mediator, and after some urging, Tarrant agreed to his emancipation. She was given a certificate stating the amount she was to receive for Caesar's freedom; this certificate was presented to the state auditor of accounts. In return, she received a warrant to the treasurer who paid her from the legislative fund. Caesar was "manumitted and set free to all intents and purposes" on November 14, 1789.[77]

The use of slaves or recently freed blacks in war resulted in judicial problems related to their treatment. In Virginia, slaves who deserted to Dunmore's "army" were occasionally recaptured. The owner sometimes took the law into his own hands and hanged the prisoners; this satisfied his anger and it also impressed the other slaves with the danger of desertion. In 1781 a recaptured slave was tried in court for waging war against Virginia. He was found guilty of treason and was sentenced to be hanged. Governor Thomas Jefferson and two judges intervened in his behalf, ruling he was not a citizen and could not commit treason.[78] Far more commonly, slaves were taken off captured British ships and their status required adjudication. Two black sailors in this situation were to be sold into slavery. The legislature of Massachusetts on September 14, 1776, ordered that they were to be treated like other prisoners of war.[79] This ruling was restated in a Massachusetts law in April 1780. Some slaves were taken by the British in raids on plantations; presumably they had no choice about accompanying the British. A group of slaves, taken off plantations in South Carolina in June 1779, were on board an English ship taken by privateers. The prize was taken to Boston, and the slaves were fed and farmed out to patriots. The original owners traveled up to Boston to reclaim their property in November 1779, and the Massachusetts court returned the slaves to their masters after the masters paid the cost to the state of maintaining the group. Occasionally, the judges in the Bay State expressed their abhorrence of the "institution" and refused to return the slaves. To support the Southerners' claim, the governor of South Carolina addressed a letter to Governor John Hancock of Massachusetts requesting his help in returning private property. Hancock dropped the case into the lap of the judiciary, which refused to return the bondsmen.

Maryland had a problem with the Negro Joe, the property of John Eden, captured by Captain Folger and placed in jail. The slave was delivered to Eden, who promised to return him if so ordered by the governor or to pay the accepted salvage fee. The Maryland Council questioned the assembly as to Joe's status, as well as that of other slaves in this predicament. Were they to be treated like other property, or were they different because they were thinking creatures who could voluntarily run away? Finally, on October 6, 1781, the Court of the Admiralty declared Joe a legal prize, and his owner, Eden, had to deliver him to the marshal.[80] George Washington, in a letter to David Ross, suggested that they wait for the owners to claim such "prizes." If they failed to come, the blacks could be sent into the country to work for food and clothes; their whereabouts would be advertised in their state's newspapers.[81] The Continental Congress on December 4, 1781, settled the problem by law. If an American recaptured a slave of a citizen or state, the original owner paid the captor up to one-fourth of the slave's value according to the laws of the state where the claim was made. If the slave was not claimed within one year and a day, he was set free.

It has been estimated that more than 100,000 slaves left the new country during and after the war. The British promised freedom to those who reached their lines. The South lost over 65,000 during the war. Others were taken with the British when they evacuated New York. Many "saved" slaves died from disease while behind the British lines. Others went off to Canada, East Florida, England, and the Caribbean (as many as 60,000 went to Jamaica).[82] Unhappily, many in the Caribbean returned to their prewar status but with British masters. Between the end of the Revolution and the end of the century, an equal number won their freedom by emancipation, particularly in the North. Those who enlisted in the Continental Army gained their freedom as promised. In some instances, it required as much as ten years to achieve this end. Many had to petition the state legislature to enforce this promise to them. In Virginia, any slave who served in place of a white man, served well, and was discharged honorably, was freed. If retaken by his old master, a jury would be impaneled to assess damages due him from his ex-master for being detained. Several states gave their black veterans bounties as well as pensions (up to $96 per year). Virginia gave its ex-slaves 100 acres of land in Kentucky and Ohio. Most sold these land grants to speculators, though, because they preferred to remain in Virginia as free men.[83]

The sudden loss of laborers in the South resulted in severe disruptions. Many planters and small farmers could not rebuild after the war and turned to the state for compensation for damages resulting from the depredations of the British in the fighting. In York County, Virginia, a court was convened on April 28, 1783, to review these claims. Three officials met with claimants to fix the value of various articles of lost property. Anne Tompkins's losses were valued at £400 for the loss of four blacks in 1780: Ned, 23; Sam, 22; Peter, 20; and Bill, 19. John Slater was owed £412 for four Negroes and a four-oared canoe. John Robinson claimed compensation for three slaves, a very fine, large, six-oared cypress boat burned by the departing British, a cart with new wheels, six oxen with good yokes and chains, one bull, eighteen head of sheep, and "one fine fowling piece mounted with steel and drilled with gold (£10)."[84] The Cumberland County Courthouse (Virginia) had similar requests:

> This day Peter Stratton came before me and made oath that he has lost four negroes which went from his plantation in this county to the British, to wit Kimball ... Joseph ... Jesse ... and Dicey ... and that these negroes were seen at York at the siege by Samuel Shepard, whose statement is attached, and that he has never recovered either of them.
> Given under my hand this 20th day of October, 1782.
>   Ben Wilson.[85]

The problems of individuals were minor compared with the dispute between the United States and Great Britain over "stolen property" which was finally settled in 1827. Article VII of the Treaty of Paris (1783) required British troops to retire from the United States without carrying away or destroying any property belonging to citizens of the United States.[86] This property included slaves who reached the British lines. However, British commanders (Dunmore, Clinton, and Cornwallis) had promised freedom and protection to all who reached them. On May 6, 1783, George Washington wrote Sir Guy Carleton, advising him that blacks were embarking on British ships on May 12, 1783. Carleton issued lukewarm orders against removal of this property. Not surprisingly, these orders were not obeyed. Washington met with Carleton at Orangetown, New Jersey, in May 1783 to try to settle the issue between them. Carleton refused to give up the blacks. He feared that these individuals might be executed or otherwise punished, which would be a "dishonorable violation of the public faith." He wanted Great Britain to compensate the original owners in the United States. Washington refused, because it would be impossible to determine their worth and properly pay the owner. Commissioners were appointed to adjudicate the controversy, but they could not solve the problem. John Adams, Gouverneur Morris, and Thomas Jefferson were equally unsuccessful. A treaty with Great Britain, formulated by John Jay in 1794, expired in 1804 without any results. The War of 1812 nullified the Treaty of Paris, and the British repeated their activities of the "First Revolution." More slaves were taken. Article I of the Treaty of Ghent, which ended the War of 1812, repealed Article VII. The problem was finally put to rest in 1827 with financial compensation.

Many slaves escaped to British lines at the siege of Savannah. These Southern slaves saw East Florida (ceded to Britain by Spain in 1763 and receded after the Revolution) as a haven. Some escapees were given to Creek chiefs by the British "King's Gifts" for their help in the Revolution. Other blacks remained among the Seminole and Creek tribes in a mild form of slavery. Still others formed black communities in Seminole lands. There was intermittent warfare between the combined forces of Seminoles and blacks, and the invading militias from South Carolina and Georgia with covert backing by the federal government. In the War of 1812 General Andrew Jackson, commanding Georgia and Tennessee militias, defeated the blacks and Seminoles. Fighting continued sporadically until 1819 when East Florida was ceded by Spain to the United States.[87]

A substantial number of ex-slaves who left New York with Guy Carleton went to Canada (Nova Scotia), Great Britain, and the West Indies. In Nova Scotia, blacks, like other immigrants, were promised free land and rations for three years as well as other aid. They settled in Digby, Annapolis, and Preston, and in Saint John, New Brunswick. Some worked in Halifax. There were 3,000 freed blacks plus 1,300 slaves who accompanied their Loyalist masters. But racial intolerance, hunger, and opposition from white workers created disillusion among the new immigrants. Many Loyalists and their slaves left. Some freed blacks elected to go to Africa. In January 1792, 1,190 left for Africa at a cost of £16,000 to Great Britain.[88]

Other blacks and Loyalists went to England. Parliament set up a commission to pay claims to recover what the Tories had lost in their flight from the United States. Blacks received little or nothing, because they "received their freedom." They had no written proof that they owned property in America.

Many poor blacks wandered the streets of London, where they were helped with donations from the Poor Black Committee supported by the businessmen of London. The problem was finally thrown into the lap of Parliament, which voted to give the indigent a dole of 6 pence per day. Henry Smeathman wanted blacks sent to Sierra Leone; he received £14 for each black shipped out. After Smeathman died, it was suggested that the blacks go to the Bahamas, but they refused because slavery under British masters still existed in the islands. Finally, Sierra Leone was accepted as the "promised land" after a good deal of propagandizing. However, there was fear among blacks about going to an area where slave trading was active. Finally 459 people left for Sierra Leone. More than half had been American slaves. Some died on the trip, others died in Africa, and still others were seized by slave traders. Two years after they left London, 120 settlers remained. By 1791, only 60 remained. In 1792, 1,100 from Nova Scotia came and founded Freetown, the capital, and infused new blood into the dying colony.[89]

At sea, anyone on board, whether a white captain or a black cabin boy, was in harm's way during a battle. The Atlantic and Caribbean did not choose their victims by color. In land warfare, few blacks were combatants. On both sides they were predominantly laborers used to build fortifications, fell trees to delay a pursuing army, repair roads, drive wagons, and perform other duties that freed soldiers for combat. In addition, they were used as fifers and drummers by both sides. Black laborers were organized into units commanded by a white supervisor. In a letter to Colonel William Moultrie on July 1, 1776, General Lee recognized the need to defend Charleston. Colonel Isaac Huger's regiment offered to work on the fort guarding the city. Lee advised that a "Corps of Blacks would have answered better, but the President and Vice-President [of Congress] think otherwise."[90] On many occasions, slaves were commandeered by American and British officers to work without being in the service. In the defense of New York, slaves worked on fortifications every day, while free blacks worked every other day. In Virginia, recaptured runaways were frequently purchased from their owners by the state for state work. In South Carolina, many who fortified Sullivan's Island with the famous palmetto logs were rented from their masters. In Charleston in 1780 every slave in the city was rounded up to build fortifications. By 1782 an army commander could requisition slaves in numbers proportional to the number held by an owner. If the owner refused, soldiers took them at rifle point. In Georgia, an army officer could impress slaves for work against their owner's wishes; however, they had to work in their own district. Georgia's legislature in September 1777 ordered that one-tenth of a plantation's slaves could be impressed for 21 days at 3 shillings per day. If a slave was injured or killed while at work, state funds paid the owner his worth.[91]

Aside from auxiliary duties, some blacks fought. Typically they were infantry privates. Occasionally they became cavalrymen or served in artillery regiments. Their lives were at risk as spies, since if caught they could be executed. There were black units from New England, but most blacks were in integrated units. Many Hessians commented on the black faces in colonial regiments. The British soldiers were more derisive: "The Rebel clowns, oh what a sight to awkward was their figure / Twas yonder stood a pious wight and here and there a nigger."[92]

Finally, the list of names of blacks who served in the Revolution, incomplete as it is, and the battles in which they fought, will not be mentioned here. The interested reader is referred to other sources.[93]

NOTES

1: The Concept of Slavery

1. Murray Eisenstedt, ed., *The Negro in American Life* (New York: Oxford Book Publishing Co., 1968), p. 1.

2. Caroline L. Shanks, "The Biblical Anti-Slavery Argument of the Decade, 1830–1840," *Journal of Negro History* 16:2 (April 1931), p. 141.

3. Rayford W. Logan, "The Attitude of the Church Toward Slavery Prior to 1500," *Journal of Negro History* 17:4 (Oct. 1932), pp. 469, 478.

4. Peter M. Bergman, *The Chronological History of the Negro in America* (New York: Harper and Row, 1969), p. 141.

5. Michael I. Cassity, "The Mohammedan Slave Trader," *Journal of Negro History* 13:4 (Oct. 1928), p. 478.

6. Nathaniel Weyl, see "Historic Roots of Slavery" in Murray Eisenstadt, ed., *The Negro in American Life* (New York: Oxford Book Pub. Co., 1968), pp. 4–10.

7. Cassity, "Mohammedan Slave Trader," pp. 486, 487, 488.

8. William Renwick Riddell, "Observations on Slavery and Privateering," *Journal of Negro History* 15:3 (July 1930), pp. 337ff.

9. Winthrop D. Jordan, *White Over Black* (Chapel Hill: University of North Carolina Press, 1968), p. 51.

10. Oscar Handlin and Mary F. Handlin, "Origins of the Southern Labor System," *William and Mary Quarterly*, 3d series, 7:2 (April 1956), p. 204; *Publications of the Colonial Society of Massachusetts*, vol. 5, pp. 226–30; Bennett H. Lerone, Jr., *The Shaping of Black America* (Chicago: Johnson Publishing Co., 1975), p. 43.

11. "Indenture Agreement July 23, 1696," in New York Historical Society 1885, vol. 18, pp., 569–70.

12. Lerone, *Shaping of Black America*, p. 42.

13. *Ibid.*, p. 45.

14. W. F. Craven, "Introduction to the History of Bermuda," *William and Mary Quarterly* 17:3 (July 1937), pp. 317–62.

15. Alden T. Vaughan, "Blacks in Virginia: A Note on the First Decade," *William and Mary Quarterly*, 3d series, 29:3 (July 1972), p. 475.

16. George Ducas and Charles Van Doren, eds., *Great Documents in Black American History—The Life of Olaudah Equiano, the African—Gustavers Vassa* (New York: Praeger Publishers, 1970), p. 3.

17. William Loren Katz, *Eyewitness: The Negro in American History* (New York: Pitman Publishing Co., 1974), p. 20.

18. Michael I. Cassity, *Legacy of Fear* (Westport, Conn.: Greenwood Press, 1985), pp. 14–15.

19. *Ibid.*

20. *William and Mary Quarterly* 20:2 (Oct. 1911), p. 148.

21. Cassity, *Legacy of Fear*, pp. 16, 17.

22. Leslie H. Fishel and Benjamin Quarles, *The Negro American* (New York: William Morrow, 1967).

23. William T. Alexander, *History of the Colored Race in America* (Palmetto Publishing, 1887; reprint, New York: Negro University Press, n.d.), p. 133.

24. Jordan, *White Over Black*, pp. 67, 68.

25. *The New York Historical Society Quarterly* 55:1 (Jan. 1971), p. 14.

26. Robert Goldston, *The Negro Revolution* (New York: Macmillan, 1968), p. 67.

27. Robert Dale Owen, *The Wrong of Slavery* (Philadelphia: J.P. Lippincott, 1864), pp. 24, 27–29, 31.

28. Peter M. Bergman, *The Chronological History of the Negro in America* (New York: Harper & Row, 1969), p. 3.

29. Carl N. Degler, "Slavery and the Genesis of American Race Prejudice," in August Meier and Elliott Rudwick, eds., *The Making of Black America* (New York: Atheneum Press, 1969), pp. 92–93.

30. Rodney D. Carlisle, *Prologue to Liberation* (New York: Appleton-Century-Crofts, 1972), p. 33.

31. Jordan, *White Over Blacks*, pp. 6, 29, 31.

32. Ducas and Van Doran, *Great Documents in Black American History*, pp. 15–21.

33. Fishel and Quarles, *The Negro American*, pp. 97–98.

34. Charles W. Simmons and Barry W. Morris, eds., *Afro-American History* (Columbus, Ohio: Charles E. Merrill Publishing Co., 1972), pp. 39–40.

35. Cassity, *Legacy of Fear*, p. 16.

36. Jordan, *White Over Black*, p. 486, 491.

37. *Ibid.*, pp. 482, 499, 500, 538.

38. Cassity, *Legacy of Fear*, pp. 26–29.

39. T.R. Davis, "Negro Servitude in the United States," *Journal of Negro History* 8:3 (July 1923), 247–83.

40. Fishel and Quarles, *The Negro American*, pp. 91–92.

41. Katz, *Eyewitness*, p. 95.

42. Gilbert Osofsky, *The Burden of Race* (New York: Harper & Row, 1967), pp. 104–8.

2: *African Roots*

1. Leslie H. Fishel and Benjamin Quarles, *The Negro American* (New York: William Morrow, 1967), pp. 2, 3.

2. Murray Eisenstadt, ed., *The Negro in American Life* (New York: Oxford Book Publishing Co., 1968), p. 2.

3. John Hope Franklin, *From Slavery to Freedom* (New York: Alfred A. Knopf, 1947), pp. 11–20.

4. Kenneth G. Goode and Winthrop Jordan, *From Africa to the United States and Then* (Glenview, Ill.: Scott, Foresman, 1969), pp. 5–12.

5. Fishel and Quarles, *The Negro American*, pp. 11–13.

6. Melvill J. Herskovitz, "The African Heritage" in Eric Foner, ed., *America's Black Past* (New York: Harper Row, 1970), p. 28.

7. Franklin, *From Slavery to Freedom*, pp. 13–27.

8. Leslie H. Fishel and Benjamin Quarles, *The Black American* (New York: William Morrow, 1970), pp. 14–16.

9. Franklin, *From Slavery to Freedom*, pp. 27–31.

10. Fishel and Quarles, *The Negro American*, p. 14.

11. Fishel and Quarles, *The Black American*, p. 3.

12. Leslie J. Pollard, "Aging and Slavery: A Gerontological Perspective," *Journal of Negro History* 66:3 (Fall 1981), pp. 229–35.

13. Franklin, *From Slavery to Freedom*, pp. 32–33.

14. Lerone Bennett, Jr., *Before the Mayflower—A History of Black America* (Chicago: Johnson Publishing Co., 1969), pp. 26–27.

15. Mabel Morshach, *The Negro in American Life* (New York: Harcourt, Brace & World, 1966), pp. 24–25.

16. Booker T. Washington, *The Story of the Negro* (London: T. Fisher Unwin Co., 1907), pp. 67–70, 71.

3: The Slave Trade

1. Booker T. Washington, *The Story of the Negro* (London: T. Fisher Unwin Co., 1909), pp. 85–86.

2. Merl R. Eppse, *The Negro, Too, in American History* (Chicago: National Educational Publishing Co., 1938), pp. 24, 25, 26.

3. Saunders Redding, *They Came in Chains* (Philadelphia: J.P. Lippincott, 1950), p. 12.

4. L.P. Jackson, "Elizabethan Seamen: The African Slave Trade," *Journal of Negro History* 9:1 (Jan. 1924), pp. 3–14.

5. George Frederick Zook, "The Company of Royal Adventurers Trading Into Africa," *Journal of Negro History* 4:2 (April 1919), pp. 139, 143.

6. *Ibid.*, p. 163.

7. John Hope Franklin, *From Slavery to Freedom* (New York: Alfred A. Knopf, 1947), pp. 50–51.

8. William T. Alexander, *History of the Colored Race in America* (Palmetto Publishing, 1887; reprint, New York: Negro University Press, n.d.), p. 126.

9. Robert Dale Owen, *The Wrong of Slavery* (Philadelphia: J.P. Lippincott, 1864, reprint 1968), p. 32.

10. Peter M. Bergman, *The Chronological History of the Negro in America* (New York: Harper & Row, 1969), p. 24.

11. Leslie H. Fishel and Benjamin Quarles, *The Negro American* (New York: William Morrow, 1967), p. 16.

12. Earl Conrad, *The Invention of the Negro* (New York: Paul S. Eriksson, 1966), p. 9.

13. Eric Williams, "From Capitalism and Slavery," in Eric Foner, ed., *America's Black Past* (New York: Harper & Row, 1970), p. 33.

14 Bergman, *Chronological History*, p. 75.

15. Mabel M. Smythe, *The Black American Reference Book* (Englewood Cliffs, N.J.: Prentice Hall, 1971), p. 14

16. Robert Goldston, *The Negro Revolution* (New York: Macmillan, 1968), p. 46.

17. Eppse, *The Negro, Too*, p. 66.

18. Lerone Bennett, Jr., *Before the Mayflower—A History of Black America* (Chicago: Johnson Publishing Co., 1969), pp. 15–16.

19. Daniel C. Littlefield, "The Colonial Slave Trade to South Carolina—A Profile," *South Carolina Historical Magazine* 91:2 (April 1990), pp. 68–69.

20. James C. Lydon, "New York and the Slave Trade, 1700–1774" *William and Mary Quarterly*, 3d series, 35:2 (April 1978), pp. 376, 377, 384, 391.

21. Elizabeth Donnan, "The New England Slave Trade After the Revolution," *New England Quarterly* 3:2 (1930), pp. 253–57.

22. Herbert S. Klein, "North American Competition and the Characteristics of the African Slave Trade to Cuba, 1790–1791," *William and Mary Quarterly*, 3d series, 18:1 (1971), pp. 86, 88, 90, 91.

23. Redding, *They Came in Chains*, pp. 14–15.

24. Washington, *The Story of the Negro*, pp. 57, 60.

25. Franklin, *From Slavery to Freedom* (New York: Alfred A. Knopf, 1947), pp. 54–55.

26. Thomas R. Frazier, ed., *Afro-American History—Primary Sources* (New York: Harcourt, Brace & World, 1970), pp. 1–16.

27. John H. Bracey, Jr., et al., eds., *The Afro-Americans* (Boston: Allyn & Bacon, 1912), pp. 9, 10–12.

28. Washington, *The Story of the Negro*, p. 103.

29. Virginia Bever Platt, "'And Don't Forget the Guinea Voyage'—The Slave Trade of Aaron Lopez of Newport," *William and Mary Quarterly*, 3d series, 32:4 (Oct. 1975), p. 606.

30. Owen, *The Wrong of Slavery*, pp. 56–57.

31. A note about tonnage of ships that carried the slaves. Originally, tonnage was a measure of capacity or weight. A tun was a large cask used to transport wine, which filled to the top weighed 2,240 pounds (a long ton). In the eighteenth century, a ton became a measure of capacity based on this formula:

$$\frac{\text{Keel Length} \times \text{Inside Beam} \times \text{Depth of Hold}}{94}$$

The tonnage of a slaver out of Liverpool was about 209. According to the Dolben Act of Parliament (1788), the number of slaves per ton was set at 1.6. See Charles Garland and Herbert S. Klein, "The Allotment of Space for Slaves Aboard Eighteenth Century British Slave Ships," *William and Mary Quarterly*, 3d series, 42:2 (April 1985), pp. 240, 241.

32. Falconbridge Alexander, "An Account of the Slave Trade on the Coast of Africa," Bracey, et al., eds., *The Afro-Americans*, pp. 12–16.

33. George Ducas and Charles Van Doren, eds., *Great Documents in Black American History—The Life of Olaudah Equiano, the African—Gustavus Vassa* (New York: Praeger Publishers, 1970), pp. 40–50.

34. Williams D. Pierson, "White Cannibals, Black Martyrs, Fear, Depression and Religious Faith," *Journal of Negro History* 72:2 (April 1977), pp. 147–150.

35. *Ibid.*, pp. 152–60.

36. Goldston, *The Negro Revolution*, p. 37.

37. Owen, *The Wrong of Slavery*, p. 64.

38. Darrold D. Wax, "Preferences for Slaves in Colonial America," *Journal of Negro History* 58:4 (Oct. 1973), pp. 374, 378, 391, 393.

39. Platt, "'And Don't Forget the Guinea Voyage,'" p. 617.

40. *Letter Book of Hugh Hall*, publication of the Colonial Society of Massachusetts, vol. 32, 1833–37, p. 517; *Diseases of Slaves on Shore* (Portland, Me.: Atheneum Press, 1984).

41. J. Hall Pleasants, ed., *Archives of Maryland*, vol. 52 (Baltimore: Lord Baltimore Press, 1935), p. 576.

42. *Archives of Maryland*, no. 26, Sept. 26, 1704, p. 289.

43. Percy S. Flippen, "William Gooch, Successful Royal Governor of Virginia," *William and Mary Quarterly*, 2d series, 5:4 (Oct. 1925), p. 235.

44. *Archives of Maryland*, vol. 63, Acts of the Assembly 1771–73, Nov. 30, 1771, p. 32.

45. *New Jersey Archives* (Newark, N.J.: Daily Advertiser Printing House, 1882), vol. 4, letter from Brigadier Hunter, governor of New Jersey, Aug. 27, 1714, p. 196.

46. Benjamin Quarles, *The Negro in the Making of America* (New York: Collier Books, 1964), pp. 44–45.

47. William Renwick Riddell, "Encouragement of the Slave Trade," *Journal of Negro History* 12:1 (Jan. 1927), pp. 23–25.

48. Alexander, *History of the Colored Race in America*, p. 151.

49. *Ibid.*

50. Alexander, *History of the Colored Race in America*, pp. 151, 152.

51. Eppse, *The Negro, Too*, pp. 142–43.

52. Charles H. Wesley, "Manifests of Slave Shipments Along the Waterways, 1808–1864," *Journal of Negro History* 27:2 (April 1942), pp. 158–59.

53. Franklin, *From Slavery to Freedom*, p. 153.

54. P.R. Standenraus, "Victims of the American Slave Trade, a Document," *Journal of Negro History* 51:2 (April 1956), p. 148.

55. Goldston, *The Negro Revolution*, p. 102

56. William Loren Katz, *Eyewitness: The Negro in American History* (New York: Pitman Publishing Co., 1967), p. 57.

57. *Ibid.*, p. 15.

58. Eppse, *The Negro, Too*, p. 170.

59. Darrold D. Wax, "Black Immigrants—The Slave Trade in Colonial Maryland," *Maryland Historical Magazine* 73:1 (Spring 1978), pp. 31, 37, 39.

60. Daniel C. Littlefield, "Charleston and Internal Slave Redistribution," *South Carolina History Magazine* 87:2 (April 1986), pp. 93, 94, 97.

61. Michael A. Stevens, "'To Get as Many Slaves as You Can.' An 1807 Slaving Voyage," *South Carolina History Magazine* 87:3 (July 1986), p. 187.

62. Smythe, ed., *Black American Reference Book*, p. 22

63. Philip S. Foner, *History of Black Americans* (Westport, Conn.: Greenwood Press, 1985), pp. 43, 46, 48, 49.

4: The Slave's Life in Colonial America

1. John Solomon Otto and Augustus Marion Burns, "Black Folks and Poor Buckras," *Journal of Black Studies* 14:2 (Dec. 1983), pp. 189–90.

2. Philip S. Foner, *History of the Black American* (Westport, Conn.: Greenwood Press, 1983), pp. 88–89.

3. Mrs. Henry Rowe Schoolcraft, *Plantation Life* (1852–60; reprint New York: Negro University Press, 1969), pp. 34–36.

4. Johann Martin Bolzius, "Answers a Questionnaire on Carolina and Georgia," *William and Mary Quarterly*, 3d series, 14:2 (April 1957), p. 236.

5. Gail Gibson, "Costume and Fashion in Charleston, 1769–1782," *South Carolina History Magazine* 82:3 (July 1981), p. 233.

6. Schoolcraft, *Plantation Life*, p. 112.

7. Otto and Burns, "Black Folks and Poor Buckras," p. 193.

8. Helen Jones Campbell, "The Syms and Eaton Schools and Their Successor," *William and Mary Quarterly* 20:1 (Jan. 1940), p. 6.

9. Bolzius, "Answers a Questionnaire," p. 236.

10. Schoolcraft, *Plantation Life*, pp. 49, 50.

11. Thomas C. Parramore, "The 'Country Distemper' in Colonial North Carolina," *North Carolina Historical Review* 48:1 (Jan. 1971), pp. 45–49.

12. Martin Kaufman, "Medicine and Slavery, an Essay Review," *Georgia Historical Quarterly* 63:3 (Fall 1979), pp. 381–83.

13. "Letter from W. Byrd, May 31, 1737," *William and Mary Quarterly* 1:3 (July 1921), p. 195.

14. Donald Jackson and Dorothy Twohig, eds., *The Diaries of George Washington*, vol. 1 (Charlottesville, Va.: University of Virginia Press, 1979), p. 231.

15. Franklin Frazier, "The Negro Slave Family," *Journal of Negro History* 15:2 (April 1930), pp. 198–259.

16. Jackson and Twohig, *Diaries of George Washington*, vol. 6, p. 263.

17. Kaufman, "Medicine and Slavery," p. 387.

18. Lorenzo Greene, "Slave-holding New England and Its Awakening," *Journal of Negro History* 13:4 (Oct. 1928), p. 504.

19. Robert L. Douglas, "Myth or Truth: A White and Black View of Slavery," *Journal of Black Studies* 19:3 (March 1989), p. 346.

20. Franklin Frazier, "The Negro Slave Family," *Journal of Negro History* 15:2 (April 1930), pp. 250–51, 246.

21. John Hope Franklin, *From Slavery to Freedom* (New York: Alfred A. Knopf, 1947), p. 178.

22. Saunders Redding, *They Came in Chains* (Philadelphia: J.P. Lippincott, 1950), p. 82.

23. "Trivia," *William and Mary Quarterly*, 3d series, 9:1 (Jan. 1952), p. 85.

24. Frazier, "The Negro Slave Family," pp. 241–42.

25. Schoolcraft, *Plantation Life*, pp. 39–41.

26. Franklin, *From Slavery to Freedom*, p. 198.

27. Elizabeth A. Fenn, "'A Perfect Equality Seemed to Reign.' Slave Society and Jonkonnu," *North Carolina Historical Review* 65:2 (April 1988), pp. 127–47.

28. Northrup, "Interstate Slave Trade," pp. 61–63.

29. Schoolcraft, *Plantation Life*, p. 16.

30. Jeffrey J. Crow, "Tory Plots and Anglican Loyalty. The Llewelyn Company of 1777," *North Carolina Historical Review* 55:1 (Jan. 1978), p. 4, note.

31. William S. Price, Jr., "'Men of Good Estates'—Wealth Among North Carolina's Royal Councillors," *North Carolina Historical Review* 99:1 (Jan. 1972), p. 77.

32. Schoolcraft, *Plantation Life*, pp. 227–28.

33. C.W. Harper, "House Servants and Full Hands. Fragmentation in the Ante-Bellum Slave Community," *North Carolina Historical Review* 55:1 (Jan. 1978), pp. 42–58.

34. *Ibid.*, pp. 42–43, 45.

35. Jessie W. Parkhurst, "The Role of the Black Mammy in the Plantation Household," *Journal of Negro History* 23:3 (July 1938), pp. 350–69.

36. Robert Goldston, *The Negro* (New York: Macmillan, 1968), p. 68.

37. Francis L. Hunter, "Slave Society in the Southern Plantation," *Journal of Negro History* 7:1 (Jan. 1922), pp. 5–6.

38. Kenneth G. Goode and Winthrop D. Jordan, *From Africa to the United States and Then* (Glenview, Ill.: Scott, Foresman, 1969), p. 58.

39. Otto and Burns, "Black Folks and Poor Buckras," p. 194.

40. Leslie H. Fishel, and Benjamin Quarles, *The Negro American* (New York: William Morrow, 1967), p. 109.

41. William Loren Katz, *Eyewitness: The Negro in American History* (New York: Pitman Publishing Co., 1974), p. 34.

42. Philip D. Morgan. "Work and Culture: The Task System and the World of How (?) Country Blacks, 1700–1800." *William and Mary Quarterly*, 3d series, 39:4 (Oct. 1982), pp. 563–69.

43. Bolzius, "Answers a Questionnaire," pp. 233–34.

44. Fishel and Quarles, *The Negro American*, pp. 110–11.

45. James M. Clifton, "Golden Grains of White Rice Planting on the Lower Cape Fear," *North Carolina Historical Review* 50:4 (Oct. 1973), p. 369.

46. Bolzius, "Answers a Questionnaire," pp. 233–36, 251.

47. Foner, *History of Black Americans*, pp. 31–32.

48. William T. Alexander, *History of the Colored Race in America* (Palmetto Publishing, 1887; reprint, New York: Negro University Press, n.d.), p. 142.

49. Foner, *History of Black Americans*, p. 33

50. Goode and Jordan, *From Africa to the United States*, p. 49.

51. Northrup, "Interstate Slave Trade," pp. 54–55.

52. Bolzius, "Answers a Questionnaire," pp. 255–56.

53. Foner, *History of the Black American*, p. 62.

54. Ronald Lewis, "Slavery on Chesapeake Iron Plantations Before the American Revolution," *Journal of Negro History* 59:3 (July 1974), pp. 242–48.

55. Charles B. Drew, "David Ross and the Oxford Iron Works—A Study of Industrial Slavery in the Early 19th Century," *William and Mary Quarterly*, 3d series, 31:2 (April 1974), pp. 195, 197–200, 205–8.

56. E.M. Landers, Jr., "Slave Labor in South Carolina Cotton Mills," *Journal of Negro History* 38:2 (April 1953), pp. 161–62.

57. Foner, *History of Black Americans*, pp. 60–61.

58. S. Sydney Bradford, "The Negro Ironworker in Ante-Bellum Virginia," *Journal of Southern History* 25:2 (May 1959), pp. 195, 196, 199.

59. Loren Schweninger, "Slave Independence and Enterprise in South Carolina, 1780–1865," *South Carolina History Magazine* 93:2 (April 1992), pp. 112, 118, 121.

5: *Africans in New England*

1. G.W. Williams, *History of the Negro Race in America* (New York: Bergman Press, 1883), p. 173.

2. Carl N. Degler, "Slavery and the Genesis of Race Prejudice," in August Meier and Elliott Rudwick, eds., *The Making of Black America* (New York: Atheneum Press, 1969), p. 104.

3. William T. Alexander, *History of the Colored Race in America* (Palmetto Publications, 1887; reprint, New York: Negro University Press, n.d.), p. 168.

4. John Hope Franklin, *From Slavery to Freedom* (New York: Alfred A. Knopf, 1947), p. 100.

5. Edmund S. Morgan, "The Puritan Ethic and the American Revolution," *William and Mary Quarterly*, 3d series, 24:1 (Jan. 1967), pp. 22–23.

6. Lorenzo J. Greene, "Slave-holding New England and Its Awakening," *Journal of Negro History* 13:4 (Oct. 1928), p. 501.

7. Merl R. Eppse, *The Negro, Too, in American History* (Chicago: National Educational Publishing Co., 1938), p. 47.

8. Lerone Bennett, Jr., *The Shaping of Black America* (Chicago: Johnson Publishing Co., 1975), p. 29.

9. Winthrop D. Jordan, "The Influence of the West Indies on the Origins of New England Slavery," *William and Mary Quarterly*, 3d series, 18:2 (April 1961), p. 247.

10. John Hope Franklin, *From Slavery to Freedom*, 3rd ed. (New York: Vintage Books, 1969), p. 105.

11. Robert C. Twombly and Robert H. Moore, "Black Puritan—The Negro in Seventeenth Century Massachusetts," *William and Mary Quarterly*, 3d series, 24 (April 1967), pp. 240–41.

12. Williams, *History of the Negro Race in America*, p. 208.

13. Franklin, *From Slavery to Freedom* (1947), pp. 107–8.

14. Lawrence W. Towner, "The Sewall-Saffin Dialogue on Slavery," *William and Mary Quarterly*, 3d series, 21:1 (Jan. 1964), pp. 42–45.

15. Lawrence W. Towner, "A Fondness for Freedom—Servant Protest in Puritan Society," *William and Mary Quarterly*, 3d series, 19:2 (April 1962), p. 218.

16. Towner, "The Sewall-Saffin Dialogue," p. 48.

17. Williams, *History of the Negro Race in America*, p. 218.

18. Greene, "Slave-holding New England," p. 527.

19. Publication of conference held Nov. 6–7, 1981 by the Colonial Society of Massachusetts (Portland, Me.: Atheneum Press, 1984), vol. 62, pp. 29, 107–25.

20. Williams, *History of the Negro Race in America*, pp. 228–31.

21. Kenneth W. Porter, "Three Fighters for Freedom," *Journal of Negro History* 28:1 (Jan. 1943), pp. 51–52.

22. William Loren Katz, *Eyewitness, the Negro in American History* (New York: Pitman Publishing Co., 1974), p. 42.

23. Publication of the Colonial Society of Massachusetts, 1922–24, vol. 25, p. 253.

24. Peter M. Bergman, *A Chronological History of the Negro in America* (New York: Harper & Row, 1969), p. 48.

25. Elaine MacEacheren, "Emancipation of Slavery in Massachusetts—A Reexamination," *Journal of Negro History* 55:4 (Oct. 1970), pp. 301–3.

26. William O'Brien, "Did the Jennison Case Outlaw Slavery in Massachusetts?" *William and Mary Quarterly*, 3d series, 17:2 (April 1960), pp. 224–33.

27. Robert M. Spector, "The Quok Walker Cases (1781–83): The Abolition of Slavery and Negro Citizenship in Early Massachusetts," *Journal of Negro History* 53:1 (1968), pp. 12–16.

28. Eppse, *The Negro, Too*, p. 54.

29. Greene, "Slave-holding New England," p. 495.

30. *Ibid.*, pp. 516–17.

31. *Ibid.*, pp. 531–32.

32. Eppse, *The Negro, Too*, p. 56.

33. Williams, *History of the Negro Race in America*, pp. 309–11.

34. J. Kevin Greffagenino, "Vermont Attitudes Toward Slavery: The Need for a Closer Look," *Vermont History* 45:1 (Winter 1997), p. 31.

35. John Page, "The Economic Structure in Revolutionary Bennington," *Vermont History* 49:2 (Spring 1981), p. 72.

36. Jon T. Anderson, "Royall Tyler's Reaction to Slavery and the South," *Vermont History* 42:4 (Fall 1974), p. 301.

37. Williams, *History of the Negro Race in America*, p. 436.

38. Jordan, "The Influence of the West Indies," p. 245.

39. John Russell Bartlett, ed., *Colonial Records of Rhode Island* (Providence: Anthony Knowles & Co. Printers, State Printer, 1860), vol. 3, p. 493.

40. John Russell Bartlett, *Colonial Records of Rhode Island*, vol. 6, p. 64.

41. Williams, *History of the Negro Race in America*, p. 272.

42. Albert T. Klyberg, "Rhode Island and the American Nation," *Rhode Island History* 46:3 (Aug. 1987), p. 87.

43. Christian McBurney, "The South Kingston Planters: Country Gentry in Colonial Rhode Island," *Rhode Island History* 45:3 (Aug. 1981), pp. 81–86.

44. J.R. Bartlett, *Colonial Records of Rhode Island*, vol. 5, pp. 176–77.

45. J.R. Bartlett, *Colonial Records of Rhode Island* (Providence: A. Crawford Greene State Printer, 1862), vol. 7, pp. 257–63.

46. J.R. Bartlett, *Colonial Records of Rhode Island* (Providence: Jackson Cooke & Co. Printer to State, 1864), vol. 8, p. 618.

47. J.R. Bartlett, *Colonial Records of Rhode Island* (Anthony Alfred Printer to State, 1864), vol. 9, p. 738.

48. J.R. Bartlett, *Colonial Records of Rhode Island* (Providence: Providence Press Co., 1865), vol. 10, p. 7.

49. *Ibid.*, p. 85.

50. Eppse, *The Negro, Too*, p. 55.

6: *Africans in the Middle Atlantic Colonies*

1. Morton Wagman, "Corporate Slavery in New Netherlands," *Journal of Negro History* 24:1 (Winter 1980), pp. 34–35.

2. William Renwich Reddell, "The Slave in New York," *Journal of Negro History* 13:1 (Jan. 1928), pp. 58–59.

3. Wageman, "Corporate Slavery," pp. 37–39.

4. Joyce D. Goodfriend, "Burghers and Blacks: The Evolution of a Slave Society at New Amsterdam," *New York History* 59:2 (April 1978).

5. Wagman, "Corporate Slavery," pp. 37–39.

6. Oliver A. Renk, "The People of New Netherlands. Notes on Non-English Immigration to New York in the Seventeenth Century," *New York History* 62:1 (Jan. 1881), pp. 33–34.

7. Goodfriend, "Burghers and Blacks," pp. 138–39.

8. William T. Alexander, *History of the Colored Race in America* (Palmetto Publishers, 1987; reprint, New York: Negro University Press, n.d.), p. 135.

9. Sheldon D. Cohen, "Elias Neau, Instructor to New York's Slaves," *New York Historical Society Quarterly* 55:1 (Jan. 1971), pp. 15–17.

10. John Hope Franklin, *From Slavery to Freedom* (New York: Alfred A. Knopf, 1947), pp. 89–90.

11. New York Historical Society (Publication Fund, 1893) vol. 78, p. 285.

12. Oscar R. Williams, "The Regimentation of Blacks on the Urban Frontier in Colonial Albany, New York City, and Philadelphia," *Journal of Negro History* 63:4 (Fall 1978), p. 330.

13. Edwin Olson, "The Slave Code in Colonial New York," *Journal of Negro History* 19:2 (April 1944), p. 150.

14. Williams, "The Regimentation of Blacks," p. 333.

15. Edwin Olson, "Social Aspects of the Slave in New York," *Journal of Negro History* 26:1 (Jan. 1941), p. 66.

16. New York Historical Society (Publication Fund, 1892) vol. 15, p. 196.

17. New York Historical Society (Publication Fund, 1893) vol. 26, p. 188.

18. New York Historical Society (Publication Fund, 1896) vol. 29, pp. 113–14.

19. New York Historical Society (Publication Fund, 1897) vol. 30, pp. 53–54.

20. *Ibid.*, p. 167.

21. New York Historical Society (Publication Fund, 1901) vol. 33, p. 42.

22. New York Historical Society (Publication Fund, 1896) vol. 29, p. 84.

23. New York Historical Society (Publication Fund, 1900) vol. 3, pp. 121–22.

24. New York Historical Society (Publication Fund, 1901) vol. 34, p. 17.

25. Leo H. Hirsch, Jr., "New York and the Negro from 1783–1865," *Journal of Negro History* 16:4 (Oct. 1931), p. 385.

26. *Ibid.*, p. 386.

27. *Ibid.*, pp. 388, 391.

28. Merl R. Eppse, *The Negro, Too, in American History* (Chicago: National Educational Publishing Co., 1938), p. 51.

29. Spencer Crew, "Black New Jersey Before the Civil War," *New Jersey History* 99:1, 2 (Spring-Summer, 1981), pp. 67–86.

30. Alexander, *History of the Colored Race in America*, p. 135.

31. Marion Thompson Wright, "New Jersey and the Negro," *Journal of Negro History* 28:2 (April 1943), pp. 162–65.

32. William A. Whitehall, ed., New Jersey Archives 1683 (Newark: Daily Advertiser Printing House, 1881), vol. 13, p. 82.

33. John W. Gibson and W.H. Crogman, *Progress of a Race* (1902; Miami: Mnemosyne Publishing Co., 1969), p. 50.

34. Wright, "New Jersey and the Negro," pp. 165–69.

35. Whitehall, New Jersey Archives, 1st series, vol. 3, p. 473.

36. Wright, *New Jersey and the Negro*, pp. 165–69.

37. Simeon F. Moss, "The Persistence of Slavery and Involuntary Servitude in a Free State, 1685–1866," *Journal of Negro History* 35:3 (July 1950), p. 301.

38. Lee Callegaro, "The Negro's Legal Status in Pre–Civil War New Jersey," *New Jersey History* 85:3, 4 (Fall-Winter 1967), p. 168.

39. Moss, "The Persistence of Slavery," pp. 290, 292.

40. Arthur Zilversmit, "Liberty and Property—New Jersey and the Abolition of Slavery," *New Jersey History* 88:4 (Winter 1970), p. 216.

41. Franklin, *From Slavery to Freedom*, p. 94.

42. Moss, "The Persistence of Slavery," p. 294.

43. W. Frederic, ed., New Jersey Archives (Trenton: John L. Murphy Pub. Co., 1891), 1st series, 1744, vol. 15, p. 384.

44. Wright, "New Jersey and the Negro," pp. 157–99.

45. Zilversmit, "Liberty and Property," p. 223.

46. Moss, "The Persistence of Slavery," p. 306.

47. Eppse, *The Negro, Too*, p. 53.

48. Gary B. Nash, "Slaves and Slave Owners in Colonial Philadelphia," *William and Mary Quarterly*, 3d series, 30:2 (April 1973), p. 225.

49. G.W. Williams, *History of the Negro Race in America* (New York: Bergman Press, 1883), p. 313.

50. Nash, "Slaves and Slave Owners," pp. 251–55.

51. Franklin, *From Slavery to Freedom*, p. 96.

52. Debra Newman, "Black Women in the Era of the American Revolution in Pennsylvania," *Journal of Negro History* 61:3 (July 1976), p. 280.

53. Franklin, *From Slavery to Freedom*, p. 96.

54. Pennsylvania Archives, 4th series, p. 343.

55. Darrold Wax, "Africans on the Delaware—The Pennsylvania Slave Trade, 1759–1765," *Pennsylvania History* 50 (Jan. 1983), p. 38.

56. Newman, "Black Women," p. 279.

57. Franklin, *From Slavery to Freedom*, p. 97.

58. New York Historical Society, collections for year of 1929 (Printed 1930), vol. 62.

59. Jean R. Soderbund, "Black Women in Colonial Pennsylvania," *Pennsylvania Magazine of History and Biography* 107 (Jan. 1983), pp. 50, 57.

60. *Ibid.*, pp. 62, 64.

61. Semuel Hazard, ed., Pennsylvania Archives (Philadelphia: Joseph Sevarns & Co., 1853), 1778, 1st series, vol. 7.

62. Newman, "Black Women," pp. 281, 282.

63. Ibid., p. 281.

64. Ibid., pp. 276–89.

65. *Ibid.*, p. 277.

66. G.W. Williams, *History of the Negro Race in America*, p. 249.

67. Franklin, *From Slavery to Freedom*, pp. 57–58.

7: *Africans in the South*

1. Lerone Bennett, Jr., *The Shaping of Black America* (Chicago: Johnson Publishing Co., 1975), pp. 6–8.

2. William Loran Katz, *The Negro in American History* (New York: Pitman Publishing Co.), p. 20.

3. J.B. Boddie, "Edward Bennett of London and Virginia," *William and Mary Quarterly* 13:2 (April 1933), p. 118.

4. William Montgomery Sweeney, "Gleanings from the Records of (Old) Rappahannock County and Essex County, Virginia," *William and Mary Quarterly* 18:3 (July 1938), p. 310.

5. Eric Foner, *America's Black Past* (New York: Harper & Row, 1970), p. 66.

6. Bennett, *The Shaping of Black America*, p. 34.

7. Lerone Bennett, Jr., *Confrontation Black & White* (Chicago: Johnson Publishing Co., 1965), pp. 29–32.

8. Michael I. Cassity, *Legacy of Fear* (Westport, Conn.: Greenwood Press, 1985), p. xx.

9. *Ibid.*, pp. 26–28.

10. Bennett, *Confrontation Black & White*, p. 19.

11. Merl R. Eppse, *The Negro, Too, in American History* (Chicago: National Educational Publishing Co., 1938), p. 46.

12. Leslie H. Fishel and Benjamin Quarles, *The Negro American* (New York: William Morrow, 1967), p. 19.

13. Winthrop Jordan, "Modern Tensions and the Origins of American Slavery," in Carlos E. Cortes, Arlen I. Ginzburg, Alan W. F. Green, and James A. Joseph, *Three Perspectives on Ethnicity* (New York: G.P. Putnam's Sons, 1976), p. 32.

14. Leslie H. Fishel and Benjamin Quarles, *The Black American* (New York: William Morrow, 1970), p. 20.

15. Bennett, *The Shaping of Black America*, p. 67.

16. Leonard Stavisky, "The Origins of Negro Craftsmanship in Colonial America," *Journal of Negro History* 32:4 (Oct. 1947), p. 420.

17. James H. Brewer, "Negro Property Owners in Seventeenth Century Virginia," in August Meier and Elliott Rudwick, eds., *The Making of Black America* (New York: Atheneum Press 1969), p. 202.

18. Adele Hast, "The Legal Status of the Negro in Virginia, 1705–1765," *Journal of Negro History* 54:3 (July 1969), pp. 218–19, 225–26, 232.

19. *Journal of Negro History* 61:1 (Jan. 1976), pp. 89–90.

20. *William and Mary Quarterly* 8:1 (July 1899), p. 35.

21. *Virginia Gazette*, April 21, 1775, in *William and Mary College Quarterly* 8:1 (July 1899), p. 35.

22. G.W. Williams, *History of the Negro Race in America* (New York: Bergman Publishing Co., 1883), pp. 127–31.

23. Cassity, *Legacy of Fear*, p. 30.

24. William T. Alexander, *History of the Colored Race in America* (Palmetto Publishers, 1887; New York: Negro University Press), p. 137.

25. Saunders Redding, *They Came in Chains* (New York: J.P. Lippincott, 1950), p. 45.

26. *William and Mary Quarterly*, series 1-10-11, 1901–1903, 10:3 (Jan. 1902), pp. 177–78.

27. Williams, *History of the Negro Race in America*, pp. 127–28.

28. Donald M. Sweig, "The Importation of African Slaves to the Potomac River 1732–72," *William and Mary Quarterly*, 3d series, 42:4 (Oct. 1985), pp. 577–81.

29. Jane Chapman Slaughter, "Reverend Philip Slaughter—A Sketch," *William and Mary Quarterly* 16:3 (July 1936), p. 445.

30. Peter M. Bergman, *A Chronological History of the Negro in America* (New York: Harper & Row, 1969), p. 46.

31. R. Wilton Moore, "George Mason, the Statesman," *William and Mary Quarterly* 13:1 (Jan. 1983), p. 16.

32. Alexander, *History of the Colored Race in America*, pp. 189, 199–201.

33. Russell R. Menard, "The Maryland Slave Population 1658–1730—A Demographic Profile of Blacks in Four Counties," *William and Mary Quarterly*, 3d series, 32:1 (Jan. 1975), pp. 30–31.

34. Elizabeth Merritt, ed., *Archives of Maryland*, Proceedings of the Provincial Court 1675–1677, vol. 66 (Baltimore: Maryland Historical Society, 1954), p. 94.

35. Merritt, *Archives of Maryland*, Provincial Court 1679–1680, vol. 69, p. 34.

36. Alexander, *History of the Colored Race in America*, p. 133.

37. Whittington B. Johnson, "The Origins and Nature of African Slavery in

Seventeenth Century Maryland," *Maryland Historical Magazine* 73:3 (Sept. 1978), pp. 237–38.

38. Cassity, *Legacy of Fear*, pp. 20–21.

39. *Ibid.*, pp. 32–33.

40. Merritt, *Archives of Maryland*, Provincial Court 1675–1677, vol. 66, p. 291.

41. Bergman, *The Chronological History of the Negro in America*, p. 19.

42. William H. Browne, ed., *Archives of Maryland*, Proceedings and Acts of the Assembly of Maryland, September 1681, vol. 7 (Baltimore: Maryland Historical Society, 1889), p. 203.

43. Robert G. Schoufeld and Spencer Wilson, "The Value of Personal Estates in Maryland 1700–1710," *Maryland Historical Magazine* 58:4 (Dec. 1963), p. 342.

44. Williams, *History of the Negro Race in America*, p. 246.

45. Bernard Christian Steiner, ed., *Archives of Maryland*, Proceedings of the Provincial Court, 1658–1662, vol. 41 (Baltimore: Maryland Historical Society, 1922), pp. 204–77.

46. J. Hall Pleasants, ed., *Archives of Maryland*, Proceedings of the Provincial Court, 1663–1666, vol. 49 (Baltimore: Maryland Historical Society, 1932), pp. 489–91.

47. Pleasants, *Archives of Maryland*, Proceedings of the Provincial Court, 1663–1666, vol. 49, p. 521.

48. William H. Browne, ed., *Archives of Maryland*, Proceedings of the Council of Maryland 1754–1765, vol. 31 (Baltimore: Maryland Historical Society, 1911), pp. 409–10.

49. Johnson, "The Origins and Nature of African Slavery," pp. 241, 242.

50. J. Hall Pleasants, ed., *Archives of Maryland*, Proceedings and Acts of the Assembly of Maryland 1752–1754, vol. 50 (Baltimore: Maryland Historical Society, 1933), p. 142.

51. Elizabeth Merritt, ed., *Archives of Maryland*, Proceedings of the Provincial Court 1670–1675, vol. 65 (Baltimore: Maryland Historical Society, 1952), pp. 331–32.

52. J. Hall Pleasants, ed., *Archives of Maryland*, Journal and Correspondence of the State Council 1781–1784, vol. 49 (Baltimore: Maryland Historical Society, 1931), p. 547.

53. J. Hall Pleasants, ed., *Archives of Maryland*, Proceedings and Acts of the Assembly, 1755–1756, vol. 52 (Baltimore: Maryland Historical Society, 1935), p. 460.

54. J. Hall Pleasants, ed., *Archives of Maryland*, Proceedings and Acts of the Assembly, 1757–1758, vol. 55 (Baltimore: Maryland Historical Society, 1938), p. 527.

55. Bernard Christian Steiner, ed., *Archives of Maryland*, Proceedings and Acts of the Assembly 1733–1736, vol. 39 (Baltimore: Maryland Historical Society, 1919), p. 387.

56. Benjamin Quarles, "Freedom Fettered—Blacks in the Constitutional Era in Maryland, 1776–1810," *Maryland Historical Magazine* 84 (Winter 1989), p. 302.

57. Booker T. Washington, *The Story of the Negro* (London: T. Fisher Unwin Co., 1909), p. 193.

58. Lorena S. Walsh, "Rural African Americans in the Constitutional Era in Maryland, 1776–1810," New York Historical Society for the year 1929 (1930), pp. 338–39.

59. Bernard Christian Steiner, ed., *Archives of Maryland*, Act of the Assembly 1694–1729 (Baltimore: Maryland Historical Society, 1918), vol. 38, p. 51.

60. William H. Browne, ed., *Archives of Maryland*, Proceedings of the Council of Maryland 1732–1753 (Baltimore: Maryland Historical Society, 1908), vol. 28, p. 92.

61. William H. Browne, ed., *Archives of Maryland*, Letter of Governor Sharpe, May 5, 1761, vol. 9 (Baltimore: Maryland Historical Society, 1890), p. 514.

62. J. Hall Pleasants, ed., *Archives of Maryland*, Proceedings and Acts of the Assembly, 1763, vol. 58 (Baltimore: Maryland Historical Society, 1941), p. 512.

63. Bernard Christian Steiner, ed., *Archives of Maryland*, May 15, 1734, Proceedings and Acts of the Assembly 1733–1736, vol. 39 (Baltimore: Maryland Historical Society, 1919), p. 465.

64. J. Hall Pleasants, ed., *Archives of Maryland*, Proceedings and Acts of the Assembly 1752–1754, vol. 50 (Baltimore: Maryland Historical Society, 1933), p. 479.

65. William H. Browne, ed., *Archives of Maryland*, Proceedings of the Council of Maryland 1761–1770, vol. 32 (Baltimore: Maryland Historical Society, 1912), p. 95.

66. Eppse, *The Negro, Too, in American History*, p. 50.

67. *Ibid.*, p. 57.

68. M. Eugene Sermons, "The Legal Status of the Slave in South Carolina 1670–1740," *Journal of Southern History* 28:4 (1962), pp. 462–67.

69. Wylie Sypher, "Hutcheson and the 'Classical' Theory of Slavery," *Journal of Negro History* 24:3 (July 1939), pp. 267–73.

70. Alexander, *History of the Colored Race in America*, p. 134.

71. Sanford Winston, "Indian Slavery in the Carolina Region," *Journal of Negro History* 19:4 (Oct. 1934), p. 432.

72. Eppse, *The Negro, Too*, p. 57.

73. Williams, *History of the Negro Race in America*, pp. 293–301.

74. *Ibid.*

75. *Ibid.*

76. *Ibid.*

77. Franklin, *From Slavery to Freedom*, pp. 78–79.

78. Sermons, "The Legal Status of the Slave," p. 469.

79. Donald J. Senese, "The Free Negro and the South Carolina Courts 1790–1860," *South Carolina Historical Magazine* 68:3 (July 1967), p. 42.

80. Herbert Aptheker, "South Carolina Poll Tax 1737–1895," *Journal of Negro History* 31:2 (April 1946), pp. 131–39.

81. Franklin, *From Slavery to Freedom*, p. 78.

82. *Ibid.*, p. 80.

83. George C. Rogers, ed., "The Letters of William Loughton Smith to Edward Rutledge, June 8, 1989, to April 28, 1794," *South Carolina History Magazine* 70:1 (Jan. 1969), p. 46.

84. Bergman, *A Chronological History of the Negro in America*, p. 83.

85. Leslie H. Fishel and Benjamin Quarles, *Negro America* (New York: William Morrow, 1967), pp. 85–86.

86. Philip Africa, "Slaveholding in the Salem Community 1771–1851," *North Carolina Historical Review* 54:3 (July 1977), pp. 271, 275, 276, 279.

87. Jerry L. Surratt, "The Role of Dissent in Community Evolution Among Moravians in Salem 1772–1860," *North Carolina Historical Review* 52:3 (1975), p. 250.

88. James A. Padgett, "The Status of Slaves in Colonial North Carolina," *Journal of Negro History* 14:3 (July 1929), p. 303.

89. Franklin, *From Slavery to Freedom*, p. 81.

90. Franklin, *From Slavery to Freedom*, p. 82.

91. Padgett, "The Status of Slaves," p. 300.

92. Cassity, *Legacy of Fear*, p. 55.

93. Alan D. Watson, "North Carolina Slave Courts 1715–1785," *North Carolina Historical Review* 60:1 (Jan. 1983), p. 25.

94. Padgett, "The Status of Slaves," p. 305.

95. John Hope Franklin, "The Enslavement of Free Negroes in North Carolina," *Journal of Negro History* 29:4 (Oct. 1944), p. 406.

96. Padgett, "The Status of Slaves," p. 307.

97. Franklin, *From Slavery to Freedom*, p. 81.

98. Williams, *History of the Negro Race in America*, p. 304.

99. Watson, "North Carolina Slave Courts," pp. 28–31.

100. Padgett, "The Status of Slaves," pp. 304–9.

101. *Ibid.*, p. 312.

102. Fishel and Quarles, *Negro America*, p. 115.

103. *Ibid.*

104. Watson, "North Carolina Slave Courts," pp. 34–36.

105. *Ibid.*, p. 319.

106. *Ibid.*, p. 324.

107. Williams, *History of the Negro Race in America*, p. 316.

108. Randall M. Miller, "The Failure of the Colony of Georgia Under the Trustees," *Georgia Historical Quarterly* 53:1 (March 1969), pp. 2–4.

109. *Ibid.*, pp. 1–17.

110. Darrold W. Wax, "Georgia and the Negro Before the Revolution," *Georgia Historical Quarterly* 51:1 (March 1967), pp. 62–67.

111. Miller, "The Failure of the Colony of Georgia," p. 9.

112. Franklin, *From Slavery to Freedom*, p. 82.

113. Miller, "The Failure of the Colony of Georgia," pp. 1–17.

114. Darrold W. Wax, "New Negroes Are Always in Demand. The Slave Trade in Eighteenth Century Georgia," *Georgia Historical Quarterly* 68:2 (Summer 1981), pp. 193–200, 203.

115. Franklin, *From Slavery to Freedom*, p. 84.

116. William L. Withuhn, "Salzburgers and Slavery. A Problem of Mentalitè," *Georgia Historical Quarterly* 68:2 (Summer 1984), p. 189.

117. C. Robert Haywood, "Mercantilism and Colonial Slave Labor 1700–1763," *Journal of Southern History* 23:4 (Nov. 1957), p. 459.

118. Withuhn, "Salzburgers and Slavery," pp. 173–92.

8: The Freedmen

1. Peter M. Bergman, *A Chronological History of the Negro in America* (New York: Harper & Row, 1969), p. 82.

2. William H. Browne, ed., *Archives of Maryland*, Proceedings of the Assembly of Maryland 1684–1692, vol. 13 (Baltimore: Maryland Historical Society, 1894), p. 309.

3. Sumner Eliot Madison, "Manumission by Purchase," *Journal of Negro History* 33:2 (April 1948), p. 155.

4. Juliet E.K. Walker, "Pioneer Entrepreneurship: Patterns, Processes and Perspectives. The Case of the Slave Free Frank on the Kentucky Pennyroyal, 1795–1819," *Journal of Negro History* 68:3 (Summer 1983), pp. 289, 295, 298, 299, 301.

5. Madison, "Manumission by Purchase," pp. 146–47, 149.

6. *William and Mary Quarterly* 2d series, 2:4 (Oct. 1922), pp. 274–75.

7. Harry B. Yoshipe, "Slave Manumissions in New York," *Journal of Negro History* 26:1 (Jan. 1941), pp. 92–93, 105.

8. *Ibid.*

9. John Russell, "Colored Men as Slave Overseers in Virginia," *Journal of Negro History* 1:3 (July 1916), p. 233.

10. Ross M. Kemmel, "Free Blacks in Seventeenth Century Maryland," *Journal of Negro History* 71:1 (Spring 1976), p. 20.

11. Charles H. Wesley, "Negro Suffrage in the Period of Constitution, 1787–1865," *Journal of Negro History* 32:2 (April 1947), p. 147.

12. Gilbert Osofsky, *The Burden of Race* (New York: Harper & Row, 1967), pp. 62–54.

13. Leon F. Litwack, "The Federal Government and the Free Negro, 1790–1860," *Journal of Negro History* 43:4 (Oct. 1958), p. 62.

14. Rodney P. Carlisle, *Prologue to Liberation* (New York: Appleton-Century-Crofts, 1972), pp. 84, 85.

15. Michael I. Cassity, *Legacy of Fear* (Westport, Conn.: Greenwood Press, 1985), pp. 107–8.

16. Lorenzo J. Greene, "New England Enterprises," in Charles W. Simmons and Barry W. Morris, eds., *Afro-American History* (Columbus, Ohio: Charles E. Merrill Publishing Co., 1972), pp. 8–11.

17. Carlisle, *Prologue to Liberation*, p. 87.

18. Wesley, "Negro Suffrage in the Period of Constitution," p. 151.

19. Litwack, "The Federal Government and the Free Negro," pp. 263, 270, 272.

20. Kenneth G. Good and Winthrop D. Jordan, *From Africa to the United States and Then* (Glenview, Ill.: Scott, Foresman, 1969), pp. 41–42.

21. Booker T. Washington, *The Story of the Negro* (London: T. Fisher Unwin Co., 1909), p. 199.

22. Leslie H. Fishel and Benjamin Quarles, *The Negro American* (New York: William Morrow, 1967), p. 128.

23. Luther P. Jackson, "Early Life of the Negro in Virginia," *Journal of Negro History* 25:1 (Jan. 1940), p. 27.

24. Mabel M. Smythe, ed., *Black American Reference Book* (Englewood Cliffs, N.J.: Prentice Hall, 1976), p. 29.

25. Richard Randolph, "Black and Free," in Charles W. Simmons and Barry W. Morris, eds., *Afro-American History* (Columbus, Ohio: Charles E. Merrill Publishing Co., 1972), p. 76.

26. John H. Russell, "Colored Men as Slave Owners in Virginia," *Journal of Negro History* 1:3 (July 1916), p. 235.

27. John Hope Franklin, *From Slavery to Freedom* (New York: Alfred A. Knopf, 1947), p. 221.

28. Loren Schweninger, "John Carruthers Stanly and the Anomoly of Black Slaveholding," *North Carolina Historical Review* 67:2 (April 1990), pp. 159, 161, 163, 165, 169, 175, 182.

29. R. Halliburton, Jr., "Free Black Owners of Slaves. A Reappraisal of the

Woddson Thesis," *South Carolina History Magazine* 76:3 (July 1975), pp. 130, 133, 134, 135.

30. C. Ashley Ellegon, "Free Jupiter and the Rest of the World—The Problems of a Free Negro in Colonial Maryland," *Maryland Historical Magazine* 66:1 (Spring 1971), pp. 1, 2, 3–4.

31. "Document of a Petition of Free Negroes in South Carolina (1791)," *Journal of Negro History* 31:1 (Jan. 1946), pp. 98–99.

32. Robert Goldston, *The Negro Revolution* (New York: Macmillan Publishers, 1968), p. 95.

33. "Petition from Free Blacks to the United States House of Representatives, 1797," in Thomas R. Frazier, *African American History Primary Sources* (New York: Harcourt Brace, 1970), pp. 253–56.

34. Eric Foner, *America's Black Past* (New York: Harper & Row, 1970), p. 160.

35. James F. Browning, "The Beginnings of Insurance Enterprise Among Negroes," *Journal of Negro History* 22:4 (Oct. 1937), p. 418.

36. *Ibid.*

37. Horace Fitchett, "The Traditions of the Free Negro in Charleston, South Carolina," in August Meier and Elliott Rudwick, eds., *The Making of Black America*, 1 (New York: Atheneum Press, 1969), pp. 209, 210, 212–213.

38. Bergman, *A Chronological History*, p. 70.

39. Philip S. Foner, *History of Black Americans* (Westport, Conn.: Greenwood Press, 1983), p. 185.

40. Frazier, *Black American History Primary Sources*, pp. 46–50.

41. Harry E. Davis, "Documents Relating to Negro Masonry in America," *Journal of Negro History* 21:4 (Oct. 1936), pp. 412–13, 421.

42. *Ibid.*, p. 426.

43. Franklin, *From Slavery to Freedom*, p. 161.

44. Lerone Bennett, Jr., *Confrontation Black and White* (Chicago: Johnson Publishing Co., 1965), p. 53.

45. Frazier, *African American History Primary Sources*, p. 31.

46. Foner, *History of Black Americans*, pp. 218, 219, 220–21.

47. Franklin, *From Slavery to Freedom*, pp, 159, 160.

48. Rodney P. Carlisle, *Prologue to Liberation* (New York: Appleton-Century-Crofts, 1972), p. 91.

49. Frazier, *African American History Primary Sources*, pp. 32, 33–34.

50. *Ibid.*, pp. 36, 39, 40.

51. Franklin, *From Slavery to Freedom*, pp. 154, 155.

52. Mukhter Ali Isani, "The British Reception of Wheatley's Poems on Various Subjects," *Journal of Negro History* 66:2 (1981), pp. 155–57.

53. Franklin, *From Slavery to Freedom*, p. 155.

54. Henry S. Baker, "Benjamin Banneker, the Negro Mathematician and Astronomer," *Journal of Negro History* 3:2 (April 1918), pp. 103, 105, 107, 109, 112.

55. Margaret Barley Tinkson, "Caviar Along the Potomac," *William and Mary Quarterly*, 3d series, 8:1 (Jan. 1951), p. 103.

56. H.N. Sherwood, "Paul Cuffee," *Journal of Negro History* 8:2 (April 1923), pp. 156, 157–58, 162.

57. *Ibid.*, pp. 174, 198, 206.

58. Gary B. Nash, "New Light on Richard Allen—The Early Years of Freedom," *William and Mary Quarterly*, 3d series, 46:2 (April 1989), pp. 336, 337.

59. Richard Randolph, "Social Origins of Distinguished Negroes, 1700–1865," *Journal of Negro History* 40:3 (July 1955), pp. 221–25.

60. William Loren Katz, *Eyewitness, the Negro in American History* (New York: Pitman Publishing Co., 1967).

61. Randolph, "Social Origins," pp. 220, 229.

9: Colonization

1 Paul J. Scheips, "Lincoln and the Chiriqui Colonization Project," *Journal of Negro History* 37:4 (Oct. 1952), p. 419.

2. H.N. Sherwood, "The Formation of the American Colonization Society," *Journal of Negro History* 2:3 (July 1917), p. 209.

3. Winthrop D. Jordan, *White Over Black* (Chapel Hill: University of North Carolina Press, 1968), p. 546.

4. Lerone Bennett, Jr., *The Shaping of Black America* (Chicago: Johnson Publishing Co., 1975), p. 133.

5. George R. Woolfolk, "Turner's Safety Valve and Free Negro Westward Migration," *Journal of Negro History* 50:3 (July 1965), p. 190.

6. Sherwood, "The Formation of the American Colonization Society," pp. 209–28.

7. *Ibid.*, pp. 212, 219.

8. W.R. Riddell, "The Slave in Upper Canada," *Journal of Negro History* 4:4 (Oct. 1919), pp. 372–73.

9. George Washington Williams, *History of the Negro Race in America* (New York: Bergman Publishing Co., 1883), pp. 86–88.

10. Sheldon H. Harris, "An American's Impression of Sierra Leone, 1811," *Journal of Negro History* 47:1 (Jan. 1962), pp. 35–41.

11. Frankie Hutton, "Economic Considerations in the American Colonization Society's Early Effort to Emigrate Free Blacks to Liberia, 1816–1836," *Journal of Negro History* 48:4 (Oct. 1983), p. 377.

12. Hollis R. Lynch, "Negro Nationalism in the New World Before 1862," in August Meier and Elliott Rudwick, *The Making of Black America*, vol. 1 (New York: Atheneum, 1969), p. 46.

13. Douglas P. Seaton, "Colonizers and Reluctant Colonists—The New Jersey Colonization Society and the Black Community, 1815–1848," *New Jersey History* 96: 1, 2 (Spring-Summer 1978), p. 10.

14. Robert J. Williams, "Blacks, Colonization and Anti-Slavery—The Views of Methodists in New Jersey, 1816–1860," *New Jersey History* 102:3-4 (Fall-Winter 1984), p. 52.

15. Charles I. Foster, "The Colonization of Free Negroes in Liberia, 1816–1835," *Journal of Negro History* 38:1 (Jan. 1953), pp. 43–44.

16. Eugene Portlette Southall, "Arthur Tappan and the Anti-Slavery Movement," *Journal of Negro History* 15:2 (April 1930), p. 165.

17. Philip S. Foner, *History of Black Americans* (Westport, Conn.: Greenwood Press, 1983), pp. 290–91.

18. Sherwood, "The Formation of the American Colonization Society," pp. 222–24.

19. Martin Robinson Delany, *The Condition, Elevation, Emigration and Destiny of the Colored People in the United States* (New York: Arno Press and *New York Times*, 1968), pp. 31–45.

20. Lynch, "Negro Nationalism," p. 47.

21. Abraham Camp's letter in *Journal of Negro History*, 10:2 (April 1925), pp. 155–56.

22. Charles I. Foster, "The Colonization of Free Negroes in Liberia, 1816–1835," *Journal of Negro History* 38:1 (Jan. 1953), pp. 50, 51.

23. Southall, "Arthur Tappan," pp. 166–67.

24. John William Gibson and W.H. Crogman, *Progress of a Race* (Miami, Fla.: Mnemosyne Publishing Co., 1969), p. 28.

25. Hutton, "Economic Considerations," pp. 381–83.

26. Aaron Stopak, "The Maryland Colonization Society: Independent State Action in the Colonization Movement," *Maryland Historical Magazine* 63:3 (Sept. 1968), pp. 275–74, 279, 282.

27. *Ibid.*, pp. 290, 291, 296–97.

28. Booker T. Washington, *The Story of the Negro* (London: T. Fisher Unwin Co., 1909), pp. 244–45.

29. William Allen Poe, "Georgia's Influence on the Development of Liberia," *Georgia Historical Quarterly* 57:1 (Spring 1973), p. 5

30. Memory F. Mitchell, "Off to Africa—With Judicial Blessing," *North Carolina Historical Review* 53:3 (July 1976), pp. 266–67, 274.

31. Williams, *History of the Negro Race in America*, pp. 95–96.

32. W. Wayne Smith, "A Marylander in Africa—The Letters of Henry Harmon," *Maryland Historical Magazine* 69:4 (Winter 1974), pp. 399–404.

33. *Ibid.*

34. Louis R. Mehlinger, "The Attitude of the Free Negro Toward African Colonization," *Journal of Negro History* 1:3 (July 1916), p. 301.

35. William H. Pease and Jane H. Pease, "Organized Negro Communities," *Journal of Negro History* 47:1 (Jan. 1962), pp. 19–32.

10: Opposition to Slavery in Colonial America

1. Paul Funkelman, "The Kidnapping of John Davis and the Adoption of the Fugitive Slave Law of 1793," *Journal of Southern History* 56:3 (Aug. 1990), pp. 400–20.

2. Leslie H. Fishel and Benjamin Quarles, *The Negro American* (New York: William Morrow, 1967), pp. 34–35.

3. Andrew Oliver and James B. Peabody, eds., Publication of the Colonial Society of Massachusetts, vol. 8 (Boston: Colonial Society of Massachusetts, 1990), p. 288.

4. Joseph Conforti, "Samuel Hopkins and the Revolutionary Anti-Slavery Movement," *Rhode Island History* 38:2 (May 1979), pp. 39–41.

5. Nwabueze F. Okoye, "Chattel Slavery as the Nightmare of the American Revolutionaries," *William and Mary Quarterly*, 3d series, 37:1 (Jan. 1980), p. 22.

6. Herbert Aptheker, *Essays on the History of the American Negro* (New York: International Publishers, 1945), p. 75.

7. Herbert Aptheker, "The Quakers and the Negro Slavery," *Journal of Negro History* 25:3 (July 1940), p. 332.

8. Roger Sappington, "Dunker Beginnings in North Carolina in the Eighteenth Century," *North Carolina Historical Review* 46:3 (July 1969), p. 231.

9. Fishel and Quarles, *The Negro American*, p. 28.

10. Henry J. Cadbury, "An Early Quaker Anti-Slavery Statement," *Journal of Negro History* 22:4 (Oct. 1937), pp. 488–93.

11 Aptheker, "The Quakers and Negro Slavery," p. 338.

12. Winthrop D. Jordan, *White Over Black* (Chapel Hill: University of North Carolina Press, 1968), pp. 273–74.

13. Fishel and Quarles *The Negro American*, pp. 30–32.

14. Aptheker, "The Quakers and Negro Slavery," pp. 348–50.

15. Kenneth L. Carroll, "Religious Influences on the Manumission of Slaves," *Maryland Historical Magazine* 56:2 (June 1961), pp. 178–83.

16. Kenneth L. Carroll, "Nicholites and Slavery in Eighteenth Century Maryland," *Maryland Historical Magazine* 19:2 (Summer 1987), pp. 126–29.

17. Peter Kent Opper, "North Carolina Quakers, Reluctant Slaveholders," *North Carolina Historical Review* 52:1 (Winter 1975), pp. 37, 40, 42.

18. Jeffrey Brooke Allen, "The Racial Thought of White North Carolina Opponents of Slavery, 1789–1876," *North Carolina Historical Review* 59:1 (Jan. 1982), p. 52.

19. Jordan, *White Over Black*, p. 359.

20. H.J. Cadbury, "Another Early Quaker Anti-Slavery Document," *Journal of Negro History* 27:2 (April 1942), p. 214.

21. John M. Mechlin, "The Evolution of the Slave Status in American Democracy," *Journal of Negro History* 2:2 (April 1917), p. 120.

22. Conforti, "Samuel Hopkins," pp. 42–43.

23. Benjamin Quarles, *The Negro in the Making of America* (New York: Collier Books, 1964), p. 58.

24. John Lofton, "Enslavement of the Southern Mind, 1775–1825," *Journal of Negro History* 43:2 (April 1958), p. 134.

25. Unattributed document in *Journal of Negro History* 14:4 (Oct. 1929), p. 378.

26. Fishel and Quarles, *The Negro American*, p. 67.

27. Benjamin Quarles, "Freedom Fettered—Blacks in the Constitutional Era in Maryland," *Maryland Historical Magazine* 87 (Winter 1989), p. 299.

28. Anita Aidt Guy, "The Maryland Abolition Society and the Promotion of the Ideals of the New Nation," *Maryland Historical Magazine* 84 (Winter 1989), pp. 342–43.

29. Quarles, "Freedom Fettered," p. 299.

30. Quarles, *The Negro in the Making of America*, p. 57.

31. Unattributed document in *Journal of Negro History* 6 (1921), pp. 322–26.

32. Carroll, "Religious Influences," pp. 187–92.

33. Allen, "The Racial Thought," p. 53.

34. William Howard Kenney, III, *The Significance of Revivalism in S.C. 1738–41* in *South Carolina Historical Magazine* 71:1, pp. 1–16.

35. Lofton, "Enslavement of the Southern Mind," 43:2 (April 1958), p. 137.

36. Thomas E. Drake, "Joseph Drinker's Plea for the Admission of Colored People to the Society of Friends, 1795," *Journal of Negro History* 32:1 (Jan. 1947), pp. 110, 111–12.

37. Washington's letter to Capt. Thompson in *Journal of Negro History* 2:4 (Oct. 1917), p. 411.

38. Washington's will in *Journal of Negro History* 2:4 (Oct. 1917), p. 420.

39. Merl R. Eppse, *The Negro, Too, in American History* (Chicago: National Educational Publishing Co., 1938), p. 39.

40. Washington's letter to Robert Lewis in *Journal of Negro History* 2:4 (Oct. 1917), p. 419.

41. John D. Gillard, "Lafayette, Friend of the Negro," *Journal of Negro History* 19:4 (Oct. 1934), p. 361.

42. Eppse, *The Negro, Too*, p. 96.

43. William Loren Katz, *Eyewitness: The Negro in American History* (New York: Pitman Publishing Co., 1974), p. 41.

44. Lerone Bennett, Jr., *Confrontation Black and White* (Chicago: Johnson Publishing, 1965), p. 48.

45. Linda Grant DePauw, "Land of the Unfree: Legal Limitations in Liberty in Pre-Revolutionary America," *Maryland Historical Magazine* 68:4 (Winter 1973), p. 366.

46. Eppse, *The Negro, Too*, pp. 132–33.

47. John R. Howe, Jr., "John Adams' Views of Slavery," *Journal of Negro History* 49:3 (July 1964), pp. 202–5.

48. Eppse, *The Negro, Too*, p. 135.

49. "Thomas Jefferson's Writing on Virginia," *Journal of Negro History* 3:1 (Jan. 1918), pp. 57–58.

50. Jordan, *White Over Black*, pp. 434–60.

51. Leslie H. Fishel and Benjamin Quarles, *The Negro American* (New York: William Morrow, 1967), pp. 65–66.

52. "Thomas Jefferson's Writings on Virginia," pp. 68–71.

53. George Livermore, *Negroes as Slaves, Citizens and Soldiers* (New York: Burt Franklin Publishing Co., 1968), p. 17.

54. "John Madison's Writings About Negroes," *Journal of Negro History* 6 (1921), pp. 74–100.

55. *Ibid.*

56. Unattributed document in *Journal of Negro History* 4:1 (Jan. 1919), p. 41.

57. "Benjamin Franklin and Freedom," *Journal of Negro History* 4:1 (Jan. 1919), pp. 42, 44.

58. *Ibid.*, pp. 48–49.

59. *William and Mary Quarterly* 8:2 (April 1928), p. 116.

60. John T. Gillard, "Lafayette, Friend of the Negro," *Journal of Negro History*, 19:4 (Oct. 1934), pp. 355, 356–57.

61. *Ibid.*, pp. 358–60, 362–63, 369.

62. Livermore, "Negroes as Slaves," p. 96.

63. Unattributed document in *Journal of Negro History* 1:4 (Oct. 1929), p. 379; Bennett, *Confrontation Black and White*, p. 48.

64. Katz, *Eyewitness*, p. 50.

65. Lofton, "Enslavement of the Southern Mind," p. 133.

66. Okoye, "Chattel Slavery," p. 24.

67. Shane White, "Impervious Prayers: Elite and Popular Attitudes Toward Blacks and Slavery in the Middle Atlantic States, 1783–1810," *New York History*, 67:3 (July 1983), p. 264.

68. Kempes Schnell, "Slavery Influences on the Status of Slaves in a Free State," *Journal of Negro History* 50:4 (Oct. 1965), pp. 258–59.

69. Lerone Bennett, *The Shaping of Black America* (Chicago: Johnson Publishing Co., 1975), p. 119.

70. Aptheker, *Essays on the History of the American Negro*, pp. 77–78.

71. Ruth Bogin, "'Liberty Further Extended'—A 1776 Anti-Slavery Manuscript by Lemuel Haynes," *William and Mary Quarterly*, 3d series, 40:1 (Jan. 1983), pp. 85–93.

72. Katz, *Eyewitness*, p. 35.

11: Miscegenation

1. James Hugo Johnson, "Documentary Evidence of the Relations of Negroes and Indians," *Journal of Negro History* 14:1 (Jan. 1929), pp. 21–22.

2. Lerone Bennett, Jr., *Confrontation Black and White* (Chicago: Johnson Publishing Co., 1965), p. 22.

3. Publication of the Colonial Society of Massachusetts, vol. 29 (Boston: Colonial Society of Massachusetts, 1933), Records of Suffolk County Court 1671–1680, pp. 185, 232, 233, 809.

4. Publication of the Colonial Society of Massachusetts, vol. 59 (Portland, Me.: Atheneum Press, 1982), p. 46.

5. Alan D. Watson, "Women in Colonial North Carolina: Overlooked and Underestimated," *North Carolina Historical Review* 58:1 (Jan. 1981), p. 4.

6. Herbert Moller, "Sex Composition and Correlated Culture Patterns of Colonial America," *William and Mary Quarterly*, 3d series, 2 (April 1945), p. 134.

7. Carter G. Woodson, "The Beginnings of the Miscegenation of the Whites and Blacks," *Journal of Negro History* 3:4 (Oct. 1918), pp. 339–41.

8. Michael I. Cassity, *Legacy of Fear* (Westport, Conn.: Greenwood Press, 1985), pp. 34–35.

9. Woodson, "Beginning of Miscegenation," pp. 346–48.

10. Winthrop D. Jordan, *White Over Black* (Chapel Hill: University of North Carolina Press, 1968), p. 171.

11. *Ibid.*, p. 471.

12. Kenneth G. Goode and Winthrop D. Jordan, *From Africa to the United States and Then* (Glenview, Ill.: Scott, Foresman, 1969), p. 174.

13. Publication of the Colonial Society of Massachusetts, vol. 29 (Boston: Colonial Society of Massachusetts, 1933), Records of Suffolk County Court 1671–1680, p. 1067.

14. Jordan, *White Over Black*, pp. 155–56.

15. Pearl M. Graham, "Thomas Jefferson and Sally Hemings," *Journal of Negro History*, 46:2 (April 1961), pp. 89–99.

16. Kenneth W. Porter, "Relations Between Negroes and Indians Within the Present Limits of the United States," *Journal of Negro History*, 17:3 (July 1932), pp. 295, 299–304, 310, 323.

17. Kenneth W. Porter, *The Negro on the American Frontier* (New York: Arno Press and *New York Times*, 1971), pp. 15, 28–31.

18. C.G. Woodson, "The Relations of Negroes and Indians in Massachusetts," *Journal of Negro History* 5:1 (Jan. 1920), p. 45.

19. Johnston, "Documentary Evidence," pp. 19, 38.

20. Henry T. Malone, "Cherokee-White Relations on the Southern Frontier in the Early Nineteenth Century," *The North Carolina Historical Review* 34:1 (Jan. 1957), p. 10.

21. Lerone Bennett, Jr., *Before the Mayflower—A History of Black America*, 4th ed. (Chicago: Johnson Publishing Co., 1969), p. 269.

12: Slave Rebellion and Black Codes

1. Daniel E. Meaders, "South Carolina Fugitives as Viewed Through Local Colonial Newspapers with Emphasis on Runaway Notices (1732–1801)," *Journal of Negro History* 60:2 (April 1975), p. 291.

2. Wesley H. Wallace, "Property and Trade: Main Themes of Early North Carolina Advertisements," *North Carolina Historical Review* 32:4 (Oct. 1955), p. 452.

3. Michael P. Johnson, "Runaway Slaves and the Slave Communities in South Carolina, 1799–1830," *William and Mary Quarterly*, 3d series, 38:3 (July 1981), pp. 418–20.

4. Marvin L. Michael, Kay Cary and Loren Lee Cary, "Slave Runaways in Colonial North Carolina, 1748–1775," *North Carolina Historical Review* 63:1 (Jan. 1986), pp. 12–14, 18, 32–36.

5. Alan D. Watson, "Impulse Toward Independence: Resistance and Rebellion Among North Carolina Slaves, 1750–1775," *Journal of Negro History* 63:4 (Oct. 1978), pp. 320, 323.

6. Saunders Redding, *They Came in Chains* (New York: Lippincott, 1950), p. 85.

7. *Journal of Negro History* 63:4 (Fall 1978).

8. *Ibid.*

9. *Journal of Negro History* 1:2 (April 1916).

10. Lorenzo J. Greene, "The New England Negro as Seen in Advertisements for Runaway Slaves," *Journal of Negro History* 29:2 (April 1944), 128–31.

11. C.W.A. David, "The Fugitive Slave Laws of 1739 and Its Antecedents," *Journal of Negro History* 9:1 (Jan. 1924), pp. 18, 21–23.

12. Meaders, "South Carolina Fugitives," pp. 288–319.

13. David, "The Fugitive Slave Laws," p. 20.

14. W. Renwick Riddell "The Slave in New York," *Journal of Negro History* 13:1 (Jan. 1928), p. 82.

15. Meaders, "South Carolina Fugitives," pp. 294, 297.

16. Bernard Christian Steiner, ed., *Archives of Maryland*, Proceedings and Acts of the Assembly, 1737–1740 (Baltimore: Maryland Historical Society, 1921), vol. 40, pp. 95, 425.

17. William M. Miecek, "The Statutory Law of Slavery and Race in the Thirteen Mainland Colonies of British America," *William and Mary Quarterly*, 3d series, 2 (April 1977), pp. 273, 274.

18. Paul Hamlin and Charles E. Baker, eds., New York Historical Society, vol. 79, pp. 271, 272.

19. New York Historical Society, vol. 79, Oct. 14, 1704.

20. Watson, "Impulse Toward Independence," p. 323.

21. William Loren Katz, *Eyewitness: The Negro in American History* (New York: Pitman Publishing Co., 1974), p. 34.

22. Lowry Ware, "The Burning of Jerry—The Last Slave Execution by Fire in South Carolina," *South Carolina Historical Magazine* 91:2 (April 1990), p. 100.

23. Riddle, "The Slave in New York," p. 69.

24. Betty Wood, "'Until He Shall Be Dead, Dead, Dead'—The Judicial Treatment of Slaves in Eighteenth Century Georgia," *Georgia Historical Quarterly* 71:3 (Fall 1987), pp. 379–83.

25. Lerone Bennett, Jr., *Confrontation Colored and White* (Chicago: Johnson Publishing Co., 1965), p. 31.

26. Harvey Wish, "American Slave Insurrections Before 1861," *Journal of Negro History* 22:3 (July 1937), pp. 300–3.

27. Redding, *They Came in Chains*, p. 29.

28. Herbert Aptheker, *Essays in the History of the American Negro* (New York: International Publishers, 1945), pp. 11–13.

29. *Archives of Maryland*, June 1740, vol. 40, p. 425.

30. Oscar R. Williams, "The Regimentation of Blacks on the Urban Frontier in Colonial Albany, New York City and Philadelphia," *Journal of Negro History* 63:4 (1978), p. 332.

31. Marion D. deB. Kilson, *An Analysis of Slave Revolts in the United States* in August Meier and Elliott Rudwick, eds., *The Making of Black America* (New York: Atheneum Press, 1969), pp. 165, 169, 171.

32. Redding, *They Came in Chains*, p. 55; John Hope Franklin, *From Slavery to Freedom* (New York: Alfred A. Knopf, 1947), p. 189.

33. Charles H. Bowman, Jr., "Archibald Monk—Public Servant of Sampson County," *North Carolina Historical Review* 47:4 (Oct. 1970), p. 344, note.

34. Franklin, *From Slavery to Freedom*, p. 91.

35. Riddell, "The Slave in New York," pp. 70–81.

36. Paul Hamlin and Charles E. Baker, eds., New York Historical Society, vol. 78, Supreme Court Province of New York 1691–1704, pp. 321–22.

37. Ferenc M. Szasz, "The New York Slave Revolt of 1741—A Re-Examination," *New York History* 48:3 (July 1967), pp. 218–27.

38. *Ibid.*

39. Booker T. Washington, *The Story of the Negro* (London: T. Fisher Unwin Co., 1909), pp. 91–92.

40. New York Historical Society, 1918, vol. 51, p. 225.

41. Katz, *Eyewitness*, p. 36.

42. Donald D. Wax, "The Great Risque We Run," *Journal of Negro History* 67:2 (1982), p. 136.

43. Franklin, *From Slavery to Freedom*, p. 80.

44. Wax, "The Great Risque We Run," pp. 138, 139, 140, 142, 144.

45. Douglas R. Egerton, "Gabriel's Conspiracy and the Election of 1800," *Journal of Negro History* 56:2 (May 1992), pp. 192–93.

46. Bert M. Mutersbaugh, "The Background of Gabriel's Insurrection," *Journal of Negro History* 68:2 (Spring 1983), pp. 209–10.

47. Egerton, "Gabriel's Conspiracy," pp. 196–211.

48. *Ibid.*, pp. 211–13.

49. John M. Lofton, Jr., "Denmark Vesey's Call to Arms," *Journal of Negro History* 33:4 (Oct. 1948), pp. 396–402.

50. Washington, *The Story of the Negro*, p. 182.

51. Lofton, "Denmark Vesey's Call to Arms," pp. 404–17.

52. Richard C. Wade, "The Vesey Plot: A Reconsideration," *Journal of Southern History* 30:2 (May 1964), pp. 150–60.

53. Philip S. Foner, *History of Black Americans* (Westport, Conn.: Greenwood Press, 1983), p. 145.

54. Wish, "American Slave Insurrections," p. 317.

55. *Ibid.*, p. 314.

56. Redding, *They Came in Chains*, p. 92.

57. Vincent Harding, *The Other American Revolution* (Los Angeles: Center for Afro-American Studies, UCLA, 1980), pp. 34–35.

58. Redding, "They Came in Chains," p. 93.

59. Charles W. Simmons and Barry W. Morris, eds., *Afro-American History* (Columbus, Ohio: Charles E. Merrill Publishing Co., 1972), pp. 53–55.

60. Robert N. Elliott, "The Nat Turner Insurrection as Reported by the North Carolina Press," *North Carolina Historical Review* 38:1 (Jan. 1961), pp. 4–16.

61. *Ibid.*, p. 16.

62. Aptheker, *Essays in the History of the American Negro*, pp. 62–66.

63. Leslie H. Fishel and Benjamin Quarles, *The Negro American* (New York: William Morrow, 1967), pp. 20–26.

64. *Ibid.*, p. 23.

65. *Ibid.*, p. 25.

66. *Ibid.*, p. 26.

67. *Ibid.*, p. 25.

68. Watson, "Impulse Toward Independence," pp. 317–20.

69. New York Historical Society, vol. 80.

13: Blacks and Christianity

1. John M. Mecklin, "The Evolution of the Slave Status in American Democracy," *Journal of Negro History* 2:3 (April 1917), pp. 117, 118.

2. William H. Browne, ed., *Archives of Maryland*, Proceedings and Acts of the Assembly of Maryland, 1684–1692, vol. 13 (Baltimore: Maryland Historical Society, 1894), pp. 505–6.

3. William K. Riddell, "The Slaves in New York," *Journal of Negro History* 13:1 (Jan. 1928), p. 66.

4. Robert Goldston, *The Negro Revolution* (New York: Macmillan, 1968), p. 42.

5. Herbert L. Ganter, "Documents Relating to the Early History of the College of William and Mary and to the History of the Church in Virginia," *William and Mary Quarterly* 9:4 (Oct. 1939), pp. 460, 469.

6. Leslie H. Fishel and Benjamin Quarles, *The Negro American* (New York: William Morrow, 1967), p. 36.

7. Earl Conrad, *The Invention of the Negro* (New York: Paul S. Eriksson, 1966), p. 34.

8. Gilbert Osofsky, *The Burden of Race* (New York: Harper and Row, 1967), p. 34.

9. William Loren Katz, *Eyewitness to the Negro in North American History* (New York: Pitman Publishing Co., 1944), p. 23.

10. Osofsky, *The Burden of Race*, p. 4.

11. Henry J. Cadbury, "Negro Membership in the Society of Friends," *Journal of Negro History* 21:2 (April 1934), pp. 152–56.

12. David T.J. Morgan, "Scandal in Carolina: The Story of the Capricious Missionary," *North Carolina Historical Review* 47:3 (July 1970), pp. 234–35.

13. Vebert Faith, "The Society for the Propagation of the Gospel in Foreign Parts: Its Work for the Negroes in America Before 1783," *Journal of Negro History* 18:2 (April 1933), pp. 171–212.

14. New York Historical Society, 1880, vol. 13, p. 348.

15. *Ibid.*

16. *Ibid.*, p. 175.

17. Faith, "The Society for the Propagation of the Gospel in Foreign Parts," p. 175.

18. Peter M. Bergman, *A Chronological History of the Negro in America* (New York: Harper and Row, 1969), p. 40; Samuel Clyde McCullough, "Dr. Thomas Bray's Trip to Maryland: A Study in Militant Anglican Humanitarianism," *William and Mary Quarterly*, 3d series, 2 (Jan. 1945), p. 31.

19. Samuel Clyde McCullough, "James Blair's Plan of 1699 to Reform the Clergy of Virginia," *William and Mary Quarterly*, 3d series, 4:1 (Jan. 1947), p. 85.

20. Jerome W. Jones, "The Established Virginia Church and the Conversion of Negroes and Indians, 1620–1760," *Journal of Negro History* 56:1 (Jan. 1961), pp. 18, 21, 23.

21. Luther P. Jackson, "Religious Development of the Negro in Virginia from 1760–1860," *Journal of Negro History* 16:2 (April 1931), p. 171.

22. C.W. Birnie, "The Education of the Negro in Charleston, South Carolina, Before the Civil War," *Journal of Negro History* 12:1 (Jan. 1927), p. 3.

23. Faith, "The Society for the Propagation of the Gospel," pp. 177–78.

24. *Ibid.*, pp. 199–200.

25. Birnie, "The Education of the Negro," p. 14.

26. Faith, "The Society for the Propagation of the Gospel," p. 206.

27. *Ibid.*

28. Allan Gallary, "The Origin of Slaveholders' Paternalism—George Whitefield, the Bryan Family and the Great Awakening in the South," *Journal of Southern History* 53:3 (Aug. 1987), pp. 380–91.

29. *Ibid.*

30. Lewis M. Purefoy, "The Southern Methodist Church and the Proslavery Argument," *Journal of Southern History* 32:3 (Aug. 1966), pp. 325–41.

31. G.R. Wilson, "The Religion of the American Slave: His Attitude Toward Life and Death," *Journal of Negro History* 8:1 (Jan. 1923), pp. 57.

32. J.D. Hartzell, "Methodism and the Negro in the United States," *Journal of Negro History* 8:3 (July 1923), pp. 301, 302.

33. Walter H. Brooks, "The Priority of the Silver Bluff Church and Its Promoters," *Journal of Negro History* 7:2 (April 1922), pp. 172, 173, 182, 185.

34. John W. Davis, "George Liele and Andrew Bryan, Pioneer Negro Baptist Preachers," *Journal of Negro History* 3:2 (April 1918), pp. 119–27.

35. Loretta Funke, "The Negro in Education," *Journal of Negro History* 5:1 (Jan. 1920), p. 1.

36. J. Hall Pleasants, ed., *Archives of Maryland*, vol. 50 (Baltimore: Maryland Historical Society, 1933), p. 201.

37. Pleasants, *Archives of Maryland*, vol. 50, p. 198.

38. B.T. Washington, *The Story of the Negro* (London: T. Fisher Unwin, 1909), p. 271.

39. Wilson, "The Religion of the American Slave," pp. 64–65.

40. Osofsky, *The Burden of Race*, pp. 39, 41.

41. Philip S. Foner, *History of Black Americans* (Westport, Conn.: Greenwood Press, 1983), pp. 85, 97.

42. Rodney P. Carlisle, *Prologue to Liberation* (New York: Appleton-Century-Crofts, 1972), p. 19.

43. R.A. Carter, "What the Negro Church Has Done," *Journal of Negro History* 11:1 (Jan. 1926), p. 1.

44. Foner, *History of Black Americans*, pp. 49, 121.

14: Blacks in War

1. Department of Defense, *Black Americans in Defense of Our Nation* (Washington, D.C.: U.S. Government Printing Office, 1985), p. 23.

2. Bernard C. Nelty and Morris J. MacGregor, eds., *Blacks in the Military, Essential Documents* (Wilmington, Del.: Scholarly Resources, Inc., 1981), p. 24.

3. Marvin Kay and William S. Price, Jr., "'To Ride the Wood Mare': Racial Buildup and Militia Service in Colonial North Carolina, 1740–1775," *North Carolina Historical Review* 57:4 (Oct. 1980), p. 385.

4. Kenneth W. Porter, *The Negro on the American Frontier* (New York: Arno Press and *New York Times*, 1971), p. 157.

5. Peter M. Bergman, *A Chronological History for the Negro in America* (New York: Harper and Row, 1969), p. 35.

6. William Loren Katz, *Eyewitness: The Negro in American History* (New York: Pitman Publishing Co., 1974), p. 27.

7. Leslie H. Fishel, Jr., *The Black American* (New York: William Morrow, 1970), p. 7.

8. Philip S. Foner, *Blacks in the American Revolution* (Westport, Conn.: Greenwood Press, 1975), p. 68.

9. *Ibid.*, p. 50.

10. Lerone Bennett, Jr., *Before the Mayflower: A History of Black America* (Chicago: Johnson Publishing Co., 1969), pp. 52, 53.

11. C.W. Williams, *History of the Negro Race in America* (New York: Bergman Press, 1883), p. 330.

12. Sidney Kaplan and Emma Kaplan, *The Black Presence in the Era of the American Revolution* (Amherst, Mass.: University of Massachusetts Press, 1989), p. 17.

13. Philip T. Drotning, *Black Heroes in Our Nation's History* (New York: Cowles Book Co., 1969), pp. 15–18.

14. John Hope Franklin, *From Slavery to Freedom* (New York: Alfred A. Knopf, 1947), p. 27.

15. John S. Butler, *Equality in the Military: The Black Experience* (Saratoga, Calif., Century Twenty-One Publishing, 1980), p. 12.

16. Merl Eppse, *The Negro, Too, in American History* (Chicago: National Educational Publishing Co., 1938), p. 77.

17. W.B. Hartgrove, "The Negro Soldier in the American Revolution," *Journal of Negro History* 1:2 (April 1916), pp. 113, 114.

18. Leslie H. Fishel, Jr., and Benjamin Quarles, *The Negro American* (New York: William Morrow, 1967), p. 56.

19. Sylvia R. Frey, "Between Slavery & Freedom—Virginia Blacks in the American Revolution," *Journal of Southern History* 49:3 (Aug. 1983), pp. 377–78.

20. Benjamin Quarles, "Lord Dunmore as Liberator," *William and Mary Quarterly*, 3d series, 15 (Oct. 1958), pp. 495–98.

21. Benjamin Quarles, "Lord Dunmore," in August Meier and Elliott Rudwick, eds., *The Making of Black America* (New York: Atheneum, 1969), p. 126.

22. *Ibid.*, pp. 129–33.

23. *Ibid.*

24. Frey, "Between Slavery and Freedom," p. 387.

25. Benjamin Quarles, "Lord Dunmore," *William and Mary Quarterly*, 3d series, 15 (Oct. 1958), pp. 503–6.

26. William Alexander, *History of the Colored Race in America* (Palmetto Publishing, 1887; reprint, New York: Negro University Press, n.d.), p. 332.

27. Fishel and Quarles, *The Negro American*, p. 58.

28. George Fenwick Jones, "The Black Hessians, Negroes Recruited by the Hessians in South Carolina and Other Colonies," *South Carolina Historical Magazine* 83:4 (Oct. 1982), pp. 291–302.

29. New York Historical Society, 1882, vol. 15, p. 39.

30. Peter Maslowski, "National Policy Toward the Use of Black Troops in the Revolution," *South Carolina Historical Magazine* 73:1 (Jan. 1972), p. 5; Williams, *History of the Negro Race in America*, p. 338.

31. Nelty and MacGregor, eds., *Blacks in the Military*.

32. Hartgrove, "The Negro Soldier," pp. 117–18.

33. Maslowski, "National Policy," pp. 8–14.

34. Fishel and Quarles, *The Negro American*, pp. 652–53.

35. Foner, *Blacks in the American Revolution*, p. 173.

36. John Hope Franklin, *From Slavery to Freedom*, 3rd ed. (New York: Vintage Press, 1969), p. 136.

37. Nelty and MacGregor, eds., *Blacks in the Military*, p. 63.

38. Kaplan and Kaplan, *The Black Presence*, p. 90.

39. Foner, *Blacks in the American Revolution*, p. 102; Williams, *History of the Negro Race*, p. 345.

40. John Russell Batlett, ed., "Records of the State of Rhode Island and Providence Plantations in New England," vol. 8 (Providence: Cooke Jackson & Co., Printers to the State, 1863), p. 641.

41. *Ibid.*, p. 359

42. *Ibid.*, p. 361.

43. Lorenzo J. Greene, "Some Observations on the Black Regiment of Rhode Island in the American Revolution," *Journal of Negro History* 37:2 (April 1952), pp. 153–62.

44. Records of the State of Rhode Island, vol. 9, 1780–1783, p. 582.

45. Katz, *Eyewitness*, p. 57.

46. Records of the State of Rhode Island, vol. 10, 1784–1792, p. 44.

47. H. Aptheker, *Essays in the History of the American Negro* (New York: International Publishers, 1945), pp. 98–100.

48. Robert J. Clough, "Black Men in the Early Jew Jersey Militia," *New Jersey History* 88:4 (Winter 1970), pp. 228–29.

49. New York Historical Society, 1875, vol. 8, p. 397.

50. Bernard Christian Steiner, ed., *Archives of Maryland*, Proceedings of the Provincial Court 1658–1662, vol. 41 (Baltimore: Maryland Historical Society, 1922), pp. 148, 167.

51. Bernard Christian Steiner, ed., *Archives of Maryland*, Journal and Correspondence of the State Council, vol. 45 (Baltimore: Maryland Historical Society, 1927).

52. William L. Calderhead, "Thomas Carney, Unsung Soldier of the American Revolution," *Maryland Historical Magazine* 84 (Winter 1989), p. 319.

53. Hartgrove, "The Negro Soldier," pp. 110–13.

54. *Archives of Maryland*, vol. 45, July 3, 1781, p. 494.

55. Nelty and MacGregor, eds., *Blacks in the Military*, p. 16.

56. Luther P. Jackson, "Virginia Negro Soldiers and Seamen in the American Revolution," *Journal of Negro History* 27:3 (July 1942), p. 252.

57. George Livermore, *Negroes as Slaves, Citizens, and Soldiers* (New York: Bart Franklin, 1962), p. 137.

58. New York Historical Society, vol. 1–4, 1871–1874, p. 425.

59. Franklin, *From Slavery to Freedom*, p. 134.

60. E. Wheeler, "Militia—Development and Organization of the North Carolina Militia," *North Carolina Historical Review* 41:3 (July 1964), p. 310.

61. Robert A. Olwell, "'Domestic Enemies': Slavery and Political Independence in South Carolina, May 1775–March 1776," *Journal of Southern History* 55:1 (Feb. 1989), pp. 22–24, 35, 36.

62. Livermore, *Negroes as Slaves*, p. 99.

63. M. Foster Farley, "The South Carolina Negro in the American Revolution, 1775–1783," *South Carolina Historical Magazine* 79:2 (April 1978), pp. 75–76, 77.

64. Hartgrove, "The Negro Soldier," p. 123.

65. Foner, *Blacks in the American Revolution,"* p. 142.

66. New York Historical Society, vol. 8, 1875, pp. 497–99; G. Terry Sharrer, "Indigo in Carolina, 1671–1796," *South Carolina Historical Magazine* 72:2 (April 1971), p. 98.

67. New York Historical Society, vol. 2, 1872, pp. 114–17.

68. New York Historical Society, vol. 2, 1872, p. 188.

69. Fishel and Quarles, *The Negro American*, p. 51.

70. Bergman, *A Chronological History*, p. 55.

71. Kaplan and Kaplan, *The Black Presence*, p. 118.

72. *Ibid.*, p. 147.

73. Harold D. Langley, "The Negro in the Navy and Merchant Service, 1798–1860," *Journal of Negro History* 52:4 (Oct. 1967), p. 275; Department of Defense, *Black Americans*, p. 37.

74. Drotning, *Black Heroes*, p. 32.

75. J. Hall Pleasants, ed., *Archives of Maryland*, Journal and Correspondence of the State Council, 1781, vol. 47 (Baltimore: Maryland Historical Society, 1930), p. 111.

76. Quarles, *The Negro in the American Revolution* (Chapel Hill: University of North Carolina Press, 1961), pp. 63, 64.

77. Fishel and Quarles, *The Negro American*, p. 53.

78. Kaplan and Kaplan, *The Black Presence*, p. 138.

79. Williams, *History of the Negro Race*, pp. 379, 380.

80. Bernard Christian Steiner, ed., *Archives of Maryland*, Journal and Correspondence of the State Council, 1780–1781, vol. 45 (Baltimore: Maryland Historical Society, 1927), p. 435.

81. *Journal of Negro History*, 2:4 (Oct. 1917), p. 413.

82. Benjamin Quarles, "The Negro Response," in Melvin Drummer, ed., *Black History: A Reappraisal* (Garden City, N.J.: Anchor Books, 1968), pp. 132–46.

83. Jackson, "Virginia Negro Soldiers," p. 280; Williams, *History of the Negro Race*, p. 410.

84. Catherine C. Shield, "Losses of York County Citizens in the British Invasion, 1781," *William and Mary Quarterly* 15:2 (April 1935), p. 173.

85. J.A.C. Chandler and E.G. Swen, eds., "Records from the Old Jail at Cumberland County Court House, Virginia," *William and Mary Quarterly* 12:1 (Jan. 1932), p. 39.

86. Arnett G. Lindsay, "Diplomatic Relations Between the United States and Great Britain Bearing on the Return of Negro Slaves, 1788–1828," *Journal of Negro History* 5:4 (Oct. 1920), pp. 392–406.

87. Kenneth Wiggins Porter, "Negroes and the Seminole Wars, 1817–1818," *Journal of Negro History* 36:3 (July 1951), pp. 251–78.

88. John N. Grant, "Black Immigrants Into Nova Scotia, 1776–1815," *Journal of Negro History* 58:3 (July 1973), pp. 255–56.

89. Mary Beth Norton, "The Fate of Some Black Loyalists of the American Revolution," *Journal of Negro History* 58:4 (Oct. 1979), pp. 404–19.

90. New York Historical Society, Major General Charles Lee's Papers, vol. 2, 1870, pp. 104–5.

91. Quarles, *The Negro in the American Revolution*, p. 195.

92. Department of Defense, *Black Americans in Defense of Our Nation*, p. 32.

93. *Afro-Americans '76*, by Eugene Winslow (Chicago: Afro American Publishing Co., 1975); *Black Heroes in Our Nation's History*, by Philip T. Drotning (New York: Cowles Book Co., 1969); *The Black Presence in the Era of the American Revolution*, by Sidney Kaplan and Emma Kaplan (Amherst, Mass.: University of Massachusetts Press, 1989); *The Colored Patriot of the American Revolution*, by William C. Nell (Y.B. Yerrinton, 1855); *For Black Seamen: Essays on the History of the American Negro*, by H. Aptheker (New York: International Publishers, 1945).

The number of servicemen from each state was taken from William T. Alexander's book *History of the Colored Race in America*, originally published by Palmetto Press in 1887. Original figures were found in the New Hampshire Historical Society Records, 1824. The number of slaves in each state in 1775 came from *A Chronological History of the Negro in America*, by Peter M. Bergman (New York: Harper and Row, 1961).

INDEX

287